Media Policy in a
Changing Southern Africa

Media Policy in a
Changing Southern Africa
Critical reflections on media reforms in the global age

Edited by
Dumisani Moyo and Wallace Chuma

UNISA PRESS
PRETORIA

© 2010 University of South Africa
First edition, first impression

ISBN 978-1-86888-569-5

Published by Unisa Press
University of South Africa
P O Box 392, 0003 UNISA

Book Designer: Dawid Kahts
Editor: Isabelle Delvare
Indexer: Hannalie Knoetze
Typesetting: Marlé Oelofse
Printer: Harry's Printers

CONTENTS

TABLES

FIGURES

Policing the media in Southern Africa in the global era:

An introduction

Wallace Chuma and Dumisani Moyo

A great deal of continuity and change have characterised media and communication policy-making in Southern Africa over the past two decades. Across the sub-region, rapid political and economic developments of the 1990s spawned the adoption of 'second generation' reforms aimed at opening up the media to diverse and pluralistic interests in the context of ongoing democratisation projects. In many cases these reforms assumed a 'public' outlook and character, in the sense that both state and non-state actors participated in their formulation. They were also different from the first cycle of 'reforms' that accompanied the attainment of independence from colonial rule, which, by and large, were characterised by the retention of colonial media policy with cosmetic modification.

It is important to note that non-state actors have been among the key players in both the conception and delivery of the most successful media and communications policies in the region. From the Windhoek Declaration, through the robust media reform advocacy of national chapters of the Media Institute of Southern Africa, to the militant lobbying of South Africa's media activists during the Conference for a Democratic South Africa (Codesa) talks, it is clear that the character of the current policies in most of Southern Africa owes much to the input of civil society. The inclusion of explicit provisions for media freedom in constitutions, the passing of freedom of information legislation and the creation and legislation of independent media regulators, among other policy initiatives, were processes in which civil society – more than it ever had or could before – played the role of midwife.

It also needs to be noted that the reforms of the 1990s were in a major way influenced by the end of the Cold War, which created a unipolar world in which the United States and its Western allies shifted their African policies to focus on democratisation, liberalisation and good governance. With the new foci being presented as prerequisites for donor funding and other forms of support, most African governments embraced liberalisation of sorts across the spectrum of politics and economics, to varying degrees. Media reforms in Africa during this period and thereafter should be viewed against this backdrop, and should also be positioned against the backdrop of the globalisation of new information and communication technologies (ICTs). American- and European-based donors, with the backing of their governments, supported civil society advocacy for media reform in areas such as the liberalisation of the airwaves, the independence of regulators and the legislation of freedom of information.

Naturally, and as this volume illustrates, different countries in Southern Africa responded in ways both different and similar to internal and external pressures for media reform. As Chakravartty and Sarikakis (2006) remind us, recent changes in the communication and media landscapes, as well as policy responses to these changes, have not been experienced as homogeneous processes across the globe, but have been influenced by cultural, social and political contexts. It is therefore important, in communication and media policy analysis, to 'develop tools for making macro-level observations of patterns without losing sight of the micro-levels of realities of experience' (Chakravartty & Sakikakis 2006: 3).

It is clear from this collection of essays that the promise of a far-reaching and profound 'opening up' of media to all – a promise made in most media/communication policy documents across the region – is not about to be realised. In fact, it is as if the momentum for further policy reform has been lost, at a time when corporate hierarchies and the state appear set on reversing some of the gains of the earlier decade. From the Zimbabwean government's 'musical chairs' approach to media reforms during the mid-1990s and its subsequent, concerted efforts to 'capture' the mediated public sphere, through the corporate domination of South Africa's ostensibly public-service media, to Zambia's 'stop-go' approach to broadcasting regulation, the case studies in this collection point not only to the gains made by non-state actors, but also to new threats to media freedom and diversity in Southern Africa.

In the era of the global dominance of neo-liberal orthodoxy, it is interesting that states in Southern Africa have remained key actors in the policy process within their territorial borders. While not immune to the influences of regional and global pressures or to local clamours for enhanced media freedom and access, states in Southern Africa, with a few exceptions, continue to drive – at their own pace – the process of communication reform (Kupe 2007). Largely as a result of this, the fate of the public service broadcaster in various countries remains inextricably bound to the whims of the state. There is a sense of convergence in the ways in which both democratic and non-democratic regimes in the region reluctantly approach issues around the independence and autonomy of public broadcasters and broadcasting regulators. Notably, public broadcasters have remained in the clutches of state control, and broadcasting regulators are generally staffed with loyal appointees who are at the beck and call of the ruling elites. The perceived role of broadcasting institutions as engines of nation-building and identity formation in a post-colonial dispensation has created justification for this continued state control – a justification that is often spuriously masked in the discourses of 'public interest' and 'national interest'.

The aim of this book

This collection of essays is an effort to bring debate on media policy reform back to the centre, to initiate a stocktaking exercise as it were; in Chinua Achebe's terms, to try and find out 'where the rain began to beat on us'. It offers regional case studies that examine the political economy of media reform over a period covering roughly two decades. And it goes further than this. The chapters in this collection look to the future, taking stock of what has been 'hit and missed' and looking at the possibilities for transcending the current uncertain phase (where, depending on how one looks at it, the glass is either half full or half empty). They do this in the interest of expanding the mediated public sphere to include everyone, in a context where the reigning orthodoxy emphasises exclusion.

This volume takes the debate on media reforms to a new level as we believe that, following a certain degree of policy 'maturation', it is important to reflect on new possibilities. The book builds on a great deal of other research and many other published works on media reform in Southern Africa and globally. Much of this previous work is very useful. Tawana Kupe's *Broadcasting Policy and Practice in Africa* (2003) is a case in point, focusing as it does on the constraints and opportunities in broadcasting policy-making in Africa, mostly during the 1990s era of deregulation, privatisation and convergence. Elizabeth Barratt and Guy Berger's (2007) edited volume, *50 years of Journalism: African media since Ghana's Independence*, looks back and reflects on the gains that media in Africa have made as institutions of the public sphere since 1957. Francis Nyamnjoh's (2005) *Africa's Media: Democracy and the Politics of Belonging* pays particular attention to Cameroon's media practice and policy, while drawing generalisations and comparative notes for the continent. These, and other earlier works not mentioned here, to some extent inform some of the debates raised in this book.

A major strength of this book is that it looks at policy-making in various media sectors, including broadcasting, print and the new information and communications technologies (ICTs).

Many cases, one debate: A comparative perspective

This book is a melting pot of a range of debates and ideas around media policy-making in Southern Africa over the past few decades, and brings together scholars from different research traditions and different parts of the world. The point, though, is not to melt everything into a single homogeneous product, but to bring diverse – though in many ways connected – perspectives between its covers. Although the chapters focus on specific country cases, we have decided to organise them in a way that allows the reader not only to pick and choose different aspects of interest but also to draw connections between them. These connections draw from the various themes emerging from the chapters, which inform the wider media policy debate in the region. It is more helpful to conceptualise these themes as some form of research questions that have guided the various authors in the writing process. The book illustrates remarkable convergences and divergences in the patterns and experiences of media-policy reform across the region.

One fundamental question that has preoccupied most of the chapters in this book is why there has been a persistent culture of state dominance in the media and communications policy-making process, despite years of struggle for recognition and participation by non-state actors. Several chapters address this question at various lengths and depths: Windrich's chapter on broadcasting reform in Zimbabwe, Phiri's chapter on Zambia, and Dumisani Moyo's comparative chapter on Zambia and Zimbabwe confirm the thesis that policies are path-dependent: once they are set on a particular course, something of substantial strength will be needed to deflect them from that course (Peters 1999). Windrich, for instance, closely traces the historical changes and continuities in Zimbabwe, and illustrates that monopoly ownership and control of broadcasting has been a regime obsession from Ian Smith to Robert Mugabe, who both made it a site of contest in the battle for the control of the hearts and minds of their subjects. Similarly, Phiri argues that an obsession with power and control has been the constant factor in determining Zambian policy-making from Kaunda, through Chiluba, and up to the Mwanawasa regime. He concludes his chapter by arguing that a form of 'media-phobia' – born from an understanding of the power of the media – has tended to drive successive Zambian administrations away from genuinely transforming the media in fulfilment of their founding promises.

What comes out clearly in most of the chapters in this book is that, contrary to arguments about the 'retreating state' or the 'weak or failed state' that is giving in to global and even local forces, the state in Southern Africa remains at the centre of policy-making and only expediently accommodates input from non-state actors. Chakravartty and Sarikakis (2006), in their discussion of globalisation and media policy, argue that the role of the state 'has been transformed [but] ... is not necessarily diminished in the face of globalisation' (ibid: 10). As we pointed out earlier, the flurry of policy debates and reforms in the region since the 1990s was initiated by these non-state actors, only to be usurped by the state subsequently.

The question of why efforts to transform state broadcasters into public-service broadcasters in the entire region seems to have reached a dead end is a central one in contemporary media and communications policy debate. It is a question that is also inextricably linked to the failure of the democratisation project in the region, as evidenced by reversals in countries such as Zimbabwe, Kenya, Malawi and even South Africa. What Larry Diamond (2008) has described as an era of 'democratic recession' appears to be evident in the region, where governments appear keener on the form rather than the substance of democracy. Several scholars have written on how the wave of democratisation in most developing countries has given way to superficial forms of democracy: Joseph (1999, 2003), Diamond (1999), and Bratton and Van de Walle (1997), among others, have used terms such as 'pseudo democracy,' 'virtual democracy,' and 'electoral democracy' in an attempt to capture the hollowness of the emerging forms of imitative democracy. Few of these scholars, however, have attempted to make connections between this superficial democracy and its implications for public policy, particularly in the media sector. We argue that the superficial nature of democracy in most countries in the region has meant that media policy reforms – supposedly meant to strengthen the democratic process – have been equally superficial. Just as most of the countries have embraced electoral democracy as some form of window dressing to hide dictatorial tendencies, so too has a tendency developed of imitating media policies and regulations that are perceived as acceptable to Western donor countries. Thus, while freedom-of-information or access-to-information laws, and laws purportedly establishing public-service broadcasters and even independent regulatory authorities have been introduced, little has been done to implement them. Dumisani Moyo argues that some of these reforms were introduced to placate vocal critics and donors, and not for the expansion of the public sphere as such. He also shows, however, that the superficiality of the reforms notwithstanding, some of them have had far-reaching – albeit unintended – consequences in terms of opening up hitherto closed communicative spaces.

South Africa, which for some time served as a model of how to transform a state broadcaster into a genuine public-service broadcaster, appears to have developed a situation characterised by two distinct centres of power. A combination of state interference and over-commercialisation is tending to remove the broadcaster from its role of serving the public interest as expected of a typical public-service broadcaster. Duncan and Glenn's chapter looks at critical turning points in South African television policy-making since the 1990s, and argues that these historic moments represented missed opportunities for coming up with policies that could have ushered in a more democratic and robust television system for the country. All these opportunities, including the multiparty negotiations in the run-up to the first democratic elections, the Triple Inquiry of the Independent Broadcasting Authority (IBA) into the nature of public broadcasting, the establishment of the second free-to-air channel, e.tv, to name a few, were squandered in the 'rush for commercialism' and marketisation.

Duncan and Glenn argue that, contrary to perceptions among media scholars and activists that South Africa provides a model for the region in terms of having put in place a three-tier system with public service broadcasting at the core – based on models advanced by John Keane (1991) and James Curran (1991) – South Africa rather is a typical example of 'how not to establish three tiers of broadcasting.' They argue that the fact that all the tiers have been permeated by commercialisation implies that South Africa has ended up with a single tier of broadcasting, one that is commercial through and through. Theirs is not a universally accepted position, however. Wallace Chuma, for example, contends that, its imperfections notwithstanding, the three-tier system still offers a model for the region. His chapter argues that while television has arguably become 'captive' to commercial imperative – the extent to which values of public service have been abandoned in the process remains debatable – radio still remains an important entry point into the mediated public sphere for the majority of South Africans because of access in all three tiers.

The refusal by the Zambian government to appoint the boards for the Independent Broadcasting Authority and the Zambian National Broadcasting Corporation as required by new laws passed in 2002, is clear testimony to the reluctance of ruling elites to create an environment conducive to the emergence of vibrant public-service broadcasting institutions. Apart from informing, educating and entertaining, such institutions have the capacity to play a watchdog role, and this scares many governments whose human rights records are questionable. As Phiri eloquently puts it: 'A free media is inquisitive; it investigates and poses questions. A free media also prints and broadcasts dissenting voices. All this makes Zambian governments jittery because they would no longer be in control of what will be said or revealed. They find it hard to go to bed peacefully not knowing what tomorrow's headlines will announce.'

These fears in part explain the policy paralysis that seems to characterise the kingdom of Swaziland. Richard Rooney argues that the failure to come up with democratic media policies in Swaziland is largely to do with the peculiarity of Swaziland as the only surviving monarchy in the region. The chapter argues that the conservatism of the Swazi monarchy, and its general distrust of the media, are the key explanatory factors for the piecemeal media reform that has taken place in that country over the past two decades. The chapter illustrates that despite the international pressures for liberalisation and deregulation, the response from Southern African countries has been uneven, and has certainly been shaped by domestic political dynamics.

Zimbabwe's seemingly endless crisis has also raised media policy-related questions that have begged thorough analytical engagement. To what extent, for instance, have media policies in that country been a factor in the multifaceted crisis gripping the country since the turn of the century? What suitable policy directions can be proffered for a post-crisis Zimbabwe? Last Moyo's chapter addresses the former question by looking at the link between structure and content in the Zimbabwean media landscape and illustrating how a weakly conceived media structure can lead to an impoverished public sphere. It illustrates how a state-dominated media landscape can be manipulated for propagandistic ends on the one hand; and on the other hand how privately owned media operating under a restrictive environment can be manipulated by corporate and oppositional interests to pursue a narrow discourse.

Last Moyo departs from the common approach of saying that government media is bad and privately owned media is good, and illustrates that both sides report from certain ideological positions that lead to these polarised perceptions. The public (or rather, government-controlled) media frame their reporting within a 'nationalist,' and 'patriotic' perspective, while the privately owned media emphasise the discourses of human rights and property rights. The result is a rise of two irreconcilable forms of journalism, which the author calls 'patriotic journalism' and 'anti-establishment journalism.' Both have their problems.

Similarly, Wallace Chuma's chapter looks at the tensions in media policy-making in contemporary Zimbabwe and argues that the unfolding Zimbabwean crisis calls for new thinking on how the media should be structured in that country to create a sound basis for democratisation. Chuma notes that post-2000 media and communication policies in Zimbabwe have led to an erosion of the nominal agency powers of journalistic practice, leaving the profession at the mercy of political and socio-economic power hierarchies. Echoing Last Moyo in this volume, Chuma argues that in the obtaining, polarised climate, the media have become 'tribunes for competing elites in capital, civil society and the state.' Like Windrich, and Dumisani Moyo in this volume, Chuma emphasises the point that the continuities in media policy from colonial to post-colonial have entrenched the state as the dominant actor in shaping both media systems and journalistic practice. The chapter ends by making invaluable policy suggestions for a post-crisis Zimbabwe, drawing from and adapting the model advanced by James Curran (2002) and the South African post-apartheid reform process.

Another pertinent question relates to the role of non-state actors already alluded to earlier. What gains, for example, have non-state actors made in policy-making in the region? Various chapters in this book address the role of civil society in media and communications policy debate in the region, and there is consensus that civil society has gained considerable space in which to leverage policy reforms. However, this space and the degree of accommodation from the state vary from country to country, and everywhere the state retains the power to have the final say-so. Phiri, Jere and Dumisani Moyo, for example, recount from different angles the role of the Media Institute of Southern Africa (Zambia) in influencing policy direction by drafting its own media bills, the core features of which reappeared in the government bills. The refusal by the Zambian government to accept these bills and to implement the new laws, however, points to the fact that the success of civil society interventions depends largely on the willingness of the executive to grant such a space.

James Zaffiro focuses on the role of the media, civil society and the state in the realisation of media and communication objectives of Botswana's Vision 2016 programme, whose tenets include greater democratisation, transparent governance, enhanced access to ICTs, and a robust media system. Zaffiro explores the development of media policy in Botswana, identifying constraints and opportunities for both state and civil society actors in the policy process. His key argument is that the state in Botswana needs to open up policy discussions and decisions to a range of civil society actors, and should free the public-service media from state control. To realise the goals of Vision 2016, Zaffiro argues, there is the need for journalistic professionalism and journalism training in Botswana, and increased civil society support for media-reform initiatives.

Why has the universal access goal in the provision of ICTs in the region remained a mirage? In their chapter, Sethunya Mosime and Sarah Chiumbu explore the evolution of ICT policy in Botswana, paying particular attention to the tensions between liberalisation and universal access. They contend that while the ICT policies represent a symbolic expression of noble intentions on the part of the state, the realities of fiscal limitations and a small, inward-looking private telecommunications sector militate against the realisation of universal access to ICTs by the majority of Botswana's population. Mosime and Chiumbu also cite case studies in other parts of the world, including South Africa and the United States, to illustrate the tensions between universal access and market liberalisation of media. In the same vein, Robert B Horwitz and Willie Currie argue that the privatisation – rather than the liberalisation – of South Africa's telecommunications sector was done in haste and at the expense of service delivery, and at a huge cost to the poor. They trace the development of the post-apartheid telecommunication policy from White Paper through to legislation, and identify the process as highly flawed. Among other things, it retained the monopoly of Telkom, worsened telecommunication service delivery and opened up opportunities for rent-seeking under the ideological aegis of black economic empowerment (BEE).

To what extent has neo-liberal global communications policy influenced policy directions and outcomes in the region? In a comparative study, Dumisani Moyo analyses the trajectory of the broadcasting policy reform processes in Zambia and Zimbabwe. He argues that, despite regional and global pressures in both countries, the policy-making processes remained nationally determined, with the state playing a key role.

There is no consensus in the book, however, as to the nature and extent of external influences. For example, while the globalisation of market liberal policies is often blamed for the commercial models that have emerged in countries such as South Africa, Duncan and Glenn make the compelling argument that 'the marketisation of television (in South Africa) is a chosen strategy, rather than policy trajectory imposed in response to external, objective constraints …' Far from affirming the thesis that a liberalised media environment would lead to foreign domination in developing nations (Paterson 1994) – a fear that seems to have influenced the strict ownership regulations developed in Zimbabwe – Duncan and Glenn's chapter illustrates that South Africa did not become a haven for foreign multinationals after liberalisation, as the country turned out to be less attractive to foreign investors than had been anticipated. Instead, it is South African corporations that have been going global.

Finally, whither media policy-making in Southern Africa? One of the major contributions of this book is that some of the authors have taken the trouble to proffer suggestions and solutions regarding the policy paralysis experienced in particular countries. Policymakers and civil society actors alike will find it interesting to engage with these contributions. While the suggestions are country-specific, they address what appear to be universal concerns about the future direction and opportunities for policy reform in the region. Chuma's chapter on Zimbabwe, for instance, painstakingly develops what could be a blueprint for a long-awaited 'new Zimbabwe,' carefully borrowing from a mix of Western models and South African experience. Through their critique of the South African experience, Duncan and Glenn's chapter also provides warnings and suggestions for future policy directions.

The editors are especially grateful to Prof Tawana Kupe, the Dean of Humanities at the University of the Witwatersrand for providing financial assistance through his Dean's discretionary fund towards the copy editing of this volume, and to Isabelle Delvare who worked tirelessly to make this book more readable. We also wish to acknowledge financial support from the Emerging Researcher Programme at the University of Cape Town (UCT). Most especially, we wish to thank all the contributors to this collection for their cooperation and persistent commitment to making this project successful, and hope that you, the reader, will find it insightful and enjoyable.

References

Barratt, E. and G. Berger, eds. 2007. *50 Years of Journalism: African Media Since Ghana's Independence*. Johannesburg: African Editors' Forum.

Bratton, M. and N. van de Walle. 1997. *Democratic Experiments in Africa: Regime Transitions in Comparative Perspective*. Cambridge: Cambridge University Press.

Chakravartty, P. and K.Sarikakis. 2006. *Media Policy and Globalization*. Edinburgh: Edinburgh University Press.

Curran, J. 2002. *Media and Power*. London and New York: Routledge.

Diamond, L. 2008. The Democratic Rollback: The Resurgence of the Predatory State. *Foreign Affairs*, March/April 2008.

——. 1999. Introduction. In *Democratisation in Africa*, ed. L. Diamond and M.F. Plattner. Baltimore and London: The Johns Hopkins University Press.

——. 1996. Is the Third Wave Over? *Journal of Democracy* 7(3).

Joseph, R. 1999. Africa, 1990–1997: From Abertura to Closure. In *Democratisation in Africa*, ed. L. Diamond and M.F. Plattner, 3–17. Baltimore and London: The Johns Hopkins University Press.

——. 2003. Africa: States in Crisis. *Journal of Democracy* 14 (3).

Kupe, T. ed. 2003. *Broadcasting Policy and Practice in Africa*. Johannesburg: Article 19.

——. 2007. Southern Africa: 50 Years of Media. In *50 Years of Journalism: African Media Since Ghana's Independence*, ed. E. Barrat, E. and G. Berger, 136–147. Johannesburg: African Editors' Forum.

Nyamnjoh, F.B. 2005. *Africa's Media: Democracy and the Politics of Belonging*. London and New York: Zed Books; Pretoria: University of South Africa Press.

Paterson, C. 1994. Broadcasting for National Development in the New South Africa. Paper presented at the annual conference of the Association for Education in Journalism and Mass Communication, 10–14 August, in Atlanta, Georgia, United States.

Peters, G. 1999. *Institutional Theory in Political Science: The 'New Institutionalism'*. London and New York: Continuum.

Politics, privatisation and perversity in South Africa's telecommunications reform programme[1]

2

Robert B. Horwitz and Willie Currie

Background

The first all-race, democratic election in South Africa in 1994 brought to power the ANC, and also a mandate to transform nearly all South African institutions away from their apartheid pedigree and point of reference. The process to reform telecommunications ensued soon after the electorate voted in the ANC as the dominant partner in a government of national unity. Following an unusual participatory, consultative policy process, Parliament passed comprehensive legislation in 1996 to revamp the sector, roll out telephone service to the previously disadvantaged, and establish an independent regulator to oversee the reform. Government thereupon sold a 30 per cent equity stake in the state-owned telecommunications incumbent network operator, Telkom, to help facilitate the expansion of telephone services into under-serviced areas and populations (Republic of South Africa 1996a).[2]

More than ten years have now elapsed since the passage of the Telecommunications Act of 1996. By most accounts, the reform of South African telecommunications has been at best a bare success and at worst a medium-term failure. The act granted Telkom a five-year period of exclusivity to expand the network and prepare itself for eventual competition. Telkom, essentially managed by its equity partner Thintana Communications – itself a partnership between the American telecommunications giant SBC Communications (now, after merger, renamed AT&T), with a 60 per cent stake, and Telekom Malaysia, with 40 per cent – satisfied the letter of its roll-out obligation to build some 2.8 million new lines, but not the spirit of its universal service mandate. Telkom's high prices for installation, rental, and calls (and sociologically inappropriate billing mechanisms in rural areas) resulted in the disconnection of the vast majority of the new lines.[3] Thus, whereas access to telephone service in South Africa has improved considerably since 1996, gains in connectivity have been accomplished almost entirely through the market-led growth of pre-paid mobile telephony rather than through the legislatively mandated roll-out of the fixed line network by the incumbent operator.

Despite massive investment and construction, in the ten years from 1996 to 2006 the number of fixed-line subscribers increased from some 3.92 million to just under 4.71 million. In a population estimated at between 44 million and 47 million, this represents a current penetration rate of just 10 per cent (and falling). In the same time period, the number of mobile subscribers increased from under a million to over 19 million (Telkom 1997; ITU 2005; US Securities and Exchange Commission 2006: 9, 15).[4] Yet, notwithstanding the impressive growth of mobile telephones, prices for telecommunications services in South Africa – including mobile ones – are strikingly high by international comparisons to countries with roughly similar characteristics. The graph below, assembled from the research of James Hodge (2005a, 2005b) and Efficient Research (2004), illustrates these high prices. A key conclusion to be drawn is that mobile telephony, not Telkom, did increase access to communications, but that high prices constrained use. The growth and flexibility of value-added network services (VANS), including Internet access, have been constrained not just by high prices for leased lines, but by a highly litigious and sometimes predatory Telkom. This is not simply a sectoral problem. Because telecommunications are an input into virtually all productive activities, high tariffs and constrained service offerings are now recognised as a tax on industry and a drag on economic growth.[5]

Table 2.1 summarises the findings of a comparison of South African telecommunications prices with those of 14 other countries. The comparison included a group consisting of international 'best practice' countries (e.g. Canada and South Korea); and another group comprising countries similar to South Africa in terms of input costs, geographical dispersion of the population, income dispersion and level of development (e.g. Brazil and Morocco).

Table 2.1: Comparison of telecommunications pricing

Product	South African pricing compared with that in surveyed countries
Business asynchronous digital subscriber line (ADSL) broadband	The most expensive of the 15 countries sampled, and more than 9 times as expensive as the cheapest country surveyed.
Domestic leased lines	The most expensive of 12 countries surveyed, and 102% more expensive than the average price sampled.
International leased lines	Approximately 3 times higher than the next most expensive country sampled, and 31 times more expensive than the cheapest country out of 11 sampled.
Retail ADSL broadband	The most expensive of the 15 comparison countries.
Monthly fees for Internet service providers (ISPs)	The fourth-most expensive in the comparison group of 13 countries (but highest when calculated according to purchasing power parity).
Business international peak calls	The fifth-cheapest of the 15 comparison countries.
Peak local calls	The most expensive of the 15 countries sampled, and 199% more expensive than the average price.
Mobile-to-fixed-line calls	The second-most expensive of 15 countries surveyed, and 107% higher than the average price.
Retail off-peak local calls	The second-most expensive of 14 countries sampled, and 79% more expensive than the average price.
Off-peak mobile calls	The fifth-most expensive of 15 countries sampled, and 37% more expensive than the average price.

Source: Hodge, J. 2005. Telecommunications Prices in South Africa: An International Peer Group Comparison. Johannesburg: South Africa Foundation.

The Regulator, initially known as the South African Telecommunications Regulatory Authority (SATRA), then as the Independent Communications Authority of South Africa (ICASA) when SATRA and the Independent Broadcast Authority merged in 2000, has not been particularly effective. Its authority has been limited through a cumbersome dual jurisdictional structure with the Ministry of Communications

(MoC). And the government's mistrust of the Regulator's independence has resulted in efforts to control it. The MoC itself had a structural conflict of interest as both the policy-maker for the sector and the custodian of the state's considerable shareholding in Telkom. As a result, policy in the sector has unfolded in fits and starts, marked by many controversial incidents and abrupt reversals of strategy, the cancellation of ICASA regulations by the Minister, and the delay of competitive entry, notably in the licensing of a third mobile operator and a second network operator.[6]

In short, South African telecommunications has been a sector plagued by poor policy and monopolistic behaviour. This chapter explores the South African telecommunications sector ten years after its reform legislation and tries to account for the relative failure of that reform. As always in policy and regulatory matters, the story is dense and complicated. It can, however, be distilled into three interrelated themes:

1. Privatisation – the selling of a state infrastructural asset to a private party – won out over liberalisation – opening the sector to entry and fostering conditions for competition. This is best seen in three developments:

    a. The initial legislation of 1996, which eliminated the liberalisation timetable worked out in the preceding White Paper policy process in favour of ministerial discretion, largely in order to satisfy the demands of Telkom's strategic equity partner, Thintana Communications.

    b. Telkom's ongoing utilisation of its monopoly over the backbone network and its invocation of its legal exclusivity in order to inhibit the growth of competitive VANS and Internet service providers (ISPs); and the relative inability of the Regulator to combat either Telkom's predatory designs over upstream and downstream competitive offerings or deal successfully with the company's litigiousness.

    c. A regulatory struggle over Telkom's tariffs, in which ICASA was compelled to approve high increases in local service in order to protect the value of the company's 2003 Initial Public Offering.

    In sum, government partially privatised the incumbent network operator and, by contract and policy, protected it against competitive challenge.

2. Government's distrust of the 'state institutions supporting constitutional democracy' provided for in Chapter 9 of the South African Constitution, including institutions with various degrees of independence from government, such as the Auditor General, the South African Human Rights Commission, and ICASA. The ANC-led government has been leery about permitting real independence for these 'Chapter 9' institutions, and, at least in the case of ICASA, has not provided adequate operating resources. The Regulator not only

suffered from having to do many difficult tasks quickly without adequate human skills capacity, but was also in effect not permitted to develop and exercise those capacities because its authority and budget were so often undercut by the Ministry and the Department of Communication (DoC). That environment, in which a duly constituted democratic body was largely foiled in its efforts to do its job, dovetailed with the larger political environment of ANC actions to consolidate political power in 1996, with a relative lack of transparency in decision-making and with the discouragement of public criticism generally speaking – the last-mentioned the legacy of the ANC's exile culture of democratic centralism. In short, ANC political culture undermined independent regulation of the telecommunications sector.

3. Societies in transition from one political and economic orientation to another are particularly subject to 'rent-seeking' behaviour, especially where the privatisation of state assets is concerned. Privatising state assets is often a high-stakes, complicated process with few reliable institutional controls or applicable precedents. The debacle of privatisation in the former Soviet Union stands as a startling example of how clever former bureaucrats and middling entrepreneurs captured key state assets for a fraction of their real value (see Barnes 2006). The privatisation process in South Africa is a far cry from that of the USSR. Still, privatisation in South Africa has taken place in a political environment distinguished by the ANC's project to create a national black bourgeoisie through black economic empowerment (BEE). The otherwise laudable goal of spreading economic opportunity and power to previously disenfranchised black South Africans coalesced with ANC efforts to place comrades in the commanding heights of the economy and, correspondingly, a small number of well-connected comrades manoeuvring for major clout in the business world. The result has been an empowerment process that enriches a very few and largely fails to benefit the masses.[7]

The article proceeds to engage these three themes through the analysis of particularly telling examples from developments and policy conflicts in the sector since 1996.

From White Paper to legislation: How privatisation subverted liberalisation

If there was a moment of 'original sin', an event that cast South African telecommunications reform along an unhappy path, it was the alteration of the White Paper as draft legislation went to Parliament in 1996. The White Paper had created a model for telecommunications reform that gave a strong emphasis to the framework and goals of the Keynesian-inspired Reconstruction and Development Programme

(RDP) of the Tripartite Alliance (the ANC, the Congress of South African Trade Unions [COSATU] and the South African Communist Party [SACP]), in particular the aim of redressing the inequity of apartheid through the provision of basic services to black people. The White Paper placed affordable telecommunications for all at the core of its vision and sought to balance 'the provision of basic universal service to disadvantaged rural and urban communities with the delivery of high-level services capable of meeting the needs of a growing South African economy' (Republic of South Africa 1996b: 17). This vision and goal was the outcome of the multi-stakeholder negotiations around the White Paper. The subsequent legislation, the Telecommunications Act of 1996, vested in the Minister several of the powers the White Paper had reserved for the Regulator and eliminated the White Paper's painstakingly achieved liberalisation timetable in favour of ministerial discretion regarding when and if various segments of the sector would be opened to competition (Republic of South Africa 1996b).[8] The changes not only delayed the liberalisation of the sector, but also created jurisdictional conflicts that were easily exploited by an opportunistic incumbent network operator – resulting in the effective doubling of the exclusivity period.

Like most incumbent operators, Telkom managed by its savvy and almost congenitally litigious equity partner, SBC Communications, was bent on maintaining its sectoral dominance and thwarting potential competitors to its service offerings and profitability. The Ministry of Communications' ambiguous brief as both policy-maker for the sector and guardian of the value of the state's shareholding in Telkom afforded opportunities for politically expedient interventions. This was seen in numerous instances, most notably in ministerial intervention in SATRA's process to award a third mobile telephone licence in 2000; in the Minister's cancellation of ICASA's draft regulations on interconnection that same year; and in pressure on ICASA to approve Telkom tariff hikes in 2002 in order to protect the value of the company's shares as the government embarked upon a public offering of shares.[9]

The usual public explanation for the changes to the White Paper concerns timing. At the same moment as the telecommunications legislation was going to Parliament in 1996, the government was trying to cement a deal for a strategic equity partner (SEP) for Telkom. The Regulator was not yet established and would not be up and running for months. More was at stake than just finding a particular SEP for Telkom; concluding this transaction would send an unambiguous signal to international investors that South Africa was a secure and desirable place to do business. Indeed, the winning bid of Thintana Communications for 30 per cent of Telkom brought US$1.2 billion to South Africa, by far the largest single infusion of foreign capital in the country in the 1990s. But, while clearly important, the timing explanation is inadequate in and of itself, given other evidence. The Minister of Posts, Telecommunications and Broadcasting, Jay Naidoo, and the Director

General of the DoC, Andile Ngcaba, were loath to cede ministerial power to the Regulator.[10] Ministry representatives and ANC parliamentarians fought very hard to limit the statutory independence of the Regulator in the final legislative debates in Parliament, arguing that SATRA, an institution of what was now a democratic government entrusted by the electorate to pursue transformation, should be 'aligned' with government, not independent of it (Republic of South Africa 1996c, 1996d).

The Telecommunications Act and the implementation of the strategic equity partner deal turned out to have serious consequences for years to come. By the time the SEP bidding came to a close, only one offer was left on the table, that of Thintana Communications. Although Deutsche Telekom and its investment-banker advisers did submit bid documents, this was little more than the appearance of a bid. At the last moment, Deutsche Telekom's board decided not to proceed with the submission. Its withdrawal amounted to a judgement that South Africa was not yet stable enough and that the profitability of an investment in Telkom was too uncertain. As a consequence, SBC, the dominant partner in Thintana Communications, gained that much more leverage. According to Jim Myers, SBC's central operative in South Africa between 1994 and 1998, the American company had made a very strong bid and, having a good understanding of South African politics in that period, had sealed the deal by 'romancing' the unions. Opposition to privatisation by the unions had put the brakes on policy reform in the sector in 1995–96. SBC flew several key South African union and government officials to San Antonio and Mexico City, where they conferred with union leaders at SBC and Telmex (another of SBC's significant investments). SBC had experience in South Africa. It had been the managing shareholder in MTN, one of the two (at the time) cellular telephone providers, with a 15.5 per cent stake. While managing MTN, SBC focused on its bid for Telkom and participated in the due diligence bid process. When it became clear that SBC was the only player left in the SEP bidding exercise, the company temporarily transferred its entire San Antonio corporate office legislative team to South Africa to help draft the Telecommunications Act, to make sure that the legislation accorded with the company's requirements (Jim Myers, interview by author, Johannesburg, 13 September 2006).[11]

It is crucial to recognise the pivotal role of SBC in the transformation of South African telecommunications. Thintana signed a 'shareholders' agreement' with the South African government in May 1997, which bound the government to terms rather favourable to the company. That document has never been released publicly – its contents remain unknown even to the Regulator. Such secrecy, presumably, is highly unusual, given that the agreement concerns a publicly owned vital infrastructural asset, in a polity where governmental transparency has been officially prized. In spite of the secrecy, several of the central provisions of the agreement can be gleaned from other documents. As part of the sale to Thintana

Communications, the then Minister of Posts, Telecommunications and Broadcasting entered into an agreement with Thintana under which the company undertook significant operational and managerial responsibilities and acquired the ability to exercise effective operational and managerial control over Telkom until May 2002. Pursuant to the agreement, Thintana had the power to staff certain management positions, including those of chief operating officer, chief financial officer and chief strategic officer. In all these provisions, SBC dominated its Telekom Malaysia partner (Thintana Communications 1997). SBC controlled Telkom by restructuring the key management committees and exercising voting supremacy within them. The individuals occupying these committee positions were seconded to Telkom from SBC and Telekom Malaysia (Telkom 1997b; Telkom SA Limited *et al.* 1997).

In addition, Thintana and the government were entitled to appoint a number of directors to Telkom's board of directors, based on their ownership of Telkom, and a number of Telkom's corporate actions were subject to specific approval by Thintana Communications and the government or their board representatives. These matters generally included business plans, annual budgets, training programmes, the payment of dividends, the performance of obligations and the exercise of rights under Telkom's Public Switched Telecommunications Services (PSTS) licence (US Securities and Exchange Commission 2006: 43–44).[12] For the five years until May 2002, Thintana was entitled to appoint a majority of the members of Telkom's operating committee, thus granting it control over most of Telkom's significant operational matters. The Shareholders' Agreement was never made public because, according to Jim Myers, some of its provisions bound the government so stringently and gave Thintana so much control that, had they become public knowledge, this would have raised huge outcry. Clauses in the Shareholders' Agreement stipulated that once the Telecommunications Act was in place, neither Telkom nor Thintana would be compelled to follow any legislation that violated the Shareholders' Agreement. This created a strong incentive for the government to prevent legislation that might violate – and make public – the Shareholders' Agreement (Jim Myers, interview by author, Johannesburg, 13 September 2006).

SBC's strategy was very clear, Jim Myers maintains: maximise the value of Thintana's investment during Telkom's five-year exclusivity period and then exit quickly. Thintana seconded 75 employees to Telkom at the highest management levels, an arrangement that not only gave it working control over Telkom but was lucrative as well. In terms of the 'Strategic Services Agreement' that accompanied these developments, Telkom was obligated to pay the seconded managers salaries *and* transfer the same dollar amount per year – averaging close to US\$1 million per SBC employee (and most of the 75 seconded managers were SBC) – to Thintana as a 'strategic services personnel fee' (Telkom SA Ltd *et al.* 1997: 9, schedules 1–3). Telkom's annual reports show that the company paid Thintana a 'management fee' in the region of R260-million per year in the middle years of its exclusivity period, which represented some 16%–17% of Telkom's net profit (Telkom 2001). [13]

Telkom's exclusivity: shield and weapon

Virtually all of Telkom's actions were oriented toward extracting value. This would not ordinarily be surprising behaviour for a company. However, because Telkom was a legally conferred monopolist, its explicit mandates were to expand telecommunications service to the previously disadvantaged and to develop advanced services for South African businesses. Of course, it was also charged with protecting its own value and preparing itself for eventual competition, and *this* was the mandate the company pursued with vigour. Telkom worked to police and even augment the exclusivity over the fixed-line network it was granted by the Telecommunications Act. Together with the PSTS licence, the act authorised Telkom to provide, on an exclusive basis, national long-distance, international and local-access telecommunication services; public payphone services; telecommunication facilities for the provision of VANS and private telecommunications networks (PTNs); and telecommunication facilities comprising fixed lines for the mobile cellular telephone operators (Minister of Communications 1997a). Among other things this meant that providers of VANS and Internet services were required by law to purchase leased lines and other means of telecommunications access from Telkom. But Telkom itself competed directly in the VANS, Internet access provider (IAP), and Internet service provider (ISP) markets, giving it the power and the incentive to favour its own offerings and/or hinder those of competitors. An early instance of this coalesced around Internet access.

The controversy over Internet access provides a window on how Telkom, even prior to coming under SBC's control but very much in keeping with the hard-nosed, litigious orientation of its future SBC manager, exploited its exclusivity claims to engage in anti-competitive practices and, beyond that, to use litigation to impose costs and delay.[14] Internet access in South Africa – as has been the case in many countries – developed originally in the universities and largely beyond the range of Telkom's corporate radar (Janisch & Kotlowitz 1998; Lewis 2005). Using network infrastructure leased from Telkom, private ISPs had propelled South Africa to one of the 20 most Internet-connected countries in the world by the mid-1990s (Salaman 1998; ISPA undated). The Internet did come to Telkom's attention, and it launched SAIX, its own IAP, in June 1996 at a tariff considerably lower than other IAPs. In November of that year Telkom introduced Intekom, a dial-up ISP. The private IAPs and ISPs, galvanised by the prospect of Telkom entering its markets even as it was also the company from which they had to lease lines to gain access to the backbone network, formed a trade association, the Internet Service Providers' Association

(ISPA). The association lodged a complaint with the Competition Board, South Africa's competition and antitrust agency, after the launch of SAIX, alleging that Telkom was unfairly leveraging its control of basic voice and data networks to engage in predatory pricing. The Competition Board initiated a process to define a policy framework for the Internet industry, but Telkom refused to provide audit information on the cost structure of SAIX and rejected the board's jurisdiction in favour of the newly established SATRA.[15]

At SATRA, Telkom filed a counter-complaint that commercial ISPs were in contravention of its sphere of exclusivity, and asked the Regulator to amend its licence to recognise Internet as part of its PSTS monopoly. ISPA argued that Telkom's complaint was indefensible in terms of any reasonable interpretation of the Act, which expressly identified the provision of e-mail as a VANS in the competitive arena (Republic of South Africa 1996a: section 40[2]). Accordingly, in one of its first rulings, SATRA decreed in October 1997 that access to the Internet would be applied under VANS licences and that Telkom had no claim to exclusivity with regard to the provision of Internet access (SATRA 1997). Telkom then challenged SATRA's ruling in the Pretoria High Court, claiming that SATRA had no legal basis for its decision. Although the court found for Telkom because of procedural violations on the part of SATRA, Telkom and the ISPs came to a commercial *modus vivendi* and Telkom declined to proceed further legally (*Telkom* v. *Maepa* 1998). Still, because all South African Internet providers must lease lines from Telkom, and because dial-up access is subject to high, metered call tariffs, Internet use has weakened. If in the mid-1990s South Africa's Internet connectivity was fourteenth in the world, a decade later it dropped to thirty-seventh (ISPA 2006).[16]

As part of the effort to thwart competition by expanding the ever-increasing shadow of its exclusivity, Telkom also challenged the private data networks offered by VANS providers as a breach of its legal monopoly. Telkom's PSTS licence gave it the right to contractually bind VANS providers to lease from it, with no resale, and no provision of voice. VANS were legally constrained from prompting or assisting users to bypass the PSTS. The relationship between Telkom and VANS providers began amicably enough. Members of the South African VANS Association (SAVA) used to meet with a number of Telkom business managers once a month. By May 1999, with the ascension of SBC's Tom Barry as Telkom's Chief Operating Officer, Telkom managers were told to stop meeting with SAVA. Telkom now saw VANS, and particularly their provision of virtual private networks (VPN), as an express threat to Telkom's hold on its largest corporate clients (Mike van den Bergh, past president of the South African VANS Association, interview by author, Johannesburg, 4 September 2006).[17] Telkom complained to SATRA that some VANS providers were offering services in violation of the company's exclusivity rights. Telkom insisted that a VPN constituted a PSTS service. Unhappy with SATRA's demurral on this question, Telkom began sending letters to VANS providers requiring them to confirm that they were not using Telkom's infrastructure for purposes that violated Telkom's exclusivity. The letters specified various practices that, if followed, would severely curtail VANS services. The letters indicated that if the providers and customers could not so stipulate, Telkom could suspend provision of its leased infrastructure and would refuse to supply additional bandwidth to the VANS providers. Telkom in fact stopped supplying leased lines to AT&T in September 1999 (which prompted a complaint from the US Trade Representative that Telkom was in breach of international trade agreements) and refused to lease additional lines to VANS providers.

At the same time, Telkom's own VANS offerings were priced differently and more favourably than its competitors': Telkom priced a digital leased line according to speed, distance and the whole circuit; the price for its own VANS offerings was distance independent and charged customers for just half the circuit. Moreover, Telkom insisted that its VANS offering could bundle voice and data, whereas legally its competitors' offerings could not. Telkom increased the price of digital 2Mb leased lines by more than 20 per cent each year from 1998 to 2000. This resulted in a 4 to 1 price differential on a national VPN (Melody et al 2003: 32–33; Mike Van den Bergh, interview by author, Johannesburg, 4 September 2006; Makhaya & Roberts 2003: 52–53). Telkom actions were also not just designed to capture VANS market share. They were oriented, according to a study commissioned by the Department of Communications (DoC), toward protecting its legacy data services, in particular frame relay and dial-up PSTN and ISDN (Finnie et al 2003: 77). The Department for Trade and Industry (DTI) early on understood the problem of Telkom's ability to bottle up access to the network backbone. A high-level delegation from DTI, including its Director General, Alistair Ruiters, approached Andile Ngcaba, Director General of the DoC, in 2000 about high telecommunications prices and businesses having a hard time obtaining appropriate data telecommunication services. DTI wanted to open up the backbone network to allow two more network operators, in large part to accommodate the data communication needs of the 500 major South Africa corporations. Despite assurances from Ngcaba, nothing came of the proposal even after repeated written inquiries (Dave Kaplan, DTI economist, interview by author, Cape Town, 10 September 2006; Alan Hirsch, DTI economist, interview by author, Pretoria, 15 September 2006).[18]

SAVA's subsequent complaint regarding Telkom's anti-competitive behaviour was upheld by a SATRA cease-and-refrain determination of 10 September 1999, and a formal judgment of 26 June 2000 ordering Telkom to supply additional bandwidth to VANS providers – both of which Telkom took to court on review and won on procedural grounds (*Telkom* v. *Mayimele-Hashatse* 2000; *Telkom* v. *Dikgale* 2001). In the midst of this fracas, SATRA sent finalised interconnection and facilities leasing guidelines to the Minister, guidelines that spelled out Telkom's common carrier obligations and specified a pricing formula. The Minister approved and published the guidelines in March 2000, but abruptly withdrew them a month later, on the basis that there had been insufficient public consultation and that the merger between the Independent Broadcasting Authority (IBA) and SATRA required further postponement so as to allow the IBA to participate in the process. Widespread speculation was that Telkom's unhappiness with the chosen pricing methodology and provisions for interconnection lay behind the Minister's cancellation of the policy (DoC 2000a, 2000b; Cohen 2003). ICASA also convened an inquiry on the status of VPNs, determining them to be part of VAN services (ICASA 2001). But with the resolution of the matter frustrated by ICASA's problems following legal procedure, SAVA filed the complaint against Telkom with the Competition Commission (the replacement of the Competition Board). In February 2004 the Commission found that Telkom had engaged in anti-competitive actions, and fined the company R3.7 billion (Competition Commission 2004). Telkom appealed the decision on jurisdictional grounds (reversing itself and claiming only ICASA had proper jurisdiction). The matter remains unresolved as of this writing. The point in the VANS controversies was that Telkom refused to provide facilities on the basis of its own interpretation of the Act and its PSTS licence. Two government oversight bodies deemed Telkom's actions anti-competitive, and an important Cabinet Ministry – Trade and Industry – clearly concurred. Telkom essentially paid no heed to the fact that there was a Regulator statutorily authorised to make determinations regarding facilities and licences, and the company challenged jurisdiction at every turn. If that failed, Telkom could exercise its *ex parte* influence on the Ministry to cancel regulations that it found particularly irksome, in this case the Regulator's 2000 interconnection and facilities leasing guidelines.

Distrust of independent government institutions: Joint jurisdiction, weak regulator

All democracies possess various institutions – at some remove from the elected government – that exercise oversight of certain economic, social, and governmental activities. Regulatory agencies are among these institutions. The independent regulation of telecommunications, moreover, is required in a number of international and regional agreements. In any instance of oversight of this type, there is a balance to be struck between policy-making and regulation, even though there is an element of arbitrariness to the distinction. South Africa's balance between policy-making and regulation of the communications sector was bound up in the politics of the ANC's consolidation of power and the need to confront the faltering economy in the mid-1990s. Two consequential matters shaped the ANC's outlook during 1995–1996:

the National Party went into opposition, and it became clear that hitherto efforts to manage the economy under the Reconstruction and Development Programme (RDP) were not working. With the departure of the National Party from the Government of National Unity, the ANC was now in the position to assume genuine political power – and was now fully responsible for policy failures. The RDP, understood generally as a Keynesian-inspired plan of growth through redistribution, had represented a blend of approaches and mix of compromises rather than a coherent set of economic policies (Republic of South Africa 1994).

By the mid-1990s, the South African economy was hit by the fallout of the previous several years of apartheid budget deficits and political instability. Capital flowed out of the country, the national debt was up considerably, and the rand fell sharply against foreign currencies. Business investment had not materialised. A shift from the RDP's Keynesian orientation to fiscal stabilisation and a focus on growth underlay the adoption of the Growth, Employment and Redistribution (GEAR) macroeconomic strategy, which had features of a locally imposed IMF-style structural adjustment policy (Republic of South Africa 1996g; Gelb 1998; Hirsch 2005).

GEAR may well have been a shrewd macroeconomic plan to deal with the vagaries of South Africa's difficult post-apartheid economic situation as the country faced the realities of globalisation. Alan Hirsch, among others, makes a robust case for GEAR's success, as well as consideration of the circumstances where the implementation of fiscal discipline was too stringent.[19] For our purposes in this paper, it was the *way* GEAR was adopted that is of note. Notwithstanding the strong culture of consultation and transparency in the politics of the Tripartite Alliance, the ANC leadership presented GEAR to its COSATU and SACP partners and civil society structures as a 'non-negotiable' *fait accompli*. Accompanying, even part and parcel of, the ANC's consolidation of political power, the imposition of GEAR was an important moment in the transformation of the broader political and ideological environment. That environment was one in which the ANC leadership, annoyed by the time and effort required for consultation, and intent on understanding itself as the government entrusted with a mission from the electorate, dovetailed with the old ANC exile culture of democratic centralism. It marked the beginning of the centralisation of power in the presidency and of governing largely from above (Gumede 2005). The new ideological atmosphere manifested itself as deep suspicion of the putative independence of the Chapter 9 institutions.

In the case of the telecommunications Regulator, it meant establishing a kind of joint jurisdiction. In the terminology of scholars of the sector, this entailed 'regulatory dualism' (Gillwald 2003) and the 'capture' of the Regulator from the beginning by the government (Cohen 2003). As seen above, the Telecommunications Act gave the Minister the responsibility for issuing Telkom licences and determining if and when various parts of the sector would be open to competition. The Act also gave the Minister power over interconnection policy and Telkom tariffs for an initial three-year period. The Minister retained the power to invite and endorse applications for major licences and to approve certain regulations drafted by the Regulator. The Act empowered the Regulator to assess licence bids and make recommendations to the Minister, but it could not award a licence – the Regulator merely 'issued' a licence on approval by the Minister. Only in the case of non-restricted licences, such as VANS and PTNs, could the Regulator take a decision on its own. The Minister may issue policy directions. The Minister does not have the power to *issue* regulations, but retains the power to *approve* certain regulations, without which the regulations cannot be promulgated. Because of this structure, real power, in the estimation of Nkateko Nyoka, former chief executive officer of ICASA, lies in the *interpretation* of policy, a prerogative that rests with the Minister. And the Ministry is open – if only by virtue of its shareholding in Telkom – to industry (especially Telkom) lobbying (Nkateko Nyoka, interview by author, Johannesburg, 14 September 2006).[20]

When they could not control the Regulator structurally, the Ministry and the political establishment endeavoured to control it by two other means: through the process of appointment onto the ICASA Council, and via the budget. Although statutorily the appointment to Council was made by the President on the recommendation of the Parliamentary Portfolio Committee on Communications, in reality it was primarily the Ministry and the DoC that put forward nominees. The Portfolio Committee published a public call for nominations and then held public interviews using a shortlist. The Ministry and the DoC made sure that surrogates nominated preferred candidates, after which they lobbied the ANC parliamentary committee caucus, known as the Parliamentary Study Group. (And even then the Ministry – twice – tried to get Parliament to give it power of appointment.) It is widely understood that some Council members have been 'political animals', to use the term of SATRA's former Council chairperson, Nape Maepa; in other words, the minions of the Ministry or of the DoC's director general, typically consulting with their government sponsors before votes. In the third cellular licence deliberations in particular, it appeared as if certain ICASA councillors were acting on instructions from the executive arm of government rather than applying their own minds to the issue before them (Nape Maepa, interview by author, Johannesburg, 4 September 2006).[21]

The dynamic was explained in a more subtle manner by Mandla Langa, who was chairperson of the ICASA Council from 2000 to 2005. Langa indicated that what matters in South African politics is who sends the policy, not necessarily the policy itself, reflecting in complicated fashion the ongoing metric of political capital in internal ANC relations (Mandla Langa, interview by author, Johannesburg, 5 September 2006).[22] Exiles and former Robben Island prisoners have more political capital than other ANC leaders, even those who carried on the anti-apartheid struggle inside the country in the 1980s – and trust flows through these ANC networks of political capital. The political establishment, until recently organised around President Mbeki, has cultivated these networks of trust through the appointment process at all levels of government (Mbeki appointed not only cabinet ministers but also all directors general of departments) and extends to the award of state contracts, tenders, and privatisations (Gumede 2005: 40–41).[23] Indeed, the practice of democratic centralism in the post-apartheid period is clearly signalled by government's frequent use of the word 'deployment' when appointing people to various posts. ANC cadres have typically been 'deployed' to serve in various institutions at the behest of the ANC, suggesting that they have been answerable to those who appointed them. This 'deployment' has been into the business sector as well as the political sphere.

With regard to the Regulator's budget, ICASA is classified as a Schedule 3 institution by the Treasury, which requires that the Regulator's budget come through the budget of the DoC. As Nkateko Nyoka avers, the department typically required the Regulator to make the case regarding its budgetary needs, but would not listen to reason and would automatically cut the amount requested. In Nyoka's view, the monies allocated were a little more than half of what was necessary to do the job properly. An inadequate budget also adds to the Regulator's political losses: without money, it cannot properly litigate court challenges, especially challenges made by companies with deep pockets, such as Telkom (Nkateko Nyoka, interview by author, Johannesburg, 14 September 2006).

The consequences of dual jurisdiction and the subjugation of the Regulator are perhaps best seen in the struggle over Telkom's tariffs. These tariffs were administered under a price-cap regime, the now standard international model for regulating the prices of dominant network operators. According to the model, the operator's tariffs may be increased to cover the expected effects of inflation on the company's costs of providing a designated basket of services, but must be decreased to cover expected improvements in its productivity. The Minister set the initial price cap productivity figure in May 1997 at a very conservative 1.5 per cent.[24] This ministerial determination also stated that future reviews of the rate regime should not have a material adverse impact on Telkom or its ability to meet the universal and access obligations set out in its licence (Minister of Communications 1997b). ICASA commenced an inquiry on the rate regime in December 2000. Its inquiry found that the initial productivity factor was set too low and that residential customers were highly vulnerable to Telkom's rate rebalancing. ICASA concluded that rate rebalancing had already been taken too far and that residential customers were subsidising Telkom's competitive VANS and other business services (Thornton & Hodge 2006: 205). Moreover, the Regulator was convinced that Telkom had abused the use of inflation forecasts. On the key matter of the productivity factor, ICASA recommended setting the figure at 5 per cent. This figure itself represented just an informed guess because Telkom had failed to produce regulatory accounts as required by law. Once again, Telkom did not (or could not, because of the bundled nature of its services) make costing information available. Fearful that Telkom would litigate yet again, ICASA reduced the productivity figure to 3 per cent (Ibid: 206). Even so, Minister Ivy Matsepe-Casaburri did not approve the regulations. She sent them back to ICASA with a recommendation to return to the productivity factor of 1.5 per cent – a recommendation with which the Regulator complied (Stones 2001).

Even after winning in the price cap struggle, Telkom refused to abide by ICASA's rate regime regulations. Employing a gap in the law and the timing of the new regulations, Telkom published tariff increases before the new regime fell into place. Using a productivity factor of zero per cent, Telkom's published tariffs effectively increased rates by 5.5 per cent. Telkom also removed the 50 km–100 km band from the call structure, turning all such calls into long-distance ones.

Facing continuing court challenges, ICASA reached an out-of-court settlement with Telkom, allowing the company to implement its tariff increases in exchange for a promise to keep its subsequent increases below the maximum permissible by the rate regime regulations. Telkom also agreed to a special lifeline service for emergency calls. The Minister approved and published the amended rate regime regulations in 2002 (DoC 2002).[25]

The result of Telkom's ability to cajole the Minister and defy the Regulator was that, for example, prices for a local three-minute call at peak times between 1997 and 2002 increased by 26 per cent per year. These increases were in part responsible for so many customers dropping off the wire-line network. It bears repeating that Telkom cut off 2.1 million lines from the poor, lines that with some pricing ingenuity presumably might have been kept in place for emergency and incoming calls. Telkom's triumph on the rate regime issue was yet another instance when privatisation trumped liberalisation and independent regulation, the White Paper's basic goal of telephone service to the poor was abrogated, and the rational growth of the sector was undermined.[26] The immediate reason for ministerial interference in, and the Regulator's acquiescence on, rates was the perceived need to maintain the value of the government's shares in the upcoming Telkom initial public offering (IPO) (Mandla Langa, interview by author, Johannesburg, 5 September 2006). The IPO of government-held Telkom shares (initially planned for 2001, but put off until 2003) would bring a higher share price and more revenue to the treasury.

The subjugation of the Regulator's independence had other, unforeseen consequences. When approval for a second network operator (SNO) was finally secured after years of delay, government officials, including ICASA councillors, went abroad hoping to entice foreign communication operators to bid. Cable &

Wireless, in his bemused recollection, almost ran Mandla Langa out of its corporate office, saying that it would never come in on the SNO deal owing to South Africa's protectionist and non-independent regulatory structure. An article in the *Mail&Guardian*, quoting unnamed former ICASA councillors, claimed that British Telecom had also declined to make a bid for the SNO, for similar reasons (Dawes 2004). In general, South Africa had a great deal of trouble attracting viable bidders for its third mobile operator and its second network operator, adding considerably to the delay of these services.

Privatisation in societies in transition: 'Rent-seeking' and black economic empowerment

What joint jurisdiction and limitation on the Regulator's independence and efficacy did secure was Telkom's financial health and the guarantee of lucrative profits for its Thintana partner. Telkom's operating revenues rose consistently every year. Its net profits and earnings per share dropped in 2000, then rose steadily and soared in 2004 and in the two years thereafter. It is difficult to settle on hard and fast numbers, because in each annual report Telkom 'restates' or adjusts the numbers from previous years. Nonetheless, the following provide a pretty accurate picture of trends:

Table 2.2: Telkom, US Securities and Exchange Commission

	Operating revenue (Rbn)	Net profit (Rbn)	Earnings per share (cents)
1997	15.8	1.79	458.0
1998	19.2	2.4	448.5
1999	22.7	2.35	421.2
2000	27.1	1.5	290.2
2001	31.4	1.6	294.6
2002	34.2	1.2	343.8
2003	37.3	1.7	292.3
2004	41.1	4.7	823.9
2005	43.7	6.8	1 246.7
2006	48.3	9.3	1 744.7

Source: Telkom annual reports, various years; US Securities and Exchange Commission (2006).

Listed on the Johannesburg Stock Exchange and the New York Stock Exchange in March 2003, Telkom's share price reflected its monopoly position and its rising profit levels. In the words of the company's own corporate profile (Telkom 2005), the share price 'has more than trebled in value over the past two years ... This performance reflects Telkom's financial stability, track record in growing market share, and ability to balance the pursuit of growth opportunities with the interests of employees, customers and communities.' In fact, this is corporate-speak for the fact that monopolistic power empowered Telkom to thwart competition and realise high profits.

As for Thintana Communications, its 30 per cent stake of Telkom purchased in 1997 for R5.45 billion (US$1.26 billion), was sold in two tranches in 2004: a 14.9 per cent stake in June for R6.1 billion (US$1.02 billion) and the remaining 15.1 per cent stake in November 2004 for R6.6 billion (about US$1.1 billion). It is difficult to track the final value of Thintana's investment beyond the figures stated above. Simpiwe Piliso (2006a) wrote in the *Sunday Times* that Thintana had realised R15 billion between management fees and share sales at the time it sold 14.9 per cent of Telkom (just under half of its stake) in June 2004.

The South African treasury may have benefited in the short run from the initial privatisation and the March 2003 sale of government-held (share-price-sheltered) Telkom stock. The latter sale also represented South Africa's biggest attempt to spread share ownership to the black majority through what was known as the 'Khulisa share scheme'.[27] But in the view of most analysts, and consonant with the analysis of this paper, the exchange of liberalisation and competition for privatisation was damaging to the larger economy.[28] Who else gained from a set of arrangements that, by any reasonable reckoning, did not much benefit residential telephone users or would-be users, Internet surfers, businesses requiring sophisticated data services, or the potential electronic services and ICT companies enamoured of the DTI? Here the brief history of telecommunications after 1996 intersects with some of the patterns of South African black economic empowerment (BEE).

The conversion of South Africa from its apartheid legacy naturally had to extend not just to politics and government but also to the economy and the internal workings of business. Nearly all business and other organisations have initiated processes that bring the previously disadvantaged into leadership, ownership, and management positions. This is what is understood by the widely used term, 'transformation.' But the initial pattern of transformation functioned largely to produce a small group of extremely wealthy black businessmen: enrichment rather than empowerment. Because most of this group consisted of ANC comrades with excellent political connections, there is reason to understand the phenomenon as a conscious political project to seed ANC members into the commanding heights of the economy in a kind of 'political machine' or political clientelism project.

A few ANC discussion documents speak openly of establishing a national black bourgeoisie.[29] But this may be too 'conspiratorial' a view. Suffice it to say that in the wake of the ascendance of the ANC's business elite, in a situation where the government has no clear grand social transformation project (notwithstanding the ANC's paper on such), rent-seeking and clientelism – which are legitimated in terms of post-apartheid restitution, deracialisation, and black economic empowerment – can thrive. The topic of the 'gravy train' or of quick, politically derived, enrichment is a constant feature of contemporary South African everyday conversation and news reports. Rent-seeking behaviour prompted Parliament to pass the Broad-based Black Economic Empowerment Act in 2003 in order to establish controls over the transformation process and help spread out its benefits (Republic of South Africa 2003). Still, insider rent-seeking has impacted on, and continues to affect, the telecommunications sector. A couple of examples will suffice.

The 1996 Telecommunications White Paper did not address the issue of a strategic equity partner (SEP) and the matter was left to the Minister for Posts, Telecommunication and Broadcasting. Since the Tripartite Alliance was deeply divided on the issue of the privatisation of state-owned enterprises, it fell to the Minister to work out a *modus vivendi* with the trade unions. President Mandela replaced Minister Pallo Jordan with former COSATU General Secretary Jay Naidoo because, in the judgment of many observers, Jordan had not been able to get the unions on board in terms of the SEP.[30] Recall that SBC, in the words of Jim Myers, 'romanced' the unions. One particular amorous interlude involved Communications Workers Union (CWU) chief, Tlhalefang Sekano. Sekano was elected president at the union's founding in 1996, when the Posts and Telecommunications Workers' Association (POTWA) merged with other smaller unions to create the CWU. Sekano's slate defeated that of POTWA's incumbent president, Lefty Monyokolo, who was known to be firmly opposed to the privatisation of Telkom. Sekano was one of those union leaders whom SBC took to San Antonio and Mexico City in 1996–1997, and who presumably helped convince the CWU rank and file to go along with that particular SEP. Sekano was not just president of the CWU; he also became executive chairman of the Communication Workers' Investment Company, and a member of the Board of Directors of Ucingo Investments, which held 3 per cent of the ordinary shares of Telkom until 17 September 2003, when it was sold. Sekano was brought onto the Telkom Board of Directors in 2001, a period when Telkom was retrenching tens of thousands of unionised workers. He left the board in 2004 (making approximately R96,000 in fees per annum for his service to the board). Telkom's annual report for 2005 (Telkom 2006) states that Sekano was also the chairperson of Letlapa Security and a director of Telesafe Security. Letlapa Security owned an interest in Telesafe Security, a security company that provides physical security to Telkom. Telkom paid R16 million and R39.3 million to Telesafe

Security for these services, in the years ended 31 March 2005 and 31 March 2004 respectively. There is no smoking gun of corruption here. Yet the overall impression created is that some union officials, approving the privatisation of Telkom and acquiescing to, if not collaborating with, the outsourcing and downscaling processes led by Telkom management, benefited from them personally under the aegis of BEE.

The director general of the DoC, Andile Ngcaba, who had a long history in the sector, clearly carried out a sectoral version of black economic empowerment. As Postmaster General in 1996, he awarded a data-switch licence to Vula Communications, days *before* the passage of the Telecommunications Act in 1996. The original owners of Vula were drawn from a BEE group that participated in the White Paper process; the licence presumably was their reward for loyalty to Ngcaba. Vula became Wireless Business Solutions (WBS) following the sale of a portion of the company to a strategic equity partner to save it from collapse, following two years of interconnection negotiations that failed to result in commercial agreement. WBS got involved with Uthingo, which was awarded the lucrative contract to operate the national lottery. Interestingly, Tlhalefang Sekano had been a director, since 1999, of Wireless Business Solutions.

Ngcaba was at the centre of most of the policy in the telecommunications sector for more than a dozen years. He clearly favoured Telkom as the agent of bringing telecommunication services to the previously disadvantaged, and acted to protect Telkom so as to defend the universal service obligation. Ngcaba was also described by one insider as 'always scheming about the sector to support his comrades'. But he also served his own interests in a spectacular way at the end of his government tenure. While still director general of the DoC, Ngcaba devised a strategy to bid for Thintana's shares if and when they came available. He even showed Jim Myers a compact disc featuring the plan and asked him to arrange a meeting with SBC. Myers refused. SBC also refused to meet with Ngcaba while he was still in the government (Jim Myers, interview by author, Johannesburg, 13 September 2006). Ngcaba left the department in December 2003, to take up the position of chairperson of Dimension Data, an information and communication technology (ICT) supplier. His ascent to Dimension Data gave that company an entry point into government and private ICT procurement, inasmuch as a transformation charter of ICT companies put in place a BEE procurement policy such that signatories promised to procure 70 per cent of eligible procurement from excellent, good and satisfactory BEE contributors (ICT Empowerment Charter Working Group 2005).

Thintana sold 14.9 per cent of its stake of Telkom in June 2004 to South African and certain international institutional investors. Soon thereafter, it announced its intention to sell its remaining 15.1 per cent stake. In November a consortium led by Ngcaba, which included Gloria Serobe of Women Investment Portfolio Holdings and Smuts Ngonyama, the ANC national spokesman, concluded an agreement to acquire Thintana's remaining interest in Telkom for several billion rand. Originally making separate bids, both Ngcaba and Ngonyama asked for government backing for their respective offers. According to a solid press account, President Mbeki urged the two consortia to co-operate.[31] When the merged consortium – the Elephant Consortium – couldn't get its structure in place before Thintana's deadline, the shares were bought and 'warehoused' by the Public Investment Corporation (PIC), which manages R600 billion of public servants' pension funds (Piliso 2006a). When the story broke, public outcry was such that the government then asked the PIC to ensure a 'proper' empowerment process, which led to the merged consortium's stake being reduced to 10.1 per cent, of which the Elephant Consortium agreed to allocate another 3.37 per cent for further broad-based economic empowerment (PIC 2005).

The hue and cry was raised not just by the usual critics, who saw Andile Ngcaba as the architect of a series of sweetheart policies that had protected Telkom's monopoly and placed Ngcaba himself in pole position to benefit from the deal by playing off the government's conflicting interests. The deal was also denounced by COSATU and some ANC leaders (Dawes 2004; Rose 2005). Not surprisingly, non-ANC members of the Parliamentary Portfolio Committee on Communications were scathing about Ngcaba and the sector generally, and about how the latter had suffered under ANC control.[32]

Toward a conclusion: Telecommunications as an early moment in a pattern of poor service delivery

Despite the intricacies of the situation as delineated in this account of the reform of South African telecommunications since 1996, there are a few important lessons that can be drawn from it. The choice of privatisation over liberalisation and competition led to the entrenchment of the incumbent network operator. The Shareholders' Agreement and related contracts gave Thintana Communications, and more specifically SBC, the power to obstruct competition and realise monopoly rents. The case of South Africa is mostly in keeping with the conclusion drawn from surveys of telecommunications reform in developing countries – that privatisation without regulation does not improve service and may even decrease mainline penetration and connection capacity (see Wellenius 1993; Wallsten 1999). In South Africa, privatisation, though only partial, essentially created a private monopoly in place of the previous state monopoly, and also a government jealous about the value of its remaining share of the monopoly. Because the institutional arrangement undermined independent regulation, it operated in a fashion ironically not unlike the old apartheid link between the government and the licensee (the Post Office), albeit now with power having shifted from the government to the licensee (Telkom), and, more accurately, to the strategic equity partner (SBC). SBC did bring management smarts to Telkom, elevating its profitability and share price considerably. But this was accomplished largely through monopoly power. Indeed, Telkom and Thintana's profitability meant the transfer of huge resources from the broader economy to shareholders. High telecommunications prices and limited service offerings created a drag on general economic growth. And contrary to its central mandate, Telkom failed to increase teledensity.

Monopoly in and of itself does not necessarily produce such results, of course. But monopoly without effective oversight or regulation almost invariably does. The close-to-congenital distrust the ANC-led government displayed toward independent agencies weakened regulation and hence intensified the incumbent's power. An additional factor in an incumbent's increasing power comes into play when the ministry responsible for safeguarding the government's residual financial interest in the incumbent is also the ministry making policy for the sector. The South African experience shows that the incumbent will tend to have the ministry's ear, not least because the Ministry is keenly attentive to the company's share price in the event of future public offerings. It may also be the case here – and this is speculative given the secret nature of the contract – that the Shareholders' Agreement explicitly forbade any governmental body from pursuing policies whose effect would liberalise the sector and hence 'harm' Telkom. Finally, the retention of government control through joint jurisdiction and the sabotage of effective regulation created opportunities for rent-seeking ANC comrades – opportunities strengthened through subsequent privatisations and legitimated by the goal of BEE.[33]

These issues – privatisation policy, the monopoly power of the incumbent, rent-seeking through BEE – must be seen as interrelated. It is rather astonishing to realise that, even as Telkom disconnected 2.1 million lines during its exclusivity period, ICASA, the Universal Service Agency, the Parliamentary Portfolio Committee, the DoC and the Office of the President all essentially said and did nothing. This failure represents a systemic failure of the democratic institutions of the country, which, at the broadest level, can be attributed to the ANC's legacy of democratic centralism and the concentration of political power at the top.[34] The only organisation to pay attention was COSATU, which called two general strikes over privatisation policy generally. These actions, however, accomplished little. The primary concrete reason for the systematic failure seems to lie with the government's single-minded commitment to privatisation. The ANC leadership fought successfully to position South Africa's economy favourably with respect to globalisation, but the costs were carried by the poor alone. In this respect, the failure of telecommunications reform presaged a broader story of poor service delivery in post-apartheid South Africa. Although some gains have been made in the provision of housing, water, and electricity, more than 5,000 protests at the local level about service delivery –

many of them violent – were reported during the 2005 financial year (BBC 2007). One can only wonder about the extent to which Telkom's privatisation and failed service delivery to the poor contributed to the current bitter leadership succession struggle in the ANC, which has pitted the adherents of GEAR and BEE as a black-middle-class project against those who still support the RDP and BEE as broad-based empowerment for the poor.

There is a related issue, one that goes beyond South Africa. South Africa is the most powerful country in Africa. It is seen as a model, both economically and politically. The South African telecommunications reform formula became dominant in Southern Africa and elsewhere in Africa during the latter part of the 1990s. Hence the 'privatisation trumps liberalisation' model for all intents and purposes became accepted as 'best practice' in the Southern African Development Community (SADC) Protocol on Transport, Communication and Meteorology of 1996. And the model's general guidelines likewise and in essence were adopted by the Telecommunications Regulators' Association of Southern Africa (TRASA), an organisation inaugurated in September 1997 (SADC 1996; TRASA undated). It remains to be investigated whether, and to what extent, the problems that plague the South African telecommunications sector have effectively been exported to the rest of Africa.

References

African National Congress. 1996. The state and social transformation: An ANC discussion document. http://www.anc.org.za/ancdocs/policy/s&st.html (accessed 17 June 2008).

ANC *see* African National Congress.

Barnes, A. 2006. *Owning Russia: The struggle over factories, farms, and power.* Ithaca: Cornell University Press.

BBC *see* British Broadcasting Corporation.

British Broadcasting Corporation. 2007. Protests turn violent in South Africa. Video, 21 September. http://search.bbc.co.uk/cgibin/search/results.pl?scope=all&edition=i&q=pr otests+turn+violent+in+SA&go.x=25&go.y=10&go=go (accessed 7 January 2008).

Business Day. 2000. Telecoms body says the minister acted illegally and that its regulations still stand. http://www.businessday.co.za/Articles/TarkArticle. aspx?ID=276155 (accessed 17 June 2008).

——. Non-stop flip-flops, 22 October 2001.

——. Telkom proves empowerment is cash in hand, 6 March 2004.

Cohen, T. 2003. Rethinking (reluctant) capture: South African telecommunications and the impact of regulation. *Journal of African Law* 47: 65–87.

Competition Commission. 2004. Competition Commission refers Telkom complaint to tribunal. Media Release 24 February. http://www.compcom.co.za/resources/Media%20 Releases/Media%20Releases%202004/Jan/Med%20Rel6%20of%20%2024Feb%20 2004.asp (accessed 20 June 2008).

Dawes, N. 2004. Telkom: How Andile Ngcaba served himself. *Mail&Guardian Online* http://www.mg.co.za/articlepage.aspx?area=/insight/insightnational&articleid=141775 (accessed 20 June 2008).

Department of Communications. 2000a. Interconnection guidelines issued by the authority in terms of section 43 of the Telecommunications Act of 1996. *Government Gazette*, vol. 417, no. 20993 (March 15), Notice 1259. http://www.polity.org.za/html/govdocs/notices/2000/not1259.html (accessed 12 January 2008).

——. 2000b. Facilities leasing guidelines issued by the authority in terms of section 44 of the Telecommunications Act of 1996. *Government Gazette* 21108 GN R1680, Notice 1260. http://www.polity.org.za/html/govdocs/notices/2000/not1260.html (accessed 12 January 2008).

——. 2002. Regulations: Manner of determining fees and charges for telecommunications services in the public switched telecommunications services (PSTS) sector. *Government Gazette* 23986, Notice R1333. http://www.ICASA.org.za/SearchResults. aspx?Page=91&Criteria=Manner%20of%20Determining%20Fees%20and%20 Charges%20for%20Telecommunications%20Services%20in%20the%20Public%20 Switched%20Telecommunications%20Services%20(PSTS)%20Sector (accessed 14 June 2008).

DoC *see* Department of Communications.

Efficient Research. 2004. An international comparison of South African telecommunications costs and the possible effect of telecommunications on economic performance; and a report on Telkom's financial statements and comparisons with selected local and international companies. http://www.hellkom.co.za/ (accessed 17 March 2008).

Finnie, G., C. Lewis, D. Lonergan, C. Mendler and D. Northfield. 2003. *South African communications, 2002–2008: Market review and analysis*. Pretoria: Yankee Group.

Gelb, S. 1998. The politics of macroeconomic reform in South Africa. Paper presented to the Conference on Democracy and the Political Economy of Reform, 16–18 January, in Cape Town, South Africa.

Gillwald, A. 2003. Good intentions, poor outcomes: Telecommunications reform in South Africa. *Telecommunications Policy* 29: 469–491.

Gillwald, A. and S. Esselaar. 2004. South African ICT sector performance review. http://link.wits.ac.za/research/research.html (accessed 23 May 2008).

Gillwald, A. and S. Kane. 2003. South African telecommunications sector performance review. http://link.wits.ac.za/research/research.html (accessed 23 May 2008).

Gumede, W. M. 2005. *Thabo Mbeki and the battle for the soul of the ANC*. Cape Town: Zebra Press.

Gush, H. and J. Ginsberg. 2003. South Africa raises $500 mln in Telkom IPO, 4 March. http://pages.stern.nyu.edu/~igiddy/cases/telkomsa.htm (accessed 22 January 2008).

Hellcom. http://www.hellcom.co.za (accessed 18 June 2008).

Hirsch, A. 2005. *Season of hope: Economic reform under Mandela and Mbeki*. South Africa and Canada: University of KwaZulu-Natal Press and International Development Research Centre.

Hodge, J. 2005a. *Telecommunications prices in South Africa: An international peer group comparison*. Johannesburg: South Africa Foundation.

Hodge, J. 2005b. *Reforming telecommunications in South Africa: Twelve proposals for lowering costs and improving access*. Johannesburg: South Africa Foundation.

Horwitz, R. B. 2001. *Communication and democratic reform in South Africa*. New York: Cambridge University Press.

ICASA *see* Independent Communications Authority of South Africa.

ICT *see* Information and Communication Technologies Empowerment Charter Working Group.

Independent Communications Authority of South Africa. 2001. Findings and conclusions on the S27 enquiry whether a virtual private network (VPN) constitutes a managed data network (MDNS) or not. http://www.ICASA.org.za/SearchResults. aspx?Page=91&Criteria=VPN (accessed 12 June 2008).

Information and Communication Technologies Empowerment Charter Working Group. 2005. ICT empowerment charter – final version. http://www.ictcharter.org.za/draft.htm (accessed 12 June 2008).

Institute for Justice and Reconciliation. 2006. 2006 Economic transformation audit: Money and morality. http://www.polity.org.za/pol/home/?show=95682; http://www. transformationaudit.org.za/ (accessed 28 May 2008).

Internet Service Providers' Association. Undated. http://www.ispa.org.za/news/ press060606-02.shtml (accessed 17 June 2008).

ISPA *see* Internet Service Providers' Association.

ITU *see* International Telecommunications Union.

International Telecommunications Union. 2005. Mobile cellular subscribers per 100 people pdf Files for 2001–2004. http://www.itu.int/ITU-D/ict/statistics/ (accessed 11 June 2008).

Janisch, H. N. and D. M. Kotlowitz. 1998. African renaissance, market romance: Post-apartheid privatisation and liberalisation in South African broadcasting and telecommunications. Columbia Institute of Tele-Information. http://www.vii.org/ papers/romance.htm (accessed 12 June 2008).

Lewis, C. 2005. Negotiating the net: The internet in South Africa (1990–2003). *Information Technologies and International Development* 2: 1–28.

Makhaya, G. and S. Roberts. 2003. Telecommunications in developing countries: Reflections from the South African experience. *Telecommunications Policy* 27: 41–59.

Mbeki, T. 2005. State of the nation. http://www.info.gov.za/speeches/2005/05021110501001.htm (accessed 4 June 2008).

Melody, W. H. 2002. Assessing Telkom's 2003 price increase proposal: Price cap regulation as a test of progress in South African telecom reform, and e-economy development. *Link Centre policy research paper*, 2. http://link.wits.ac.za/research/wm20021130.htm (accessed 14 June 2008).

Melody, W. H., W. Currie and S. Kane. 2003. Preparing South Africa for information society 'e-services': The significance of the VANS sector. *The Southern African Journal of Information and Communication* 4. http://link.wits.ac.za/journal/journal4.html (accessed 20 June 2008).

Minister of Communications. 1997a. Licence issued to Telkom SA Ltd to provide public telecommunications services under section 36 of the Telecommunications Act, 1996. *Government Gazette* 17984, Notice 768 of 1997.

——. 1997b. Ministerial determination on fees and charges for telecommunication services. *Government Gazette* 17984, Notice 772 of 1997 (7 May).

——. 2001. Telecommunications Act – policy directions (26 July). http://www.polity.org.za/html/govdocs/policy/telecomms.html (accessed 12 May 2008).

Mokaba, P. 1997. On leadership. Unpublished discussion paper in preparation for the ANC's 50th National Conference.

Mouffe, C. 2000. *The democratic paradox*. London: Verso.

MyADSL. 2006. Telkom's monopoly costs SA economy R50 billion. http://www.mybroadband.co.za/nephp/?m=show&id (accessed 11 January 2008).

Parkin, K. ed. 2006. *Mandela: The authorised portrait*. London: Hodder Moa and Blackwell.

PIC *see* Public Investment Corporation.

Piliso, S. 2006a. How ANC bigwigs jostled for Telkom. *Sunday Times*, 15 October.

——. 2006b. ANC defends state role in Telkom deal. *Sunday Times*, 15 October.

Public Investment Corporation. 2005. Announcement of the Elephant Consortium–Telkom deal (5 May). http://www.pic.gov.za/ur/Telkom.Announcement.pdf (accessed 20 June 2008).

Regulateonline.org. 2006. South Africa: Telecommunications policy costs users. (http://www.regulateonline.org/index.php?option=content&task=view&id=813&Itemid=32&relaItemid=643 (accessed 3 December 2007).

Republic of South Africa. 1994. *White Paper on Reconstruction and Development*. Cape Town: Government Printer.

——. 1996a. *Telecommunications Act (Act No. 103 of 1996)*. Cape Town: Government Printer.

——. 1996b. Ministry for Post, Telecommunications and Broadcasting. *White Paper on Telecommunications Policy*. Pretoria: Ministry.

———. 1996c. Ministry for Post, Telecommunications and Broadcasting. *Submission to the Portfolio Committee on Communications on the Telecommunication Bill* (28 October). Pretoria: Government Printer.

———. 1996d. Ministry for Post, Telecommunications and Broadcasting. *Telecommunications regulatory regime: An international comparison of legislation (16 October)*. Pretoria: Ministry.

———. 1996e. Portfolio Committee on Communications, National Assembly. *Amendments to Telecommunications Bill* (B 85A-96). Cape Town: Committee.

———. 1996f. Debates of Parliament, National Assembly. Telecommunications Bill (second reading debate). Remarks of the Minister for Post, Telecommunications and Broadcasting (30 October). [Unrevised copy: tape 220, disk 178; tape 240, disk 198.]

———. 1996g. *Growth, Employment and Redistribution: A Macroeconomic Strategy*. Pretoria: Government Printer.

———. 2001. *Telecommunications Amendment Act (Act No. 64 of 2001)*. Cape Town: Government Printer.

———. 2004. *Broad-based Black Economic Empowerment Act (Act No. 53 of 2003)*. Pretoria: Government Printer.

———. 2006. *Electronic Communications Act (Act No. 36 of 2005)*. Cape Town: Government Printer.

———. 2007. Parliament. *Report of the ad hoc Committee on the Review of Chapter 9 and Associated Institutions*. Cape Town: Government Printer.

Rose, R. 2005. Telkom: COSATU leans on affiliate. *Business Day*, 9 May.

SADC *see* Southern African Development Community.

Salaman, A. 1998. Internet statistics. http://www.dns.net/andras/stats.html (accessed 17 November 2007).

SATRA *see* South African Telecommunications Regulatory Authority.

South African Telecommunications Regulatory Authority. 1997. Pronouncement – P0001 (14 October). Johannesburg: SATRA.

Southern African Development Community. 1996. Protocol on Transport, Communication and Meteorology. http://www.iucnrosa.org.zw/elisa/SADC-Protocols/transport_ protocol.html (accessed 14 December 2007).

Stones, L. 2001. Minister 'meddled' in ICASA's proposals: Plan would have benefited users, but restricted Telkom's overall rate hikes. *Business Day*, 6 November.

Telecommunications Regulators' Association of Southern Africa. Undated. http://www. trasa.org.bw/index.php (accessed 18 April 2008).

Telkom. 1997a. *Annual report 1996*. Pretoria: Telkom.

———.1997b. *Written resolutions of all the directors of Telkom SA Limited (with exhibits)*. Pretoria: Telkom.

———. 2001. *Annual report 2000*. Pretoria: Telkom.

——. 2003. *Annual report 2002*. Pretoria: Telkom.

——. 2005. Corporate profile. http://www.telkom.co.za/common/aboutus/index.html (accessed 3 January 2008).

Telkom Ltd v. *M Mayimele-Hashatse NO, SATRA, SAVA* (TPD, 17 April 2000, Case No. 27451/1999, unreported).

Telkom SA (Limited) v. *Maepa and Others*. 1998. Transvaal Provincial Division 25840/97 High Court of South Africa. (8 April).

Telkom SA Limited, Thintana Communications LLC, SBC International Management Services, Inc and Telekom Management Services SDN.BHD. 1997. Strategic services agreement. http://www.telkom.co.za/pls/portal/docs/page/contents/minisites/ir/docs/exhibit10_2.pdf#search=%22telkom%20strategic%20services%20agreement%22 (accessed 12 January 2008).

Telkom SA Ltd v. *H Dikgale NO, ICASA, SAVA* (TPD, 20 March 2001, Case No. 19341/2000, unreported).

The Arms Deal Virtual Press Office. 2007. Various contributions. http://www.armsdeal-vpo.co.za/ (accessed 15 June 2008).

Thintana Communications LLC. 1997. Amended and restated limited liability company agreement. Pretoria: Thintana.

Thornton, L. and J. Hodge. 2006. Telecommunications pricing regulation. In *Telecommunications law in South Africa*, ed. L. Thornton, Y. Carrim, P. Mtshaulana and P. Reyburn, 200–214. Johannesburg: STE Publishers.

TRASA *see* Telecommunications Regulators' Association of Southern Africa. United States Securities and Exchange Commission. 2006. Form 20-F: Telkom annual report pursuant to section 13 or 15(d) of the Securities Exchange Act of 1934 (filed 4 August).

——. 2000. SBC Communications, Inc. Form 10-K (31 December).

Walsten, S. J. 1999. An empirical analysis of competition, privatization, and regulation in telecommunications markets in Africa and Latin America. Policy Research Working Paper 2136. Washington, DC: World Bank.

Wellenius, B., R. Saunders and J. Warford. 1993. *Telecommunications: World Bank experience and strategy*. Washington, DC: World Bank.

Yacoob, S. and K. Pillay. 2006. Licensing. In *Telecommunications law in South Africa*, ed. L. Thornton, Y. Carrim, P. Mtshaulana and P. Reyburn, 132–171. Johannesburg: STE Publishers.

Turning points in South African television policy and practice since 1990

3

Jane Duncan and Ian Glenn

This chapter analyses the turning points in television policy and broadcast market strategies that have led to key changes in television practice in South Africa since 1990. We try to identify and understand legislative and financial pressures shaping decisions, and the power of arguments for liberalisation that have led to major, painful changes at the British Broadcasting Corporation and other public broadcasters (see Born 2005); and argue that, in many ways, South Africa has missed major opportunities to use broadcasting for national development, the development of a public sphere or the shaping of an informed citizenry. We identify some of the key policy decisions broadcasters have made and also moments in the history of television transformation when South Africa faced competing policy choices that could have set in motion very different courses of action.

In 2001, Robert Horwitz cautioned about the dangers of what he termed a 'commercialising juggernaut' eclipsing the public service nature of the South African media system, which he maintained was necessary to redress the legacies of the country's apartheid past (Horwitz 2001: 137–177). In 2002, Clive Barnett identified the central policy issue facing post-apartheid media as 'whether and how [liberalisation] can be regulated and made consistent with the aims of nation building, development, democratisation and cultural diversity' (Barnett 2002: 44). By that stage he had already concluded that broadcasting had been subordinated to the broader globalisation imperatives of economic policy (Barnett 2000: 83–84); in other words, that liberalisation had trumped public service objectives. In this chapter we argue that the evidence from television policy and practice gives credence to Horwitz and Barnett's views, and identify the moments in post-apartheid television history when policy makers and practitioners could have gone one of two ways, but chose marketisation.[1] It should be noted that these conclusions relate to television; a rather different set of conclusions could be arrived at in relation to radio, which is on the whole a less costly and more accessible medium than television.

At the outset of South African broadcasting's transition, the liberation movement agreed that there should be three tiers of broadcasting: commercial, community and public service (Omroep oor Radio Freedom 1991: 67). We argue that the country's media system has become characterised by the dominance of commercial television within the three tiers of broadcasting, with even community and public service television forced to follow commercial imperatives as subsidiary elements.

The effect of these policy choices is that the South African television system has become characterised by uneven development, with those who participate in the economic mainstream having access to a plurality of television services and to viewing options that expand all the time as the multi-channel environment matures. For them, media reform has been a consumer success, but at the expense of a fragmented share of common viewing experiences. Elihu Katz (1996: 22–33) has argued that increasing choice and segmentation of news and current affairs viewing, in particular, damages the sense of a shared public political culture. We will return to the particular problems posed by television news.

Free-to-air services have delivered South African content successfully, while largely maintaining their financial viability, although this content shows signs of reproducing South African society's dualistic character. But South Africans who were never in, or who have fallen out of, the economic mainstream, still remain grossly underserved by television. Attempts to address the dualistic nature of South African television have run into serious difficulties. Since 2002, there has been evidence of a popular backlash against the marketisation of television.[2] It remains to be seen whether this backlash will take a progressive form, involving the re-establishment of public service principles in the broadcasting system, or a conservative form, entailing attempts to control 'indecent' and 'offensive' content. There are indications of both trends in recent debates on the state of South Africa's television system.

Negotiations and South African television

Television came to South African shores quite late (in 1976), owing in part to the ruling National Party's nervousness about the potentially subversive impact of the medium. Television was introduced initially for white English and Afrikaans speakers, then was extended to black people, and broadcast in Zulu, Xhosa, Sotho and Tswana (Paterson 1994b). A channel was also established in the 'homeland' of Bophuthatswana in the mid-1980s. This meant that when political negotiations around a new dispensation ensued, television was dominated by the then state broadcaster, the South African Broadcasting Corporation (SABC). Television was funded from a mix of advertising and television licence fees (the radio licence fee was abandoned in 1982). The SABC's reliance on advertising was so great that it could barely be compared to public broadcasters in other parts of the world.[3]

An exception was the encrypted satellite subscription service, M-Net, set up by the major newspaper groups. The Ministry of Home Affairs sanctioned the establishment of M-Net in 1986 in an attempt to compensate these groups for loss of advertising revenue to state television, but with the proviso that M-Net not run television news. Their current affairs programme, *Carte Blanche*, based on the US show *60 Minutes*, has, however, been a major influence on local news, and was for five years in a row rated as the single most influential news source in the country (Schreiner 2006).

Rising costs associated with the running of television services led to the SABC posting a deficit by 1986. Management read the international trends, and began to recognise that liberalisation was inevitable, which meant that competition for ad spend would increase. Programming costs also spiralled upwards, driven partly by the weakening of the rand and competition for sports programming from M-Net. In 1990, the SABC embarked on a massive restructuring exercise to 'shift the emphasis from a bureaucratic corporation to an effective, commercialised, market-orientated entity' (SABC 1989: 10).

The SABC was divided into an internal market system, where services were unbundled into business units and made to operate on a profit-and-loss basis. Services were rationalised, leading to massive retrenchments. By 1991, these changes led to the SABC almost doubling the profit it had earned in 1990, but at the expense of internal stability.

However, further restructuring became a source of tension between the SABC and the government on the one hand, and the liberation movement on the other hand. Sensing the heightened possibility of unilateral restructuring being imposed on the broadcasting sector, progressive organisations grouped together into the Campaign for Open Media, which was launched in January 1990. In the same year, the Minister of Home Affairs decided to speed up the restructuring of broadcasting, and appointed a Task Group to advise Cabinet on broadcasting policy, and to chart the way forward for an 'orderly development of the broadcasting industry'. This mandate seemed to be a euphemism for the liberalisation of the sector: an approach that reproduced shifts towards liberalisation in the broader economy.[4]

The establishment of the Task Group was controversial in the liberation movement, owing to the lack of transparency in the setting up of the group. It precipitated the establishment of the Campaign for Open Media (COM), whose mandate was to ensure the lifting of State of Emergency media regulations, the repeal of censorship laws, and the opening up of the airwaves under public control.[5] Also, the apartheid government was accused of attempting to pre-empt a negotiated change in broadcasting, to entrench the sector's power in white hands. The Task Group came up with two main findings: firstly, that the control of broadcasting should be taken away from the government and handed to an independent regulator; and secondly, that more broadcasters should be allowed to operate (Duncan 2002: 121). The implementation of these findings was frozen, but COM succeeded in ensuring that broadcasting was placed as an item on the agenda of multiparty negotiations. The liberation movement realised that a new vehicle was needed to ensure well co-ordinated responses to negotiations, which led to the formation of the Campaign for Independent Broadcasting (CIB) in 1992.

The fact that the pro-liberalisation line of thinking of the government coincided with that of the liberation movement paved the way for a consensus on what Horwitz has termed the 'negotiated liberalisation' of broadcasting at the multiparty negotiations on broadcasting's transition (Horwitz 2001). The CIB busied itself with ensuring that negotiations addressed the establishment of the regulator and the appointment of the first independent SABC Board.

The Jabulani! Freedom of the Airwaves Conference, held in Amsterdam in August 1991, resolved that the broadcasting system should be conceptualised on three levels. Public service broadcasting had to include programming that educates, entertains and informs; had to cater for all tastes and interests; and had to be geographically comprehensive. The public broadcaster would be governed by a Charter that ensured the broadcaster's accountability to the public, and impartiality and independence from government. Commercial broadcasting would operate for profit by providing advertisers with access to consumers, while community (or participatory) broadcasting would be controlled by communities of interest or geographic communities, to enable them to 'express their concerns without outside interference'. The Jabulani! conference started from the premise that 'the public broadcaster should form the core of the broadcasting system and set the standard for all broadcasting' (Balch et al. 1991: 67).

By 1992, when multiparty negotiations began in earnest, television services consisted of TV1, the country's first channel; CCTV, which was a merger between the two channels focusing on black audiences; and an extra channel used mainly for educational services, TSS.

Negotiations focused on the appointment procedures of the SABC Board, and on the drafting of the Independent Broadcasting Authority Bill (passed into law in 1993). The eventual set of guidelines for the appointment of the Board was actually concluded in bilateral negotiations between the African National Congress (ANC) and the apartheid government (Fokane, cited in FXI 2008: 10). The details of the bill were thrashed out in an Independent Telecommunications Authority technical committee consisting of nine members, with the bill passing through seventeen stages and eight drafts. The Independent Broadcasting Authority Act contained many important elements that suggested that a progressive South African television system was possible, such as the recognition of three tiers of broadcasting, limitations on foreign ownership and cross-media control, and the need for an independent broadcasting regulator. However, the act deferred the major policy work until after the transition, when the Independent Broadcasting Authority (IBA) was expected to conclude inquiries into three issues: the role and responsibility of the public broadcaster; cross-media ownership; and local content. This became known as 'the Triple Inquiry'.

At the time, Chris Paterson put forward the provocative argument that American pressure and influence during the negotiations had led to the 'Americanisation' of the broadcasting sector, with commercial media set to make gains at the expense of public service broadcasting (Paterson 1994a). He argued that the bulk of the spectrum would be open to commercial broadcasters. Also, according to the act, only 20 per cent of programming had to be of local origin, which, Paterson argued, would pave the way for US and European conglomerates to come in and take over. Paterson's arguments are assessed later on in this chapter.

Post-apartheid television policy and regulation: The Triple Inquiry

The Triple Inquiry was held from 1994 to 1995, in an attempt to begin the process of post-apartheid broadcasting-policy development, as there were dangers in the IBA regulating the sector in a policy vacuum.

The inquiry had strong input from a range of stakeholders. One common thread of the submissions was that the SABC should be streamlined to make way for other services, but that its remaining services should be freed from dependence on advertising as a major source of revenue.[6] This argument formed the basis of a submission by a group of thirteen non-governmental organisations and professional associations.[7] These bodies proposed the establishment of what they called a two-tier structure for broadcasting services, operating at the national and provincial levels. This structure would take advantage of the fact that the interim Constitution of South Africa gave provinces the competency to run their own provincial public broadcasters (MBC 1994).[8]

In order to achieve a balance between the provincial and national levels, the group argued, the SABC's television channels should be reduced from three to two, with regional windows for provincial news and other programmes (MBC 1994: 44). These services would be freed from advertising and funded differently. Provinces would also exercise their constitutional power to set up provincial public broadcasters.

The group reasoned that three channels would lead to the SABC overextending itself and that a 'leaner and meaner' SABC would be better placed to meet challenges internationally. It also argued for a five-year period over which to phase out advertising and replace it with a government grant complemented by a levy on electricity. The purpose of the government grant would be to insulate the SABC from international technological and national commercial pressures, and to enable it to 'reconstitute the national and provincial public broadcasting services as genuine public services in the country' (MBC 1994: 50).

The IBA accepted some of these arguments and recommended that the SABC reduce its terrestrial channels from three to two by 1997. To prepare for privatisation, the SABC would shift informational and educational programming from its third channel to the other two, in the process repositioning this channel to operate a satellite service. This service would be re-licensed as a private channel. The IBA also proposed that the desirability of provincial public broadcasting be investigated, and that the provinces be served by the national public broadcaster through provincial windows in the meantime. Because it considered provincial television not to be financially viable, it argued that provincial programming needs should be met by the existing national SABC channels. To this end it proposed the establishment of hour-long windows, to be funded by the government.

Most significantly in terms of the Triple Inquiry, the IBA did not accept the arguments for institutional funding for the SABC. Rather, it argued that the corporation should continue to derive its funding from a mix of sources, namely advertising and sponsorship, licence fees, a government grant, and other income derived from activities such as merchandising its products and leasing its facilities. In addition, the IBA said, Parliament should provide funding for specific projects (Independent Broadcasting Authority, 1995).

While the report was important in that it recognised that public funding was necessary for the fulfilment of the public mandate, it also marked a significant retreat from the call for ongoing government funding for the SABC as a whole, and an acceptance of the 'reality' of advertising as a significant source of revenue. This important concession allowed the government to continue shying away from funding the SABC as an entity. Also, the funding for 'special projects' could be discontinued easily.

The Triple Inquiry proposals were debated in Parliament. After intense lobbying by the SABC, Parliament allowed the corporation to retain all three television stations. It appeared to have been convinced by the SABC's argument that the corporation needed three channels to deliver on its mandate of offering services in all eleven official languages, while maintaining financial viability. The SABC argued, further, that research pointed to the fact that South African audiences self-divided into three market segments based on language groupings. It said that SABC 1 would service the Nguni language group, SABC 2 the Sotho language group and SABC 3 English. It was anticipated that SABC 3 would operate as a commercial channel that would cross-subsidise the other two channels. The result was that SABC 3 ended up as a strange, hybrid creature in a legal and regulatory limbo: a public service commercial channel, with no clear mandate or rules, driven only by the expectation of turning a profit to fund the public service channels, SABC 1 and SABC 2. In time, this led to complaints from rival commercial channels irked that they had to play by rules on advertising limits or local content which SABC 3 could ignore.

The status of Afrikaans was, at the time, unclear, and this lack of clarity had negative financial consequences owing to the fact that the SABC lost ad spend for Afrikaans programming (Barnett 2000: 72–73). The IBA's argument for special project funding[9] for the SABC was, however, accepted, and Parliament was expected to provide this on a triennial basis (Portfolio Committee on Communications 1994).

Parliament amended a section in the IBA's report, calling for significant public service, language and local content obligations, by amending 'significant' to read 'some' (Portfolio Committee on Communications 1994: 6). Parliament's Committee responsible for legislative oversight and review of broadcasting matters, the Portfolio Committee on Communications, amended the IBA's proposal that no newspaper group might control a radio or television station if it owned more than 15 per cent of total newspaper readership, if the licence area overlapped substantially with the circulation area of the newspaper. This requirement was relaxed to 20 per cent. In response, the IBA reiterated its stance that the broadcasting market was too small to sustain four advertiser-driven television channels, and that the viability of existing channels would be threatened if public funding were not made available to free advertising up for commercial channels. It also noted that the committee's relaxation of the cross-media ownership rule was not supported by international precedent (IBA 1995: 3).

Parliament's selective adoption of the Triple Inquiry report was, arguably, the most significant turning point of all for post-apartheid television, in that it set the television system on an overwhelmingly commercial path: a point that has also been argued by Horwitz (2001). The government was obligated to fund the SABC for a short period only, while the SABC was allowed to retain all three channels. This landed the SABC in a policy framework that clearly separated the three tiers of broadcasting from one another, setting each tier on a separate but complementary path of development.

This collapse of will on the part of Parliament was in line with the development of the government's controversial fiscal austerity plan, the Growth, Employment and Redistribution Plan (GEAR)[10], released later that year. GEAR's logic also had a persuasive impact on the Department of Communications' review of broadcasting policy in 1997, which led to the publication of the White Paper on Broadcasting Policy in 1998. By this stage the department had asserted its muscle over the IBA, by claiming back the right to make policy; this shift in policy-making power from the IBA back to the government would have allowed the government to ensure an alignment between broadcasting policy and macro-economic policy (Duncan 2001: 103–111). The policy recognised the fact that post-apartheid broadcasting transformation had done little to extend media diversity to the majority of South

Africans, and that the system still exhibited a duality whereby those who were well-off had access to a plethora of services, while large sections of the population, who were less well-off, did not. It attempted to address this duality by encouraging the globalisation of broadcasting, so that the fruits of global participation could be used to meet development objectives. It also stated that the South African broadcasting system should be predominantly South African in character, and argued that in the broadcasting system 'language choice and diversity should be comparable for all South Africans' (DoC 1998: 17–18). The document indicated that the SABC was expected to gear itself for financial self-sufficiency, sending the corporation the unambiguous signal that it could not expect ongoing public funding.

The SABC after the Triple Inquiry report

Soon after the adoption of the Triple Inquiry report, the SABC repositioned and re-launched its three television channels, in an attempt to move them away from the separation of white and black audiences on different channels and to emphasise a nation-building role (Teer-Tomaselli 2001:118). According to Barnett, it had initiated this repositioning even before the Triple Inquiry debates were completed, reflecting confidence (even arrogance) on the SABC's part that the IBA's television proposals would be rebuffed (Barnett 2000: 76). But the SABC soon ran into major financial problems for a multitude of reasons,[11] leading to the corporation posting a deficit of R60 million for 1996. In response to these developments, the IBA argued that the SABC's public service obligations would be unsustainable unless 'it is given an opportunity to implement a long-term financial rescue plan which relies exclusively on the public broadcaster generating a surplus through advertising and licence fees' (Independent Broadcasting Authority 1997: 6). This comment marked a shift in thinking for the Regulator from its timid proposal of project funding, as it signalled that the IBA was willing to consider the SABC surviving without any government funding, especially given the fact that the corporation had reacted with hostility to its downsizing proposal. This intellectual retreat was to be repeated over and over again in different institutions in the coming months, including the SABC itself.

In an attempt to address the crisis, the SABC launched a resources review, which was outsourced to McKinsey Management Consultancy. The review focused mainly on television, and largely left radio untouched. It advocated that the SABC stop being a programme producer,[12] and instead become a publisher broadcaster.[13] This meant that the SABC would outsource all its programme production except for news, which was redefined as its core business. McKinsey also recommended a review of the programming mix on television to increase advertising revenue, and further recommended that the regional windows should be closed down.[14] In line with these recommendations, the SABC Board approved a television strategy focusing on the 'core business' of news and current affairs. Magazine programming would be outsourced and religious programming would be reduced. Approximately one third of the workforce was retrenched at the time. The IBA also acceded to a reduction in the level of local content, from 50 per cent to 30 per cent, delaying the 50 per cent quota for five years.

These recommendations led to the SABC turning a profit in just six months, but at the expense of the public service mandate. In fact, the outsourcing of content destroyed the SABC's ability to develop strong content skills in particular genres, and harmed the distinctiveness of the services. It also destroyed what might have been one of the SABC's greatest strengths: the ability to draw on the synergies with radio and the undoubted popularity of many of its radio presenters and talk-show hosts. While other broadcasters then used, and still use, the popularity of radio figures to boost television viewership, the SABC seemed blind to this possibility. Arguably, the new direction also inflated the SABC's programming costs: the evidence that the outsourcing of content production saves money is contested in television research (Duncan 2002: 117; Etzioni-Halevy 1987).

It was not long before the SABC again posted a deficit. This underlined the fact that the corporation was simply unable to afford self-sufficiency, and showed that the cross-subsidisation arrangement was profoundly misguided. SABC 3, as the public commercial service, was meant to cross-subsidise the two public service channels, in spite of the fact that SABC 3 was making a loss and SABC 1 was making a profit.[15] The cumulative effect of Parliament's and the government's decisions has been that the SABC operates one fully commercial and two quasi-commercial channels. This development has subverted the government's intention of splitting the SABC's services into public and public commercial services, with the latter cross-subsidising the former, in an attempt to create a space where public services could grow unhindered by commercial considerations. As a result, the economics of language[16] dictated that English, and to a lesser extent Afrikaans, continued to dominate the airwaves: a reality that – according to Neville Alexander – would contribute to condemning the country to perpetual mediocrity (Alexander 2000).[17]

In spite of its financial problems, the SABC recognised that local content was enormously popular with South African audiences, and was therefore an underexploited source of revenue. The corporation's success with the local production, *Suburban Bliss*, which headed the audience appreciation index for adults in 1998 (Teer-Tomaselli 2001: 132–133), suggested that the local content quotas could be used to attract large audiences, and, in time, create increased revenue. The Independent Communications Authority of South Africa (ICASA), which superseded the IBA after a merger with the South African Telecommunications Regulatory Authority (SATRA), also began to recognise the commercial potential of South African content. In line with the White Paper, it argued that television content should be overwhelmingly South African.[18] ICASA concluded that all stations needed to be regulated, to ensure that they were predominantly South African. To that end, ICASA issued regulations increasing South African television content quotas from 30 per cent to 55 per cent for public broadcasting; from 20 per cent to 35 per cent for commercial free-to-air services; and from 5 per cent to 8 per cent for terrestrial subscription services.[19]

By that stage, some of the most adventurous programming was coming out of SABC Education, which used its subsidy from the Department of Education to develop a new genre of educational drama in an attempt to address the harsh realities that many learners faced in schools, such as sexual harassment, drug and alcohol addiction, and lack of educational resources. This genre was exemplified by the hugely popular but controversial[20] programme, *Yizo Yizo*. The programme was first flighted in 1999, with a sequel produced and flighted in 2002, and contributed to building an appetite for South African drama. By that stage, experiments with the genre of educational drama had pointed to its possibilities: these experiments included the less gritty *Soul City*, which promotes health and social change and which was first flighted in 1994, and *Tsha Tsha*, an HIV/AIDS-related series that began in 1993. The SABC has also commissioned long-running local drama programmes that maintain high audience ratings, such as *Isidingo*, *Generations*, *Sewende Laan* and *Muvhango*, with the last series contributing greatly to the SABC's ability to meet its marginalised languages quota.[21]

This new generation of soap-type dramas has enabled the SABC to achieve what many thought impossible at the onset of post-apartheid media transformation: namely to attract and maintain audiences, and meet local content quotas, while delivering audiences to advertisers successfully. The SABC's now well-established formula involves the localisation of the soap genre, based on the normalisation of middle-class lifestyles. A programme such as *Isidingo* seems to have shifted its emphasis away from the conflicts between labour and management in a mine and towards interpersonal intrigues; while *Muvhango* has commercialised its fairly realistic dramatisation of the contradictions between rural and urban life in an attempt to compete for ratings with *Generations*.[22]

Product placement for products such as Sasko Flour have become more evident as the series has developed, and in 2007 a host of older, more experienced actors were replaced by younger, more attractive actors. As Amanda Ngudle has argued: 'While *Muvhango* started looking conservative and old, the past few months have seen it take on a younger, trendier look, which meant increasing the number of young people in the soapie. Before that … *Generations* led the race with eye-candy characters (Ngudle 2007).[23] These trends towards the commercialisation of local content are under-researched, and any comments on them are necessarily anecdotal, but they do suggest that Paterson's prediction at the onset of post-apartheid television of an Americanisation of the system needs to be modified somewhat (Paterson 1994a: 22).[24] Nevertheless, to the extent that Paterson equates 'Americanisation' with 'commercialisation', his argument does have credence. While it could be argued that the country has achieved a television system that is predominantly South African in nature, rather than American, the SABC's experience with soaps does raise questions about which South Africans are addressed in the country's local content regime, and the extent to which the identities constructed are inclusive in nature. In the case of lifestyle programmes such as *Top Billing* and *Pasella*, the SABC has simply resorted to the fairly flagrant commercialisation of content, offering for a fee an equivalent of unannounced advertorials to showcase products.

The SABC has also recognised that local content has the potential to be sold on to other African countries. In 1998, the corporation launched its subscription pay channel, Africa-2-Africa, and SABC Africa (a news-orientated channel), with the intention that they should become leading content providers on the continent. The bulk of Africa-2-Africa's programming was drawn from the SABC's archives, and SABC Africa used the corporation's existing news infrastructure to generate content (Ndlovu 2003: 303–304). This predominance of South Africa in the content called into question the SABC's professed objective of encouraging inter-African debate. Moreover, the SABC's policy of outsourcing content production hampered its ability to reach Africa on the DSTV platform. After a complaint from a local producer, who saw a programme he had produced – with local rights only – broadcast in Namibia, the SABC was forced to withdraw its offerings on DSTV outside South Africa, as in many cases it had not negotiated for the required international rights.

An analysis of television advertising suggests that other opportunities were missed in the rush to commercialisation, and that, even in advertising, public service messages were crowded out. Millward Brown South Africa (formerly Impact Information) has records of how South Africans of all races rate every new television advertisement broadcast in the country. Until quite recently, there were marked differences in response between black and white respondents in the 'most-highly-rated-ever' band of advertisements. Among white South Africans, high-cost advertisements with high production values, often with sophisticated humorous stereotypes ('Boet' and 'Swaer' in the Castrol advertisements, the David Kramer Volkswagen bus advertisements, the Sun City advertisements) have tended to be the most highly rated, while among black South Africans, many of the most-highly-rated advertisements were public service advertisements from the mid-1990s: an advertisement about HIV/AIDS featuring a singing nurse; and information on the new Constitution, or on voting. This suggests a hunger for useful information and help in understanding the burdens and possibilities of new citizenship – a hunger that subsequent developments did not adequately address. Some experiments in adventurous content, especially local content, that have risen above the dualism of the television system, and have even attempted to critique the complexities of South Africa's transformation, have been contentious. In some cases, they have even raised the ire of the authorities, and have either been discontinued or been censored. One of the earliest controversies concerned John Pilger's documentary, 'Apartheid did not die', which focused on how historic compromises agreed to by the ANC and the apartheid regime during multiparty negotiations compromised the ANC-led government's ability to redress the legacy of apartheid. In 2006 the SABC commissioned a documentary on President Thabo Mbeki, but then refused to flight it, arguing that the documentary was 'incurably defamatory'. In April 2007, the SABC withdrew a documentary on circumcision, entitled '*Emthunzini we Ntaba*', after complaints that it exposed circumcision secrets. Then in the same month, the SABC delayed the screening of 'After Nine', a drama based on a black gay man in a straight relationship (*The Star* 2007). These incidents implied that the SABC was reluctant to defend its own editorial independence or the editorial integrity of its commissioned filmmakers: hardly a recipe for encouraging cutting-edge local productions.

In relation to news and current affairs, the performance of the SABC as a public broadcaster has been a mixed one. Controversies over alleged bias towards the government intensified once the SABC Board chaired by Vincent Maphai was replaced by a new board in 2003 (chaired by Eddie Funde). The appointment of the new board was widely seen as controversial, with opposition parties accusing the ANC of stacking it with its appointees. This appointment process followed an ANC resolution on communications adopted at the party's 2002 conference. In the resolution, it lamented the commercialisation of the SABC, and resolved to establish a publicly funded broadcasting system by 2012. This resolution followed a period of vigorous commercialisation under the leadership of Peter Matlare, who managed to stabilise the SABC's finances. But this was at the expense of the public service mandate. Those services that targeted 'uneconomic' audiences, namely women, rural people and the elderly, were marginalised; and whole formats, such as radio drama, were dropped as they were too expensive to maintain.[25] These developments led to a public backlash against the SABC.

In response, the DoC proposed, through the Broadcasting Amendment Bill, that the Minister of Communications had to approve the SABC's editorial policies, thereby subjecting the broadcaster's editorial content to government control. Also, the Bill proposed that two state broadcasters, under direct government control, should be established independently of the SABC. While it is true that the ANC and the government were attempting to address a very real problem of over-commercialisation, this seemed to have translated into a deliberate strategy at the time to deploy people into the SABC, once the department lost the battle for direct control over the editorial policies. Since then, the SABC has developed distinct statist tendencies.

Once it assumed office in 2003, the new board declared its preference for what it called 'development journalism',[26] and controversies surfaced about the extent to which it had become a mouthpiece of the government and the ruling party. Quantitative studies have largely affirmed the SABC's professionalism in news production, in spite of accusations of bias against its managing director, Snuki Zikalala, which reached their height in 2006 when allegations surfaced of his having blacklisted certain political commentators.[27] These studies found that while SABC news had greatly increased the extent of its reporting on the government, and on the President in particular, its reporting had been largely neutral (Media Monitoring Project, cited in Skinner 2007: 125). At times this had even tended toward negative coverage of the government and the ruling ANC – though not as negative as in other media.[28] The overall findings led the Media Monitoring Project (MMP) to state that it challenged 'views perpetuated in some media that the SABC is biased in favour of government and the ANC' (Skinner 2007: 125). Yet qualitative studies have painted a rather different picture, pointing to subtle biases in editorial decision-making.

For instance, a qualitative report on SABC current affairs, commissioned by the News and Current Affairs Department from the organisation Plus 94 Research, contains a finding that focus group participants had observed that SABC current affairs programmes were not considered to be credible in the eyes of SABC listeners and viewers, with the exception of *Special Assignment* (Plus 94 Research 2007). The report was based on the findings of 20 focus groups held around the country. It states that 'the SABC current affairs credibility was thought not to be convincing and perceptions of external control persisted'. On the handling of politics, with the exception of *Special Assignment*, 'there was a widespread feeling in these group discussions that the subject of politics is any journalist's landmine given the political climate in the country and in the ruling party when this study was conducted. This was said to be the challenge the SABC must overcome.' The report went on to state that 'there was a deeply held view among respondents that the SABC current affairs tend to cover up and treat government officials with kid gloves' (Plus 94 Research 2007: 15–19).

Corinna Arndt's qualitative study (2007) also exposes pressures on the internal independence of SABC journalists. In her study, she analyses the institutional culture inside the SABC's News and Current Affairs Department and attempts to understand how this culture impacts on the SABC's independence. She claims (correctly) that this approach is missing in the current debate, which generally tends to focus on formal structures and policies (which appear to protect the Corporation's independence). Based on her fieldwork involving interviews with current and ex-SABC employees, she argues that the SABC's independence is under pressure from within the corporation, and that these threats come from the board and from management.

Arndt argues that these structures 'manage dissent … using pressure and rewards that, in combination, appear to effectively stifle independent thinking and hence work against editorial independence, and a professional ethos integral to the SABC's public broadcasting mandate' (2007: 89). In a climate of uncertainty, where managers and even board members dabble in decision-making that should be left to journalists, there is a growing tendency to self-censor to please the powers that be internally and externally, particularly when it comes to controversial decisions that may offend the government or the ruling party.

While the differences between the findings of the quantitative and qualitative studies need to be more fully understood, it is worth noting that most of the recent editorial disputes[29] have been about current affairs and programming rather than news, which implies that the SABC produces news fairly proficiently, but is weak when it comes to providing high quality analysis and discussion of news stories. According to Lesley Cowling and Caroline Hamilton, the 'blacklisting' controversy revealed a clash of competing models of journalism. On the one hand there was the 'journalistic model', which visualises the media as a mediator between the public and the government, and on the other the 'majoritarian position', which sees the public as being represented by Parliament, and therefore the national interest and the public interest as being co-terminous (Cowling and Hamilton 2008: 31). Cowling and Hamilton's paper deals with the clash of these two models in relation to the SAFM programme, *AM Live*. They argue that the programme sought to increase the diversity of commentary to include voices from civil society. However, this experiment in constructing a diverse, informed public clashed with an attempt by SABC news management to corporatise commentary through its draft policy on the use of commentators. This policy sought to narrow the range of commentators to include mainly those located in recognised institutional settings, such as universities. The conflicting views culminated in an on-air clash between the SABC's spokesperson, Kaizer Kganyago and *AM Live* presenter, John Perlman, which precipitated a commission of enquiry into the existence or otherwise of a 'blacklist'.

The conflation of the SABC's nation-building agenda with a statist agenda arguably led to a situation where President Thabo Mbeki was considered by SABC management to be the embodiment of the development agenda, which attempted to redress the legacies of poverty and inequality under apartheid. The most troubling editorial decisions the SABC made more recently related to the controversies surrounding Mbeki, and also the former and current deputy presidents of the country. These incidents suggested a climate of deference towards Mbeki, coupled with an aversion to risk-taking in relation to Jacob Zuma. Quantitative studies, which focus on news only, have not monitored the SABC's coverage of such controversial issues across a variety of programming genres. Moreover, qualitative data considers only what is broadcast, not what is not produced for broadcast. To do so would require a contextual analysis, in which key news stories during a particular period are identified and compared with the SABC's coverage of them. Also, the increase in the number of government and ANC-related stories and their increasing prominence in the news line-up is in itself significant, even if bias cannot be proved, in that SABC news is engaging in agenda-setting, and communicating the message that 'development' is synonymous with the government and the ruling party. Such agenda-setting limits the chances that other actors in the development field will be considered agenda-setters (which would enhance their chances of attracting support), and constructs as normative the dominance of ANC rule.

The twists and turns of regional and local television

The final version of the Constitution ruled out the possibility of provincial public broadcasting, as it removed the power that provinces had in the interim constitution to establish provincial public broadcasters. Furthermore, Parliament decided in response to the Triple Inquiry report that all provincial broadcasters should be subsumed into the SABC. This constitutional change, coupled with the SABC's financial woes, meant that provincial television receded into the background. In any event, the possibility of provincial television was met with some suspicion by the SABC and the Independent Broadcasting Authority (IBA), who felt that it might undermine the building of a common national identity. While they resisted the push for regional television and even regional news, on the grounds that all national languages had widespread constituencies and had the right to be heard nationally, the situation of a multi-lingual news division has been a complex one.

At one point, SABC Television News attempted to reproduce the same national news across the various languages, in an attempt to unify the citizenry and educate it about what were felt to be the most pressing issues of the day. The competition from South Africa's first private free-to-air channel, e.tv news, and the awareness of regional interests among different news teams over time led to a change from what one might call the Habermasian notion of a public sphere[30] at the time of the former Head of News Allister Sparks to a more de-centralised, federal notion of news and news priorities under his successor, Jimi Matthews. The result has been that there are often startling differences in news coverage between television news stations covering different languages, even though they share news collection and editing resources. In retrospect, it might have been preferable to maintain provincial or regional television news stations able to focus on local issues, and perhaps also able to stimulate the growth of smaller local production teams and production facilities.

A faltering attempt is being made in this direction. The matter of regional television was revisited again in 2002, when the DoC introduced legislation in Parliament to set up two parallel state broadcasters in an attempt to address the language deficits on SABC television.[31] This motivation was supported by the ANC, which argued at its National Congress in 2002 that South Africa needed a publicly funded media system. The system was to be established by 2012, as the sector was too heavily dominated by advertiser-driven media. This model was necessary 'in order for public and community media to serve as vehicles to articulate the needs of the poor, rural people, women, labour and other marginalised constituencies' (African National Congress, 2002).

In an attempt to move towards this model, the ANC resolved that two new regional television stations would be established, to be run on a non-commercial basis – a resolution that was then implemented by the DoC. In proposing these services, the department was attempting to address the skewed nature of television resulting from the economics of advertising. All television stations derive the bulk of their advertising revenue from reaching viewers who have means. In South Africa, this means viewers classified as being in the upper Living Standard Measures (LSMs).[32] These realities of ad spend have an impact on the prioritisation of audiences by television owners; SABC 1 identifies LSM 5.1 as the centre of its target audience, while SABC 2 targets LSM 5.7 and SABC 3 targets LSM 6.3. E.tv has set LSM 5.5 as its target. Yet according to the statistics for 2006 of the South African Advertising Research Foundation, some 59.3 per cent of the population fell in LSM 5 and below.[33] This means that for economic reasons these services do not really consider about half of South Africa's population to be a target audience: hardly a justifiable situation for a broadcasting system geared towards universality and diversity (DoC undated: 17).

The move to establish the regional television stations proved to be controversial, as it was interpreted as an attempt to achieve greater government control over broadcasting, under the guise of addressing language equity. Parliament arrived at a compromise arrangement whereby the two stations would be run by the SABC, and would become known as SABC 4 and 5 (Tleane and Duncan 2003: 170–173). In terms of the Broadcasting Amendment Bill of 2002, which proposed to bring these two stations into being, the SABC was directed to apply to ICASA for licences for these services. ICASA was also given the power to decide whether these services should be allowed to receive advertising. However, the whole train of events was troubling: ICASA was basically reduced to issuing the licences, and the developments marked a turn towards parliamentary licensing by legislative fiat. This is a trend that continues to this day, and threatens the independence of the regulator, which in terms of the Constitution should have sole powers to regulate broadcasting.[34]

In an attempt to assert some level of independence, and fight its reduction to a mere rubber stamp of the legislature, ICASA decided to use the opportunity to revisit the idea of regional television, and in 2003 conducted a feasibility study on community, commercial and public service regional television, and also held public hearings. The study confirmed the Regulator's long-held view that commercial regional television would not be viable in South Africa, and, if introduced, would result in the fragmentation of the advertising cake to the detriment of existing broadcasters (ICASA 2005: 3). ICASA decided to license only public regional services, and also indicated that programming in English would not be allowed, as these services were designed to promote marginalised languages; in any event, English was well catered for on national services. ICASA also ruled out advertising on these services.

Following the release of the policy paper, the SABC submitted its applications for the two public regional stations. Ironically, in the public hearing, the SABC argued that SABC 5 would require the re-establishment of in-house production infrastructure that had been dismantled when the SABC stopped providing regional television. The SABC also proposed an analogue terrestrial roll-out, although frequencies would need to be harvested from commercial and community television (including e.tv).

ICASA rejected this suggestion, noting that, in some areas, frequencies were so scarce that only a single frequency remained available. It argued that 'it may, in some cases, be impossible to provide additional analogue coverage for the proposed regional services equivalent to that achieved for existing analogue services. Significant gaps may exist in the coverage areas' (ICASA 2005: 4). This has led to the suggestion that the roll-out of the stations may have to wait for digital migration. But a more significant obstacle has arisen, which has led to ICASA granting but not issuing the licences – namely a lack of clarity about whether government would provide funding. It would appear that, in hatching the idea of the stations, the DoC did not lobby the Ministry of Finance sufficiently for funding. This led to the Minister of Communications indicating in 2004 that her department would finalise a public-private partnership model for the regional stations (ICASA 2004: 15). A solution options analysis report commissioned by the department recommended that either the stations be run as joint ventures with private businesses, or that all their operations be outsourced to a private party. The department has been advised to invite expressions of interest in the stations (DoC, undated: 47). ICASA also reversed its initial decision not to allow advertising on the services. Even in the 2008/9 budget, there was no indication of any support from the treasury for these developments, though some political observers felt that the call for SABC 4 and SABC 5 enjoyed ANC support and was likely, as ANC policy, to obtain funding in due course.

The public television situation that South Africa has ended up with can only be described as perverse. Initially, the IBA had recommended two non-commercial television services for the SABC. Largely owing to the fact that government would not commit to ongoing public funding, the broadcaster has now landed up with five channels, two of which have been mothballed owing to a lack of clarity about frequencies and funding, and all of which are semi-commercial in nature. In fact, SABC 4 and 5 may even become private-sector-run initiatives, which will call into question their very identity as public stations.

Community television

Local community television has become the Cinderella of the television system. Attempts to establish community television via SABC regional windows have been unsettled by the commercialisation of public broadcasting, which has frustrated the attempts of community media organisations to establish partnerships with the SABC. Since the mid-1990s, the community media sector has argued that there exists a 'natural partnership' between itself and public broadcasting: both sectors have a shared vision of a non-commercial, public-interest broadcasting that addresses audiences as citizens rather than consumers. Karen Thorne has argued that in the climate of fiscal austerity that prevailed in the late 1980s, community media had to develop strategies for self-sustainability that included pursuing this partnership with the SABC. Community television initiatives argued strongly for the establishment of SABC regional services, so that the sector could contribute local-level programming. Thorne argued that this arrangement could benefit both the SABC and community television: the SABC's programming capacity would be boosted, while the latter would have access to airtime and other production resources (Thorne 1998: 228–230). In time, this could have resulted in a truly independent community television sector.

However, the partnership – which was cemented in a record of understanding between community media and the SABC – faltered, owing to 'ongoing uncertainty about the SABC's financial future, the restructuring of the SABC and the fact that the IBA chose, after much debate, not to enshrine the partnership in the SABC's licence conditions' (Thorne 1998: 229). This failure to secure an agreement led the community television advocacy group, the Open Window Network (OWN), to seek a partnership with private television. In making these arguments to ICASA in the context of public hearings into the establishment of private television, OWN (1997: 5) noted that 'community television has been waiting patiently at the back of the queue of South African broadcasting policy reform', and wanted some attention. It accused the IBA of failing to develop a holistic broadcasting policy that recognised community television's right to exist. The IBA's 1997 position paper on private television was silent on the issue (IBA 1997). Seemingly, another turning point in television policy was that neither the public broadcaster nor the first private free-to-air television channel were obliged by ICASA to support the community television sector, making the establishment of a community television sector even more difficult.

Community television only really got off the ground in 2007, when ICASA licensed Soweto Community Television (SCTV) for one year. SCTV was actually launched in 2000, and registered as a Section 21 company in 2004. According to the station's application to ICASA: 'It is a live channel that combines the immediacy of talk radio with the relevance of a daily city newspaper and the entertainment of a TV show.' Its programming breakdown, however, betrays a bias towards music and talk shows (which account for 84.5 per cent).

The station also has other troubling features, especially some concerning public participation. While the station's licence states that 'the licencee must establish and maintain formal structures which will facilitate the participation of the community in the control, management, operational and programming aspects of the broadcasting service' (ICASA 2007), SCTV seems to operate like a closed corporation. According to its Articles of Association, it has a Board consisting of a chairperson, an honorary treasurer, a secretary, a managing director and three other members or delegates appointed by its affiliated organisations (who these are is unclear). The station is obliged to hold an annual general meeting, but the quorum for such a meeting is 'at least three members of the Board'. It is difficult to see how such a structure enables community participation. The station sees community participation taking place rather at the level of programming, with community members co-opted to participate in the daily operations of the broadcasting and production facility. The station's initial start-up costs were also reportedly being covered by the local television production company, Urban Brew, which is also providing technical support. It also remains to be seen whether the station will, in time, develop independence from this commercial television producer (Byrne 2007).

In commercial terms, community television could become quite lively given the absence of regional television and news. An additional possibility is that of community stations becoming regional advertising houses, as they are allowed to advertise even more than other television stations (as long as their advertising is not aimed making a profit). But the original vision of community television as the embodiment of non-commercial, community-driven initiatives has been lost, at least for the foreseeable future.

The establishment of private free-to-air television

In 1995, in its Triple Inquiry report, the IBA signalled its intention to license a new private television channel early in 1998. In 1996, following public hearings, it released its position paper on commercial television. In it the IBA argued that it intended to place a 30 per cent local-content obligation on private television (IBA 1997). Had the SABC not been financially disabled in the way it was in 1996, the development of South Africa's local content industry could have been much more advanced than it is.

After a competitive process involving seven applicants, the first private free-to-air licence was granted to Midi TV in March 1998. The IBA had signalled that ownership and control by previously disadvantaged South Africans would be a significant consideration in who obtained the licence; and indicated, in its reasons for awarding the licence to Midi, that it was impressed with the group's empowerment credentials. In terms of its licence conditions, issued in March 1998, 'historically disadvantaged groups' means, *inter alia*, black (African, Coloured and Indian) South Africans, women and disabled people. Midi demonstrated ownership by historically disadvantaged people in all these categories. The IBA also allowed Midi to introduce local content incrementally.[35]

The first few months after the awarding of the licence can only be described as a comedy of errors. The station began broadcasting in October in the absence of finalised licence conditions. When the conditions were finalised for the initial six-hour broadcast period, Midi argued that some of the conditions were unrealistic, such as the restriction on advertising and the requirement to broadcast news and information in IsiZulu, IsiXhosa, SeSotho and SeTswana. The station also experienced major problems in getting its news programmes off the ground, because it claimed that its broadcasting equipment was being held up by customs officials. This delay led to the IBA declaring in December that the station was in breach of its licence conditions (Midi Television 1999: 6–7).

In an attempt to address the growing crisis, Midi TV applied to the IBA to relax some of its licence conditions. Possibly the most significant change it requested the IBA to endorse was to its ownership structure. The original shareholding structure had consisted of a variety of local companies and empowerment initiatives, representing workers, youth and the disabled, as well as ownership by the American multinational, Time Warner. The IBA had been especially impressed by the involvement of the South African Clothing and Textile Workers' Union and the Mineworkers' Investment Corporation, as their involvement held out the possibility that dividends would be broadly distributed among workers. And although a weak point had been that Midi TV had failed to demonstrate a commitment to women's empowerment, that feature had been shared by other applicants as well.

In 1999, this ownership structure changed. Time Warner transferred its shares into South African Television Holdings, while all the other shareholders in Midi transferred their shares (accounting for 80% of the total number of shares) to Sabido Investments, a wholly owned subsidiary of Hosken Consolidated Investments (HCI). At the time, the IBA expressed concern about the fact that the restructuring of Midi's shareholding would reduce the diversity of its owners. In return, Midi argued that the minority shareholders were not able to provide their portion of funding (MCU 2002: 1–2). In an attempt to prevent the dilution of the original intention behind the granting of the licence, namely to ensure ownership and control by persons from historically disadvantaged groups, the IBA ruled that the change in the ownership structure could be allowed only on condition that the empowerment component of the licensee or of its South African shareholder not be reduced.

In spite of this condition, in 2000 the Rembrandt company acquired a significant stake in Sabido – which accounted for the bulk of the empowerment ownership – and in Midi, which meant that the control of the station was now shared by Rembrandt and HCI. The IBA's Broadcast Monitoring and Complaints Commission found Midi TV guilty of contravening its licence conditions by failing to seek regulatory approval for entering into the Rembrandt deal. However, when Midi applied to ICASA to condone the sale, ICASA agreed. In its reasons, it noted that the economic climate had worsened significantly since the time when Midi had made its initial promise of performance. It said that the weakness of the rand had inflated Midi's costs to three times the amount of R450 million it had expected as shareholder funding. The contraction of ad spend had also left Midi with shortfalls in income. In 2003, ICASA agreed to the amendment, providing the station remained controlled by black empowerment entities (Langa 2003).

A leading media-law expert, Justine White, argued strongly against the IBA's allowing of the amendment. She cited a statement made by Midi in its application for amendment that 'the parties were aware, at the time of preparing and submitting the bid, that most of them did not have the financial resources that would be required in order to meet their respective funding obligations towards Midi TV (Proprietary) Limited'. White read this as an admission that Midi had misled the IBA about the merits of its application, which had been granted in the face of stiff competition partly because of the empowerment credentials of the bidders. She argued that the IBA should not have granted the licence to Midi in the first place, and that the licence should be revoked (White 1999: 7–9). ICASA did not heed White's argument and endorsed a situation that reduced the station's empowerment base. In any event, it would appear that the diversity of shareholding of e.tv was built on a false economy.

In 2001, Time Warner sold its stake in e.tv, as it was concerned that it would never own a controlling stake in the station.

After these major changes, e.tv stabilised. In terms of taste, it was an odd mix from close to the outset. The early broadcasting of high-quality drama series such as *The West Wing* and the promise of Warner material gave way to a plethora of low popular culture items: imported wrestling shows, *Walker, Texas Ranger*, soft porn and action movies. Where e.tv undoubtedly succeeded was in bringing a new vitality and informality to television news and current affairs. Research suggests that many young black South Africans find e.tv's informal and direct English easier to understand than the often formalised and slightly archaic language of African language stations (Ndlovu 2005).

E.tv has certainly used its news programmes and its investigative current affairs programme, *Third Degree*, hosted by Debora Patta, as a sign of its feisty independence from government. With much of its news audiences taken away by this competitor, SABC 3 was forced to move its news broadcasting from 8 p.m. to 7 p.m., to go head to head with e.tv's news. The advertising slogan that perhaps caught the new station's tone best was in response to the up-market pretentiousness of SABC 3's 'So much better' slogan. E.tv came back with 'So much badder' – no doubt in mischievous reference to its late-night soft-porn broadcasts, but also to a slightly mocking attitude to high culture.

By 2002, e.tv was meeting, and even exceeding, its licence conditions in relation to language and local content, informationals, children's programming and drama. Although it exceeded slightly the limitation on advertising, the regulator declared its satisfaction with the performance of the station (MCU 2002). The Monitoring and Complaints Unit reported similar results in 2003. In 2004, e.tv became profitable for the first time, and according to the station, returned annual average profits of 25 per cent until 2008. The station broadcasts two daily South African dramas (*Rhythm City* and *Scandal*), and also provided unprecedented coverage of the King Commission of Enquiry, the Hefer Commission and the judgements in the Schabir Shaik and Jacob Zuma trials. As a commercial station with some public service obligations, the station can be considered a success story. It has expanded news and entertainment opportunities for viewers in the LSM 5.5 band and above (its target audience), and shows that local content can be delivered successfully within a commercial television framework.

The one area where it has fallen down is meeting its licence condition on provincial diversity, given that the bulk of its commissioned programmes comes from the Western Cape and Gauteng. In an attempt to correct this problem, e.tv has conducted hearings in other provinces to encourage programming proposals: an approach that has yielded some fruit. Largely, e.tv has been quick to correct shortfalls in meeting its licence conditions. For instance, when it recorded an indigenous language shortfall in its drama programmes in 2005, it replaced the producers of both *Backstage* and *Scandal*.

E.tv has provoked controversy with its late-night adult films, which led to Parliament summoning it to account for its actions. In 2005, the Portfolio Committee on Home Affairs organised a public hearing on what it termed 'pornography in the media'. The committee argued that it was duty-bound to call the hearing as it had received complaints about the films. E.tv did not attend, resulting in calls by members of the committee for the station to be subpoenaed, as it was considered to be the guiltiest in purveying 'pornography'. Later that year, e.tv finally appeared before the committee and argued that its programming schedule was entirely in keeping with ICASA regulations. Some parliamentarians brought up the possibility of children staying up to watch the films and likened this to child abuse, and accused the station of arrogance. In a later session the Chairperson, Patrick Chauke, argued that Parliament should pass a law to 'protect our nation, our people' from the onslaught of pornography. Reportedly, Chauke commented that if the committee were to ban pornography in the media, and the Constitutional Court were to declare the ban unconstitutional, then 'one should perhaps consider amending the Constitution'.

These threats were to culminate in a draft amendment to the Film and Publications Act, which attempted to subject the media, including broadcasters, to pre-publication censorship by the Film and Publications Board. At the time of writing, the Bill had been referred back to Parliament by the President, owing to concerns about its constitutionality. Parliament has amended the Bill, which is now with the President for ratification. Not all the concerns raised by media organisations about overlapping jurisdictions between ICASA and the Board have been addressed, which means that the Bill may need to be referred to the Constitutional Court. The move towards pre-publication censorship strongly suggested an attempted return to the sort of morality-based censorship of broadcasting content that was done away with at the end of apartheid.

Convergence, digital migration and the liberalisation of subscription services

Teer-Tomaselli (2001) has identified the nation-building project that is central to the SABC's mandate as being essentially modernist, and in contrast with the postmodernist trend towards particularist, ethnic or 'lifestyle' programming. The explosion of media possibilities enhanced by digitisation could be a potential crisis for all broadcasters in that there is an emerging trend among youth not to watch programmed viewing, but instead to access content on demand, in the form of DVDs, 'ripped' or copied content (often illegally obtained) or on the Internet, and on handheld devices including cell phones. Increasingly, commercial television operators are arguing that multi-channel television, and the segmented audiences it creates, are the future of television, as opposed to the universal, single-channel environment of the past. The Regulator claims to be ready for this development. According to its Chairperson, Paris Mashile, ICASA has 'already liberalised the content market, and created the necessary seedbed for a multi-channel environment to flourish' (Mashile 2008: 4). Yet, as Elihu Katz, the founder of Israeli television, has pointed out, segmentation damages the possibilities for a public sphere (Katz 1996: 22–33).

The pay-television channel, M-Net, was – to use the words of veteran media activist and former Rand Daily Mail editor Raymond Louw – 'born in sin' when the apartheid government conceded its establishment to compensate South Africa's newspaper groups for loss of advertising to the country's first SABC television channel, which started broadcasting in 1976.[36] In 1995, the IBA allowed M-Net a two-hour slot – from 5 p.m. to 7 p.m. each day and known as 'open time' – when it could broadcast unencrypted free-to-air content in order to attract advertising and new viewers. In 1989, M-Net SuperSport was launched (and then re-launched in 1992) as a stand-alone brand. A multi-channel satellite service was launched in 1995, called DStv, and operated by MultiChoice, to complement M-Net.

When M-Net's Chief Executive Officer, Glen Marques, gave a presentation at a South African Communication Association (SACOMM) conference in Stellenbosch in 2003, he included a quote from Rupert Murdoch about sport being the 'battering ram' for pay television. In a sport-mad nation, M-Net and – subsequently – DStv have managed to control and shape the television coverage of sport (with e.tv's over-ambitious foray into World Cup Soccer coverage the exception that proves the rule).

Recently, ICASA decided to embark on the process of liberalising the subscription market, long dominated by MultiChoice. ICASA advertised for applicants and received eighteen applications. The objective of licensing new entrants is to provide competition in the subscription market without threatening the existing subscriber base of DStv, which boasts the wealthiest South Africans, who are mainly white: 52.2 per cent of its subscribers fall into the LSM 10 band and 26.8 per cent into the LSM 9 band.

A number of applicants argued that the black-middle-class market is underserved by DStv. E.sat, which was one of four subscription-television groups licensed in 2007, intends to provide subscription services to this market, given that its sister business e.tv has a significant share of this market. Many of the channels licensed through this process will be compiled locally, unlike the 'pass-through' of DStv, which has mostly internationally packaged channels. The consortiums that were granted licences were those that were already active in broadcasting, namely MultiChoice and e.sat, with the exception being on-Digital Media. Another successful applicant was Telkom TV, a sister company of the telecommunications parastatal, Telkom. Walking on Water, a small initiative intending to focus on the Christian community, was also granted a licence. The awarding of these licences suggests that those operators who have a foot in the door, either in media or telecommunications, are the ones best poised to take advantage of the possibilities of digitisation and convergence. Others may face ever-increasing barriers to entry.

The major problems for new entrants into the digital multi-channel environment are scarcity of content and the general presupposition that there is a large, under-served black market in the LSM 5–9 bands. This implies an intention on the part of these services to generate local content, but it is unclear where this content will come from. At the time of the ICASA submissions midway through 2006, the number of Compact DStv's subscribers was 50,000, the majority of them black. Many of the potential entrants argued that the R199 Compact subscription would open the door to their cheaper (usually R100–R150) packages, which would service this community.

By early 2008, these projections looked increasingly unlikely and optimistic. MultiChoice, in part through its seemingly extravagant bid for PSL soccer rights, managed to increase its number of Compact DStv subscribers from 50 000 to 230 000 between September 2006 and March 2008 and thereby to remove one of the key potential selling points for rival services. If indeed there was a viable new group of black entrants into the subscription television market, willing to pay R100 or more, it seems that MultiChoice has already seized the lion's share of this group. Moreover, most of the other applicants will be competing with one another for this group. If and when SABC 4 and SABC 5 enter the market, they are likely to find themselves in a very competitive environment from the point of view of both content and audiences.

One successful applicant that has anticipated this problem, and altered its strategy in response to new developments, is e.sat. The commercial success of e.tv has led the station to develop ambitious plans for the future. It has decided to change from being a platform supplier to being a multi-channel operator: hence the establishment of e.sat.

In December 2007, the station reached an agreement with MultiChoice to distribute a 24-hour e-news service on the DStv platform. E.sat intends to produce a number of channels for the DStv platform (Hamlyn 2008: 1). In doing the deal, it gave up its ambition of being an African-wide platform, as envisaged in its ICASA submission for a subscription licence, clearly having decided that it would be difficult, if not impossible, to compete with DStv technologically and to replicate the massive effort of establishing marketing and legal agreements across Africa. What this deal did for MultiChoice was to give it a 24-hour African news channel, thus trumping one of the ambitions of other new entrants such as Telkom Media. It is thus not surprising that e.sat decided to climb onto the DStv bandwagon.

The Telkom group has the huge potential advantage of being able to offer cable television instead of, or in addition to, satellite television, and also a three-in-one combination of television, internet and telephone through already existing cables into the home. However, it seems likely that if it uses its pre-existing monopoly telephone rights for broadcast purposes, it may well be challenged to share this access with other groups. It is also not clear how the Telkom group or other licencees will find content able to entice new viewers, given the very high levels of satisfaction reported by most DStv subscribers.

In time, free-to-air services will also have to catch up with subscription-based services and go digital. South Africa's highly unequal economic situation means that there is a vast social need for quality free-to-air broadcasting, as subscription services are simply unaffordable (DoC 2007: 4–5). While opening up the subscription market is likely to change this picture somewhat – by increasing the television opportunities of those falling within LSM 6 and above – over half the population (which is located in LSM 5 and below) will remain dependent on free-to-air services. These services are particularly difficult to migrate to digital.

In 2005, the Department of Communications (DoC) established a Digital Migration Working Group to develop a national strategy for the migration of analogue to digital broadcasting. Digital switch-on took place on 1 November 2008, to be followed by a dual illumination period[37] of three years. The 2010 Soccer World Cup, which South Africa is hosting, will be used as an opportunity to encourage audiences to invest in high-definition television. Multiplexing will allow at least six digital channels to be made available in future on a channel that would otherwise provide only one channel on an analogue platform. Given the liberalisation of subscription services, the interoperability of set top boxes in unscrambling digital signals will become a key topic for debate and resolution. Affordability of set top boxes is also a key concern. The DoC has already predicted that 4.5 million households will be unable to afford set top boxes at any price and may well require subsidy or risk being shut out of the broadcasting environment entirely. In August 2008, Cabinet approved the Broadcasting Digital Migration Policy, and has also agreed to help approximately 5 million of the poorest households, by providing up to 70 per cent of the cost of set-top boxes (BuaNews 2008).

Conclusion: South Africa's one tier of broadcasting

As has been argued, South Africa has faced particular periods in post-apartheid television history when it could make strategic choices about the nature of the television system. These periods included the initial multiparty negotiations; the IBA's Triple Inquiry into the nature of public broadcasting and Parliament's response to this; the establishment of e.tv and the attempts to establish SABC 4 and SABC 5; and the drive towards convergence and multi-channel television. The trend has been one of policy choices that have favoured marketisation, and more lately a statist approach to correcting the negative effects of this marketisation.

The African Charter on Broadcasting, developed in 2001, recognises three tiers of broadcasting and calls for their establishment in African media systems.[38] South Africa is often taken as a model in that regard. We would argue on the basis of the evidence presented in this chapter that South Africa is an example of how not to establish three tiers of broadcasting. While there can be no doubt that the country's transition to democracy has resulted in an unprecedented diversification of services, this diversification has taken place only to the extent that all tiers of broadcasting have adapted to the commercial sector. This development differs fundamentally from the resolution taken at the Jabulani! Freedom of the Airwaves Conference in 1991, that public broadcasting should form the core of South African broadcasting. Instead, commercial broadcasting has come to form the core of the system. This has led to divisions opening up between the 'television haves' and the 'television have-nots'.

By marrying Pierre Bourdieu's concept of symbolic capital[39] with David Harvey's concept of accumulation by dispossession,[40] we could arrive at a characterisation of the South African television system as one marked by accumulation by symbolic dispossession in South Africa (and, increasingly, in the Southern African sub-region). In other words, the overwhelming reliance of the television system on commercial sources of funding has concentrated an ever-increasing number of services in the LSM bracket of bands 5 and above: as a result, their symbolic capital has grown. Those who fall in the bracket of LSM 4 and below are severely underserved by television: their symbolic capital has not grown, and may even have shrunk. This symbolic relationship was well captured by an advertisement for the new DStv services, in which a young black man is put in the nightmarish position of being in a corporation in which all the others, including the window-cleaners, share a set of references to which he is oblivious – because he does not have subscription television.

While accumulation by symbolic dispossession has taken place within South Africa, the country's media are also setting up similar relationships of unequal exchange with other Southern African countries.

What are the implications of such enclaves in South Africa's television system? Guy Berger (2002) has argued in relation to media reform, that 'The bottle, of course, is admirably half-full or disappointingly half-empty depending on whether one looks at the past or the future. But it indisputably contains a lot more liquid than it did before 1994.' Berger's approach is useful, as it focuses debate on the gains that have been made from apartheid to democracy in non-absolutist terms. But what Berger does not take into account is the inherently unstable nature of such a deeply divided television system. This instability could lead to progressive claims for a more equitable television system, or conservative counter-claims for more state control of broadcasting content. The fragmentation of public space fuelled by media segmentation may further reinforce social divisions, in the process consigning to the dustbin of history the idealistic notion of a 'public sphere' constituted by a united South African nation.

Could different policy choices have been made? Were there externalities driving decision-making, which imposed constraints? While the scope for what has been termed 'progressive manoeuvrability'[41] – or the policy space to achieve a people-centred global economic order rather than a purely profit-centred order – may have looked very bleak in 1996, when Parliament took such significant decisions on the future of television, the same cannot be said now. The countries that have championed policies generally associated with the 'Washington consensus' are on the defensive, having led the global economy into recession. The growing global influence of

China, India and Brazil has meant that global politics are not as unipolar as they were in 1990. These developments mean that scope for redistributive policies, including in the media, has grown, although the ability of different countries to implement such policies may be constrained by the global financial crisis.

South Africa's television system is not extroverted, and in fact is characterised by extensive local ownership, control and content. Paterson's warning about foreign multinationals coming into South Africa and buying up local television has not really materialised. Though this is not for want of their trying, South Africa proved to be less attractive to foreign investment than hoped for at the time of the drafting of the White Paper, for a variety of complex reasons. Rather, South African companies have become multinational, and have bought into the media systems of other African countries. Also, broadcasting is not subject to the General Agreement on Trade in Services, so there is no multilateral pressure on South Africa to open up its markets. South Africa's relative strength as a sub-regional economy gave it significantly more scope for 'progressive manoeuvrability' – also in relation to broadcasting – than other Southern African countries. Extensive national ownership and control of television gives South Africa the scope to be much more daring in its television policy and practice than has been the case.

Furthermore, the argument that South Africa cannot afford to fund public broadcasting owing to other pressing demands on the fiscus, needs to be questioned. As Finance Minister Trevor Manuel pointed out in 2005, 'South Africa has bundles of cash available to ramp up the development of infrastructure, but doesn't have the imaginative and detailed plans needed to make the necessary upgrades to its urban and rural areas a reality' (Manuel quoted in Legassick 2007: 138).

All these factors, combined, suggest that the marketisation of television is a chosen strategy, rather than a policy trajectory imposed in response to external, objective constraints, or even an unintended outcome of well-meaning policy-makers. In 2002, COSATU argued that there existed a longstanding (pre-1994) plan to implement unpopular measures – captured in the regime's outright neo-liberal normative economic model of 1993 – and that the ANC had taken a policy decision that it might have to continue with implementing this plan. COSATU further argued that, as early as 1994, the ANC had predicted the possibility that material conditions might arise in the country that might necessitate the implementation of this plan, and was already considering the likely effects of implementing such a plan on its support base. According to COSATU, the ANC had noted that anger and resistance in the democratic movement were the most likely responses. If events at the latest ANC conference – where Thabo Mbeki was deposed by Jacob Zuma – are anything to go by, then it would appear that this anger and resistance are indeed on the rise.

South Africa should undertake a re-think of its television policies and practice: a rethink that will be of significance to the whole Southern African sub-region, given the increasing interconnectedness of television systems. The Jabulani! conference provided some guidance on essential elements for a South African broadcasting system when it argued that public broadcasting must form the core of the system, to set the standard for all broadcasting. As things stand, the notion that the SABC could set the standard for broadcasting appears to be somewhat far-fetched. Elements of the core could also include publicly regulated commercial media, although these should not constitute the most important constituents of the core.

Public broadcasting will be able to take its place at the centre of the broadcasting system only if it is resourced appropriately (from public funds), and boosted by measures to upgrade its independence and accountability. These services should reach the mass of South Africans, providing common platforms for debate irrespective of LSM. It is important that the public elements of the system should not be conceptualised as 'top-ups' for commercial services, addressing audiences hitherto neglected by commercial media: rather, concerted efforts need to be made to establish a space where all South Africans can meet and deliberate on the pressing issues of the day. There are real dangers in not having such a shared public space, and the further fragmentation of this space may exacerbate social instability.[42] As James Curran has argued, such services would offset 'the particularistic features of the rest of the media system by providing a common symbolic environment which reinforces ties of mutuality' (Curran 1991: 105).

This media system should also contain a number of peripheral sectors, addressing particular audiences and drawing on different models of journalism. Currently, the professional model is taken to be the normative model of journalism, with development journalism having become the model associated with the SABC. A redesigned television system should make space for a multiplicity of journalistic models at its periphery, including advocacy journalism and even political-party-linked media. The development of more detailed policy proposals are beyond the scope of this contribution. What we need to recognise, though, is that much more daring policy alternatives are needed. If South African policy-makers develop the appetite for confronting honestly the deficits in the existing television system, then another television system is possible.

References

African Charter on Broadcasting. 2001. Paris: UNESCO.

African National Congress. 2002. Media in a democratic society. Downloaded from http://www.anc.org.za/ancdocs/history/conf/conference51/index.html (accessed 20 February 2008).

——. 2007. Commission reports and draft resolutions. Downloaded from http://www.anc.org.za/ancdocs/history/conf/conference52/index.html (accessed 20 February 2008).

Alexander, N. 2000. Transcribed speech on language and the SABC, delivered at the Freedom of Expression Institute's Stock-taking Conference on the SABC, 4–5 November, Parktonian Hotel, Braamfontein.

Arndt, C. 2007. *Managing Dissent: Institutional Culture and Political Independence in the South African Broadcasting Corporation's News and Current Affairs Division.* Unpublished MA dissertation, University of Cape Town, South Africa.

Banda, F. 2006. An appraisal of the applicability of development journalism in the context of public service broadcasting. Paper presented at the South African Broadcasting Corporation 'News content planning' workshop, Johannesburg, 21 October 2006.

Barnett, C. 2000. Language equity and the politics of representation in South African media reform. *Social Identities* 6(1): 63–90.

——. 2001. Media, scale and democratisation. In *Media, democracy and renewal in Southern Africa*, ed. H. Dunn and K. Tomaselli, 41–53. Colarado Springs: International Academic Publishers.

Berger, G. 2001. Deracialisation, democracy and development: Transformation of the South African media. In *Media, Democracy and Renewal in Southern Africa*, ed. H. Dunn and K. Tomaselli, 151–180. Colarado Springs: International Academic Publishers.

Bond, P. (ed.). 2007. *Beyond enclavity in African economies: The enduring work of Guy Mhone*. Durban: Centre for Civil Society.

Bourdieu, P. 1984. *Distinction: A social critique of the judgement of taste*. London: Routledge & Kegan Paul.

BuaNews. 2008. Digital broadcasting one step closer. http://www.southafrica.info/about/media/bdm-070808.htm (accessed 16 March 2009).

Byrne, C. 2007. Loxion kulcha: Soweto TV takes the lead. *Mail&Guardian*, 6 November.

Cowling, L and C. Hamilton. 2008. Thinking allowed/aloud: Pursuing the public interest in radio debates. Paper presented at the conference, Paradoxes of the Postcolonial Public Sphere, 28–31 January, at the University of the Witwatersrand, Johannesburg, South Africa.

Curran, J. 1991. Mass media and democracy. In *Mass media and society*, ed. J. Curran and M. Gurevitch, 82–117. Kent: Edward Arnold.

Department of Communications. Undated. Draft solution options analysis report.

Department of Communications. 1998. *White Paper on broadcasting policy*. Pretoria: Author.

DoC *see* Department of Communications.

Duncan, J. 2002. *Broadcasting and the national question: South African broadcasting in the age of neo-liberalism*. Johannesburg: Freedom of Expression Institute and Netherlands Institute for Southern Africa.

——. 2006. From national to global apartheid: Ten years of broadcasting in a democratic South Africa. In *Media in South Africa: A cross-media assessment*, ed. A. Olorunnisola. New York: Edwin Mellen Press.

——. 2008. Executive overstretch: South African broadcasting independence and accountability under Thabo Mbeki. *Communicatio* 34(1): 21–52.

Etzioni-Halevy, E. 1987. *National Broadcasting under Siege*. New York: St. Martin's Press.

Freedom of Expression Institute. 2008. *The Broadcasting Independence Handbook*. Johannesburg: Author.

FXI *see* Freedom of Expression Institute.

Gemini Consulting. 2000. Overarching analysis and recommendations. Unpublished paper.

Habermas, J. 1989. *The Structural Transformation of the Public Sphere: An Inquiry into a Category of Bourgeois Society*. Cambridge, Massachusetts: Massachusetts Institute of Technology Press.

Hamlyn, M. 2007. E.tv to launch 24-hour news. *News24*, 12 December. http://www.news24.com/News24/Entertainment/Local/0,2-1225-1242_2237516,00.html (accessed 3 February 2008).

Harvey, D. 2003. *The New Imperialism*. Oxford: Oxford University Press.

Horwitz, R. 2001. *Communications and democratic reform in South Africa*. Cambridge: Cambridge University Press.

IBA *see* Independent Broadcasting Authority.

ICASA *see* Independent Communications Authority of South Africa.

Independent Broadcasting Authority. 1995. *Triple Inquiry report into the protection and viability of public broadcasting, cross-media ownership and local content*. Johannesburg: Author.

——. 1995. Reply to principle questions raised at hearings of Parliamentary Committee on Communications, 10 November 1995. Unpublished paper.

——. 1997. Position paper for the introduction of the first free-to-air private television service in South Africa. Unpublished paper.

Independent Communications Authority of South Africa. 2002. South African content on television and radio: position paper and regulations. Johannesburg: Author.

——. 2004. Oral hearings on SABC licence application (SABC 5), held at Holiday Inn, Cape Town. Transcript.

——. 2005. Application for two regional public television licences by the South African Broadcasting Corporation in terms of Section 22A of the Broadcasting Act, No. 4 of 1999. Unpublished paper.

——. 2007. Community television broadcasting licence. Unpublished document.

Katz, E. 1996. And deliver us from segmentation. *Annals of the American Academy of Political and Social Science* 546(1): 22–33.

Langs, M. 2003. Application by Midi TV (Pty) Ltd for the amendment of the terms and conditions of its broadcasting licence – ruling and reasons. Unpublished document.

Legassick, M. 2007. Flaws in South Africa's 'first' economy. *Africanus* 37(2): 111–144.

Louw, P. E. ed. 1993. *South African Media Policy: Debates of the 1990s*. Bellville: Anthropos.

Marais, H. 1998. *South Africa: Limits to Change*. Cape Town: University of Cape Town Press and Zed Books.

Mashile, P. 2009. Creating public awareness about the pending digital switchover: The Authority's roadmap to engage consumers. Unpublished opening address for the Digital Broadcasting Switchover Forum, 3–5 February, Sandton Sun Hotel, Johannesburg.

MBC *see* Media and Broadcasting Consultants.

McKinsey and Associates. 1993. Public service broadcasters around the world. Unpublished report.

MCU *see* Monitoring and Complaints Unit.

Media and Broadcasting Consultants. 1994. Joint submission to the Independent Broadcasting Authority's Inquiry into the protection and viability of public broadcasting services in a democratic South Africa. Unpublished submission, 10 June.

Media Tenor. 2006. The SABC: A five-year content analysis of new bulletin trends. http://www.mediatenor.co.za/#SABCFiveYears.pdf (accessed 4 April 2008).

Midi Television. 1999. Application in terms of Section 52(1)(c) of the Independent Broadcasting Authority Act (Act 153 of 1993) to amend its licence conditions. Unpublished document.

Monitoring and Complaints Unit, ICASA Broadcasting Division. 2002. *Annual Monitoring Report: Midi Television*. Unpublished report.

Mosco, V. 1996. *The Political Economy of Communication*. London: Sage Publications.

National Assembly of South Africa. Written reply to question no. 1834, from Ms. P. De Lille (ID). (Internal question paper no. 43/2007, 9 November 2007.)

Ndlovu, M. 2003. The South African Broadcasting Corporation's expansion into Africa: South African media imperialism? *Communicatio* 29 (1&2): 297–311.

Ngudle, A. 2007. Local soaps are lekker. *Sowetan*, 20 July. http://www.sowetan.co.za/News/Article.aspx?id=525324 (accessed 2 April 2008).

Omroep oor Radio Freedom.1991. *Jabulani! Freedom of the Airwaves: Towards Democratic Broadcasting in South Africa*. Amsterdam: African-European Institute.

Open Window Network. 1997. Submission to the Independent Broadcasting Authority on the private television discussion document. Unpublished paper.

OWN *see* Open Window Network.

Paterson, C. 1994a. Remaking South African broadcasting – in America's image. *Extra!* Jan/Feb: 22–23.

Paterson, C. 1994b. Broadcasting for National Development in the New South Africa. Paper presented at the annual conference of the Association for Education in Journalism and Mass Communication, 10–14 August, in Atlanta, Georgia, United States.

Plus 94 Research. 2007. *Qualitative overview of current affairs programmes*. Unpublished research report for SABC News and Current Affairs division.

Portfolio Committee on Communications. 1996. Report of the Portfolio Committee on Communications on the Independent Broadcasting Authority's report on the protection and viability of public broadcasting services, cross-media control of broadcasting services and local television content and South African music. Unpublished report.

SABC *see* South African Broadcasting Corporation.

Schreiner, W. 2006. *Carte Blanche* remains most quoted medium in South African media in 2005. http://www.mediatenor.co.za/newsletters.php?id_news=48 (accessed 20 February 2008).

Skinner, K. ed. 2007. *Meeting their Mandates? A Critical Analysis of South African Media Statutory Bodies*. Cape Town: Open Society Foundation for South Africa.

Smith, R. 2003. *Yizo Yizo* and essentialism. In *Shifting Selves: Post-apartheid Essays on Mass Media, Culture and Identity*, ed. H. Wasserman and S. Jacobs, 249–266. Cape Town: Kwela Books.

South African Broadcasting Corporation. 1989. *Annual Report*. Johannesburg: Author.

——. 2004. *Editorial Policies*. Johannesburg: Author.

——. 2006a. *Social report: Let the beneficiaries speak*. Johannesburg: Author.

——. 2006b. *Commission of Enquiry into Blacklisting and Related Matters: Report*. Published on the *Mail&Guardian* website, 14 October.

South African Broadcasting Corporation Strategy Team. 1997. Maximising the SABC's advertising revenue. Presentation to Steering Committee, 19 March.

Soweto Community Television. 2007. Application to ICASA: community television broadcasting licence. Unpublished document.

Teer-Tomaselli, R. 2001. Nation building, social identity and television in a changing media landscape. In *Culture in the New South Africa*, ed. R. Kriger and A. Zegeye,117–138. Cape Town: Kwela books and South African History Online.

Teer-Tomaselli, R. and K. Tomaselli. 2001. Transformation, nation-building and the South African media, 1993–1999. In *Media, Democracy and Renewal in Southern Africa*, ed. H. Dunn and K. Tomaselli, 123–150. Colorado Springs: International Academic Publishers.

Thorne, K. 1998. Community media – a price we can afford? In *Media and Democracy in South Africa*, ed. J. Duncan and M. Seleoane, 211–245. Pretoria: Human Sciences Research Council and Freedom of Expression Institute.

Tleane, C. and J. Duncan. 2003. Public broadcasting in the era of cost recovery: a critique of the South African Broadcasting Corporation's crisis of accountability. Johannesburg: Freedom of Expression Institute.

White, J. 1999. Representation by Justine White in respect of application in terms of S.52 of the Independent Broadcasting Authority Act by Midi Television (Proprietory) Limited T/A E.TV. Unpublished submission.

Wortley, B. and S. Bolton. 2002. Portfolio Committee on Communications Hearings into Transformation of the Advertising and Marketing Industry, Advertising Transformation Index, 12 November. Unpublished presentation.

Zita, L. 2000. Criticism of Mbeki's governance built on shaky foundations. *City Press*, 25 June.

Broadcasting in Zimbabwe:

An historical perspective

4

Elaine Windrich

Unlike the other British colonies that made the transition from Colonial Office rule to independence, Zimbabwe did not evolve from the 'colonial' to the 'post-colonial', at least not in the strict sense of those terms. Instead, it was transformed from rule by the white minority – first by the British South Africa Company and then by the white settlers in the 'self-governing colony' of Southern Rhodesia – to rule by the African majority. What this meant for broadcasting was that policy decisions were not determined in London but in Salisbury and, later, Harare, although the British Broadcasting Corporation (BBC) did exert some influence intermittently over the years. However, broadcasting policy did not remain constant throughout the period of white rule. With the advent of the Rhodesian Front (RF) in 1964, the prevailing convention that left broadcasting free of political influence and control, which in effect amounted to the toleration of dissent within the well-defined limits of white Rhodesian politics, gave way to the imposition of total control. Not that these differences affected the African majority, since they were excluded from participation in the determination of broadcasting policy whatever the political affiliation of the governing party. Once in power, however, the government elected by the majority made up for the historic deprivation by following the precedent set by the RF. Broadcasting may have been transferred from the white minority to the black majority, but total party control remained.

This chapter traces the institutional history and development of broadcasting in Zimbabwe since its beginning in the colonial era, and illustrates how history has tended to repeat itself over the years. It uses archival and institutional research to explore and analyse the development of broadcasting in Zimbabwe. This historical narrative is necessary to understand the shifts in policy that have taken place and the practices in the country's broadcasting sector, which are discussed in subsequent chapters on Zimbabwe in this volume. The chapter makes a number of key arguments: first, that monopoly of political power, by both the Smith and the Mugabe regimes, explains continued monopoly of broadcasting in Zimbabwe; second, that the prevailing political environment has, to a great extent, shaped the policy, structure and content of broadcasting; and third, that the legacy of the RF's censorship and propaganda has come to define broadcasting control and uses under Mugabe's ruling ZANU PF party.

Although Southern Rhodesia saw itself as conforming to the BBC model of radio broadcasting – to 'inform, educate and entertain' – this was a pretence as it catered almost exclusively for its 'European' listeners. For this audience, which represented a mere five per cent of the population but the main source of the broadcasting licence fee, a Southern Rhodesia Broadcasting Service was established in Salisbury in 1941. Under the control of the postmaster general, it was to provide a formal structure for the voluntary public service broadcasting begun by employees of the Post Office during the previous decade (Zaffiro 2002: 41–42). The black majority, however, only became radio listeners in large numbers after the Second World War, with the establishment of the Central African Broadcasting Station (CABS) in Northern Rhodesia (an expanded successor to the wartime Radio Lusaka) and the invention of relatively cheap battery-operated radio receivers known as 'saucepan specials' (Smyth 1984: 195–201).

As soon as planning for post-war broadcasting in central Africa began, the government of Southern Rhodesia insisted upon maintaining control of all English-language broadcasting for the white minority, leaving the provision of a service for the black majority to CABS. This division of responsibility on the basis of race was agreed to at a meeting of the Central African Council (a short-lived experiment in regional co-operation) in 1945. Although CABS founder Harry Franklin had proposed some sharing of the broadcasting services to avoid duplication and reduce the overall costs, the Salisbury delegation rejected the proposal as outside interference in matters 'impinging on politics or policy concerning race interests' (Franklin 1963: 36). Consequently, during the following decade the Africans living in Southern Rhodesia were provided with broadcasts in the vernacular languages and in English not by their own government, but by the Colonial Office in Northern Rhodesia, which founded, financed and administered CABS.

CABS: The art of the possible

Although CABS was based in Lusaka, its broadcasts were recorded locally, throughout the Rhodesias and Nyasaland. For this purpose, teams of broadcasters were sent out to the rural areas to collect folklore, narratives, music and song for radio programmes, thereby contributing some 80 per cent of the total broadcasting output. As a result, it became the first radio station in Africa broadcasting exclusively to an African audience and employing Africans at every level of its operations. By covering such a wide area and using prominent African singers and instrumentalists – such as Andreya Masiye, who recorded the experience in his memoirs (see Masiye 1977) – it succeeded in establishing the largest record collection of African music in the world. CABS also provided a news service for its listeners, which included local, regional, continental and international news of relevance to an African audience. Special programmes were designed for women listeners as well. CABS's Salisbury branch started women's radio home-craft clubs that recorded talks, competitions, music and songs at the meetings of these clubs, leading to the formation of additional branches by other interested listeners and readers of its monthly African Listener (Smyth 1984: 199). Staff exchanges organised by the Salisbury liaison organisation invariably resulted in a transformation of the Southern Rhodesians sent to Broadcasting House in Lusaka. Arriving quite resigned to their 'subservient role in society', they soon became bitter critics of their home government and the racial situation in their own country. Two of these exchange visitors (Harry Nyela and Barnabus Tshabalala) were among the station's most popular broadcasters (Kerr 1998: 115–116).

Also contributing to the popularity of CABS was the innovative practice of providing tape recorders at all of the district administration information offices, through which members of the local community were encouraged to respond to the radio programmes. This they did in great numbers, as did many of the listeners in the Lusaka area who had open access to Broadcasting House for comments and discussions. In measuring the audience for these broadcasts, estimates ranged from about 150,000 at the beginning of the 1950s to more than a million, half of them in Southern Rhodesia, by the end of the decade (Zaffiro 2002: 46, 50). Whether the count was for the number of radio receivers purchased or the number of listeners to each set (calculated on the basis of 10 listeners per radio receiver), the general consensus seemed to be that radio listening had become 'a normal habit for many central Africans' (Kerr 1998: 130).

For this success, credit must go to the extraordinarily talented and dedicated staff at Broadcasting House, which was prepared to work with African artists, producers and technicians and train them in broadcasting skills (ibid: 116). Besides Franklin, who had initiated the establishment of CABS and the production of the 'saucepan specials', thereby earning the praise of Labour Colonial Secretary Arthur Creech Jones (Armour 1984: 377), there were Michael Kittermaster, who had studied African languages and African music as well as broadcasting, and Peter Fraenkel, who grew up in Northern Rhodesia as a refugee from Nazi Germany and later became head of the BBC European Service. They were known throughout central Africa for their touring recording studios, which enabled them to reflect African views and opinions to a wider African audience. Kittermaster also conducted the first 'audience research' in Africa to determine what was understood and what was most popular among African listeners, as a result of which programmes, especially educational and English language ones, were adapted to meet listeners' needs and demands (Kittermaster 1954: 42–46) Fortunately for posterity, they were also prolific writers who provided a record of broadcasting in central Africa at the time (Fraenkel 1959, 2005). In addition, their achievements in creating a broadcasting service 'refreshingly free from racial prejudice and official paternalism' (Roberts 1976: 210) prompted one observer to lament that there was nothing comparable for 'Europeans' to help them understand the world they lived in, especially the impact of African nationalism and the 'wind of change' sweeping over the continent (Powdermaker 1962: 253).

Unfortunately, however, these achievements were short-lived and their very success was their undoing. For the decade of CABS's ascendancy coincided with the political turmoil that was generated by the establishment of the Central African Federation (CAF) demanded by the ruling white minority, and by its subsequent dissolution as a result of the overwhelming opposition of the African majority. As a multi-racial island in a sea of racial tension and hostility, CABS was particularly vulnerable, blamed by the white settlers and their local press for fomenting African opposition to their cause and obliged by their British paymasters (the Conservative government which had imposed CAF) to give the new experiment in 'partnership' a fair hearing. But this directive was incompatible with local reality, as CABS discovered when its efforts to recruit African speakers favouring Federation (to 'balance' the majority opposing it) produced a representative of the Capricorn Africa Society who, after arriving in Lusaka, promptly joined the African National Congress (Fraenkel 1959: 170).

Increasingly under pressure from both sides, CABS had the choice of retaining the loyalty of its African audience, hitherto encouraged 'to get their frustrations off their chest, to voice criticism and to ask awkward questions', or of its government, but certainly not of both (Fraenkel 2005: 196; Armour 1984: 391). The climax to this dilemma came soon after the establishment of the Federal Broadcasting Corporation (FBC) in Salisbury in 1958, which proceeded to usurp the functions of CABS and confiscate its best equipment. The final blow was the Rhodesian police raid on Broadcasting House to seize tapes and records of songs alleged to contain 'hidden nationalist messages'. In protest, Kittermaster resigned and Fraenkel soon followed, leaving Franklin, who had already quit over the imposition of Federation, as a spokesman for African interests in 'Legco', the colonial legislative assembly (Kerr 1998: 120).

As with the Southern Rhodesia Broadcasting Corporation (SRBC), the FBC was, as one critic put it, 'unabashedly European centered in its sense of audience, mission, content and management' (Zaffiro 2002: 30). Despite its obligations to the eight million Africans in the territories, not a single African was appointed to the board of governors (even after Franklin's objections) and no Africans were recruited for the senior levels of management (Franklin 1949: 175). In any case, the FBC was short-lived, for soon after it began broadcasting in 1958 the first cracks in the edifice of the Federation itself began to appear. With the outbreak of demonstrations and riots in Nyasaland and the threat of violence engulfing the whole region, the Conservative government which had imposed Federation on an unwilling African majority finally yielded to the 'wind of change' proclaimed by its prime minister by accepting the right of its member territories to secede. As a result of the subsequent dissolution, broadcasting (along with the other shared services) reverted to the governments of the three territories, soon to include the independent ones of Zambia and Malawi. Thus, with the demise of CABS in Lusaka, Southern Rhodesia would become responsible for providing an African service along with the long-established 'European' one. But in doing so, it would reverse the achievements of CABS by denying African listeners a voice in either the making or the receiving of the broadcasts directed at them.

The Rhodesian Broadcasting Corporation: Rhodesian Front (RF) control

In accordance with the terms of the dissolution, the SRBC (soon to become the RBC) inherited the studios for the English-language service in Salisbury and the new African service studios in Harare township, along with the studios, offices and transmitter stations located in Bulawayo and the other larger towns. It also inherited from the FBC (whose 'management committee' for the dissolution became its first board of governors) a set of guidelines and principles to be observed by the 'new' Rhodesian broadcaster, which included many of the same staff as its predecessor. Heading the list was the requirement that the corporation would be 'autonomous, independent in matter of policy and non-political', although it came under the control of a government ministry and its traditional policy had been to support the government of the day, whether at the federal or territorial level. Also a requirement was that news, features and current affairs were to be 'factual and balanced' but 'framed in a manner calculated to assist in maintaining law and order in this multi-racial society' (Stephens 1965: 23). In effect, the status quo (i.e. white minority control) would be maintained, although the justification for it would be offered in the African languages as well. Control of the message would pass from the Native Affairs Department to the newly created Ministry of Information (MOI).

While the status quo was supposedly assured by the continuance of much the same personnel and the reiteration of many of the same platitudes, it soon became obvious that the newly elected RF government was determined to mould broadcasting in its own party image. Gone was even the pretence of 'partnership' espoused by the United Federal Party (UFP) to win support for the Federation. Instead, broadcasting would be used to legitimise white minority rule and the unfettered right of the RF to maintain it. The justification for this policy was that it was necessary to balance the so-called 'monopoly press'. Although the Argus Press of South Africa did indeed own all of the main newspapers through its local subsidiary, the Rhodesian Printing and Publishing Company, the RF's real concern was that it had been a traditional supporter of the UFP, the party of Godfrey Huggins, Roy Welensky and Edgar Whitehead which, under various party labels, had ruled the country for most of its history as a 'self-governing colony'. Nor was there a case for balancing a monopoly press until the RF contributed to one by banning most of the alternative publications, including the African Daily News, the liberal Central African Examiner, various church-based ones such as Moto and Umbowo and even the right-wing Rhodesian Property and Finance for being critical of the RF's 'mafia tactics' against its opponents (Windrich 1981: 57).

Under RF control, broadcasting became the voice of the ruling party, as opposition spokesmen and other dissenting voices were denied access to the public airwaves. The first major change had been in the appointment of party loyalists to top positions at the RBC, headed by the director-general and the board of governors, irrespective of their lack of qualifications for the job. The combined radio and television newsroom was particularly vulnerable in this regard. As the more independently minded broadcasters resigned or were removed, in came the placemen and the South African propagandists recruited by the new Minister of Information, Pieter van der Byl, including Ivor Benson and Harvey Ward of the notoriously racist Candour League. Once these appointments were in place, all other changes automatically followed, since they were the arbiters of what could and could not appear on the RBC. Even the white opposition parties which succeeded the UFP were harassed and marginalised, especially if they opposed a unilateral declaration of independence (UDI), which most of them did. Their access to the RBC was limited to the legally specified time limits allocated to political parties during elections and even this was often circumscribed (ibid: 37–38). As for the black opposition, it soon disappeared from view altogether, with its parties banned by the new Prime Minister, Ian Smith, in 1964 and their leadership detained or driven into exile. Thereafter, the only African voices allowed on the air were those of the 'tribal' chiefs and the other government functionaries supporting RF rule.

As a result of these measures, the most frequently heard voices on the RBC were those of RF ministers. Often backed by allegedly non-political civil servants, their main function was to extol the virtues of white rule and to warn of the dire consequences of the dreaded alternative. Another theme was anti-communism, which was used to vilify the African nationalists as pawns of Soviet or Chinese imperialism. As the war accelerated during the 1970s, this theme was extended to the guerrilla armies of the Zimbabwe African National Union (ZANU) led by Robert Mugabe and the Zimbabwe African People's Union (ZAPU) led by Joshua Nkomo.

They were portrayed as 'communist terrorists', threatening to destroy 'Christian civilisation' and the 'Rhodesian way of life'. Much of the war propaganda on the RBC also featured 'victories' for the white-led security forces. Such claims appeared in the military communiqués of 'Combined Operations', measured in kill ratios of at least ten or even twenty to one, which were included in the daily news bulletins (see Frederikse 1984).

While RBC propaganda may have succeeded in fooling its white listeners, most of whom supported the RF to the bitter end, it had no such effect on the African majority. For them, alternative voices could be heard on the 'bush radio', fed by families and friends in the rural areas where the fighting was going on, and on the clandestine broadcasts of ZANU and ZAPU in exile. ZANU's Voice of Zimbabwe, along with ZAPU's Voice of the Revolution, had been broadcasting on and off since the late 1950s, beginning in Egypt when Nasser provided a base for African nationalist parties. From there they moved on to the Front-Line States, as Tanzania, Zambia and Mozambique became independent with broadcasting facilities of their own, which could be used by the liberation movements. Also available for those with access to shortwave radio were the voices of the international broadcasters – the BBC, Radio Netherlands, Radio Moscow, the Voice of America and others – offering a version of reality to counteract the propaganda of the RBC.

The Zimbabwe Broadcasting Corporation: ZANU control

High hopes for the unshackling of Rhodesian broadcasting accompanied the transformation of Rhodesia into Zimbabwe in 1980, when Mugabe's ZANU party won an overwhelming majority in the independence elections. The new information minister, Nathan Shamuyarira, was no stranger to the practice of government censorship, having been a victim of it himself when he was editor of the banned African Daily News. Although the ministry was thoroughly reorganised in terms of personnel, with ZANU cadres replacing nearly all of the white civil servants, its structure remained largely intact. The old RBC may have given way to the new Zimbabwe Broadcasting Corporation (ZBC) but broadcasting was still under the control of the MOI, as were the newspapers (the Zimbabwe Newspapers Group, Zimpapers) and the news agency (the Zimbabwe Inter-Africa News Agency, ZIANA).[1]

One innovation, however, was the Zimbabwe Mass Media Trust, which was intended to allay the impression of direct government control of the media. Composed of 'the great and the good' (in accordance with the BBC model), this allegedly independent watchdog was endowed with responsibility for monitoring media output and performance, and advising the government on information policy. In practice, however, the trust was completely dependent upon the government for providing its finance and administration. In addition, its membership, although self-renewing, was subject to government approval and its advisory powers were never exercised (at least not publicly) to criticise or cast doubt upon the wisdom of government policy during the two decades of its existence. This was certainly the case with regard to broadcasting policy, even though some of its members also served on the board of governors of the ZBC.

Although the changes in broadcasting after 1980 were generally regarded as long overdue, especially the recruitment of Africans at all levels of employment (from the news readers and commentators to the director-general), many of the old problems remained. Ironically, the new Mugabe government (enlarged to include representatives of ZAPU and the white opposition) suffered from some of the same disabilities as the RF when it came to power for the first time. Foremost of these was the lack of experienced broadcasters who knew how to operate a credible national broadcasting system. Those who had any experience at all knew only about the clandestine broadcasting from exile, the main purpose of which was to appeal to the African listener to support the liberation movements and join the guerrilla forces of ZANU and ZAPU. But this was scarcely a relevant qualification for broadcasting in a multi-racial and multi-party society pledged to national reconciliation by its new leadership. Nevertheless, those who had been with the Voice of Zimbabwe were thrust into nearly all of the top positions in management and operations at the ZBC. Over the years, their numbers were supplemented by graduates from the newly created training programme for media personnel – the Zimbabwe Institute of Mass Communications (ZIMCO) – at the Harare Polytechnic. ZIMCO, however, was staffed mainly by party loyalists, including a director (Tafataona Mahoso) who, while training Zimbabwe's future journalists, also served as a party propagandist for the ZBC and Zimpapers. In addition, as chairman of the Media and Information Commission (MIC) in later years, he shut down four independent newspapers.

Also a casualty of inexperienced broadcasters was programme content, which again recalled the deficiencies of the RBC. Just as the RBC had filled its airwaves with RF ministerial pronouncements, the ZBC continually featured ZANU ministers (especially then Prime Minister Mugabe) extolling the government's achievements. While some of these, such as the expansion of education and health facilities, were indeed commendable, the undue emphasis on the ministerial role in making them happen conveyed the impression of party propaganda. But 'developmental' or 'sunshine' journalism required that only the success stories should make it on the ZBC, leaving anything suggesting failure or 'Afro-pessimism' unseen or unheard. Ministers were never called to account for their incompetence or corruption and government policies were never subjected to critical analysis, for to do so would incur the wrath of the MOI.

Another example of continuity was the ruling party's monopoly of the airwaves of what was a public broadcaster, which had also been the case under RF control. Once again, opposition parties kept off the air by the RBC were denied access by the ZBC. Although both regimes paid lip service to the legal requirement of equal coverage during election campaigns, this obligation was never observed in practice. Not that there was much organised opposition for either to overcome, as they both won every electoral contest in their virtual one-party states. But even after 1999, when the political situation was transformed by the emergence of a credible political opponent, the ZBC still continued to practise its politics of exclusion. As a succession of election-observer reports revealed, the ZBC provided overwhelming coverage of ZANU PF's campaigns –more than 90 per cent of the total output – while denigrating the opposition parties in much of the remaining time (MMPZ 2000:8; 2003: 58, 63). Furthermore, these violations of internationally accepted electoral practices have not ceased despite the government's endorsement of the new electoral charter adopted by the Southern African Development Community (SADC) in 2004, which requires equal access to the media.

The ZBC was also used by the ruling party to suppress unwelcome or embarrassing news and information, especially in times of crisis, such as the violence inflicted upon the people of Matabeleland during the 1980s. Although such attempts at censorship were often undermined by the reporting of foreign journalists or international broadcasters, in this case the ZBC was not deterred from promoting the official line – that the government was waging a campaign to eradicate ZAPU 'dissidents' and their Ndebele supporters, who were allegedly trained and supported by agents of the apartheid regime. When this campaign was finally concluded with a 'unity accord' at the end of 1987 – by which time an estimated 20,000 lives had been lost (see CCJP 1997) – ZAPU ceased to exist as a party and its leadership was co-opted by ZANU to form a new Patriotic Front (ZANU PF). For the ZBC this meant that former ZAPU officials included in the new government could now appear on the airwaves as ministerial spokesmen for government policy.

While peace prevailed during the ensuing decade, except for the harassment and intimidation associated with ZANU PF's conduct of election campaigns, it was a peace very much on the ruling party's terms as far as broadcasting was concerned. No changes were made to open up the airwaves to other parties or alternative views, despite the commissioning of a BBC report on the best means of doing so (Moyo 2004: 20). In practice, the only concession, and a minor one at that, was the leasing of a television channel to consortiums of ZANU PF supporters, including Joy TV. But the leases restricted the station to providing music and other entertainment and a very limited news service, and even this was removed as a result of the 'restructuring' of the ZBC beginning in 2001. As this episode revealed, ZANU PF could continue to preserve its monopoly of broadcasting as long as it preserved its monopoly of political power.

The new challenges

The first challenge to ZANU PF's monopoly of power came at the end of the 1990s, with the formation of the Movement for Democratic Change (MDC) headed by trade union leader Morgan Tsvangirai. The immediate consequence of the new alignment of political forces was that ZANU PF suffered its first electoral defeat, losing the February 2000 referendum on the new constitution it had devised to enhance Mugabe's already formidable powers, including the power to confiscate white-owned farmland. In retaliation for this rebuff, and to prevent losses in the upcoming parliamentary election, Mugabe unleashed a campaign of violence and intimidation against the MDC, spearheaded by war veterans and the party's youth militia. Also targeted were the white landowners whose farms were occupied as an integral part of ZANU PF's electoral campaign in the rural areas, where most of its supporters live. Leading the campaign on the propaganda front was the new Minister of Information, Jonathan Moyo, a former critic of Mugabe from the University of Zimbabwe who had been recruited to the constitutional commission to promote the abortive constitution. Once in power, however, and especially as Mugabe's 'spin doctor', he soon avenged the electoral setback by rivalling his RF predecessor (Pieter van der Byl) in the harassment and deportation of journalists and the imposition of draconian censorship legislation.

One of the first issues confronting the newly reorganised MOI (now a government department in the Office of the President) arose over the government monopoly of broadcasting. Although broadcasting had always been a government monopoly in Zimbabwe, other African states were opening up their airwaves to private competitors and the possibility of Zimbabwe doing the same had been raised by previous information ministers, but to no avail (The Herald 2 Apr.1986, 20 Feb. 1997). The move to free the airwaves was initiated by Capital Radio, a group of independent broadcasters including Gerry Jackson and James Maridadi, formerly at the ZBC, and Michael Auret, son of an MDC Member of Parliament. While the group intended to broadcast a mixed programme of news, current affairs and popular music, its efforts were aborted after only a couple of broadcasts of recorded music from a studio in a prominent Harare hotel. In a portent of what was in store for private media attempting to operate outside of government control, the station was invaded by police armed with orders to seize the equipment and interrogate the would-be broadcasters.

Although Capital Radio had obtained a High Court order allowing it to broadcast, on the grounds that the ZBC monopoly was an infringement of the constitutional guarantee of freedom of expression, this reprieve was a short-lived one. As the government had done so often in the past when its authority was threatened, it enacted a presidential decree in defiance of the court order, which in this case reaffirmed the state monopoly of broadcasting. And when this decree expired (after the limit of six months), a Broadcasting Bill was rushed through the ZANU PF-dominated parliament in one sitting, to ensure that the power to decide who could broadcast remained with the information minister, as it had under RF rule (ZBC Radio 5&6 Oct. 2000).

The new Broadcasting Service Act (BSA), like the presidential decree preceding it, was also declared unconstitutional, this time by the Parliamentary Legal Committee (then headed by the late Eddison Zvobgo) but again to no avail. The Act provided for a Broadcasting Authority of Zimbabwe (BAZ) which would advise the minister on such matters as the allocation of frequencies, the issuance of licences and the establishment of broadcasting standards or codes. However, all of the members of the BAZ were appointed by the minister and the advice was merely optional. In addition, the proposal to open up the airwaves to independent broadcasters was limited to only one licence and even this offer was qualified by restrictions relating to foreign investment and political affiliation. But the most controversial provisions were that 75 per cent of programming would be local in content, and that the government would be allocated one hour a week by the licensee to publicise its achievements. Such provisions were necessary, according to Moyo, to instil loyalty and patriotism among the listeners as a defence against the alleged internal and external threats to Zimbabwe's sovereign independence (ZBC Radio 14 Oct. 2000).

With these requirements to be met, it was hardly surprising that, at the time of writing, no licence to broadcast has been issued since the enactment of the legislation in 2001. As for Capital Radio's pioneering initiative, having been refused a licence on the grounds of foreign influence and funding (Jackson is British) and having endured police harassment and intimidation, some of the broadcasters sought refuge in London. From there and as Shortwave Radio Africa, they have continued to broadcast news, current affairs and popular music to Zimbabwe, despite government efforts to silence them with jamming equipment acquired from China. Another Zimbabwe broadcaster in exile is Voice of the People, sponsored by Radio Netherlands and broadcasting similar programmes to Zimbabwe on shortwave radio. This has not been without mishap, however, since their premises in Harare were raided and looted by the police and then destroyed by a bomb that was widely attributed to state security forces (MISA-Z 29 Aug. 2002). Also broadcasting to Zimbabwe from overseas is Studio 7, sponsored by the Voice of America and presented by Zimbabwe journalists in exile, including Ray Choto, the The Standard reporter detained by the police and tortured by the military for refusing to reveal sources for his reports on dissension in the army and Zimbabwe's war in the Democratic Republic of the Congo.

Nor have community radio stations fared much better in the quest for licensing, leaving Zimbabwe as one of the few countries in Africa denying them the right to broadcast. One of the most prominent cases of denial was the projected 'Bulawayo Dialogue', which received some funding from the World Association of Community Radio Broadcasters, based in Burkina Faso (MISA-Z press releases 6 Jan. & 29 Mar. 2004). Since setting up offices and recording local music for future broadcasting, the station-in-waiting has been repeatedly raided by the police, allegedly in search of 'subversive material'. Several of its staff, including Fr Nigel Johnson, the station manager, have been detained for questioning, particularly about their links with 'Bulawayo Agenda', a local initiative that organises public meetings to discuss topical issues of concern to the city (ibid). Although a rejection of the Bulawayo application was perhaps inevitable, given the region's traditional alignment with the opposition parties, even areas with a strong ZANU PF presence, such as Masvingo and Mutare, have not succeeded in penetrating the state monopoly at the local level. Like Bulawayo, Mutare experienced harassment and intimidation, in this case with intelligence agents invading a workshop sponsored by the Media Institute of Southern Africa to discuss the setting up of a community radio station in the city (MISA-Z 21 May 2004).

In addition to ensuring the government monopoly of broadcasting, the information minister also introduced a series of 'restructuring exercises', including the change of name from ZBC to Zimbabwe Broadcasting Holdings (ZBH), which were intended to achieve administrative efficiency and financial profitability. However, there was no evidence of this occurring as a result. On the contrary, the indebtedness of ZBH continued to increase at an alarming rate over the years, until the government was finally obliged to take over the debt (Financial Gazette 24 Jun. 2002; see Manyarara 1998). The broadcasting service was also still left with a host of other problems, especially the high staff turnover resulting from job uncertainty and the periodic purges induced by financial insolvency and political expediency. In addition, ZBH continued to suffer from its antiquated equipment (90 per cent of which it regarded as obsolete), a lack of investment in research and development, and a failure to attract commercial interest for its repetitive and amateur programming (Zimbabwe Independent 3 May 2002). Besides its 'restructuring' (all of which was 'unbundled' after Moyo's sacking in 2005, when the name ZBC was restored), broadcasting was also subjected to a campaign of 'winning hearts and minds' devised by the minister to foster a 'Zimbabwean outlook'. As Moyo's 'Vision 30' had put it, the mission of ZBH was to provide 'world class programmes and services that reflect, develop, foster and respect the Zimbabwe national identity, character, cultural diversity, national aspirations and Zimbabwean and pan-African values' (Chiumbu: 30). However, ZBH did not have the personnel, facilities or finance to provide 'world class programmes' that would either satisfy the listener paying the licence fee or attract the advertising and investment to pay for the productions. Instead, to meet the 75 per cent quota required by the BSA, ZBH resorted to even more repetition of poor quality programmes, as the continual complaints in the letters column of the independent press revealed. Also provoking protests were the banning of the BBC, CNN and other international news providers (for their criticism of Mugabe and ZANU PF rule); the constant display of films glorifying ZANU's role in the liberation war; and the frequent intrusion of Moyo himself as a political commentator, a script writer and a composer and performer of party jingles and songs.[2]

Zimbabwe in crisis

Although there has always been political interference in broadcasting in Zimbabwe, as there was in Rhodesia under RF rule, it was intensified after 2000 to counter the perceived threats, both internal and external, to the ruling party's hold on power. One of the main factors responsible for this state of affairs was the crash of the Zimbabwe dollar in 1997, which was widely attributed to Mugabe's surrender to the demands of the war veterans' association for greatly increased pensions and gratuities. As the dollar fell, so too did incomes, employment and the delivery of social services, leading to 'unprecedented restlessness within the body politic', as one observer put it (see Moyo 2004: 23).

The government's response to this crisis was to proclaim the 'Third Chimurenga' (or liberation war), which was intended to divert attention from its economic mismanagement and corruption and bolster its waning popularity. The new propaganda offensive, devised by Moyo and dutifully relayed by ZBH and Zimpapers, revived memories of ZANU's historical role in the 'Second Chimurenga', but this time the enemy was not only the white minority. It also included the MDC, the non-governmental organisations (NGOs), the independent press and, externally, Britain, the European Community (EC), the Commonwealth and the United States (US). This unholy alliance, allegedly the cause of the country's economic misfortunes, was also charged with conspiring to bring about 'regime change' in Zimbabwe.

As one of the main targets of the government's offensive, the newly established independent newspaper, the Daily News (successor to the African Daily News banned by the Smith regime) was repeatedly accused of being an MDC mouthpiece financed by British interests. Its real offence, however, was that it was a government critic and that, as such, it had become the country's best-selling daily paper, far surpassing its Zimpaper rivals. But inevitably, as a result of its fearless reporting on government corruption and human rights abuses, its journalists (and also those of the Zimbabwe Independent, The Standard and the Financial Gazette) were repeatedly detained by the police and hauled before the courts on trumped-up charges contrived by the information minister. More than a hundred journalists experienced this harassment under the punitive Access to Information and Protection of Privacy (AIPP) Act and the Public Order and Security (POS) Act introduced in 2002, the latter criminalising criticism of the president and the publication of 'false reports'. Although the Daily News survived bombing by state security agents and attempts to assassinate its editor (Geoffrey Nyarota),[3] it was then denied a licence to publish by the Media and Information Commission created by the AIPP Act, despite a High Court order in its favour. Consequently, with three other independent newspapers banned as well, Mugabe's government could no longer claim (as the Smith regime had done to justify control of the RBC) that a government monopoly of broadcasting was necessary to counter the effects of a hostile independent press.

And finally, there was the criticism from the outside world to contend with, which also posed a threat to the government's hold on power. As the internal confrontations escalated after 2000 – with the land seizures by the war veterans, the government's defiance of High Court restraining orders, the purge of dissenting justices and the violence against the MDC in order to win the parliamentary and presidential elections – so too did the condemnation of the international community. Although the government's SADC partners refrained from any intervention beyond the 'quiet diplomacy' entrusted to then South African President Thabo Mbeki, other international organisations were less tolerant of the rigging of elections and the violations of human rights in Zimbabwe. After the Commonwealth Heads of Government Meeting had condemned such practices, the government retaliated by renouncing Zimbabwe's membership, thus avoiding the humiliating 'suspension' meted out to other offenders. Condemnation also came from the EC, which, along with the US, imposed so-called 'targeted sanctions' banning travel by the governing elite as well as loans and investment by international financial institutions. In addition, foreign NGOs monitoring freedom of expression, such as the Media Institute of Southern Africa, Article 19 and Reporters without Borders, repeatedly condemned the government for violations of the internationally accepted standards enshrined in the Windhoek Declaration and the covenants of the African Union and the United Nations.

The government responded to these alleged affronts to Zimbabwe's 'sovereignty' with a torrent of hate propaganda and racial abuse against the 'white racists' and 'Western imperialists', despite the fact that the Commonwealth was overwhelmingly non-white and non-Western. Britain was the main target of blame, even though it had never governed the 'self-governing colony' of Southern Rhodesia. But it provided a useful scapegoat, especially for the government's failed land reform policy, which resulted in the collapse of agricultural production and in food shortages threatening starvation. Although Britain had been the largest donor to land resettlement intended to alleviate rural poverty (it donated nearly £45 million), it cancelled any further aid on the ground that Mugabe was using the acquired farmland to reward his political cronies. This was a public humiliation that Mugabe never forgot (reinforced as it was by the frequent reprimands from Foreign Office Minister, Peter Hain) and it accounted for much of the 'hate Britain' and 'hate Tony Blair' propaganda continually appearing on the ZBC and in Zimpapers. Thus, just as it was under RF rule, Zimbabwe has become an international pariah for its denial of human rights and, in this particular case, the right to freedom of expression on the public airwaves.

Conclusions

Although broadcasting policy in Zimbabwe has been widely criticised both at home and abroad, it is not without its defenders. The government's case, endorsed by its apologists and allies, is, first, that it is only carrying on the policy of its predecessors, who also used broadcasting to promote their party. Second, that criticism from outside the country is an infringement of Zimbabwe's sovereignty, meaning its right to conduct its internal affairs without external interference. Third, that Zimbabwe is being unfairly targeted for a policy followed by many other countries, including its SADC allies. And finally, that Zimbabwe is being judged by 'Western standards' that are not applicable to Third World countries. However, the control of broadcasting by means of censorship and propaganda, which prevailed under RF rule, was a policy to be repudiated by an African majority government, not re-imposed as it was. Nor can the violation of the right to freedom of expression be justified, either by claiming that Zimbabwe is not the only offender or by asserting that the observance of this right is a Western imposition rather than a universally recognised human right.

Why the government's broadcasting policy ended up as a re-enactment of the worst excesses of white minority rule rather than as a complete break with the past has yet to be explained satisfactorily. Although Mugabe's first post-independence government set out with the best of intentions, with BBC supervision and safeguards against political interference in place, this promising start gradually gave way to ZANU control as Zimbabwe moved towards a de facto one-party state. However, this direction in the evolution of broadcasting was not unique, since other government functions and responsibilities underwent a similar transformation after independence. Whether a different outcome was ever possible now seems improbable, in view of the intolerance of criticism and opposition that has prevailed throughout Mugabe's rule. But it is indeed ironic that the only alternative or 'model' that Zimbabwe has ever experienced existed during the early years of the Colonial Office's CABS, when the African majority was encouraged 'to voice criticism and to ask awkward questions' – a right that has long ceased to exist in Zimbabwe.

References

Armour, C. 1984. The BBC and the development of broadcasting in British Colonial Africa, *African Affairs* 83(332): 359–402.

Chiumbu, S. 2004. Redefining the national agenda: Media and identity. In *Media, Public Discourse and Political Contestation in Zimbabwe*, ed. H. Melber, 29–35. Uppsala: Nordic African Institute.

Catholic Commission for Justice and Peace. 1997. *Breaking the Silence: Report on the Disturbances in Matabeleland and the Midlands, 1980–1988*. Harare: CCJP and Legal Resources Committee.

CCJP see Catholic Commission for Justice and Peace.

Fardon, R. and G. Furniss. 2000. *African Broadcasting Cultures*. New York: Praeger.

Fraenkel, P. 1959. *Wayaleshi: Radio in Central Africa*. London: Weidenfeld and Nicholson.

——. 2005. *No Fixed Abode: A Jewish Odyssey to Africa*. London: I.B. Tauris.

Franklin, H. 1949. *Report on the Development of Broadcasting to Africans in Central Africa*. Lusaka: Government Printer.

——. 1963. *Unholy Wedlock: Failure of the Central African Federation*. London: Allen & Unwin.

Frederickse, J. 1982. *None but Ourselves: Masses vs Media in the Making of Zimbabwe*. Harare: Anvil Press.

Kerr, D. 1998. *Dance, Media Entertainment and Popular Theatre in South-East Africa*. Bayreuth: Eckhard Breitinger.

Manyarara, J. 1998. Zimbabwe. In *Up in the Air: The State of Broadcasting in Southern Africa*, ed. A. Opoku-Mensah. Lusaka: Panos Southern Africa.

Masiye, A. 1977. *Singing for Freedom*. Lusaka: Longman.

Media Monitoring Project, Zimbabwe. 2000. *Election 2000: The Media War*. Harare: Author.

——. 2003. *Under Siege: Report on Media Coverage of the 2002 Presidential and Mayoral Elections*. Harare: Author.

Melber, H. ed. 2004. *Media, Public Discourse and Political Contestation in Zimbabwe*. Uppsala: Nordic African Institute.

MMP/MMPZ see Media Monitoring Project, Zimbabwe.

Nyarota, G. 2006. *Against the Grain: Memoirs of a Zimbabwean Newsman*. Cape Town: Zebra Press.

Opoku-Mensah, A. ed. 1998. *Up in the Air: The State of Broadcasting in Southern Africa*. Lusaka: Panos Southern Africa.

Powdermaker, H. 1962. *Changing Africa: The Human Situation on the Rhodesian Copperbelt*. New York: Harper & Row.

Roberts, A. 1976. *A History of Zambia*. New York: Holmes & Meier.

Smyth, R. A note on the saucepan special. *Historical Journal of Film, Radio and Television* 4(2): 195–201.

Stevens, D.A. 1965. This is Radio Rhodesia. *EBU Review*, no. 93B (September): 23.

Wedell, G. 1986. *Making Broadcasting Useful: Radio and Television in Africa in the 1980s*. Manchester: Manchester University Press.

Windrich, E. 1981. *The Mass Media and the Struggle for Zimbabwe: Censorship and Propaganda under Rhodesian Front Rule*. Gweru: Mambo Press.

——. 2001. *Broadcasting in Rhodesia/Zimbabwe. In Censorship: An Encyclopaedia*, ed. D. Jones, vol. 4. London: Fitzroy Dearborn Publishers.

Zaffiro, J. 2002. *Media and Democracy in Zimbabwe, 1931–2002*. Colorado Springs: International Academic Publishers.

Reforming the media in Zimbabwe:

Critical reflections

5

Wallace Chuma

A series of political and economic events and processes during the 1990s culminated in what is now commonly known as the 'Zimbabwe crisis', a period during which mounting threats to its legitimacy prompted the state to make a number of policy interventions in the media. This chapter examines the political economy of media policy-making in a time of crisis, devoting most attention to the post-2000 era.

Further, the chapter considers the nature and possibilities for democratic media reform in a post-crisis Zimbabwe. It addresses questions around the ideal media and communication policy options for a country emerging from a crisis linked to exhausted nationalism and a state that has historically dominated the policy-making process.

The key argument this chapter raises is that media policy reforms in Zimbabwe should be holistic, credible, and should liberate rather than limit the public sphere, long 'captured' by narrow interests of ruling elites before and after independence in 1980. I argue in favour of 'regulated pluralism' (Thompson 1995: 240). This policy approach favours the establishment of an institutional framework accommodating and securing the existence of a plurality of media organisations – by decoupling media organisations from the state, and by public intervention in the market when necessary, in the interest of protecting diversity and pluralism from being undermined by a concentration of economic and symbolic power.

I argue that one way of realising regulated pluralism in future Zimbabwean media would be to apply Curran's (2000) architecture, which consists of a multi-tiered media environment catering for differentiated audiences, while at the same time creating a genuine public service media system to which all citizens can have access. By way of illustrating how regulated pluralism can be made operational – albeit imperfectly – the chapter briefly draws on the South African media policy reform process and the structures it established, and identifies aspects that Zimbabwe's policy-makers might consider in future.

The inheritance

In 1980, Zimbabwe experienced a partially democratic transition in which the state, acting largely in the interests of the ruling party, both maintained and established a communication policy and legislative infrastructure whose main purpose was to complement the construction of Zanu PF[1] hegemony through the media.

Like a host of other inherited social institutions, the mainstream media in Zimbabwe in 1980 were tailored to serve the interests of a minority state experiencing a costly war at home and economic sanctions abroad (Windrich 1981). At independence, the South African-based Argus Press enjoyed a monopoly of the press in Zimbabwe through its subsidiary Rhodesia Printing and Publishing Company (RPP), which operated two dailies, *The Herald* and *The Chronicle*, and three weeklies, *The Sunday Mail*, the *Sunday News* and *Manica Post*. According to then Information Minister, Nathan Shamuyarira (1981), publications from this stable were 'designed from the outset to promote the cause of white settler colonialism and business interests in South Africa' (quoted in Windrich 1981: 5). Alternative publications which made an effort to provide platforms for blacks or liberal whites had been closed down under the Law and Order (Maintenance) Act and a litany of other security laws during the twilight years of the colonial regime.

Apart from the RPP publications, the print media landscape in 1980 also consisted of the financial weekly, *Financial Gazette*, launched in 1969. It had survived censorship during the repressive era of the Unilateral Declaration of Independence (UDI) mainly by staying away from political controversy. There was also the famed popular monthly magazine, *Parade*. Both the financial weekly and *Parade* were owned by local white capital, with the former targeted at the business sector readership while the latter targeted black readers and operated along the lines of South Africa's *Drum* magazine (Kupe 1997). The banned *Moto* magazine returned to the streets soon after independence, and operated as a monthly.[2]

The inherited broadcasting status quo was in many ways similar to that in the mainstream press, although it was geared towards serving the propaganda needs of the besieged colonial state in a much more pronounced fashion, especially in dealing with public opinion at home and abroad in the wake of a brutal war and economic sanctions. The Rhodesian state controlled, through the Ministry of Information, all information made available to the public by the Rhodesia Broadcasting Corporation for the 15 years of UDI (see the contributions by Elaine Windrich and Last Moyo in this volume).

The new government sought to 'transform' the media in two fundamental, yet problematic, ways. With regard to broadcasting, Rhodesian-style full state control was retained after independence. Shamuyarira wrote at the time that the rationale for the new policy on the Zimbabwe Broadcasting Corporation (ZBC) was 'to transform the state broadcasting corporation into an agency reflecting the realities of democratic rule' (quoted in Windrich 1981: 5). Most of the newly recruited staffers at the ZBC were former Zanu PF guerrilla fighters who had operated the nationalist *Voice of Zimbabwe* radio station from Mozambique and Tanzania. This ensured strict Zanu PF hegemonic control over broadcasting from the outset. It is important to note that for both the UDI and Zanu PF regimes, broadcasting – in particular radio – was a critical medium because of its pervasive reach in the country compared with other media such as the printed press. Zimbabwe is a predominantly rural country where only about 30 per cent of the population lives in cities. Because of undeveloped infrastructure and the low circulation of newspapers, radio remains the most accessible medium for its rural people, who have since 1980 been the bedrock of Zanu PF support at election time. Moyo (2004) has noted that both the colonial and postcolonial governments in Zimbabwe used broadcasting for hegemonic purposes, although this was disguised as 'national interest', 'national security' and 'national sovereignty'. In reality, however, broadcasting has always been 'rendered … a political tool in the hands of the government of the day' (Moyo 2004: 12).

Within the arena of the press, transformation occurred largely at the level of ownership, staffing and editorial re-orientation. The new government, with Nigerian aid, bought off the Argus Press shares in RPP and renamed the company 'Zimbabwe Newspapers (1980) Ltd' ('Zimpapers' in its shortened form). The new company was to be operated by a trust, the Zimbabwe Mass Media Trust (ZMMT), which was in principle autonomous, democratically constituted and tasked with transforming and rolling out the press to reach all Zimbabweans, including the majority of citizens living in the rural areas. The Trust was to take charge of broad policy guidelines and issues while individual media concerns under it would retain editorial autonomy. Against a background where the press had largely served narrow but powerful hegemonic interests of colonial minority rule, expanding the reach and orientation of the press was in principle a critical aspect of the transformation project. Immediately after assuming majority ownership of Zimpapers, the government, through the ZMMT, began a process of 'indigenising' the individual newspapers. This was done by appointing black journalists to senior editorial positions and, in some cases, insisting on editorial policies geared towards reflecting the 'developmental' programmes of a multi-racial, 'democratic' nation in the making (Chuma 2004).

As was the case with all sectors of the economy, there was no nationalisation of the private press in Zimbabwe. If the government's policy approach towards the state-controlled Zimpapers publications was clearly expounded and bordered on coercion generally, state–private press relations were characterised by indifference on the part of the former, though this was occasionally punctuated by state accusations that the private press was reluctant to transform (Saunders 1991). In general, the fact that Zanu PF enjoyed popular legitimacy during the first decade of independence, and that the private press at the time supported the state's market-friendly policies, accounts for the tolerant relationship between the two sectors at the time.

Media policy in crisis

A growing body of literature has been focusing on various aspects of what has come to be commonly known as 'the Zimbabwe Crisis'. In much of this literature, the 1990s are depicted as a policy era that provided a fertile background to the political and economic crises that beset Zimbabwe from the turn of the millennium (see, for example, Campbell 2003; Chan 2003; Bond & Manyanya 2003; Sylvester 2003; and Saunders 1999). This chapter does not engage the political economy of the Zimbabwe crisis in much detail, owing both to space and to the focus of this study. However, a brief discussion of specific policy realities and initiatives across the spectrum of politics and the economy is provided here, with a view to locating media policy in context.

The 'crisis period' in Zimbabwe began with the rise of civil society claims on the state around 1997, and continued into the new millennium, culminating in a struggle 'between democratic and sharply autocratic tendencies' (Sylvester 2003: 30). By the late 1990s, it was clear that market-oriented reforms had failed to stimulate the envisaged economic revival.[3] Unemployment, inflation and poverty shot up, resulting in constant clashes between the state and civil society organisations. In 1997 alone, for example, there were at least 55 national labour actions, involving just over 1 million worker participants (Saunders 1999: 68). This was a sharp increase over the previous 10 years, which had an average of 15 actions (ibid). Besides national strikes called by the main labour body, the Zimbabwe Congress of Trade Unions (ZCTU), demonstrations against the state were also convened around the same time by Zimbabwe National Liberation War Veterans Association (ZNLWVA), which demanded compensation for participating in the liberation struggle of the 1970s. When the state capitulated and offered hefty once-off gratuities and subsequent monthly grants, the economy took a dramatic tumble (Bond & Manyanya 2003).

In January 1998, spontaneous food riots broke out in Harare and Chitungwiza, and later spread throughout the country's main urban centres. Mass protests against the rise in the price of food and other commodities were brutally crushed by the state apparatus; at least 10 people were killed and several hundreds were arrested.[4] When *The Herald* ran an editorial comment mildly criticising the state's harsh response to the protests and challenging official claims that whites and other 'enemies of state' were behind the unrest, the paper's editor, Tommy Sithole, was instantly sacked.[5]

What was perhaps clear from the food protests and the innumerable subsequent strike actions that plagued Zimbabwe into the new millennium was that the protestors had by now broadened their range of reference. Although the predominant grievance remained the question of economic marginalisation, 'there was also a linking of (President) Mugabe's name to those of other authoritarian leaders in Africa – such as Daniel Arap Moi in Kenya, Mengistu and Mobutu' (Chan 2003:113). In May 1998, for example, University of Zimbabwe students besieged Parliament, carrying placards that likened Mugabe to Indonesia's Suharto, who had been forced to resign a few weeks earlier.

Besides economic decline and the social restlessness it created in its wake, there were three factors that contributed to the highly charged political environment of the late 1990s and eventually to the 'Zimbabwe crisis'. First, the decision by the government to deploy troops to the war in the Democratic Republic of the Congo (DRC) in August 1998 was met with stiff resistance at home. While the public press celebrated the military decision as an instance of pan-African support for the transitional government of Laurent Kabila in its effort to repel invaders, private newspapers, especially the *Financial Gazette* and *Zimbabwe Independent*, consistently blasted the decision as ill-conceived and harmful to the economy.[6] Opposition to the war intensified within both the opposition parties and civil society. The fact that the decision was taken without parliamentary approval, and also the question of whether an already ailing economy could sustain a costly war abroad, were key issues raised by the anti-war lobby. Further to these concerns, the implication of Harare elites – generals, politicians and some local businessmen – in the systematic looting of the DRC by the United Nations became a source of embarrassment for the government and a tool for civil society groups opposed to the military intervention (see Bond & Manyanya 2003).

The second issue around which the state–civil society contestation heightened was the constitutional review process of 1999. Although the government took a leading role in the process of drafting a new constitution, calls for a new constitution to replace the 1979 Lancaster Constitution dated back to the mid-1990s, and were initiated by opposition parties and civil society groups. By 1999, there appeared to be national consensus that a new constitution was needed for the country. However, different interest groups wanted the new constitution to secure their particular social and political interests. Chan (2003: 113) captured the hitherto prevailing mood in Zimbabwe with regard to a new constitution: 'Intellectuals opposed to the Government wanted it; technocrats within Zanu PF, seeking to modernise their party, wanted it; and the old guard in the ruling party, thinking it might entrench even further their own powers, wanted it.'

In May 1999, President Mugabe appointed a 396-member commission to review the Lancaster House constitution, and to undertake an outreach to gather the people's views for the drafting of a new constitution. Meanwhile, the National Constitutional Assembly (NCA), a coalition of civil society groups opposed to Zanu PF, ran a parallel exercise and produced its own draft constitution. The NCA argued that the presidential commission was dominated by ruling party members and sympathisers, and that the resulting document was likely to be a Zanu PF rather than a national constitution. The government commission's six-month outreach programme resulted in a draft, which was put to a referendum in February 2000, and got rejected. The run-up to the referendum was characterised by intense media and political campaigns for either a 'Yes' or a 'No' vote for the draft. The state and public press favoured the affirmative vote, while a host of civil society organisations, led by the NCA, wanted the draft thrown out. The rejection of the draft constitution was widely viewed as a rejection of President Mugabe and the ruling party. The 'No' vote league campaigned around the draft's provision for increased powers of the Executive as a recipe for tyranny, while for the 'Yes' campaigners the draft's provision for the compulsory state acquisition of land was its historic strength. Immediately following the rejection of the draft constitution, war veterans and ruling party youths moved on to occupy white-owned farms, setting off a series of events that contributed to the crisis immensely.

The third development to heighten the tensions between the state and civil society was the formation of the opposition Movement for Democratic Change (MDC) as a direct offshoot of the ZCTU, in September 1999. This was the political culmination of decade-old social struggles pitting the state against civil society. The coalescence of civil society into a political entity was not taken lightly by the incumbent government, as it presented the most serious threat to its political security since the merger of Zanu PF and PF Zapu[7] in 1987. State reaction to dissent from both the opposition and civil society – including the press – was more decisive than before, and assumed both legal and extra-legal forms.

The twenty-first century in Zimbabwe therefore began on a note of fierce political contestation. Besides fighting the new and highly organised opposition, the state also sought to take its 'war' to the doors of mainstream capital, which it accused of connivance with the opposition, and to civil society—including the press—which it also accused of supporting the opposition.

As the ruling party's legitimacy came under severe battering in the wake of the failure of market reforms and numerous other crises during the 1990s and beyond, the already authoritarian state became predatory and militarised. It abandoned its coaxing and limited coercion approaches of the earlier decades, and adopted brute force as a key instrument of media policy and control.

A sense of urgency characterised the state's move to introduce legislative measures to deal with sections of the media considered troublesome. As early as February 2000, the then Minister of Information, Chen Chimutengwende, had lamented that the existing media environment was 'too relaxed' and had 'allowed the penetration of media organisations with a political agenda to destroy the government and country' (*The Herald* 5 February). The minister announced that the government would introduce measures to restrict ownership of private media to local investors, among other things. In an ominous indication of things to come, Chimutengwende told journalists: 'We are not living in normal times. We therefore have to make such measures. There is a fierce battle for the hearts and minds in Zimbabwe and we just have to win it' (ibid).

Beginning in mid-2000, the structure of government communication systems underwent a radical metamorphosis. The newly created Department of Information and Publicity (DIP) replaced the Ministry of Information (which was disbanded) and oversaw the restructuring of both the ZBC and Zimpapers. The new department, which was located in the President's Office, spearheaded a process of media 'reform' characterised by a frenzy of legislative footwork.

A key advantage of the DIP, which comprised the Minister, his Permanent Secretary and a coterie of press officers, was its access to 'unlimited' funding from the President's vote. This enabled it to embark on a range of propaganda projects. At its inception, the DIP's immediate challenge was to harmonise state information policy in politically contested times. Given that existing policy then was either incoherent or simply implied through practice, the task was to articulate policy that would bring the different arms of government together into a unified information policy entity. The department's strategic location in the Presidency elevated it above other portfolios, making it the public face of the beleaguered government. In discharging its duties, it adopted a multi-pronged approach. This included fast-tracking media-oriented legislation through a malleable Parliament, multi-media information campaigns and increased control of Zimpapers and the ZBC by the state. Because of the department's profound impact on the practice of journalism in Zimbabwe, a brief discussion of specific aspects of state communication and information policy under Minister Jonathan Moyo is relevant here.

Draconian legislation

On the pretext that the state was defending a threatened sovereignty, the DIP spearheaded various laws and implemented policies without much evidence of public consultation outside the ruling party. Prior to its legislating the practice of journalism in Zimbabwe, it established a Media Ethics Committee in July 2001. The committee, whose members were handpicked by the Minister of Information, was mandated to conduct an inquiry into the state of media in the country and make recommendations. Editors of privately owned newspapers did not recognise the committee's legitimacy, citing its unrepresentative composition, and many refused to make submissions to it.

The submission of the Media Ethics Committee's report was followed by a phase of frantic law-making. As a first step, the Access to Information and Protection of Privacy Bill was published by an extraordinary Government Gazette on 30 November 2001. Twice, a parliamentary legal committee threw out the bill. In one instance, the Zanu PF chairman of the legal committee, Edison Zvobgo, described the bill as 'the most calculated and determined assault on our liberties guaranteed by the Constitution'.[8] The bill, still retaining many of its original imperfections despite having had 36 amendments, was later passed into law after a ruling party caucus had whipped dissenting members into line.

The ostensible purpose of the Access to Information and Protection of Privacy Act (AIPPA) was to make public information available to members of both the public and the press, while at the same time ensuring the right to privacy of citizens. In reality, it succeeded in making public information difficult to access, especially by the media. Further, the AIPPA was designed to silence a critical media and increase the influence of the Minister of Information on mediated communication in the country. Among its numerous provisions, the AIPPA provides for the registration of journalists by a Media and Information Commission, a body whose members are also handpicked by the Minister of Information. It also provides for the registration of media organisations by the same commission. Under the AIPPA, registration certificates for both journalists and media organisations can be cancelled at any time should the minister or the commission deem it necessary. Unaccredited journalists may not be employed anywhere in the country, and there is a fine and/or jail liability for both the journalist and the organisation breaching that legal provision.

The vesting of power in the hands of an individual minister was a key issue raised in the adverse parliamentary report that was produced by the Parliamentary Legal Committee on AIPPA, but ignored eventually when the bill was passed. The report made the following fundamental observation:

> Why does the Minister [of Information] or any Minister seek such overwhelming power from this Parliament? He would have a Commission, if the Bill passed, which could be empowered to take legal or other lawful action. All news agencies would live *in terrorem* of the Minister if this provision passes because the penalties he can impose are devastating. Should the Minister of Commerce and International Trade, or Finance be given the same powers in relation to their portfolios? They would all go around with 'certificates' in their briefcases looking for businesses to shut down 'if the Minister has reasonable grounds to believe' that such businesses are operating in contravention of some Act. These provisions are arbitrary, dictatorial and unconstitutional (Republic of Zimbabwe 2002).

The allocation of immense power to the minister and the commission had grave consequences for the media, particularly sections of the private press that were perceived to be critical of the political establishment. One of the most devastating results of the AIPPA was the closure of three privately owned newspapers in the space of just eight months. The *Daily News* and its sister weekly, the *Daily News on Sunday*, were shut down in September 2003, while the weekly *Tribune* suffered the same fate in May 2004. Although they were forcibly shut down under different circumstances – the Associated Newspapers of Zimbabwe papers were closed after the Supreme Court threw out their constitutional challenge of the AIPP Act, while the *Tribune* allegedly failed to inform the Media and Information Commission

(MIC) of changes in its shareholding – the publications were closed because of the new act.

Besides granting the public very limited access to information and rendering public bodies unaccountable to the public, AIPPA also has a provision outlawing majority foreign ownership of media in the country. This provision should be viewed against the background of the government's professed disdain for certain privately owned newspapers owned by foreign capital, with the *Daily News* the most obvious case in point.

Following AIPPA, the Broadcasting Services Act (BSA) of 2001 further entrenched the position of the Zimbabwe Broadcasting Corporation (later renamed Zimbabwe Broadcasting Holdings) as the key player in the broadcast media field. While ostensibly designed to deregulate the electronic media, the BSA created difficult conditions for new entrants, so much so that by 2008 – seven years after its inception – there were no private broadcasters in the country. Another controversial aspect of this legislation was its mandatory 75 per cent local content for broadcasters. While applauded in the local production industry as a plus for the promotion of local talent, the provision was simultaneously criticised for creating an overwhelming, low-quality sameness within ZBC programming. The BSA empowers the state-appointed Broadcasting Authority of Zimbabwe (BAZ) – the licensing authority – to interfere with the editorial content of broadcasters and to enforce adherence to the local content quotas. It also empowers the Minister of Information, through his/her control of BAZ, to amend, suspend and terminate as well as set licensing conditions for broadcasters.

The Public Order and Security Act (POSA) of 2002 was another piece of legislation passed at the height of the 'crisis' that has implications for the practice of journalism in Zimbabwe. Among its litany of deterrents to free expression, POSA criminalises the publication of 'false statements prejudicial to the State' (Section 15). In the context of a paranoid state, mild criticism can easily pass for a prejudicial statement, resulting in criminal prosecution for the individuals or organisations concerned. The duo of POSA and AIPPA became a systematic expression of the state's media policy in crisis-ridden times, predicated on – much like the Rhodesian policy during the UDI era – the need to eradicate 'the enemy within', who is supposedly being used as a puppet by the 'external enemy'.

In a political context operating on binaries, journalistic practice was reduced to being either for or against the state. (See Last Moyo's contribution in this volume.) In March 2004, the Minister of Information told *The Herald*: 'Mercenaries of any kind, whether carrying the sword or the pen, must and will be exposed and they will suffer the full consequences of the law' (*The Herald*, 11 March 2004). The perception that private press journalists were 'mercenaries' or instruments of 'regime change' has informed state media policy during the post-2000 era. While a captive state media has played a cheerleading role in relation to state activities, the private press has uncritically endorsed the opposition, in particular the MDC, and consistently bashed Zanu PF in political reportage.

The demise of journalistic agency

The dynamic tension between the agency of professional journalists and organisational or institutional structures and constraints is a subject of key interest for a critical political economy of the media (see Croteau & Hoynes 2003; and Graham & Murdock 2000). We need to examine briefly how this dynamic has played itself out in the crisis era in Zimbabwe as a result of authoritarian media policy.

One outcome of the post-2000 media and communication policies in Zimbabwe has been the erosion of the nominal agency powers of journalistic practice, leaving the profession of journalism largely at the mercy of political and socio-economic power hierarchies. The ownership factor has become a much more pronounced one in journalistic practice. Mano (2005: 76) observed that both public and private media owners during this period 'created "regimes" that undermine professional and ethical roles of journalists', leading to a scenario where journalists themselves became 'resigned to these developments, seeing them as "normal"'. The issue of journalists' declining powers of professional agency during this period also came up during interviews conducted with various members of the profession. According to Matthew Takaona of the Zimbabwe Union of Journalists (ZUJ), the fact that unemployment in the media industry was high and that employed journalists were generally wretchedly paid contributed to their easy subordination by structural constraints. He noted:

> One of the biggest problems in the media now is that we are so insecure and financially weak. As a result when one is kicked out of an organisation the next thing is probably to go back to your rural home or find a plane ticket and leave the country. You cannot go to the courts because access to lawyers is very expensive (Matthew Takaona, interview by author. Harare, April 2004).

Takaona also argued that, in a context where the levers of power were heavily skewed in favour of owners, even propaganda and hate journalism were able to thrive easily, for as long as these owners sanctioned it.

The editor of *The Sunday Mail*, William Chikoto, explained the bifurcated media framing of political life after 2000 in this way: 'It's not us journalists who are polarised … [it] is the forces behind the media that are polarised … if these forces converge, you'll find that there'll be convergence in the media as well.'[9] Another editor, Innocent Chofamba Sithole of the *Zimbabwe Mirror*, noted that his owner/ publisher's harsh responses to negative coverage of some political parties often instilled self-censorship among mostly young and vulnerable reporters.[10] Although throughout the post-colonial transition the media played the role of subordinate 'partner' in its relations with capital, civil society and the state, it was arguably in the post-2000 era that journalistic agency became almost completely subdued by structural constraints. Rather than being sites for critical-rational debate, the media during this period largely (though in varying degrees) became tribunes for competing elites in capital, civil society and the state.

The foregoing reflections show that there was a great deal of continuity in media policy from the colonial through to the post-colonial era, with the state playing the dominant role in shaping journalistic practice. It has been noted that, as its legitimacy waned amid a range of crises that began in the 1990s, the state adopted an authoritarian media policy regime whose effect was to constrain the public sphere by limiting the range of media platforms in the country. In the next section of this chapter, I will argue that, in light of the shortcomings identified in the Zimbabwean case, an ideal media system in the event of the re-democratisation of Zimbabwe will need to be nurtured at the level of both policy and practice.

The challenge of media policy

Curran (2000) has argued that an ideal media system could consist of a multi-tier system comprising both specialist and general media sectors. At the core of such a system would be a public service broadcasting system, encircled by private enterprise, social market, professional, civic and other sectoral media. At its best, such a media system, with its constituent parts organised in different ways, can 'create spaces for the communication of opposed viewpoints, and a common space for their mediation' (Curran 2000: 143).

According to Curran's architecture, the specialist media tier serves 'differentiated audiences, which enables different social groups to debate issues of social identity, group interest, political strategy and normative understanding on their own terms' (2000: 140). Serving both specialised and non-specialised audiences is the general media tier, at the core of which is public service broadcasting. Ideally, according to Curran, this tier should be able to reach and speak to heterogeneous publics in society. Further, it should be universally accessible to everyone, with content that both encourages and enables debate at all levels of society. Because of the reality of diversity in society, the specialised tiers of civic (civil society groups including non-governmental organisations), professional (media controlled by and largely addressing specific professions including the media profession), private (market-based commercial) and social (minority media, operating within the market but supported by the state), all contribute to addressing the range of information and entertainment needs of the heterogeneous publics. The underlying assumption in Curran's model is that the state itself is democratic and that, because it has the media needs of citizens at heart, it will adopt policy strategies (such as the model outlined above) that can sufficiently address these needs.

Taking note of Curran's invaluable argument and model, and drawing briefly on the South African media policy scenario, I contend that an ideal media system in a future Zimbabwe would be possible only after a dismantling of the authoritarian legal and policy infrastructure, and its replacement by a comprehensive policy that is authored by a cross-section of social interests and that creates conditions for professional media practice. Such a policy dispensation would have to provide for express media freedom in the Zimbabwe's Constitution, liberate the public media from state control by creating a genuinely publicly owned media accountable to the public through Parliament, and create enabling conditions for commercial, community and non-profit media to thrive. In addition, the broader political context in Zimbabwe – in particular the current political tensions that have polarised the country along the lines of Zanu PF and the MDC – and the poor state of the economy would need to change for the better to create these enabling conditions for the media.

Zaffiro (2000: 117) has argued that South Africa's 'ongoing experience with simultaneous political and media democratisation offers some useful lessons for Zimbabwe'. He identified, among various noteworthy aspects that Zimbabwean policy reformers may need to consider, South Africa's legal protection of free expression, its shunning of state domination of the media, and the country's creation of conditions where it is possible (although not always the case in practice) for the media to be independent of economic, editorial and legal interference.

Like Zimbabwe, South Africa went through a negotiated transition which saw the demise of apartheid and the establishment of non-racial democracy as a result of protracted negotiations between the liberation movements and the minority government. Within the arena of communication policy reform, Horwitz (2001: 20) has argued that the process of media reform from apartheid-aligned apparatuses to accountable democratic institutions 'took place via a complex political process in which civil society activism … largely won out over the powerful forces of formal market capitalism and older models of state control'. The active role of civil society in South Africa's negotiated transition therefore ensured that a media system created out of a democratic South Africa would in principle serve a range of social interests rather than just political and corporate hierarchies.

Whereas in Zimbabwe the policy formulation process was the prerogative of the emerging ruling elite from the outset, the communications policy reform process in South Africa 'constructed a genuine public sphere in which nearly all relevant parties had access and the ability to participate in ongoing discussions and negotiations in substantive rather than merely symbolic ways' (ibid: 22). Premised on a Constitution often cited as one of the most liberal in the world, South African media policy created a three-tier system in broadcasting and a multi-tier system for the press to increase both media density and in principle to broaden access to the mediated public sphere.[11] The broadcasting sector tiers include public service, commercial and community broadcasting. While community and commercial broadcasters generally target specific constituencies – defined by geography and interests – the public service broadcaster, the South African Broadcasting Corporation (SABC) carries the constitutional mandate of targeting the entire country in its diversity and in the country's 11 languages. The South African print media sector is not statutorily regulated, and consists of a multi-tier system including mainstream national, regional, local and community newspapers and magazines. With a few exceptions, the print media sector is predominantly commercially owned.

With regard to Zimbabwe, however, the emerging ruling political elite took sole charge of the policy process right from the inception of independence. In fact, even during the Lancaster House ceasefire and constitutional negotiations leading to the first democratic elections, media freedom was not given sufficient attention as a critical issue, hence the scant provision made for it in the country's Constitution.[12]

Zanu PF inherited a highly centralised state in which media policy formulation, among other things, was the sole responsibility of the state to the exclusion of all other social interests. This resulted in the continuance of authoritarian underpinnings in the new policies, their presentation to the public as democratic and transformative notwithstanding.

A democratic media and communication policy for a developing African country such as Zimbabwe would have to be a product of massive engagement between the state and social interests in civil society (including journalists' unions) and capital, among other groupings. Such a policy should be supported by legislation and constitutional provisions guaranteeing media freedom and freedom of expression. Rather than being bent on constraining media density by outlawing foreign ownership of the press and enforcing the compulsory licensing and registration of practising journalists and media houses, a democratic media policy should aim to increase media plurality and diversity. As in the South African case, policy should deliberately provide for the creation of different media outlets to serve the communication and information needs of different constituencies, including the poor and marginalised, whose information needs cannot be sufficiently addressed by market-based media. At the same time, policy should make provision for public interventions that may, from time to time, be necessary to prevent the concentration of media that can negate diversity and pluralism.

A policy trajectory would also be required, which would provide for a genuinely publicly owned public press that would be accountable not just to one set of political interests, as has been the case with Zimpapers publications since 1980. The idea of an autonomous trust remains an attractive option, but should be operationalised only when buttressed by strong and unequivocal policy and legislation, and driven by a truly representative and autonomous board of directors. Given that until now the public press has been the most pervasive print medium in the country, its decoupling from the state could, in principle, enhance its contribution to the public sphere. Ideally, the trust would have to be accountable to, and receive its (public) funding through, Parliament. A legislative provision guaranteeing both its funding and independence would ensure that it maintained an autonomous existence.

A democratic media and communication policy should be able to nurture a vibrant private commercial press and an equally vibrant community press, with the latter serving geographical areas (especially those areas with the lowest media density – i.e. rural and peri-urban areas) as well as communities with shared interests, such as professional or religious groups. Prior to the promulgation of AIPPA in 2002, there was no codified policy on the private press. As noted in this chapter, the negative provisions of AIPPA include, among others, an outlawing of foreign ownership of the media, the registration of journalists and media houses, and stringent requirements for the registration and operation of community media, especially community radio. A policy is required that will strike a reasonable balance between local and foreign ownership of the press, and will lift the litany of other requirements such as compulsory registration. The commercial press should be allowed as a matter of policy to operate unencumbered by the state. It can be regulated through either a system of self-regulation or a binding code of conduct, to be agreed upon by both the state and the media among other groups. A policy that creates a positive environment for the proliferation of community and rural media is required in Zimbabwe, not least because up to 70 per cent of the country lives in rural areas. I have noted elsewhere, regarding community newspapers in Zimbabwe, that earlier attempts at rolling out rural newspapers, done through the ZMMT, flopped partly owing to poor funding, poor management, and the exclusion of local business and civil society. A policy agenda involving the state, civil society and business is therefore a possible way to address this issue. The necessity for community media cannot be overemphasised in the case of Zimbabwe, where both the private and the public press have largely been forums for the articulation of contending elite interests, and where the press is largely an urban phenomenon (Chuma 2005: 59).

Policy initiatives promoting community and rural media should also include alternative non-market and social market media within the same band. A possible model for promoting the growth of non-market and community media in Zimbabwe could be the South African Media Development and Diversity Agency (MDDA), its flaws notwithstanding. An 'extra-market' initiative to address the media needs of marginalised and poor communities, the MDDA emerged as a partnership between the state, capital and civil society 'within the constraints of South Africa's re-entry into a global economy that privileges 'free market' solutions to developmental problems' (Pillay 2003: 401).

In a context where the mainstream media, including the public service broadcaster, is predominantly commercially funded – and therefore in practice subject to market 'tyranny' – the rationale for the MDDA is to help build the capacity of community media in areas or constituencies marginalised by the mainstream commercial media. It does so mainly through funding and training, ensuring that community media 'live up to the participatory-democratic ideals of non-profit media' by involving communities in the decision-making processes on their projects (ibid: 416). The agency receives its funding from both the state and the commercial media industry. The MDDA policy process was a drawn-out and strongly contested one, with the resulting legislation – the MDDA Act of 2002 – a significant compromise between the key partners (Pillay 2003; Skinner 2005). Although the original conception of an MDDA with a strong and transformative mandate eventually resulted in an organisation with only limited powers after intense negotiations between the mainstream media industry and government departments, the MDDA remains 'a path-breaking initiative for a developing country with limited resources' (Pillay 2003: 418).

The South African media scenario is not perfect. The country still has to contend with the reality of a mainstream media that is captive to both commercial and political centres of power, a situation that is inimical to media pluralism and diversity. But its adoption of a raft of policy interventions aimed at addressing the information needs of non-dominant and impoverished groups is laudable. These aspects, in addition to the country's creation of a multi-tier system of broadcasting and its establishment of media regulatory bodies accountable to Parliament,[13] present a possible model for policy reform in Zimbabwe.

An ideal media policy regime should arguably be informed by the desire to achieve a kind of public sphere that is beholden neither to the state nor the market. Thompson (1995: 241) calls this 'regulated pluralism'. This he defines as a principle that, on the one hand 'takes seriously the traditional liberal emphasis on freedom of expression and on the importance of sustaining media institutions which are independent of state power'; and that, on the other hand, 'also recognises that the market left to itself will not necessarily secure the conditions of freedom of expression and promote diversity and pluralism in the sphere of communication' (ibid). A policy agenda that can create enabling conditions for a robust and diverse media that approximates the public sphere should be informed by the above concerns. Both the South African model and Curran's architecture attempt to create a media system that is dominated neither by the state nor by market forces. They both have their flaws but, when considered in their totality, present competent approaches to the intricate task of media policy reform.

The challenge for journalistic practice

Media policies can only facilitate – rather than generate or represent – the multiplicity of voices so necessary for the survival of the mediated public sphere. It is the task of journalistic practice, operating in an enabling policy environment, to nurture the public sphere. In Zimbabwe, the media policy regime was designed to constrain the public sphere, while mainstream journalistic practice has also largely negated the same.

A key challenge facing journalistic practice in Zimbabwe is the development of media activism around media rights, media professionalism and the unionisation of journalists. Throughout Zimbabwe's post-colonial transition, the power of journalistic agency has been largely weakened by the country's political, and to a lesser extent, economic structures. Throughout its existence, the ZUJ, like its predecessor, the Rhodesian Guild of Journalists, has not sufficiently stood up in defence of the professional rights of its practitioners in the wake of threats from both the state and capital. ZUJ has been mostly a lame duck organisation, with neither a secretariat nor any power to protect its members, let alone the public, from violations of media freedom. The fact that the state had an active hand in its formation, and that most of its membership has consisted of state-employed journalists, has arguably added to the organisation's ineffectiveness. Despite being a member of the Zimbabwe Congress of Trade Unions (ZCTU), ZUJ has never been actively involved in the ZCTU's programmes of action (including numerous mass protests against state management of the economy and increasing state repression) – which is further testimony to its lethargic history. In 2001 many journalists from the private press left ZUJ to form a rival union, the Independent Journalists Association of Zimbabwe (IJAZ), the aim of which was to protect its members and fight state laws and policies. The successes of the IJAZ are still to be noted at the time of writing. The closure of the *Daily News* and other newspapers after 2003 whittled down both IJAZ and ZUJ's membership and adversely affected their operations. Ideally, Zimbabwe would require a vibrant journalists' body or bodies with adequate resources and power to lobby and intervene in the interest of unencumbered journalistic practice. A stronger ZUJ or IJAZ would also have to team up with organisations within civil society to present a formidable front to potential threats to media freedom and professional media practice.

The situation in Zimbabwe was not helped by the absence of institutional structures – voluntary or statutory, before 2002 – to monitor journalistic ethical conduct and provide mechanisms through which the public could interact with journalists or file complaints against unfair treatment by the media. Even after 2002, the Media and Information Commission (MIC), established by AIPPA, has revealed itself to be a very partisan body whose mandate appears to be to preside over the demise of the private press. During the period covered by this chapter, journalists in Zimbabwe were not bound by any code of conduct.[14] For media to be credible institutions of public life in Zimbabwe in future, the journalistic fraternity in the country would ideally need to come up with a Code drawn up by a range of interests including media owners and unions; members of the public; civil society groups; the state; and capital. Such a Code must bind journalists to professional practice, and compliance should be monitored by journalists' associations together with individual media houses.

Another challenge for journalistic practice in Zimbabwe, linked to the question of professionalism raised above, relates to the training of journalists. Rozumilowicz (2003: 17) argues that journalism education has a role to play in creating a media culture that promotes the proliferation of information and the tolerance of ideas. She suggests that, among other things, 'training schemes for journalists could be instituted which would instruct them in the ways of investigative journalism and a sense of professionalism in their craft'. The issue of poor training and lack of professionalism is one of concern in Zimbabwean journalism. It should be noted that, even as it established the Zimbabwe Institute of Mass Communication (ZIMCO) in 1981 to address the problem of journalistic skills shortages among blacks, the state viewed training in journalism as an arena for hegemony construction. Graduates of the sketchy six-month crash programme (later upgraded to two years), armed only with basic news-writing and interviewing skills, were hardly competent to both withstand systematic pressure from the state and to 'mediate' the transition in a more nuanced and professional manner.[15] Over the years, several media training institutions have been established in the country. However, many still suffer from lack of adequate resources, just like all the other tertiary institutions in the country at a time of profound political and economic crisis. It is plausible to argue that a better and well- resourced journalism and media training regime in Zimbabwe could lead to improved professionalism, which – coupled with progressive and democratic policy reform – could create a media system that promotes the active citizenship so central to a democracy.

Finally, the underlying assumption in my discussion of both policy and practical proposals for media reform in Zimbabwe is that there should be the political and moral will for such reforms. During the past three decades, Zimbabwe has degenerated from a state with an effective developmental thrust to one which, aside from its ubiquitous militarisation, has become weak, undemocratic and predatory (Bond & Saunders 2005). Media imbalances in a society reflect the balance of power in that society. Equally, progressive media reforms cannot happen in highly authoritarian contexts: there is always a correlation between media reform and the democratisation of the state (Price, Rozumilowicz & Verhulst 2003).

Conclusion

To nurture a vibrant media that serves the interests of democracy in the future, Zimbabwe will have to implement far-reaching changes at the levels of media policy and media practice. The process of authoring democratic policy should be inclusive, rather than confined to just one set of interests (as happened in Zimbabwe over the past three decades and earlier). The country would need to dismantle the authoritarian legal infrastructure that currently negates a free press and free expression, and put in place constitutional protections for both these freedoms. Equally, journalists would need to actively claim and exercise their agency. This they would need to do in the interest of not just the dominant groups on either side of the political divide (i.e. the ruling party and the opposition and its allies in capital) but also, and more importantly, of the smaller, weak and marginalised voices whose input into political debate and practice generally receives scant media attention. Journalists would also need to be accountable to the public through a comprehensive Code of Conduct that would ensure the fair and unbiased reportage of issues and events affecting Zimbabwean citizens.

References

Bond, P. and M. Manyanya. 2002. *Zimbabwe's Plunge: Exhausted Nationalism, Neoliberalism and the Search for Social Justice*. Pietermaritzburg: University of Natal Press.

Bond, P. and R. Saunders. 2005. Labour, the state and the struggle for a democratic Zimbabwe. *Monthly Review* 57(7): 42–55.

Calhoun, C. 1992. ed. *Habermas and the Public Sphere*. Cambridge, Massachusetts: Massachusetts Institute of Technology Press.

Campbell, H. 2003. *Reclaiming Zimbabwe: The Exhaustion of the Patriarchal Model of Liberation*. Cape Town: David Philip.

Chan, S. 2003. *Robert Mugabe: A Life of Power and Violence*. London: I.B. Tauris.

Chipika, J., S. Chibanda and P. Kadenge. 2000. *Effects of Structural Adjustment in Southern Africa: The Case of Zimbabwe's Manufacturing Sector during Phase 1 of ESAP, 1991–1995*. Harare: Sapes Books.

Chuma, W. 2004. Limiting or liberating the public sphere? Media policy and the Zimbabwe transition, 1980–2004. In *Zimbabwe: Injustice and Political Reconciliation*, ed. B. Raftopoulos and T. Savage. Cape Town: Institute for Justice and Reconciliation.

Chuma, W. 2005. Zimbabwe: The media, market failure and political turbulence. *Ecquid Novi*. 26 (1): 46–62.

Croteau, D. and W. Hoynes. 2003. *Media Society: Industries, Images, Audiences* (3rd edn). London: Pine Forge Press.

Curran, J. 1996, 2000. Rethinking media and democracy. In *Mass Media and Society*, ed. J. Curran and M. Gurevitch (2nd edn 1996, 3rd edn. 2000). London: Arnold.

Garnham, N. 1992. The media and the public sphere. In *Habermas and the Public Sphere*, ed. C. Calhoun, 395–360. Cambridge, Massachusetts: Massachusetts Institute of Technology Press.

Golding, P. and G. Murdock. 2000. Culture, communications and political economy. In *Mass Media and Society*, ed. J. Curran and M. Gurevitch (2nd edn. 1996, 3rd edn. 2000), 70–92. London: Arnold.

Habermas, J. 1992. *The Structural Transformation of the Public Sphere: An Inquiry into a Category of Bourgeois Society*. Cambridge, MA: Massachusetts Institute of Technology Press.

Hammar, A., B. Raftopoulos and S. Jensen. eds. 2003. *Zimbabwe's Unfinished Business: Rethinking Land, State and Nation in the Context of Crisis*. Harare: Weaver Press.

Herbst, J. 1990. *State Politics in Zimbabwe*. Harare: UZ Publications.

Horwitz, R.B. 2001. *Communication and Democratic Reform in South Africa*. Cambridge: Cambridge University Press.

Konrad Adenauer Stiftung. 1996. *Towards Press Freedom*. Harare: Willie Musarurwa Memorial Trust.

Kupe, T. 1997. *Voices of the Voiceless: Popular Magazines in a Changing Zimbabwe, 1990–1996*. Unpublished PhD thesis, University of Oslo.

Mano, W. 2005. Press freedom, professionalism and proprietorship: Behind the Zimbabwean media divide. *Westminster Papers in Communication and Culture*, Special Issue, Nov. 2005: 56–70.

Moyo, D. 2004. From Rhodesia to Zimbabwe: Change without change? Broadcasting, Policy Reform and Political Control. In *Media, Public Discourse and Political Contestation in Zimbabwe*, ed. H. Melber, D. Moyo and S. Chiumbu, 12–28. Uppsala: Nordic Africa Institute.

Nyahunzvi, T. 1996. Journalism training – Opportunities, limitations, institutions and funding: Harare Polytechnic Division of Mass Communication. In *Towards Press Freedom*, Konrad Adenauer Stiftung, 156-164. Harare: Willie Musarurwa Memorial Trust.

Pillay, D. 2003. The challenge of partnerships between the state, capital and civil society: The case of the Media Development and Diversity Agency in South Africa. *Voluntas: International Journal of Voluntary and Non-profit Organisations*. 14 (4): 401–420.

Price, M., B. Rozumilowicz and S.G. Verhulst. eds. 2002. *Media Reform: Democratizing the Media, Democratizing the State*. London: Routledge.

Republic of Zimbabwe. 2002. Zimbabwe Parliamentary Debates 28(46), 29 January. Government Printer. Harare.

Ronning, H. 1995. Democratisation processes in Southern Africa and the role of the media. In *Perspectives on Media, Culture and Democracy in Zimbabwe*, ed. R. Waldahl, 4-23. Oslo: Department of Media and Communication, University of Oslo.

Rozumilowicz, B. 2002. Democratic change: A theoretical perspective. In *Media Reform: Democratizing the Media, Democratizing the State*, ed. M. Price, B. Rozumilowicz and S.G. Verhulst, 9–26. London: Routledge. 2002.

Rusike, E. 1990. *The Politics of the Mass Media: A Personal Experience*. Harare: Roblaw Publishers.

Saunders, R. 1991. *Information in the Interregnum: The Press, State and Civil Society in Struggles for Hegemony, Zimbabwe 1980–1990*. Unpublished PhD thesis, Carleton University, Canada.

——. 1997. The press and popular organisations in Zimbabwe: A frayed alliance. *Southern Africa Report* 12 (3): 13–17.

——. 1999. *Dancing Out of Tune: A History of the Media in Zimbabwe*. Harare: ESP.

Saunders, R. and J. S. Saul. 2005. Mugabe, Gramsci and Zimbabwe at 25. Unpublished paper.

Shamuyarira, N. 1981. Foreword. In *The Mass Media in the Struggle for Zimbabwe*, ed. E. Windrich, 5–6. Gweru: Mambo Press.

Skinner, K. 2005. *Contested Spaces: An Analysis of the ANC Government's Approach to the Promotion of Media Development and Diversity in South Africa, with a Particular Focus on the Policy Process that led to the Formation of the Media Development and Diversity Agency (MDDA)*. Unpublished MA dissertation, University of the Witwatersrand, Johannesburg, South Africa.

Sylvester, C. 2003. Remembering and Forgetting 'Zimbabwe': Towards a Third Transition. In *Political Transition: Politics and Cultures*, ed. P. Gready, 29–52. London: Pluto Press.

Thompson, J.B. 1995. *The Media and Modernity: A Social Theory of the Media*. Oxford and Cambridge: Polity.

Windrich, E. 1981. *The Mass Media in the Struggle for Zimbabwe*. Gweru: Mambo Press.

Zaffiro, J. 2001. Mass media and democratisation of politics and society: Lessons from Zimbabwe, 1990–2000. In *Media, Democracy and Renewal in Southern Africa*, ed. K. Tomaselli and H. Dunn, 99–121. Colorado: International Academic Publishers.

Zimbabwe Human Rights NGO Forum.1999. *A Consolidated Report on the Food Riots, 19th to 23rd January 1998*. Harare: Author.

The dearth of public debate:

Policy, polarities and positional reporting in Zimbabwe's news media

6

Last Moyo

Des Freedman argues that media policy does not develop in a vacuum, but is, instead, 'purposefully created by competing political interests that seek to inscribe their own values and objectives on … the personality of media systems' (Freedman 2008: 15). Despite the perception of policy as being a benign and apolitical administrative process that is carried out in a spirit of benevolence towards citizens or the public, it is important to note that media policies and media policy-making are manifestly political and are sometimes marked by latent tensions or open conflicts between contending social forces in a given epoch and historical context.

In Africa's fledgling democracies, which are still grappling with colonial legacies and neo-colonial challenges, the trend has often been that media policy is an arena of brutal conflict in which the state bulldozes its way, working against other legitimate policy concerns in the name of national security and national interest (Nyamnjoh 2005; Blake 1997; Zaffiro 2002). Nowhere can this be a more fitting description than in Zimbabwe, where a protracted political and economic crisis has had a debilitating impact on the broader regulatory and policy regime culminating in the mortgaging of the news media's professional and ethical journalistic practice.

Most of the laws introduced by the government – such as the Broadcasting Services Act of 2001, the Public Order and Security Act (also of 2001) and the Access to Information and Protection of Privacy Act of 2002 – have been based largely on a crisis management and intervention approach, where the state single-handedly formulated media policies that excluded the input and participation of other stakeholders such as civil society, opposition parties and market forces, which it saw mostly as antagonistic. In most cases, official nationalism was and continues to be the overarching ideology that influences a policy direction through which the media are censored, silenced, or co-opted into the vanguard of defending the national interest as defined by the ruling elite. The practical manifestation of most of these policies in newsrooms has been the reduction of the news media and the profession of journalism to nothing more than mimicry and parroting of the pervasive elitist jingoism.

Those media organisations that have resisted have also been affected one way or another. For example, in 2001 Reporters Sans Frontières (RSF) noted that '20 local journalists were arrested and three correspondents of foreign press were expelled from the country for publishing stories deemed to be against the national interest' (RSF 2002:1). Again, according to the Media Institute of Southern Africa (MISA) and Amnesty International (AI), the following year a total of 44 media workers were arrested. Five were beaten up. In January 2001, the *Daily News* printing press was bombed. The offices of a prospective private radio broadcaster, Voice of the People (VOP), were bombed two years later. The state in Zimbabwe continues to use legal and extrajudicial methods as part of its armoury of paternalistic and draconian policies to contain the media and influence what they publish in the news. These policies ultimately seek to control the media's editorial content and through it the hearts and minds of media audiences. As Hutchison (1999) argues, effective media policies are always ultimately judged by how they directly and indirectly influence content, which is a key test of media behaviour or misbehaviour.

This chapter tries to address the dialectic between policy, content and agency. Whereas most of the other contributions in this volume deal directly with the question of policy as statutory principles, my focus is primarily on intended and unintended policy ramifications on the content of the news media. While policies are seen as strongly influential in determining media behaviour, media content is perceived as providing the forensics of not only the policy impact on agency, but also the broader ideological configurations that inform the given policy regimes. In other words, content can serve as a barometer for measuring the direct and indirect influence of sanctioned media policies.

Focusing on the content of the public media such as *The Sunday Mail* and Newsnet,[1] and of the private media such as *The Standard* and Short Wave Radio Africa (subsequently referred to as 'SW Radio Africa'), I contend that post-2000 media policies in Zimbabwe have seriously undermined the role of the news media as a public sphere, owing to the uncritical regurgitations of state or market propaganda that are presented in the popular idioms of everyday news on politics and society. While aggressive state intervention in media regulatory policies in the post-2000 epoch has arguably produced a culture of unquestioning loyalty and servitude in the public media, it arguably also has created hyper-adversarial responses in the private press, where negativity inspires and dominates news reports about most, if not all, government programmes.

The combined effects of Zimbabwe's paternalistic media policies and the deepening crisis in the country have culminated in subtle and sometimes flagrant manipulation of the media by the government, opposition parties, and civil society. These attempts to advance the various groups' interests are normally couched in a falsely inclusive rhetoric of nationalism and human rights. The crisis itself has polarised the nation, dividing it into camps of social and political forces that are fighting to emerge as victors in determining the direction of the country. In these circumstances the Zimbabwean media have become – for the state and the other forces – ideological apparatuses through which wars are waged, lost or won.

The interrogation of media-policy ramifications from a content perspective raises concern about not only Zimbabwean journalism's capacity to critically inform and educate citizens, but also the ability of the media as an institution to assert its autonomy and editorial independence (Waldahl, 2005; Ranger, 2005; Ronning & Kupe, 2002). As Peter Dahlgren argues, only an autonomous news media institution can play a critical emancipatory role for citizens by being 'the focal point of [their] desire for [a] good society' (Dahlgren 1993: 2). James Curran and Jean Seaton argue that media policy is seminal in nurturing a robust and effective media institution that serves to 'to inform, to mirror ... [to mediate] ... to bind, to discuss ... to challenge ... [and] to judge' (Curran & Seaton 1997: 319). The restrictive media policies in Zimbabwe have directly and indirectly created a media institution that trades in polemic, sensationalism and propaganda – the defining discourse markers of the broader crisis.

The chapter begins with an analysis of news reports on human rights and democracy in the wake of the highly restrictive media policy and socio-political polarisation challenges in Zimbabwe. The question that is central to the discussion concerns the extent to which *The Sunday Mail*, Newsnet, *The Standard* and SW Radio Africa as public spheres have been able to promote democracy and human rights in Zimbabwean politics so as to contribute to the citizens' quest for a 'good society.' To what extent do they promote or undermine democracy and human rights values, and to what extent does the socio-political and policy environment account for their actions? To deal with these questions, content analysis was used to examine the level of the coverage of good governance and human rights issues so as to extrapolate any existing patterns from the four media studied. This content analysis is then followed by a more in-depth textual analysis employing critical discourse analysis (CDA), in which the ideological roles of the news media were examined. Central to this analysis was the public sphere's normative values of an open, inclusive, democratic, fearless and critical public debate, as opposed to partisan and propagandistic reporting. In essence, the chapter tries to draw linkages between media institutions and their socio-political and policy environments through textual analysis, so as to demonstrate whether the selected media still serve as effective public spheres.

Content analysis – on the surface of news reports

The purpose of content analysis is always to paint a 'bigger picture' and delineate 'maps' about the 'the manifest content of communication' in the media (Deacon et al 1998; Kripperndorff 2004; Berger 1991; Berelson 1952). To evaluate critically the democratic role of four selected public and private news media, comparative content analysis of their editorial material was conducted between January and May 2004. The hard news and feature articles were analysed in the case of the two newspapers; for the two broadcasters, the focus was on the news bulletins. While 18 of the 22 copies of the weekly newspapers that fell within the period of study were analysed, systematic sampling comprising every Wednesday of every Week 2 and Week 4 was used for the radio broadcasters, with the starting date arrived at through a simple random selection.

Table 6.1 below summarises the results of this analysis. The column headed 'Human rights violations' focused on those articles that addressed civil and political rights issues such as police brutality; the torture and harassment of political opponents, journalists and ordinary citizens; abductions and illegal detentions; the curtailment of the freedoms of association and expression; the defiance by the state of court orders and the rule of law; and the ruling party and other organisations in the political arena. The column 'Other forms of criticism' focused on the role of the news media as watchdogs against corruption, on economic mismanagement and on other related issues. The last column, 'Defence of government', includes those articles that seemed to implicitly or explicitly justify some of the government and the ruling party's undemocratic practices in dealing with citizens.

Table 6.1: Coverage of human rights and governance issues between January and May 2004

	Content	The Standard	The Sunday Mail	SW Radio Africa	Newsnet
Human rights violations	Hard news	45	0	31	1
	Features	9	0	–	–
	Opinions	6	0	–	–
Other forms of criticism	Hard news	20	5	23	3
	Features	11	3	–	–
	Opinions	9	0	–	–
Defence of government	Hard news	0	7	0	5
	Features	0	5	–	–
	Opinions	0	10	–	–

A closer look at the table shows that *The Standard* and SW Radio Africa consistently featured civil and political rights issues, and also expressed general criticism of the government, while *The Sunday Mail* and Newsnet had a very poor performance in the same areas. For example, while *The Standard* had 45 hard news stories and nine features on human rights abuses in the period under study, *The Sunday Mail* had no stories that dealt with any civil or political rights issues on the days under study. Again, while *The Standard* had 20 hard news stories that were critical of the government and public officials, *The Sunday Mail* had only five. Of the latter, two (entitled 'Residents in for high jump' and 'Not fit for humans') criticised the local government councils that are run by opposition parties; while only one story (entitled 'Top officials involved in tractor scam') criticised corrupt public officials for using national resources for self-enrichment. It is important to note that this story was published in April 2004, when the government had introduced 'knee-jerk' anti-corruption policies to fight rampant corruption in the public and private sectors. In a different context, *The Sunday Mail* would probably not have published anything critical of the government.

In terms of civil and political rights coverage on radio, SW Radio Africa had 45 stories while Newsnet had only a single story on human rights in a period of five months. The story was about the white farmer who allegedly shot and killed a newly resettled black farmer at Riverside Farm in Manicaland.

While coverage of civil and political human rights issues and criticism of the government were clearly barely covered in the public media, *The Sunday Mail* and Newsnet also seemed to have more articles that defended the government against criticism by the private news media and civic organisations. Examples of such stories included, inter alia, 'Air Zim trashes paper's story', 'Mass action rejected, economic revival gets thumbs up', 'UK displays shocking contempt', and 'Department not offended by Paradza's ignorant remarks'.

The editorial output in Table 6.1 also appears to suggest that the news media coverage of the Zimbabwean crisis is polarised along ownership lines. The privately owned media such as *The Standard* and SW Radio Africa seemed consistently to support the human rights and democracy discourse far more than the state-controlled *The Sunday Mail* and Newsnet did. For example, while it was noted that 60% of the sampled editorial output from *The Standard* was on human rights, there appeared to be a complete blackout on the civil and political rights discourse in *The Sunday Mail*. However, a closer look revealed that 73% of the sampled content in the latter newspaper seemed uncritically to defend government policies and extra-judicial strategies used on political opponents and ordinary citizens. For example, when the police allegedly used excessive violence to stop the National Constitutional Assembly (NCA) demonstrators in February 2004, *The Standard* and other private newspapers in Zimbabwe reported how some NCA members had been severely beaten up by the police. According to *The Standard*, the NCA chairperson had been found unconscious in a pool of blood. However, *The Sunday Mail* either totally ignored the story or downplayed the issue of violence. For example, on 8 February 2004, the editor of *The Sunday Mail* also wrote an article entitled 'Ex-convict Madhuku playing to the gallery', in which he appeared to openly celebrate the alleged police brutality, accusing the demonstrators of 'engaging in conduct that [they] knew would invite the immediate and justified wrath of the law enforcement agents'.

Perhaps the consistent defence of the government by *The Sunday Mail* is the result of the vague editorial policy that stipulates that public newspapers 'need to be patriotic, supporting the national interest as projected by government' (Zimpapers Board Meeting Minutes, 7 June 1995). Clearly, in this context, the meaning of words such as 'patriotism' and 'national interest' tends to become blurred and problematic, as the terms can potentially be used by governments to curtail the editorial independence of public media. On Newsnet, the bias in approach could partly be ascribed to the fact that the station is required, by the Zimbabwe Broadcasting Corporation Commercialisation Act of 2002, to 'prioritise the needs of the state'; while the Broadcasting Services Act (BSA) of 2001 demands that it gives 'one hour cumulatively per week to the government of the day to explain its policies to the nation'. While democratically elected governments have the right to use the public media to explain their policies, this can be a problem in countries such as Zimbabwe, where the legitimacy of the government is questioned by the opposition parties and mainstream civil society owing to alleged election irregularities. This situation is made worse by the uncritical stance of certain media towards government, with journalists afraid to question government policies or to include the views of people who may be critical of the government in their news reports. As Tawanda Hondora has argued, the BSA 'is an instrument testifying to the fear within the government. It ... only serves to allow ZANU PF to churn out propaganda in its effort to retain political power' (Hondora 2003: 23).

Critical discourse analysis: Beyond the surface, into ideology

Raftopoulos argues that since the advent of the crisis in Zimbabwe, nationhood and imperialism have been some of the central and persistent ideological narratives in the news of the public media (Raftopoulos 2004: 13). In *The Sunday Mail* and Newsnet, these discourses appear to manifest themselves through the use of smaller, but nevertheless powerful, myths and binary oppositions that seek not only to reconstruct the notion of nationhood as a 'natural' rather than a culturally defined reality, but also to classify 'difference' and appropriate meanings to it, in ways that may not be favourable to other actors in the national political public sphere. Figure 1 provides an example that can be used as a basis for such an argument.

Headline: *Zimbabweans have been urged to remember fallen heroes*
            <u>9 August 2004, 20:00 News Bulletin, Newsnet</u>

Reader:
President Mugabe has urged Zimbabweans to remember and respect all the country's fallen heroes. Cde Mugabe, who was speaking during the commemoration of Heroes Day at the National Heroes Acre in Harare today, said there is need to remember that although there are few heroes lying in the national shrine, a lot more paid the supreme price and are lying in unknown caves, forests and in neighbouring countries.

Reporter:
Speaking at the national shrine, Cde Mugabe urged Zimbabweans to respect the Tomb of the Unknown soldier as it represents the unnamed and unknown soldiers who perished during the liberation struggle. The President also reminded people that it required great courage to liberate Zimbabwe adding that there is need to safeguard the country's independence and sovereignty. He said although Britain is trying to recolonise Zimbabwe using puppets, Zimbabwe will never be a colony again. The President also criticised the world's bullies who think they have the right to change governments.

Figure 6.1: Newsnet and the myths of nationhood and imperialism

From the outset, the myth or ideology of nationhood can be seen in the foregrounding of nationhood in the headline of the story called 'Zimbabweans urged to remember fallen heroes'. It is important to note that the headline does not say 'People urged' but 'Zimbabweans urged' because the former does not frame the news in a way that is ideologically consistent with nationalism. The word 'Zimbabweans' plays a critical ideological function in foregrounding nationhood as the broader context of the news narrative. Apart from the headline, the news narrative also shows that the story is framed within a nationalistic discourse that appears to be based on other constructed myths of patriotism, heroism, bravery and sacrifice prefigured through Mugabe's reference to the 'fallen heroes' who 'paid the supreme price and are lying in unknown caves [and] forests'. While the liberation struggle, indeed, represents the collective experience of the war by all Zimbabweans, it can be argued that the reconstruction of the notions of patriotism, heroism, and sacrifice as articulated by Mugabe through Newsnet, is a highly ideological process that may be directly or indirectly linked to the legitimation of the prevailing political order.

John Hartley, Tom Koch and Norman Fairclough argue that news is a great myth- or ideology-making process in which journalists unconsciously partake as agents (Hartley 1988; Koch 1990; Fairclough 1995). In the story of the news item in Figure 1 above, the myth of the 'unknown soldier', represented by the 'Tomb of the Unknown Soldier' (a symbol of patriotism and sacrifice to one's country), arguably enhances the ideological narrative of the news. The agenda of this narrative seems to be to address citizens as subjects loyal to a discourse of nationhood that may be embedded with certain elite class interests at the expense of ordinary people's political rights, such as freedom of expression and the right to have different political opinions from those who define the status quo. Yael Tamir argues that the ideology of the nation is always 'associated with the rhetoric of blood and soil, fiery exhortations to rally behind the flag, demands for total devotion and self-sacrifice and a collective feeling that sweeps away individual considerations' (Tamir 1999: 69). Thus, the ideological function of this story seems to be not only to legitimate the notion of 'Zimbabweanness' so as to make it appear natural and unquestionable, but also to set up boundaries that exclude alternative views and ways of thinking about the nature of the Zimbabwean crisis and its resolution.

At this level, it can be argued that these types of news stories from the public media play the role of 'narrativised ideology' through the 'formulaic articulation and naturalisation' of the discourse of the nation, so as to frame nationalism as the answer to the Zimbabwean crisis (see Fulton et al 2005: 150). Fairclough (1995: 91) also argues that, as narrativised ideology, news stories tend to be targeted predominantly at working class audiences because 'stories are for those who, because of their social status and education, are denied the power of exposition, while exposition is for those who have been given the right to participate in the debates that may change society'. Hence, although presented within a discourse that implies inclusion, comradeship and fellowship (i.e. nationhood), the news agenda here appears to be structured around the interests of the political elite represented by Robert Mugabe.

It is imperative to note that, because of his privileged social status, President Mugabe is the one who primarily defines Zimbabwe's political reality, the nature of the threat to the nation, and the nature of the commitments that are needed to deal with the threat; and that Newsnet attributes significance to his definition of that reality, thus showing that, as Hartley argues, 'one of the primary functions of the news in [the media] is continuously to signify myths through everyday detail of newsworthy events' (Hartley 1988: 20). The emphasis on Mugabe's characterisation of the Zimbabwean crisis, regardless of the fact that nationalism and imperialism as meta-narratives have lost their power to legitimise the ruling party's version of 'truth' to Zimbabwean citizens, clearly demonstrates how politics regulates discourse in terms of what can be said or not said. As Barker argues, discourse is 'not proliferating in an endless deferral but is regulated by power which governs not only what can be said ... but who can speak, when and where' (Barker 2001: 12).

Another good example of the ruling elite's appropriation of the ideology of nationhood and imperialism is *The Sunday Mail*'s story entitled 'We will never let Gutu go, vows Msika', published on 11 January 2004. In the story, Msika opines that the opposition Movement for Democratic Change should be ostracised by the people of Zimbabwe because it is anti-national and seeks to advance imperialism. In a statement that echoes Mugabe's earlier concerns, Msika says that 'Zimbabwe's independence did not come on a silver plate. Many Zimbabweans languished and toiled in prison and never wavered from the march towards self rule.' Thus, to the extent that *The Sunday Mail* and Newsnet can be described as myth-makers, they clearly present nationhood and resistance to imperialism as two overarching ideals that demand unquestioning loyalty from all Zimbabweans. It is interesting to note how, as politically inspired meta-narratives, they are 'violent and tyrannical in their imposition of a "totalising" pattern and a false universality of actions, [explanations] and events' (Woods 1999: 21). As Roland Barthes argued, 'myth [meta-narratives] hides nothing and flaunts nothing: it distorts: myth is neither a lie nor a confession: it is an inflection' (Barthes 1982: 116). In the Newsnet and *The Sunday Mail* stories, the inflection or distortion can be seen in the claim the Western powers, as symbolised by Britain, want to re-colonise Zimbabwe by using 'puppets' – a term that has become the public media's pejorative reference to those who dare to oppose the ruling party's version of truth. The claim that 'Zimbabwe will never be a colony again' appears not to be based on the true observation of such a political risk, but rather on the need to exaggerate the political differences between Zimbabwe and Western countries for propaganda purposes. The statement arguably has the effect of hailing the loyal and willing subjects of this discourse of nationhood and of imploring them, as Mugabe does, to 'safeguard the country's independence and sovereignty', a call which in practice has always culminated in intimidation, threats, violence and a suppression of freedoms in various political public spheres (Raftopoulos 2004; Ranger 2003; Thompson 2002).

The ideologies of nationhood and resistance to imperialism also arguably conceal the reality of the class differences brought about by the market reforms in Zimbabwe in the nineties and by the recent agrarian reforms. In performing this function of concealment, myth or ideology as a system of representation 'masks [people's] true relations to one another in society by constructing imaginary relations between people and between them and the social formation' (Phillips & Jorgensen 2003: 15). Perhaps the discourse of nationhood and resistance to imperialism in Zimbabwe might be essentially what Anthony Giddens (1996: 213) calls a 'masked expression of the interests of the dominant class'. Indeed, Raftopoulos argues that these grand narratives are simply a hegemonic ideological project of the government, which, under the current land-reform fiasco and international isolation, seeks not only to win people's hearts and minds, but also to reconstruct the post-colonial state 'in order to provide both the modality for and consolidate the accumulation drive of the ruling party elite in the country' (Raftopoulos 2004: 8). As both discourse and ideology, nationalism and imperialism seem to be in the service of the interests of the ZANU PF political and business elite, which is enriching itself through the land-reform process while the majority of Zimbabweans remain impoverished.

State media such as Newsnet and *The Sunday Mail* arguably construct and structure (unconsciously and unwittingly, perhaps) a version of reality that justifies these social actions of the elite. It is as Robert Hodge and Gunter Kress have said: 'In order to sustain the structures of domination, the dominant groups attempt to represent the world in forms that reflect their own interests, the interests of their power. But they also need to sustain the bonds of solidarity that are the condition of their dominance' (Hodge & Kress 1999: 3). These bonds of solidarity in Zimbabwe have clearly been the notions of nationalism and imperialism. For example, *The Sunday Mail*'s political editor wrote, in an article entitled 'Can someone tell Bush to shut up?', that 'over the last fours years he [i.e. Mr Bush] and his British tail part, Mr Tony Blair, have been pushing for regime change in Zimbabwe as they tried to smuggle a puppet opposition leader, Mr Tsvangirai, into power. All this was being done to protect white interests in the country' (*The Sunday Mail*, 4 April 2004). Interestingly, the entire article focuses on what the writer represents as British and American imperialism, but hardly mentions the democratic initiatives of local Zimbabweans towards legitimate regime change. Ultimately, this reporter renders the national forces and dynamics of Zimbabwean politics as insignificant and not newsworthy, while probably exaggerating the role of external forces in what the news constructs as the internal affairs of Zimbabwe.

According to Denis McQuail, news-framing is primarily about selection and salience, a process through which journalists attribute or deny value to certain things so as to create certain meaning potentials (McQuail 2005: 378–379). Thus the repetitive and consistent coverage of the so-called imperialist theme in Zimbabwean politics invariably amounts to the marginalisation of news that gives salience to the initiatives of the opposition parties and other social movements in the struggle for the re-democratisation of the country. Ian Phimister and Brian Raftopoulos argue that the discourse on imperialism may be used by the Zimbabwean public media partly for ideological purposes, to protect the ruling elite from the global norms and values of good governance and human rights that it is constantly violating. They contend that at the centre of Mugabe's strategy in counteracting international criticism for his government's human rights violations have been 'repeated attempts [by the government media] to place the Zimbabwe problem at the centre of a larger anti-imperialist … position' (Phimister & Raftopoulos 2004: 385).

Interestingly, *The Sunday Mail* and Newsnet hardly inform or educate the Zimbabwean public about the commitments that the Zimbabwe government must honour by virtue of having ratified international human rights instruments such as the United Nations Declaration (1948), the International Covenant on Civil and Political Rights (1966), and most importantly, the African Charter on Human and Peoples' Rights (1981), which require governments to adhere to principles of good governance, the observance of human rights and the respect for the rule of law. As such, the claims to absolute sovereignty by the Zimbabwean government and the criticism of the human rights discourse as being entirely imperialistic need to be subjected to critical and analytical national debate by the public media instead of being presented as the absolute truth.

Malcom Waters (2002) states that in a globalising world, governments can no longer claim to be entirely sovereign and can no longer govern their populations in an authoritarian way, hoping that they can use sovereignty as an excuse for this behaviour. Yasemin Soysal (1997: 43) argues that globalisation [together with human rights] has brought about 'global norms' and 'a world-level organising concept that disciplines states as much as it disciplines individuals.' Globalisation and its concomitant human rights discourse seem to pose new challenges for states such as Zimbabwe, which believe that they have the exclusive and absolute sovereign right to their internal affairs. Public media journalists in Zimbabwe appear to be ambivalent about the implications of globalisation and of the ratification of international human rights treaties.

The analysis of other articles in Newsnet and *The Sunday Mail* showed that their news constructed the discourse of nationhood and imperialism by creating categories and dichotomies of 'us' (i.e. the ruling party) and 'them' (i.e. all those critical of the state). These are outlined below in Table 6.2. Both sources appeared to make extensive use of these binary oppositions in the ideological representations of nationhood and imperialism in most of their stories. The prevalence of such binary oppositions shows that this discourse is interesting not only for its hegemonic purpose, but also for the ways in which the public media have recast the whole issue of national identity in a segregative manner, to include or exclude certain groups, and malign or praise other groups, so as to render citizens as either 'in-groups' or 'out-groups' in the whole nationhood project.

Table 6.2: Binary oppositions and the construction of Zimbabwean nationhood

Us	Them
Heroes	Villains
Patriotic	Unpatriotic
Revolutionaries	Anti-revolutionaries, puppets
Nationalists	Traitors, sell-outs
The People, the State	Enemies of the People, Enemies of the State

For example, *The Sunday Mail* and Newsnet both seem to recast nationhood in terms of binary oppositions that suggest deep enmity and hatred between not only the white and black races, but also the political groups, in the country. On the one hand, insiders to the myth of nationhood are described as 'comrades', 'the people', 'revolutionaries', 'patriots' and 'peace-loving Zimbabweans'; while on the other hand outsiders are vilified for their different political opinions through epithets such as 'sell-outs', 'enemies of the people', 'anti-revolutionaries', 'enemies from within', 'enemies of the state', 'detractors', 'puppets' and 'thieves.' The state-controlled media in Zimbabwe, therefore, seem to be central to the construction of a discourse that presents readers with a distorted depiction of the ruling party's political opponents. As part of narratives on nationalism and imperialism, these binary oppositions appear to stigmatise and demonise the opposition parties and social movements that are critical of the government. The latter are defined as inherently evil, while the ruling party represents everything that is good and progressive. These categories are represented simplistically by the public media as rigid, distinct, immutable and endemic, yet in reality they are a product of a media discourse that has characterised the public media since 2000.

The polarities used to construct these particular narratives of nationalism and imperialism tend to be arbitrary and unstable, and the public media are wrong to present them as simple or clearly defined. For example, given the Zimbabwean political context, the dividing line between patriotic and unpatriotic, heroes and villains, and nationalist and sell-outs, is indeed problematic and not an act of common sense as sometimes implied in the news of the public media. National interest, as the ultimate benchmark for the classification of these groups, is itself a blurred and purely restrictive concept, that only serves to limit free expression in the political public spheres of the news media and civil society. It is as Frantz Fanon observes: that 'nationalism, while vital to the emergence of Third World revolution, paradoxically limits efforts of liberation because it re-inscribes an essentialist, totalising, fetishised, often middle class specific understanding of [the] nation' (Fanon 1981: 150).

Again, the binary oppositions in the news create classification frames that privilege one category at the expense of the other, because the political identities of those who criticise the state are constructed only against those of the ruling party. As a result, Zimbabwean civil society and government opposition are not represented independently of the overarching and dominant identity of the ruling party, but are only seen as representing the absence or loss of those values that are constructed as characterising ZANU PF. As such, it can be argued that these binary oppositions create a sense of hierarchy between social classes in Zimbabwe, thus privileging the ruling elite represented through the dominant opposite. As Nick Lacey argues, 'One element in a binary opposition is always privileged over the other. This means that binary oppositions are also hierarchies, with one half dominating the other. The second term often comes to represent merely the absence of the first' (in Lacey 2000: 67). When applied to the Zimbabwean context, this means that once the opposition groups are constructed by the public news media as inferior, unstable, evil, irrational, and a threat to 'Zimbabweanness', then the state can use any means of repression – such as draconian laws and violence – to deal with them. For obvious reasons, this seriously undermines the role of the public news media as political public spheres in Zimbabwe.

Critics of the public media such as Brian Raftopoulos, Ian Phimister and Terrence Ranger have always spared the private media their criticism, perhaps because they think that the latter's representation of the crisis is non-ideological, but maybe also because they do not appear to see human rights and democracy as grand narratives that are deeply ideological in their own way. Examples of the private media such as *The Standard* and SW Radio Africa frame their news accounts not within discourses of nationalism and imperialism, but within meta-narratives of democracy, human rights and the rule of law that are deeply embedded in Western free-market politics and neoliberal globalisation. While both media have always given an alternative and counter-hegemonic perspective to that in the state media, the way they construct their discourses of democracy and human rights is contradictory and problematic because of the manner in which they uncritically apply them to the Zimbabwean situation. Just like *The Sunday Mail* and Newsnet, they have constructed oppositional myths that are based on binary oppositions that reinforce a selective and distortional human rights interpretation of the Zimbabwean crisis. The story, 'Army defies court order over farm' from *The Standard* can be used as an example to demonstrate this.

Army defies court order over farm
By Cephas Chimhete, Standard, 11 April, 2004

The Zimbabwe National Army, the police and some members of the State Security Services sealed off MDC MP Roy Bennet's Charleswood Estate in Chimanimani despite a recent High Court provisional court order barring them from interfering with operations at the farm.
Bennet's lawyer, Arnold Tsunga, told the Standard that the security agents had cordoned off the estate and were stopping people- including farm workers- from entering or leaving the coffee producing farm. Tsunga said the presence of the army and the police had thrown farming operation at the once prosperous into total disarray. "They came in trucks this morning (Friday), and sealed off the farm. At the moment no one is leaving or entering. Surprisingly, there is a provisional order granted by Justice Karwi barring them from interfering with the operations in the farm", said Tsunga, who is also the Executive Director for Zimbabwe Lawyers for Human Rights (ZLHR). The provisional order, which was granted by Justice Karwi in February, was served to the Ministry of Home Affairs, the Zimbabwe Republic Police, the ZNA and the Agriculture Rural Development Authority. According to Tsunga, the order was granted by consent when all parties were represented. "Such conduct undermines the independence of the judiciary and the administration of justice. It also fosters a culture of lawlessness in the country," noted Tsunga. He added, "We are getting worried by the wanton disregard of court orders by the authorities who have the responsibilities to enforce them..."

Figure 6.2: Instance of a construction of the human rights discourse in the private press

Denotatively, this story is simply about the collapse of the rule of law and the lack of the observance of human rights in Zimbabwe. The story exposes how, regardless of the High Court orders to the contrary, the army and other government forces invaded the Charleswood farm belonging to Roy Bennett, a Member of Parliament for the opposition. At this level, *The Standard* can be said to be playing a positive role as a watchdog against human rights abuses. However, at the connotative level, the analysis of this and other stories in *The Standard* and *SW Radio Africa* showed that their human rights discourse is based on the binary oppositions that potentially aggravate the political tension and divisions in the country. For example, this story represents the Zimbabwean crisis through the same polarities of good versus evil, order versus disorder, and victims versus perpetrators, with counter-establishment forces standing for the quest for stability and progress, and Mugabe's government representing gloom and darkness. These binary oppositions are clearly a reversal of the way *Newsnet* and *The Sunday Mail* describe the same reality. Notice how in the story, Roy Bennet, his farm workers, and the MDC represent law and order whereas the government forces represent violence, anarchy and the overall collapse and defiance of what has been constructed in the news as acceptable social norms. Discourses of the rule of law and of property rights are represented by *The Standard* as the natural order and a commonsensical way of doing things, while those who subvert this order are represented as irrational and violent criminals associated with 'lawlessness' and 'the wanton disregard of court orders'. This approach can be further demonstrated by the following story on SW Radio Africa, which was broadcast on 10 March 2004:

NEWS READER:

The Violence in Zengeza continues ahead of the parliamentary by-elections scheduled for the 27th and 28th of March. This afternoon, more than 200 Zanu PF sponsored militia stoned three houses belonging to members of the opposition including the home of James Makore, the MDC candidate. They also looted household goods and money at the candidate's house. The Zanu PF thugs invaded three houses, beat up people, and seriously injured one. Mrs Makore, the candidate's wife, told us that the militia shuttered window panes and asbestos sheets at the house and proceeded to attack neighbours.

Figure 6.3: Instance of a construction of Zanu PF in the private media

The stories in *The Standard* and on SW Radio Africa are based on the ideology of life as stable, orderly, democratic, consensual and non-violent – myths that seem to buttress a human rights ideology that is, in itself, arguably problematic and inherently contradictory. While both stories expose how the ruling party is allegedly abusing its power, their news frames and focus seem to reinforce a selective application of human rights and the rule of law. Looking beyond these two stories, both these private news organisations consistently portray ZANU PF as 'thugs', 'invaders', 'rogues', 'perpetrators of evil and injustice', an ' evil regime', a 'pariah state' and 'attackers', whereas the opposition and its supporters are always 'law abiding' and 'victims of injustice'. The framing of the news within what appears to be a dominant human rights ideology presents such classifications and perceptions of ZANU PF and the MDC as natural and obvious, but there are other competing perceptions and characterisations of the crisis that these media exclude from their news frames. For example, the human-rights-based news frames of *The Standard* and SW Radio Africa tend to be narrow and reductionist because they ignore the historical context of the Zimbabwe crisis. In the story in *The Standard*, this can be observed from the lack of historical context relating to the farm invasions; and from the dominance of human rights ideological codes or discourse markers – for instance 'court orders', 'independence of the judiciary' and 'administration of justice.' Again, the source of the story is the victim's lawyer, Arnold Tsunga, whom the reporter deliberately identifies as being also the Executive Director of Zimbabwe Lawyers for Human Rights – a title that connotes his social status and legitimacy as a news commentator on human rights issues. This effort towards legitimising him is important because it has the effect of framing the Zimbabwean crisis within a legal and human rights discourse for which the source is not only a lawyer, but also a member of a national human rights organisation. This approach delegitimises other ways of characterising the crisis, while prescribing the human rights worldview as the default view of the crisis by foregrounding Arnold Tsunga's status and assumed legal expertise.

Marianne Jorgensen and Louise Philips have argued that in meaning-making, 'power and knowledge presuppose one another' (Jorgensen & Philips 2002: 13–14). They argue that 'Power is responsible both for creating our social world ... [and for] ruling out alternative ways of being and talking' (ibid: 14). As a lawyer and a director of a human rights association, Tsunga arguably wields authority over the human rights issues in the eyes of the reader.

In February 2004, SW Radio Africa reported on the protracted invasion of Charleswood farm. It stated that women on the farm had been sexually abused, and that about 300 cattle had been stolen, by the state forces. The story was also clearly characterised by the use of binary oppositions that – like most stories in *The Standard* – foregrounded the brutality, violence, and defiance of court orders in the crisis and constructed it as simply a conflict between 'good' and 'evil' social forces. In so doing, the private media can be criticised for reinforcing negative Western stereotypes of the Third World, which are constructed within neo-liberal globalisation's corporate and government media as a place of endless crises that are caused by governments that are brutal, corrupt, and violent.

The distortions in *The Standard* and on the news bulletins of SW Radio Africa are not necessarily related to matters of fact or accuracy in their news accounts. Instead, they are related to their propensity to give prominence to conflict, drama, the bizarre and the sensational, while ignoring analytical reporting based on issues, processes and contexts. Some scholars have argued that the colonial legacy is quintessential to understanding the human rights and property rights aspects of the Zimbabwean crisis. Sachikonye (2003) and Henry Bernstein (2003) argue that while the Zimbabwean government clearly has a case to answer in relation to human rights abuses, it is imperative to acknowledge that the land issue is largely a colonial question that has exacerbated the abuse of civil and political rights.

When the acquisition of white-owned farms started in 2000, the state media represented it within the discourse of the continuation of the decolonisation agenda, and of seeking to restore the economic rights of indigenous people. In their human rights accounts, *The Standard* and SW Radio Africa appeared to downplay the issue of colonial dispossession; the constitutional constraints that stopped the government from addressing the land issue immediately after independence; and the resistance by white farmers, the IMF and the World Bank to orderly land reform in the 1990s.

According to Moyo (2005) and Sachikonye (2003), when the government tried to embark on an orderly land reform in the 1990s, Britain, the World Bank and the Commercial Farmers' Union discouraged it, arguing that resettlement of the landless masses needed to be slowed down because it 'would result in overall decline in output and in the number of people gainfully employed in agriculture' (Sachikonye 2003: 230). The private media's storytelling and reconstruction of events is therefore highly selective, excluding as it does certain issues in line not only with its own agenda-setting but also with the exigencies set by its organisational context, such as the need to make profits (see Allan 2004; Schudson 2001; Fowler 1996). As Koch argues, '[private] newspapers ... and radio stations serve first and foremost an economic function. They exist to create profits and make money for the owners through the sale of individual copies and of space ... to advertisers (Koch 1990: 23). Indeed, the human rights tragedy in Zimbabwe sells many newspaper copies and audiences to advertisers, while also attracting big donors – such as the Westminster Foundation – who pour much money into the private media institutions in the country (Bhebhe 2005; McGreal 2002). Hence, the private media's economic function of generating profits seemingly undermines its ability to provide a holistic human rights account of the crisis – one that would draw the linkages between civil and political rights, and economic rights and solidarity rights. For example, it is unable to explore the fact that respect for political and private property rights cannot be sustained in conditions of economic deprivation based on the colonial legacy.

In some cases, the private media clearly characterises the Zimbabwean crisis in religious terms – a technique that seems to further reinforce the moralistic binary oppositions that are ideal for the human rights framing of the crisis. For example, in a feature story called 'Mugabe faces the wrath of God, warns Archbishop Ncube' in *The Standard* of 25 January 2004, a journalist quotes the Archbishop as saying 'God said in his Holy Bible that you shall not kill, but Mugabe and his cabinet continue to kill. The Bible further states that you shall not steal, but Mugabe's cabinet has stolen properties belonging to white farmers who were forcibly removed from their land, that is breaking God's rules and commandments.' While the use of the Archbishop's morally authoritative voice consolidates the human rights news narrative, it also and conversely oversimplifies the Zimbabwean crisis – by ignoring the complexity of the matter as characterised by the history of colonialism in the country. In this story, Mugabe faces the wrath of God supposedly for forcibly redistributing white commercial farms. The journalist does not tell us that some of the land belonging to the white farmers was also taken by force from the indigenous people during the hundred years of British colonialism.

Ironically, most of the stories about the political crisis in *The Standard* and on SW Radio Africa are positioned against the background of an almost formulaic reference to Mugabe's 27-year rule of the country, which is always said to be the cause of the crisis. However, the same news media always ignore the colonial legacy as the broader context of the crisis in the background of stories about the land question in Zimbabwe. Nkosinathi Ndhlela argues that these sorts of oversimplifications in private media vehicles such as *The Standard* and SW Radio Africa are owing to the fact that they do not want to present complex and abstract issues to audiences because they want to sell copies. 'Media representations reduce, shrink, condense, and select, and reject aspects of intricate social relations in order to represent them as fixed, natural, obvious, and ready to consume (Ndhlela 2005: 73). Stuart Allan argues along similar lines, stating that much of the time the commercial media tend to go for personalisation, a process whereby 'an emphasis on human actors … is preferred over abstract descriptions of 'faceless' structures, forces, and institutions' (Allan 2004: 47). Personalisation focuses on personalities as protagonists of dramatic happenings, at the expense of a critical analysis of issues and processes. As a result, the news accounts of the private media seemingly reduce the Zimbabwean crisis to a personality (i.e. Mugabe), as if he (or his human rights violations) were the sole cause of the crisis.

Furedi argues that this myth is part of a neo-liberal globalisation human rights discourse that is about 'saving the Third World from itself' or 'the need of protecting ordinary people from local tyrants' (Furedi 1994: 110). In a sense, this implies that *The Standard* and SW Radio Africa may be unconsciously articulating a neo-liberal hegemonic position that, as a discourse, invariably delimits the boundaries of what can be talked about and what cannot be talked about in stories about the crisis in Zimbabwe.

Michael Foucault believed that 'discourse produces objects of knowledge in an intelligible way while at the same time excluding other ways of reasoning as unintelligible' (Barker 2001: 12).While *The Standard* and SW Radio Africa seem to deal with human rights and rule-of-law issues, they do not, however, tell the full story – especially as concerns the discourse shifts and mutations surrounding the land issue, which expose the 'double standards' of some stakeholders such as Britain, and of global institutions such as the IMF and the World Bank. They also do not question the morality or otherwise of the government paying for land (through the willing-buyer, willing-seller scheme of the 1980s) that was colonially acquired; nor do they even present the case of the poor majority who remain landless and dispossessed in post-independent Zimbabwe.

Conclusion

The rigidity of both the public and private media in restricting public debate on Zimbabwean politics to grand narratives can act as evidence of how heavily embedded in state and corporate interests these media are, at the expense of the country's citizens and of informative and educational journalism. The binary oppositions that characterise the news in *The Standard*, *The Sunday Mail*, Newsnet and SW Radio Africa reflect serious problems of 'positional' and 'unbalanced' reporting that is characterised by a lack of multi-sourcing and by an absence of diverse and plural views in the discussion of Zimbabwe's political condition. It is important to note that all the stories used as examples in this chapter depended on only one or two sources with a single homogenous view – either of the state as a human rights violator or of the opposition as puppets of the West. Yet, as I argued earlier, both positions are simplistic and have come to characterise post-2000 Zimbabwean journalism, making it almost uniformly propagandistic, boring, predictable, and uninformative.

The patriotic journalism of the public media, and the antithetical, anti-establishment journalism of the private media, seem to have produced a new breed of journalists who see themselves not as disinterested, critical or objective commentators on the conflict in Zimbabwe, but as active participants in the conflict (Moyo 2007; Ranger 2005). From this perspective, then, it can be argued that Zimbabwean journalism is now part of the crisis that urgently calls for a media policy intervention to address the structural and institutional problems that characterise Zimbabwe's polarised media landscape.

Journalistic content invariably embodies and articulates the subtle (or candid) interests of those who own and fund the media. Yet the polarisation of news accounts in Zimbabwe points to something deeper than this. It can, in fact, be said to reflect the problems of an institution that is not only losing its professional value, but that has also failed to confront its socio-political and policy environment, or to be an engine for change. As David Ward argues, the media must not always be subservient to state policy or business interests. Because the state and the market are not benign, their policies may not always have a positive impact on journalistic performance and professionalism (Ward 2004:78).

In order to restore the type of journalism that encourages cross-sectional public debates and information sharing – as opposed to propaganda manipulation – Zimbabwe urgently needs a constitution that expressly guarantees freedom of information and freedom of the press. Such freedoms will potentially provide a solid foundation upon which an autonomous media institution can stand and nurture journalism's professional identity. More importantly, they will encourage the creation of policies that can be the bedrock for an effective public sphere that encourages active citizenship, one where media audiences have certain rights or entitlements that they can claim from news media organisations in respect of content and participation.

The constitutional recognition of this independent media institution must be followed by a comprehensive legal reform programme. Laws such as the Access to Information and Protection of Privacy Act (2002) and the Public Order and Security Act (2001) have also encouraged polarised news accounts, by overly protecting public officials and public bodies against having to give timeous information to journalists. The first law is an assault on journalism and the principle of freedom of information because a public body can take as long as 30 days or more to respond to a journalist's request for information. The law has ironically made information less accessible to journalists, particularly those from the private media, thus further exacerbating the problem of polarisation. Laws such as the second one, which unduly protects the presidency against criticism by the media on perceived 'risks' or 'possibilities' of 'engendering feelings of hostilities … contempt or ridicule of the president' are clearly against the values of openness, accountability and debate, and must be repealed.

The regulatory framework can be statutory or voluntary, as long as the principles of independence and professional practice are upheld. The statutory regulatory bodies such as the Media and Information Commission and the Broadcasting Authority of Zimbabwe are not independent, nor do they represent the interests of all stakeholders in the Zimbabwean media, because the minister of information has the power to appoint and suspend members of the board. Good journalistic practice in Zimbabwe will be a product of either a reform of these bodies, or of a voluntary regulation, with self-regulation and responsibility as its advantages.

References

Allan, S. 2004. *News Culture,* 2nd ed. London: The Open University.

Barker, C. 2000. *Cultural Studies*: *Theory and Practice*. London: Sage.

Barthes, R. 1972. *Mythologies*. London: Cape.

——. 1982. *The Pleasure of the Text*. USA: Wadsworth.

Barthes, R. (author) and Sontag, S. (ed). 1982. *A Barthes Reader*. London: Routledge.

Benhabib, S. 1992. Models of public space: Hannah Arendt, the liberal tradition and Jurgen Habermas. In *Habermas and the Public Sphere*, ed. C. Calhoun, 73–98. Cambridge, MA: Massachusetts Institute of Technology Press.

Berger, G. 2001. *Configuring Convergence*. Johannesburg: New Media Lab.

Bernstein, H. 2003. Land reform in Southern Africa in world-historical perspective. *Review of African Political Economy* 30(96): 203–226.

Bhebhe, R. SW Radio Africa must be saved. *Newzimbabwe.com*, 27 May 2005.

Bignell, J. 2002. *Media Semiotics*: *An Introduction*. Manchester and New York: Manchester University Press.

Bracking, S. 2005. Development denied: Autocratic militarism in post election Zimbabwe. *Review of African Political* Economy 32(104/105): 341–357.

Bush, R. 2003. Zimbabwe left out in the cold? *Review of African Political Economy* (98)30: 535–537.

Calhoun, C. ed. 1992. *Habermas and the Public Sphere*. Cambridge, MA: Massachusetts Institute of Technology Press.

Cliffe, L. 2005. Imperialism and African social formations. *Review of African Political Economy,* 32(103): 5–7.

Curran, J. 1997. The liberal theory of press freedom. In *Power Without Responsibility*, ed. J. Curran and J. Seaton. 5th ed. London: Routledge.

——. 1999. Rethinking the media as a public sphere. In *Communication and Citizenship*: *Journalism and the Public Sphere*, ed. P. Dahlgren and C. Sparks, 27–57. London: Sage.

Dahlgren, P. and C. Sparks, eds. 1999. *Communication and Citizenship*: *Journalism and the Public Sphere*. London: Routledge.

Fairclough, N. 1989. *Language and Power*. London: Longman.

——. 1995a. *Media Discourse*. London: Arnold.

——. 1995b. *Critical Discourse Analysis*: *The Critical Study of Language*. London: Longman.

——. 2001. *Analysing Discourse*. London: Routledge.

Falk, R. 1999. *Predatory Globalisation: A Critique,* Cambridge: Polity.

Fanon, F. 1986. *The Wretched of the Earth*. Harare: Zed Books.

Feltoe, G. 2002. *A Guide to Media Law in Zimbabwe*. Gweru: Mambo Press.

Fraser, N. 1992. Rethinking the public sphere: A contribution to the critique of actually existing democracy. In *Habermas and the Public Sphere*, ed. C. Calhoun. Cambridge, MA: Massachusetts Institute of Technology Press.

Freedman, D. 2008. *The Politics of Media Policy*, Cambridge: Polity.

Fulton, H., R. Huisman, J. Murphet and A. Dunn (eds). 2006. *Narrative and Media*. London: Routledge.

Furedi, F. 1994. *The New Ideology of Imperialism*. London: Pluto Press.

Garnham, N. 1992. The media and the public sphere. In *Habermas and the Public Sphere*, ed. C. Calhoun. Cambridge, MA: Massachusetts Institute of Technology Press.

Giddens, A. 2001. *The Global Third Way Debate*. Cambridge: Polity.

Habermas, J. 1992 (1989). *The Structural Transformation of the Public Sphere*: *An Inquiry into a Category of Bourgeois Society*. Cambridge: Polity.

Hartley, J. 1982. *Understanding News*. London: Routledge.

Herman, E. S and N. Chomsky. 1999. *Manufacturing Consent: The Political Economy of the Mass Media*. London: Vintage.

Hodge, R. and G. Kress. 1999. *Social Semiotics*. Cambridge: Polity.

Hondora, T. *Analysis of the Zimbabwe Broadcast Services Act*. Harare: Media Institute of South Africa, March 2002.

Hutchinson, D. 1999. *Media Policy: An Introduction*. UK: Blackwell.

Ignatieff, M. 1999. Nationalism and the narcissism of minor differences. In *Theorising Nationalism*, ed. R. Beiner, 91−103. Albany, New York Press.

Koch, T. 1990. *The News as Myth: Fact and Context in Journalism*. Westport, CT: Greenwood Press.

Kupe, T. and D. Lush. 2005. *Crisis? What Crisis? Free expression and access to information in Zimbabwe*. Paper delivered at the Conference on International Media Support Strategies for Zimbabwe, 28−30 November, in Johannesburg, South Africa.

Krippendoff, K. 2004. *Content Analysis: An Introduction to its Methodology*. London: Sage.

Lacey, M. 2000. *Narrative and Genre: Key Concepts in Media Studies*. London: Routledge.

Loewerstern, R. and L. Moyo. 2003. *Human Rights and the Media: A Handbook*. Harare: Southern Africa Human Rights Trust.

Maruziva, D. S. 2003. Zimbabwe. *So This Is Democracy? State of media freedom in Southern Africa 2003*, 7−15. Windhoek: Media Institute of Southern Africa.

McChensey, R. 1997. The communication revolution: The market and the prospect for democracy. In *Democratising Communication? Comparative Perspectives on Information and Power*, ed. M. Bailie and D. Winseck, 57−81. New Jersey: Hampton Press.

McGreal, C. US funds penetrate Zimbabwe airwaves. *Guardian Newspaper* (UK), 24 January 2002.

McQuail, D. 2005. *Mass Communication Theory*. 2nd ed. London: Sage.

Moyo, L. 2003. Status of the media in Zimbabwe. In *Encyclopaedia of International Media and Communication*. Carlifornia: Academic Press.

———. 2007. *Digital Media, Globalisation and Human Rights: The Role of New ICTs in the Struggles for Democracy in Zimbabwe*. Unpublished PhD thesis, University of Wales.

Moyo, S. 2005. The resurgence of rural movements under neoliberalism. In *Reclaiming the Land: The Resurgence of Rural Movements in Africa, Asia and Latin America*, ed. S. Sam and P. Yeros. USA: Blackwell.

Murphy, J.W. 1989. *Technology and Human Service Delivery*. Philadelphia: Haworth Press.

Naughton, J. 2001. Contested space: The Internet and global civil society. In *Global Civil Society*, ed. H. Anheier, M. Glasius and M. Kaldor, 147–169. Oxford: Oxford University Press.

Ncube, K. 2004. Media laws and human rights in Zimbabwe. In *Human Rights and the Media: A Handbook*, ed. R. Loewerstern and L Moyo, 53–69. Harare: Souther African Human Rights Trust.

Ndhlela, N. 2005. The African paradigm: The coverage of the Zimbabwe crisis in the Norwegian media. *Westminster Papers in Communication and Culture*, Special Issue, November 2005: 71–90. London: University of Westminster.

Phillips, L. and W. Jorgensen. 2002. *Discourse Analysis as Theory and Method*. London: Sage.

Phimister, I. and B. Raftopoulos. 2004. Mugabe, Mbeki and the politics of anti-imperialism. *Review of African Political Economy* 31(101): 385–400.

Raftopoulos, B. 2007. Nation, race and history in Zimbabwean politics. Paper presented at the Conference on The Zimbabwe Economic Crisis: Towards a lasting Solution, 2 August, in Harare, Zimbabwe.

Ranger, T. 2003. Historiography, patriotic history and the history of the nation: The struggle over the past in Zimbabwe. Annual Distinguished Lecture on Africa, organised by the Interdisciplinary Research Group on Africa, 5–9 July, Ghent University, United Kingdom.

——. 2004. Historiography, patriotic history and the history of the nation: The struggle over the past in Zimbabwe. *Journal of Southern African Studies* 30 (2): 215–234, London: Routledge.

——. 2005. The rise of patriotic journalism in Zimbabwe and its possible implications. *Westminster Papers in Communication and Culture*, Special Issue, November 2005: 8–17. London: University of Westminster.

Ronning, H. and T. Kupe. 2002. The dual legacy of democracy and authoritarianism: The media and the state in Zimbabwe. In *De-Westernizing Media Studies*, ed. J. Curran and M. Park, 157–178. London: Routledge.

Sachikonye, L.M. 2003. From growth with equity to fast-track reform: Zimbabwe's land question. *Review of African Political Economy* 96: 227–240.

Saunders, R. 2000. *Never the Same Again: Zimbabwe's Growth Towards Democracy*. Harare: Haylett Printers and Packaging.

Stoneman, C. ed. 1981. *Zimbabwe's Inheritance*. Hampshire: Macmillan.

Thompson, C. 2003. Zimbabwe: Intersection of human rights, land reform and regional security. *Foreign Policy In Focus*. Interhemispheric Resource Center publication. http://www.foreignpolicy-infocus.org/commentary/zimbabwe.html

Waldahl, R. 2005. Political journalism the Zimbabwean way: Experiences from the 2000 election campaign. *Westminster Papers in Communication and Culture*, Special Issue,

November 2005: 18–32. London: University of Westminster.

Ward, D. 2004. *The European Union Democratic Deficit & the Public Sphere: An Evaluation of Public Policy*. Lancaster: IOS Press.

Willems, W. 2004. Peasant demonstrators, violent invaders: Representations of land in the Zimbabwean press. *World Development* 32(10): 1767–1783.

——. Remnants of Empire? British media reporting in Zimbabwe. *Westminster Papers in Communication and Culture*, Special Issue, November 2005: 91–108. London: University of Westminster.

Windrich E. 1981. *The Mass Media in the Struggle for Zimbabwe*. Gweru: Mambo Press.

Zaffiro, J. 2002. *Media and Democracy in Africa Zimbabwe, 1931–2002*. Colorado Springs: International Academic Publishers.

Zambia:

Policies of a media-phobic state

7

Isaac Phiri

Media policy-making in Zambia is a complex process in constant flux, because of media-phobic political regimes that have continually shifted and changed the legal and political goalposts. This chapter explores how their fear of the media's real or imagined political power drove the governments of Kenneth Kaunda (1964–1991), Frederick Chiluba (1991–2001) and Levy Mwanawasa (2001–2008) to employ various elements of legislative, judicial, executive and political tools to devise written and unwritten policies to contain and control media behaviour. The objective is to illuminate fundamental issues that may be causative to this intriguing behaviour, and to derive value for present and future media policy discourse in Zambia and possibly the Southern African Development Community (SADC) region.

The core question at hand is: Why is it that despite impressive proclamations by these successive governments (before and soon after coming to power) about the value of media autonomy in a democratic society, there is paltry evidence of a sincere commitment to the formulation and implementation of viable media policy? This study, informed by a combination of archival research and extensive unstructured in-depth conversations with media practitioners, leaders and scholars, and enriched by active observation and participation in state-media relations in Zambia, proposes that this behaviour is causally linked to the successive governments' own insecurities, which have amplified their perception of the media's political power. Thus while political actors are eager to use press freedom promises and proclamations as part of their campaign rhetoric, they recoil at the potential influence of free media once they became state actors and policy-makers.

Overview of the media industry in Zambia

Compared to, say, South Africa – the powerhouse of the SADC – the media industry in Zambia is miniscule and if not government-owned, at least state-watched. Television and radio have, as Banda (2006: 16) observed, 'continued to be the preserve of the state-owned Zambia National Broadcasting Corporation'. Television viewing in most of the country is still limited to the pro-government ZNBC Television. Almost invariably, prime-time news broadcasts start predictably with State House activities, however mundane.

The coverage of events involving opposition political actors is brief and tightly edited, and in many cases the voices of the speakers are cut out while interpretive reporting overruns the images. Informative content often comes in the form of donor-funded programmes on some development project or current affairs issue. Banda's conclusion is therefore not surprising: 'television holds a special appeal for the ruling party' (2006: 23).

Entertainment programming consists of re-runs of dated South African, Latino or Asian drama and soap operas. Recently, some West African video dramas have been aired, giving viewers a break from the mostly political content of ZNBC Television. Occasionally, old American or European action movies are plugged in for late-night entertainment.

Private free-to-air television broadcasting is limited to Muvi TV, the Trinity Broadcasting Network (TBN) and the little-known new entrants, MOBI TV and CB TV. Despite its apparent teething problems – loss of sound while on air, showing wrong images and footage, gaffes by presenters – Muvi TV does provide its viewers with content that includes voices from other political actors besides those in power. Opposition leader and presidential hopeful, Hakainde Hichilema, gave his 'independence day address' of 24 October 2007 through Muvi TV, which covered his visit to a community left homeless after court-sanctioned evictions from its township. ZNBC did not cover the event. Michael Sata, another opposition activist and presidential hopeful, has also received more airtime on Muvi TV than on ZNBC. Muvi TV also has a number of other interview programmes where ostracised voices are aired. The other two broadcasters, MOBI TV in Lusaka and CB TV in the Copperbelt Province city of Ndola, are too new to warrant analysis, save to say that their entrance indicates the potential of a well-populated network of independent broadcasters who could form alliances so as to air national broadcasts, thus bypassing the current legal restrictions.

Nonetheless, independent television broadcasting in Zambia is still limited by the fact that the operators are only licensed to reach restrictive numbers of viewers and that they are still experimental channels and therefore not taken seriously by some. TBN has a bigger reach but it is strictly religious and carries mostly American content. Further, its reputation for breakdowns and desperate appeals for financial support from its viewers makes it a far less serious player in the television industry. The minority of Zambians who can afford to purchase installation equipment and pay monthly subscription fees have additional options through DStv, GoTV and other options that satellite television can provide. But the content of these channels is so foreign and entertainment-oriented that it is of little interest to the present media policy discourse.

Radio broadcasting in Zambia, though comparatively still a tiny industry, is more vibrant. ZNBC Radio's three channels – Radio One, Radio Two and Radio Four – still dominate the national airwaves but private FM stations and community radio stations are competing strongly with the government broadcaster (Banda 2006: 96–113). Lower entry costs for investors and higher community involvement for not-for-profit broadcasters explain the vibrancy of the industry. It may have been the buoyancy in radio broadcasting that drove the momentum toward the passing of the Independent Broadcasting Authority (IBA) Act and the amendment of the Zambia National Broadcasting Corporation (ZNBC) Act in 2002. The fact that in 2008 the government was still dragging its feet about the implementation of these pieces of legislation is a matter of discussion later in this chapter.

The print media in Zambia is also skeletal. There are only three dailies: the state-run *The Times of Zambia* (hereafter referred to as *The Times*) and *The Zambia Daily Mail (*hereafter *The Daily Mail)*; and the independent, privately owned *The Post*. All three claim greater circulation than the others, as reliable figures are hard to come by. Circulation estimates dating back to 2002 may still be a good indicator, with *The Times* at 32,100, and *The Daily Mail* and *The Post* at around 40,000 each (see www.nationsencyclopedia.com/Africa/Zambia-MEDIA.html). Banda's research of 2006 cited Central Statistics Office reports that allocated the market share as follows: *The Post*, 39 per cent; *The Times,* 26 per cent; and *The Daily Mail*, 20 per cent. However, warns a footnote: 'It is to be noted that circulation figures are often inflated and circulation does not reflect readership as such' (Banda 2006a: 26).

Besides these dailies, there are at least a dozen active weekly or monthly newspapers and magazines. But many of these appear and disappear so often that it is hard to evaluate their impact on society. The National Archives, which is the official registry for periodicals, is literally an archive of many dormant titles. Limited advertising, high production costs and miniscule readership cripple the private print-media industry in Zambia. The prospects of a vibrant, independent print-media industry in the country – although favoured by relatively lax registration and regulatory demands – are remote. Little wonder, then, that the government's media policy directed at stifling the minute private press has been a gentle one.

Media policy during the Kaunda government, 1964–1991

Media policy-making during Kenneth Kaunda's reign, though not always clearly articulated, was at least synchronised. The role of the media was apparent: to uphold the status quo. In the early years after independence, experimental, competitive politics in Zambia promised some space for relatively free, competing media. However, this hope was soon dimmed by the introduction of one-party rule in 1972. Through both intelligent politicking and negotiation or, as some suspect, less than scrupulous machinations, Kaunda's United National Independence Party (UNIP) engulfed the opposition and became the powerhouse of the nation.

From then on, the state-run and only broadcasting entity, the Zambia Broadcasting Service (ZBS) parroted the messages of the government. The monopolising – and monotonous – dailies, *The Daily Mail* and *The Times*, became state chronicles. The book publishing industry, dominated by the Kenneth Kaunda Foundation (a self-revealing name) regurgitated texts of Kaunda's humanism, rehabilitated Zambian history, and published pro-government cultural and creative works and school textbooks. Cinema was censored by a film censorship board (see Balule 2004: 08). In short, media policy, understood here through UNESCO's 1972 definition of 'sets of principles and norms established to guide the behaviour of communications systems', emanated out of the Kaunda-centred deliberations of UNIP's Central Committee and was imposed on the media. The fact that the Ministry of Broadcasting and Information doubled as the source of 'national guidance' says it all.

The literature on media policy in Zambia during the one-party state is patchy. Moore's study of press freedom in Zambia is a good summation of the media policy in this era. Humanism, which Moore dubs Kaunda's 'personal philosophy,' promoted the ideals of a society in which human dignity was paramount. However, observed Moore: 'Humanism does not provide a framework for the operation of a government' and 'does not establish policy or direction to deal with the realities of an interdependent world.' The result was that 'government direction has largely been given by one man' (1991: 22). Media policy – written or unwritten – was incarnate in Kaunda and his close stalwarts. The only news source that retained autonomy was the church-run *National Mirror*. In November 1990 Kaunda was so infuriated by *National Mirror*'s reporting that he banned government advertising in the paper, an attempt to bleed the weekly to death financially. He also directed the state-run *The Daily Mail* and *The Times* to stop covering opposition events and personalities, and not to take any paid advertising from the pro-democracy movement. Ironically, Chiluba, Mwanawasa and others sued the state, arguing that President Kaunda's directive was unconstitutional and violated their rights. The High Court agreed and declared Kaunda's directive illegal (Republic of Zambia 2000). Less than one year later, Kaunda lost power to a popular movement backed strongly by the churches that owned the *National Mirror* (Phiri 2001).

Moore's study came out at about the same time that Francis Kasoma was wrapping up a similar media policy study.[1] Most of this work was an update of an earlier historiography of the press in Zambia (published in 1986), but this time he also included sections on broadcasting, book publishing, public relations and advertising, traditional media and some thoughts on media law. The most illuminating and relevant part of Kasoma's study was the summary of what he saw as 'policy bottlenecks that prevent … media organizations to achieve their goals and tasks' (1990: 85).

Firstly, Kasoma found that most top government officials 'did not fully understand the role of the media in general' and that this led to 'many wrong and bad policy decisions affecting the mass media collectively as well as individually' (ibid). Secondly, government officials had little trust in media professionals, making access to information difficult. Thirdly, the media was crippled and stifled by archaic legal restrictions and threats. Fourthly, there was a lack of coordination in public broadcasting, leading to a situation where different government ministries were duplicating efforts. For example, the Ministry of Education was packaging and broadcasting educational content. But so were the Ministry of Agriculture, the Ministry of Health and other government units. Finally, Kasoma lamented the lack of printing and broadcasting equipment and materials; and their cost when they were available.

This brief re-visitation of media policy from 1964 to 1991 is vital to present-day analysis because it affirms that while some of the 'policing' of the media changed in later years, many of the inherited limitations remain in place. Writing during Kaunda's time, Kasoma pleaded with the UNIP government not to 'force journalists [to] toe a ... line under the guise of a communication policy'. The appeal was clear: 'Mass media organizations should have the freedom to operate, the freedom to choose what to disseminate and how to disseminate it' (Kasoma 1990:100).

Sadly, at the time of writing this chapter, not much had changed. While the independent media had nominal space in which to broadcast and publish, its ability to be an effective actor in a democratic society remained severely constrained.

A United States (US) Department of State report of March 2007 catalogues arrests and harassments of media professionals in Zambia in 2006. It also contains many cases of libel and defamation against the media. According to the report, election seasons are particularly perilous. During the September 2006 elections, for example, the police attempted to close a Lusaka commercial station that was broadcasting election results live. Opposition activists stormed the offices of *The Post* for allegedly publishing inaccurate reports about their leaders.

Regarding the state media, the US report concluded that 'government exercised considerable influence ... including reviewing articles prior to publication and censuring individuals responsible for published articles or programs deemed offensive by the government' (US Department of State 2007).

The experience of Godfrey Malama, editor-in-chief of the government *The Daily Mail*, is a glaring example. Malama lost his job on 30 November 2006, soon after running a headline proclaiming that opposition figure Michael Sata – a thorn in the side of the Mwanawasa government – was leading in the 2006 polls. Mwanawasa later regained the lead and won the elections. In other words, just as it was under Kaunda's one-party state, so is it in contemporary 'democratic' Zambia (see Phiri 1999).

Media policy during the Chiluba government, 1991–2001

By the end of the 1980s, Zambians were drowning in economic woes and suffocating under Kaunda's intolerant political regime. The broadcast media aired unedited pro-government pronouncements while the print media scribbled and reprinted government press releases. The independent church-owned *National Mirror* was fighting running battles with the state and struggling to survive the financial crunch caused by the withdrawal of advertising revenue by government departments and a refusal by government sources to respond to its queries. The only government media outlet that gained popularity was Radio Mulungushi – the then newly introduced 24-hour channel that played African popular music.

Frederick Chiluba, a trade unionist turned political liberator, emerged leader of the pro-democracy Movement for Multiparty Democracy (MMD). The rhetoric was electrifying. Crowds were swayed, and so was the media fraternity. There were promises of a free media. The state-run broadcasting system would be privatised; so would the dailies. The hour had come for Zambians to say what they wanted. The government would walk away from media control. The media would finance and regulate itself. No more government subsidies and no more government gag orders either. The result of these and many other promising pronouncements by the MMD, set against the background of chronic fatigue and disillusionment with Kaunda's 27-year rule, was an overwhelming victory for the MMD in the 1991 election.

Zambia, then one of the first countries on the continent to remove a long-standing president through free and fair elections, became a 'poster boy' for African democratisation. The euphoria was contagious. Even in media circles, there was optimism that a policy would emerge that would facilitate an environment conducive to free media and democratic renewal. The appointment of Richard Sakala, then chairman of the Press Association of Zambia, as President Chiluba's media liaison officer, was read by many as a good sign. But the bubble soon burst. Not only did the new government hold on to the state-run ZNBC and the dailies, it was soon fighting running battles with the private media that it had allowed to mushroom. *The Post*, once a bedfellow of the MMD, became its arch-rival in much the same way as Kaunda had made an enemy of the *National Mirror*. Meanwhile, the ZNBC remained a parrot and *The Times* and *The Daily Mail* were tamed into lapdogs for the state. It was a case of *déjà vu*.

My 1999 examination of the state of the media in 'democratic' Zambia lamented the paralysis of the media that had taken place under Chiluba and the MMD government. It argued then that severe economic constraints, critical professional limitations and an unfavourable legal and policy environment had paralysed the media (Phiri 1999). Dumisani Moyo's 2006 doctoral thesis on broadcast policy later affirmed these observations – 'continued control of state-owned media and intimidation of the independent media' (p. 139). All the Chiluba regime did, according to Moyo, was to play a 'game of smoke and mirrors' around media policy, during which it drafted erudite papers, organised media policy workshops, appointed task forces on media reforms, read proposed media legislation in Parliament and delivered electrifying rhetoric about media freedom, but did nothing in terms of implementation.

Ministry of Information and Broadcasting (MIC) officials, however, refute the conclusion that there was hardly any movement toward clear media policy during the Chiluba years. Barker's sceptical question about Namibia, 'Is no policy a policy goal?' (2001) does not apply to Zambia, they say. MIC Senior Press Officer, Juliana Mwila, was emphatic about this when interviewed in 2007: 'We produced the country's first comprehensive media policy in 1996,' he said (Interview by author. Lusaka, 12 November 2007).

The 1996 document referred to above is of some importance to the present work because it illuminates the Zambian government's institutionalised thinking about the media. For instance, limitations in how information policy is defined are immediately apparent. It is understood as the 'provision of information to the public on all government programmes and achievement on the one hand and providing a feedback mechanism through which the public's views, opinions and suggestions are channelled to government on the other' (p.15). The state sees itself as the primary source of information, while the public plays a secondary role of giving feedback through a government-prescribed mechanism. The role of independent news-makers and media is neither included nor anticipated in this conceptualisation of media policy.

As outlined in the 1996 document, information policy goals included achieving countrywide coverage by radio and TV (obviously ZNBC), localised printing services for vernacular language newspapers, increased media outreach, the promotion of voter participation and the creation of a feedback mechanism. The other two goals are to promote the country's image and to attract tourism and international investment.

Information policy objectives include the promotion of rights to information, civic education, gender issues and HIV/AIDS awareness. Others are the more effective use of the media as an alarm system in cases of epidemic outbreaks and disasters; and as storage and publicity instruments for national events and for international promotion of the country. There is also the ambitious commitment to the creation of a 'comprehensive human and material resource development programme to strengthen capacity in the sector for improved delivery of services' (p.16).

Media policy in the document was addressed separately from general information policy and was understood to relate primarily to the operations of radio, television, and newspapers and other publications. The goals included covering the whole country with radio and television broadcasting through national and community broadcasting, the establishment of printing presses in the provinces, the upgrading of professionalism in the media and the promotion of press freedom.

The objectives of the media policy were many, but of special interest here was the plan to give state-run dailies full editorial autonomy (while retaining ownership) and making ZNBC a truly public broadcaster. These objectives represent an open admission by the government that not much had changed five years after the end of the one-party state.

The strategies the government outlined to achieve these objectives are impressive and worth close examination because they informed government behaviour in the post-Chiluba era. The government was going to attract investors into the Zambian media industry and liberally doll out TV and radio licenses. Laws impeding media freedom would be redrafted to allow greater freedom. Instead of the government policing the media, there would be self-regulating mechanisms. To top it all, the restrictive ZNBC Act of 1987 and the Broadcast Act of 1966 would be amended and repealed. New legislation would be proposed to make ZNBC 'operate more effectively as a public broadcasting service' (p. 24). Private broadcasters would be overseen by an autonomous Independent Broadcasting Authority (IBA).

According to this policy paper, the Ministry of Information and Broadcasting would be a neutral umpire – not emperor – tasked with formulating and implementing policy for the creation of an enabling environment for the full development of the media. But by 2001, when Chiluba lost power, this grand information and media policy statement was gathering dust in the archives of the ministry. Moyo's conclusion about media policy during the 10 years of the Chiluba administration is true: 'little had changed since Kaunda' (2006: 139).

Media policy during the Mwanawasa government, 2001–2007

Zambia's post-Kaunda constitution limited the President to two terms. However, as Chiluba's constitutionally mandated two-term presidency was coming to an end, he sought to change the constitution to enable him to vie for a third term. The resulting fracas was a blessing in disguise. The MMD melted and fractured. Top leaders such as Michael Sata and General Christon Tembo abandoned Chiluba and founded rival parties. Civil society was mobilised and motivated to form one front. Private media, for instance *The Post* and some commercial and community radio stations, became more vocal. Even the tamed government media woke up from its slumber. Thus by the time Chiluba's handpicked successor, President Levy Mwanawasa took office, the MMD and its government was in desperate need to redeem, reposition and rehabilitate itself. It did not help that Mwanawasa's electoral victory against the plethora of competing parties was razor-thin and challenged in the courts. Parliament was captured by the opposition. All this nurtured a transformative environment for media policy.

However, while Mwanawasa's 'New Deal' government was quick to pounce on corruption suspects – including President Chiluba – and to act on 'development' programmes, it was sluggish when it came to media policy. The new leadership 'did not consider media reform as a matter that needed urgent attention' (Moyo 2006: 172). To the contrary, the new government very quickly exhibited dictatorial tendencies toward private media operations.

Omega TV, a Lusaka broadcaster launched by Richard Sakala, former media liaison person for President Chiluba, provides a good example of this. Sakala, like his former master, was embroiled in corruption charges and was finally arrested by government law enforcement agents. 'My arrest on Friday August 2, 2002 was dramatic – it was stuff from James Bond movies,' he narrated in his planned post-imprisonment memoir. 'Soon after I was arrested, six heavily armed policemen stormed the [Omega] television station on the 23rd floor of Lusaka's Findeco House and ordered its immediate shut down' (Sakala, forthcoming).

Lawyers challenged the closure of the station but, according to Sakala, the government was 'adamant' and 'lied' in the courts that the station had broken licensing regulations. Eventually, a letter surfaced – allegedly from President Mwanawasa to the Minister of Information and Broadcasting, Newstead Zimba. 'I direct that the license that has been issued to Mr Sakala should be cancelled forthwith,' it said. The letter added that licenses should not be issued to 'people like Richard Sakala who do not mean well to this administration.' Sakala's lawyers put up a fight, but it was all futile. Omega let go of its staff and accrued rentals. The Zambian branch of the Media Institute of Southern Africa, MISA-Zambia, loaned Omega money from its 'threatened' media fund to pay for the latter's rent, but it was clear that the broadcaster had hit a dead end.

Months before the state pulled the plug on Omega Television, the media fraternity had already 'galvanized itself into action and launched a sustained campaign to resuscitate the implementation of media law reforms' (Matibini 2006: 43–44). Several factors favoured this move. As noted earlier, Chiluba's third-term bid weakened the MMD's grip on power as the presidency was won on a thin margin and Parliament lost to the opposition. Chiluba's bid had infuriated civil society and rejuvenated its activism. The position the private media, especially *The Post*, took in the third-term debate affirmed its role in society as the avenue of mass communication for voices ostracised by the state media. Thus media professionals, lawmakers and civil society activists came together to champion media-law reform.

Matibini, himself a participant and insider in the process, details the public and private events that started in January 2002 (2006: 43–50). Earlier in March, media organisations had published a document that called for the creation of an Independent Broadcasting Board; and for the repeal of the 1987 ZNBC Act and the 1966 Broadcasting Act. New legislation was called for. Ironically, these recommendations were reminiscent of the government's 1996 information and media policy document. However, there were two key differences this time. First, it was the whole media fraternity that was making these proclamations, not just the government. Secondly, there was parliamentary support to introduce this new legislation into Parliament without executive support.

The momentum towards new media policy and regulation seemed unstoppable. By the end of July, three new private bills – the Independent Broadcasting Bill, the Broadcasting Bill and the Freedom of Information Bill – were ready, and opposition MPs had pledged to present the bills to Parliament. On 1 August the bills were presented to the Speaker of the National Assembly. All was set.

Then the government started the usual tactical moves on media policy. First, Minister Newstead Zimba told Parliament that the government was committed to media reform, so there was no need for private bills. A month later, Zimba's deputy, Webby Chipili, took the media by surprise when he announced that the government had put together a task force to formulate new media law. Later, Vice-President Enoch Kavindele called a high-level meeting at which he said that the government would introduce favourable media legislation.

In October it felt as if the three private bills had survived – they were gazetted and published in the press. But in November, the government took its tactical moves to a new level. It 'borrowed heavily from the private member's bills' and rushed its own editions of the bills into the Government Gazette and the press. Instead of buying into the idea of a new broadcasting act, the government opted to patch up the ZNBC Act by 'simply removing the licensing powers … and transferring that function to IBA' (ibid: 50). By the end of 2002, the IBA Act and the ZNBC (Amendment) Act were law while the Freedom of Information Bill was still in limbo. This sent a clear message that it was difficult to go around the Zambian government when it came to media policy-making.

The amendment of the ZNBC Act and the enactment of the new IBA Act were major achievements for the media in Zambia. The ZNBC (Amendment) Act promised a broadcasting operation that would be practically free of state policing. The minister's role was limited to constituting an ad hoc committee that would 'recommend' members to a nine-member board that would run the ZNBC free of government interference. The information minister would present the nominated board members to Parliament for ratification. The board would hire a director to manage the ZNBC as a professional public broadcaster. The ZNBC's new assignment included tasks such as to 'defend democratic freedoms' and 'broadcast news and current affairs programmes which shall be comprehensive, unbiased and independent' (ibid: 373). The ZNBC would generate revenue from advertising as well as through license fees to be paid by all TV owners. In short, the corporation was primed for top performance as a true public media entity.

The IBA Act was as promising. The creation of the Authority would follow the same process as that of the ZNBC board. The information minister would create an ad hoc committee tasked with 'recommending' nine board members, and the minister would then present these names to Parliament for ratification. It was all simple and clear. As if that were not good enough, the Authority, once in operation, would 'not be subject to the direction of any other person or authority' (ibid: 340). With the government off its back, the Authority was tasked to 'promote a pluralistic and diverse broadcasting industry' and issue licenses, assign frequencies and establish high professional and ethical standards in the industry (ibid: 339–340). The Authority would be funded by Parliament and generate additional revenue from licensing fees. The only time the Authority's autonomy could be overridden was through the remote possibility of a state of emergency. In that case, the President could take over some, or all, of the broadcasting operations in the country.

The legislation of these two acts essentially brought Zambia into alignment with the African Charter on Broadcasting, which states that broadcast 'regulation should be exercised by public authorities which are protected against interference, particularly of a political or economic nature, by, among other things, an appointment process for members which is open … and is not controlled by any particular political party' (MISA 2006: 256). The media fraternity was thrilled and celebrated what appeared to be the final victory over state control of broadcasting. The government was left reeling by what appeared to be a defeat. It had been outmanoeuvred in the policy-making process and had given in to demands of media organisations and civil society. To make things worse, these bills were presented to Parliament by government itself – not as the private member bills initially intended.

The government had taken itself off the stage in the media policy arena—or had it?

Was the Mwanawasa government living up to the promises to democratise the media which previous governments had promised but never delivered on? Moyo (2006: 191) did not believe this was the case. 'I argue that the partial opening of the policy process is not in any way a sign of the erosion of state power. It is more of a 'tactical retreat' in a situation where the state remains very much in control in terms of making policies within its territorial boundaries'.

The government retreated into what looked like a sincere commitment to the implementation of these laws. The structures were created for the selection of board members for the IBA and the ZNBC. But when the proposed names were presented to the then Minister of Information and Broadcasting, Mutale Nalumango, for ratification in Parliament, she baulked. The government did not approve of some of the proposed IBA and ZNBC board members, and so would not proceed to with their ratification. She said she wanted a new list of names.

The media was infuriated. MISA-Zambia, the Media Women's Association, *The Post* newspaper and others took the minister to court. The arguments were solid: the vetting of names of proposed board members was illegal and irrational; usurped the powers of Parliament; and were in bad faith. The High Court Judge, Gregory Phiri, was persuaded by the media's case against the state and delivered a charged five-point ruling. This is worth quoting verbatim here, because it illuminates why and how good law can be a powerful tool for media reform (Republic of Zambia 2004):

a.   Does the Minister have power to appoint the directors or members of the two boards? My answer is YES she does because the law says so.

b.   Is the Minister's power to appoint the directors or members unfettered? My answer is NO because the law itself provides a specific method and specific pre-conditions for such appointments.

c.   Does the law empower the Minister to consider any other qualifications or views other than those prescribed in the two statutes? My answer is NO it does not and that if that were the intention of the legislature, the law would have specifically empowered the Minister to consider other qualifications or views.

d.   Does the law empower the Minister to substitute the names of nominee for appointment as director or members? My answer is NO because, again, if that were the intention of the legislature, the law would have specifically provided for that power.

e.   Does the law empower the Minister to veto any nominated candidate. My answer is NO, it does not.

f.   Has the Minister complied with the prescribed methods of appointment of members to the Board of Directors? My answer is NO because the Minister has not availed the National Assembly the names of the recommended appointees for ratification. As such the Boards cannot take off the ground.

The government had suffered a major legal blow. What was particularly biting was that Judge Phiri read the government's behaviour as an attempt at circumventing democratisation of the media. 'The moral of the two pieces of legislation is clearly democratic in nature – and I have taken judicial notice that Zambia has embraced democracy in its full content,' he also said. 'From reading this new law, one is left with no doubt that the law is deliberately aimed at detaching Government from direct and day-to-day control of both the public as well as the private media organizations in this country,' he added. The judgement also exposed the government's motives when he stated that the Minister's behaviour 'prevents and frustrates the vital reform of the media law in this country'. According to Judge Phiri, the Mwanawasa government was still enmeshed in the assumption that it could handle the media in the same way as the Kaunda and Chiluba administrations had done: 'I have no doubt that erroneous belief [that she had power to vet nominees] stems from the previous status of law before the reforms' (ibid).

The media fraternity was exuberant. Finally, not only had the media succeeded in getting the government to pass media reform legislation, but it had also succeeded in using the new legislation to win cases in court. This was unprecedented. For the first time, Zambia had a truly liberalised media policy. But, sadly, this was not to continue. The Mwanawasa government, which was dominated by lawyers, would not take the High Court ruling sitting down and chance losing control over the media. It regrouped and trooped to the Supreme Court.

The government's legal strategy was precise: avoid arguments over democratisation of the media, and focus on procedures instead. Its core argument before the Supreme Court was: What are the distinct functions of the ad hoc committees and the minister in the procedures leading to the appointment of the autonomous IBA and ZNBC boards? The Attorney General drew the Supreme Court's attention to the point that the job of the ad hoc appointment committee was simply to 'recommend' candidates to the minister, and that she had been under no obligation to accept all the recommendations. The minister was not just a 'rubber stamp or conveyor belt', he added (Republic of Zambia 2007).

The Supreme Court was persuaded that there was no other natural way to interpret the word 'recommend' than by what it says. Parliament had chosen the word, and the Judiciary was not about to amend the legislation. The High Court decision was set aside, with harsh commentary delivered by the Supreme Court to the lower court. 'The approach taken by the learned trial Judge amounts to nothing but the usurpation of the legislative powers of the Legislature by the Judiciary. It is not the duty of the court to edit or paraphrase the laws passed by Parliament,' it stated.

The March 2007 Supreme Court decision deflated media enthusiasm: the 'personal whims' of ministers were back in the picture. Although the IBA and ZNBC boards remained legally autonomous once they were in operation, the appointment process remains closely controlled by the government. Not only does the minister appoint members of the ad hoc appointments committee, but she also has the power to sieve the appointed candidates before presenting them to Parliament. And since Parliament is traditionally dominated by the ruling party (and those subservient to it), it is hard to see how the house can reject the names of those presented by the government. Therefore, there is a real danger that the boards, though legally independent, may be infiltrated by pro-establishment pundits masquerading as champions of media freedom. In that way, the government found its way back into the boardrooms of both the IBA and the ZNBC.

Why do Zambian governments skirt around media policy?

By the end of 2007, there was silence in government media circles and also among the private media organisations about what was going to happen to the two acts. Were the IBA Act and the ZNBC (Amendment) Act a blessing or a curse? And who was it who was blessed or cursed?

The answer to these questions is not yet clear. Obviously, the government is in a favourable position. There is a strong possibility that it will go back to Parliament and ask the legislature to edit itself, so that it is clear to all that the government can vet the names of those proposed by the Ad Hoc Appointments Committee. It is also possible that the media will lick its wounds, swallow its pride, and agree to a middle-of-the-road list of nominations to be forwarded to Parliament for ratification. What is clear, though, is that the Zambian government has the capacity and the determination to work around media policy formulation and implementation until its opponents are perilously exhausted.

The fundamental question to ask is: Why is it that despite impressive proclamations by three successive governments (before and soon after coming to power) about the value of media autonomy in a democratic society, there is little evidence of a sincere commitment to the formulation and implementation of viable media policy? Why did the Kaunda government simply clamp down on the media? Why did the Chiluba government play games that ended up with a government information and media policy paper that is of little value? Why did the Mwanawasa government, weakened by the circumstances under which it came to power, appear to support new media legislation, only to put up fierce legal fights over semantics when it came to implementation? Why is the state of the media in Zambia still more or less what it was back in 1964?

The answer is amazingly short and simple: power. President Chiluba was honest when he confessed that 'power is sweet.' Zambian governments love and support democracy when, and only when, they are in power and in full control. In general, an autonomous media represents a diffusion and dilution of this power. Suddenly, the government finds itself sharing the power of information gathering and dissemination with private (and usually, competing) actors. A free media is inquisitive; it investigates and poses intrusive questions. A free media also prints and broadcasts dissenting voices. Because they would no longer be in control of what would be said or revealed, all this makes Zambian governments jittery. They find it hard to go to bed peacefully not knowing what the next day's headlines may announce. It becomes preferable to hold onto restrictive legal regimes, and to police the media using shifting policy positions.

What is unfortunate about this behaviour by Zambian governments is that it creates and/or affirms the belief among many that those in power have a lot to hide. Thus, instead of focusing its energy on governing the country and delivering development goals, the government spends much time denying allegations of all sorts. What is even more unfortunate is that, by its own behaviour, it undermines the ability of the state media to do what it would want them to be doing: communicating its programmes and accomplishments to the people. When the people see and feel that the media are directly or indirectly state-controlled, they become sceptical about any news that is positive about the government. Their presumption is that the media carry such information simply to remain on air on in circulation. In short, the media get to be seen as state propaganda machinery.

References

Balule, B. 2004. *Undue Restriction: Laws Impacting on Media in the SADC*. Media Institute of Southern Africa: Windhoek.

Banda, F. (2006a). *Zambia: Research Findings and Conclusions*. BBC World Service Trust: London.

———. 2006b. Zambia. In *Mixed Signals: The State of Broadcasting in Southern Africa*. Lusaka: Panos Southern Africa.

Barker, J. 2001. Is no policy a policy goal? In *Media, Democracy and Renewal in Southern Africa*, ed. K. Tomaselli and H. Dunn, 13–24. Colorado Springs, USA: International Academic Publishers.

Kasoma, F. 1990. *Communication Policies in Zambia*. Tampere: University of Tampere.

Matibini, P. 2006. *The Struggle for Media Law Reforms in Zambia*. Lusaka: Media Institute of Southern Africa (Zambia).

Media Institute of Southern Africa. 2006. *So This is Democracy? The State of Media Freedom in Southern Africa, 2006*. Windhoek: Media Institute of Southern Africa.

Media Institute of Southern Africa (Zambia). 2007. MISA-Zambia disappointed with MIBS minister's remarks on public media. Press statement, available at http://www.misazambia.org.zm/ (accessed 31 March 2009).

Ministry of Information and Broadcasting Services. 1996. *Information and Media Policy*. Lusaka: Author.

Moore, R. C. 1991. *The Political Reality of Freedom of the Press in Zambia*. Lusaka: Multimedia Publications.

Moyo, D. 2006. *Broadcasting Policy Reform and Democratization in Zambia and Zimbabwe, 1990–2005: Global Pressures, National Responses*. PhD Dissertation, Department of Media and Communication, University of Oslo.

Phiri, I. 1999. Media in 'democratic' Zambia: Problems and prospects. *Africa Today* 46(2): 53–65.

———. 2001. *Proclaiming Political Pluralism: Churches and Political Transitions in Africa*. Westport, CT: Praeger Publishers.

Phiri, B. and D. Powers. 2001. Plurality and power relations in Zambian broadcasting. *Media Development* XLVIII (2): 25–30.

Republic of Zambia. 1990. *Arthur Lubinda Wina, Fredrick Jacob Chiluba and others* v. *The Attorney General* (HP/1878/1990). Lusaka: Government Printer.

——. 2004. *Fanwell Chembo et al.* v. *The Minister of Information and Broadcasting Service and the Attorney General* (2004/HP/05120). Lusaka: Government Printer.

——. 2007. *Minister of Information and Broadcasting Services and Another* v. *Chembo and Others* (76/205) [2007] ZMSC 11; SCZ No. 11 of 2007 (15 March 2007). Lusaka: Government Printer.

Sakala, R. *Rules of Men, Not of Laws*. Unpublished manuscript.

United States Department of State. 2007. *Zambia: Country Report on Human Rights Practices – 2006*. Washington, DC: Bureau of Democracy, Human Rights and Labor.

Towards a changing media policy and regulatory framework in Zambia

8

Caesar Jere

This chapter explores the impact of media policy in Zambia on the role of the media in the country's democratic process. It examines media policy and regulatory changes in Zambia in the new millennium against the backdrop of global and regional developments in the communications industry, among them corporate capitalism, digitalisation, convergence, competition and concentration. An attempt is made to explain how these factors either limit or enhance the role of the media as institutions of the public sphere in Zambia. The chapter also discusses the influence of Zambian civil society in media policy advocacy.

Since the early1990s, when Africa experienced the winds of liberal change that had earlier swept through Eastern Europe, there has been considerable democratic change in many African countries. Zambia was one of the first countries on the continent to return to multi-party politics in 1991, after 18 years of Kenneth Kaunda's one-party rule (from independence in 1964, Zambia adopted a multi-party system until 1972, when a one-party state was introduced). The coming of plural politics brought liberal policies that transformed the face of the then socialist-controlled economy to one that opened private investment across many sectors of the economy. The communications industry was no exception, as new reforms to liberalise the industry were introduced. This saw a number of new entrants into the media industry, particularly in the broadcasting arena, which had hitherto been a domain of the state. There was also a proliferation of newspapers and magazines, though many of the new titles folded up soon after being launched. This was mainly the result of lack of sustainability and poor business acumen. The affected publications include *The Chronicle, Monitor* and *The Today* newspapers; and magazines such as *Zambian Farmer, Tiyende* and *Profit*.

When the government of Frederick Chiluba ascended to power in 1991, it promised to liberalise and deregulate the media industry. This was achieved to some extent. However, in due course, Chiluba's government started backtracking on its election promise to promote media freedom and diversity. For instance, there were attempts by the state to legislate the regulation of media practice. The country recorded media violations that included the banning of a *Post* publication in 1996 and the suspension of Radio Phoenix's broadcast licence in 2000. Zambia's media-policy, legal and regulatory frameworks have since remained inadequate to respond to democratic ideals and technological changes in the communications sector. Although some attempts have been made to legislate media-friendly laws – such as the Independent Broadcasting Authority (IBA) Act of 2002 and the Zambia National Broadcasting Corporation (ZNBC) Amendment Act, also of 2002, the boards mandated by the acts to oversee the operations of the IBA and ZNBC had not been constituted at the time of concluding this chapter.

The context

It can be argued that Zambia's media policy and legal framework are insufficient to amply address governance issues in a democratic society. Adequate media policy and media-friendly laws are a prerequisite to the promotion of media freedom and the existence of pluralistic communication platforms on which democracy can thrive. The Zambian media-policy and legal frameworks fall short of adequately addressing media freedom and diversity. Furthermore, these structures also fail to effectively tackle changes in technology and market developments in the communications sector. It is therefore imperative to identify the root(s) of this problem and make recommendations towards the realisation of more favourable media policy and a regulatory framework that respond to the democratic ideals of the new millennium – namely to serve the public good, rather than parochial political or market interests. Adequate structures should also be able to respond to global changes in the communications industry.

This chapter assumes that the role of the media in the democratisation and developmental process of Zambian society is of cardinal importance. As an element of the public sphere, the media are expected to play a critical and impartial role in the creation of a public domain that accommodates divergent views. In this regard, it is expected that the media should serve the public interest and guard against undue influence by any force – political or economic. It is therefore assumed that media policy and legislation should reflect the public interest, rather than arbitrarily or deviously protect and further the interests of those who hold political or economic power (Herman & McChesney 1999; McNair 2003).

Theoretical perspectives

The theoretical and conceptual framework of this chapter is informed by the political economy of communication. It examines the interplay between the construction and consumption of media messages on the one hand, and the economic organisation of media industries on the other hand. The approach seeks to establish 'how different ways of financing and organising cultural production have traceable consequences for the range of discourses and representations in the public domain and for audiences' access to them' (Golding & Murdock 2000:76). From the onset, political economy has been concerned with analysing the scope of public intervention in the communications industry. As Golding and Murdock note,

> Classical political economists and their present-day followers start from the assumption that public intervention ought to be minimised and market forces given the widest possible freedom of operation. Critical political economists on the other hand point to the distortions and inequalities of market systems and argue that these deficiencies can only be rectified by public intervention, though they disagree on the forms that these [sic] should take (2000: 76).

The focal point of an analysis of the political economy of the media is an examination of how the different forces that influence the production and distribution of media commodities can support or limit the notion of the media as a public sphere. This requires an understanding of the system of ownership of media houses in relation to the influence and control of their operations – of how the power relations influence the production of media commodities (ibid).

Furthermore, it is also important to examine the influence of state regulation on the performance of media institutions. For instance, it is argued that in most public service broadcasting (PSB) institutions worldwide, the state has been seen to be protecting the public interest by lessening the influence of market-oriented products of commercial broadcasting (Hoynes 1994; Ang 1991). However, critics of state intervention argue that there is no good justification for such action as it erodes the principle of consumer sovereignty. Besides, cynics argue that commercial broadcasting can also provide public services (Peacock 1997).

The advocates of the market approach also argue that 'the notion of the public interest is sometimes used or seen as an ideological device designed to cloak unjustified regulatory ambitions on the part of governments or even a weapon in the assault on more fundamental liberties of expression and of business enterprise' (McQuail 1995:3).

Market concentration and competition:
global and local perspectives

Global technological advances have abetted market concentration and consolidation all over the world, among the latest being that of the Internet company America Online (AOL), 'which took over the established broadcaster and cable operator Time Warner, giving it control of Time Magazine, CNN, as well as Warner Brothers Films, Warner Records and substantial cable interests' (Levy 2001: xvii). The proliferation of media conglomerates has brought a new dimension to the debate about the misapplication of power by media proprietors. These conglomerates operate in prohibitive 'oligopolistic markets with substantial barriers to entry' (Herman & Chesney 1999:104).

The communication platforms have also spread to developing nations. India, for instance, had its first satellite transmission when CNN made an impact during the Gulf War of 1990–1991. This was followed by the introduction of a five-channel satellite transmission that Rupert Murdoch later bought off (Sakr 2001).

In Africa, South Africa's MultiChoice multi-channel satellite pay TV appears to be at the helm of cross-border transmission. MultiChoice is well established across the continent, including in Zambia.

Like other developing countries, Zambia has borne the effects of satellite 'incursions'. The national broadcaster, ZNBC, has been steadily losing its audience, especially among the educated and well-to-do elites living in metropolitan cities and towns, who have opted to switch to the satellite pay channels that offer diverse programming (Banda 2006b:101). This has pushed ZNBC to embark on a programme variation exercise in order to compete with a multiplicity of media outlets that include cross-border channels, a move likely to subtract time from its commitment as a public broadcaster (Banda 2007:29).

Apart from MultiChoice, there were two other satellite pay TV providers registered by 2007. They are Mr. Strong (My TV), beaming channels mostly from the Middle East; and Gateway Television (GTV), a British firm that was granted its broadcast licence in October 2007. The coming of GTV and My TV appeared to have signalled stiff competition in the pay TV arena. This competition has been further intensified by an influx of free-to-air decoders being sold by business houses with approved franchises.

In August 2007, GTV, which was established in some parts of Africa including Kenya and Uganda, won 80 per cent of the English Premier Soccer League broadcasting rights held by the United Kingdom's Barclays Bank, to beam live soccer sporting events in sub-Saharan Africa (including Zambia). Previously, MultiChoice had held the rights in Zambia. However, the South African firm lost the bid to GTV and only secured 20 per cent of the rights, allowing it to show just a few selected English Premier Soccer League games. This development infuriated a large number of MultiChoice 'soccer subscribers', who demanded the reimbursement of their subscription fees. Many customers indicated that they would unsubscribe from MultiChoice to join GTV, whose subscriber base reached 4 000 by December 2007 (Chitala 2007).

The British GTV company appeared to have tactfully connived with its sister British firm, Barclays Bank, to win the bid and also to offer ZNBC free-to-air rights to transmit similar English League games as those allocated to MultiChoice (Zambia). This move further weakened the position of the latter, as most viewers preferred to get the better package beamed by GTV, or alternatively to watch the games on ZNBC without having to pay. The 2008 world economic recession, which had adversely affected many businesses across the globe, again changed the state of play. GTV's parent company in the United Kingdom was forced to wind up its operations in January 2009, a development that affected its satellite companies all over the world, including that in Zambia. As a result, MultiChoice (Zambia) regained the English Premier Soccer League rights and many of the 'soccer customers' that it had lost to GTV.

In most developing nations, including Zambia, advertising has been increasing its influence in determining the content of what is shown not only on commercial television, but also on public television. Advertisers sponsor films that may not necessarily appeal to the larger public, but instead are targeted at special audiences with the capacity to purchase the goods or services advertised. The same is true for the print media, in which advertisers buy large spaces for their products and services while leaving little space for news and other content of public interest. A content analysis done in 2005 of the ZNBC main news revealed that the total time apportioned to advertisements during the main news bulletin lasting about 40 minutes was almost the same time as that allocated to the actual news items (Siame 2006). In an ideal situation, a public broadcaster should carry more news, and educational and horizon-stretching programmes, than commercial content.

In Zambia, ZNBC receives grants through Parliament to enable it to carry out its mandate as a public broadcaster. However, these finances are paltry and cannot meet the requirements of a business that is very costly. As a result, the ZNBC Amendment Act of 2002 introduced a television licence fee to supplement the income from commercial programming and rescue the public broadcaster from its financial doldrums. However, the fee levied is token (about 80 US cents per month) and the number of television sets owned by the public is still small. In 1998, only 26 per cent of Zambians owned television sets (Central Statistical Office 1998).

It can therefore be argued that advertising will remain one of the major sources of funding for ZNBC, and that this may have a lasting effect on the realisation of the ideals of PSB in Zambia, as commercial programming is intensified. However, it is worth pointing out that the notion of commercial television and radio in Zambia is a relatively new phenomenon; and so there has not yet been any real concern regarding the need for state intervention over commercial enterprises that threaten the survival of public broadcasting, as is the case in most developed Western countries. Ironically, the concern in Zambia, as in most other developing nations (Price & Verhulst 1998:23),[1] is the government's interference in the running of public media, in particular broadcasting, which should represent diverse sections of society rather than promote partisan political interests. The ruling elite's ideas and opinions continue to dominate the public media, continually promoting the group's interests and crowding out dissenting views that are in conflict with the state's political agenda. As a result the professionalism of media practitioners is at stake – they fear losing their jobs if they stand in the government's way. 'The media's accountability to the government extends as far as the everyday working conditions of reporters in that work routines are conditioned by a plethora of factors, such as fear of reprisal, job insecurity, economic uncertainty etc' (Phiri & Powers 2001). For instance, in September 2007, the then Minister of Information and Broadcasting, Mike Mulongoti, cautioned journalists working in the public media 'not to criticise government and its leaders because they have jobs to protect' (Silwamba 2007:1). On the other hand, a critical section of the private media has been widely driven by partisan interests of its own – representing mostly the political opposition and mercantile pursuits. The 2008 presidential by-election was a clear testimony to polarised reporting, with the opposition supported by the private media and the public media siding with the ruling party. It should, however, be pointed out that the private media, notably the *Post* newspaper, has been instrumental in checking the excesses of political power holders from the Kaunda era up to the current time. This state of affairs clearly demonstrates the power relations in the media industry in Zambia and is critical in analysing the political economy of the media terrain in the country.

Media policy framework

The Zambian media-policy framework is articulated in the media-policy statement drafted by the Zambia Ministry of Information and Broadcasting Services (ZMIBS) in 1996 and subsequently revised in 1999. According to this document, the broader policy objective of the ZMIBS is, 'to promote and facilitate the growth of a sustainable media industry, capable of enhancing the free flow of information and freedom of expression for national development.' The framework highlights the government's three main policy goals, which are (ZMIBS 1999):

- to increase media outreach and access to all, particularly to rural communities;

- to pursue legal reforms to enhance citizens' right to information and freedom of expression and freedom of the press; and

• to encourage private investment in the media and media support industries.

The policy envisages freedom of the press and good governance by enacting the Freedom of Information Act; turning ZNBC into a public broadcaster; turning *The Times of Zambia* and the *Zambia Daily Mail* into publicly owned newspapers not answerable to the government of the day; and increasing access to information for all as a human right (Banda 2006b: 104). The policy also addresses issues of how to improve poor media infrastructure, inadequate funding in the media industry, poor distribution of media products, capacity-building, professional ethics, gender sensitivity and promotion of the Zambian culture (ibid).

Prior to the 1996 policy, the United Independence Party (UNIP) government under the leadership of Kaunda made policy directives based on Kaunda's philosophy of humanism, in which all state apparatuses, including nationalised media, served the interests and programmes of the one-party state. These directives were clearly pronounced in 1975 by Kaunda, in a watershed speech to the national council of UNIP.

It can be argued that Zambia's media policy is outdated as it does not adequately address modern changes in the communications sector. For instance, there is hardly any attempt to redefine broadcasting in view of new, converged diffusion platforms such as the Internet, satellite transmission, mobile telephony and related technologies. The restricted radius of coverage for radio and television stations has also become questionable, in view of the digitalisation process that allows compressed radio and television signals to be conveyed instantly through the Internet all over the world. Radio and television signals from Zambia that can be accessed on the Internet in Europe and other parts of the world, have a limited radius of transmission within Zambia itself. This in effect means that the regulation of radio to cover a certain distance has become ineffective owing to the technological convergence of media platforms and diffusion services that can carry audio and video streamed data on the Internet. Radio Phoenix, Q-FM Radio and ZNBC Radio, are examples of radio stations that can diffuse their broadcasts on the Internet and can be heard from anywhere in the world (MISA 2007).

Furthermore, while modern broadcasting technology now cuts across national borders, the 1996 policy framework 'simply acknowledges the existence of satellite pay TV without addressing the need to protect local content in the face of cheaper foreign productions or to draft new regulations for such media' (Banda 2006b: 106). The policy does not address the changes in technology in the broadcasting and communications sector that have an effect on regulatory issues relating to new diffusion services and merging media platforms and their market impact. An example is that of the IBA, whose regulatory functions may prove to be invalid when it becomes operational – as it is modelled for sector-specific regulation of broadcasting.

Thus, it can be argued that broadcast policy and regulation in Zambia is inadequate, and in some cases redundant, in addressing technological changes in the communications sector.

Information and communication technology (ICT) policy

However, by adopting an ICT policy in 2005, which it subsequently launched in March 2007, Zambia appears to be progressively responding to global changes. The ICT policy framework suggests 'proposals to re-establish the regulatory framework of broadcasting to recognise convergence of technologies through the proposed Electronic Communication Authority (ECA) Bill produced in January, 2005'(MISA 2007: 127). This is aimed at establishing a merged communications regulator equivalent to the Independent Communications Authority of South Africa. Zambia's ICT policy seeks, among other things, to use ICTs to bridge the digital divide between Zambians living in the urban areas and those in the rural areas. In this regard the government, through the state-owned telecommunications company, ZAMTEL, and the national electricity supply company, ZESCO, had embarked, in the mid-2000s, on an initiative to install a fibre-optic cable system across the country. This will enable the transmission of various forms of electronic data over long distances at higher speeds, and will essentially 'feed into all forms of communication platforms – computers, television, radio, telephony and other related technologies' (Jere 2008: 202). The policy envisages the transformation of Zambia, by 2030, into an economy based on information and knowledge, which is supported by consistent development and access to ICTs by all citizens (ZMCT 2005).

The ICT policy makes suggestions to constantly review the legal and regulatory framework in relation to changes in the communications industry with a view to 'implement a flexible and dynamic technology neutral legal/regulatory and licensing framework that restricts regulation to the barest minimum; takes into account and reflects issues relating to convergence within the sector' (ICT policy 2005:49). To this effect, an ICT Act which addresses issues of technology convergence, among other issues, was enacted in August, 2009. This Act, which repealed the Telecommunications Act of 1994, will pave the way for the formation of a more effective regulator – the Zambia Information Communications Technology Authority – to replace the Communications Authority of Zambia (Chitala, 2009).

The legal framework

At the dawn of independence in 1964, the new nationalist government inherited a media system that was designed to serve the needs of the colonial settlers. In due course, the government nationalised the press and broadcasting so that they could conform to the new political order of promoting Kaunda's version of African socialism. To this effect, in 1966 an Act of Parliament was passed to form the Zambia Broadcasting Service (ZBS).

In 1972, Kaunda introduced one-party rule in order to eliminate the mounting opposition from fellow nationalists who had fallen out of his favour. The media became tools to propagate and justify the state's action of introducing the one-party state, and to solicit support from the masses. At that time, African nationalist governments, including Zambia, argued that the introduction of one-party states would eliminate conflict and unite opposing sides. It was also argued that national resources would be redirected, away from politicking and towards development (Moyo 2006: 217; Nyerere 1979).

The nationalists asserted that there were no class struggles in Africa to necessitate the formation of opposition political parties in line with Karl Marx's theory of class struggles between the bourgeoisie and the proletariat, as was the case in the Western world. They averred that Africans lived in harmony and brotherhood and that no classes existed among them (Nyerere 1979).

In propagating these political thoughts the Zambian nationalists used the media intensively, to help them garner support, eliminate opposition and achieve consensus. These arguments, some of them seemingly justifiable at that time, were later discarded at the re-introduction of political pluralism in the early 1990s (Mwanakatwe 1994). In 1991 multi-party politics were re-introduced after pressure on the Kaunda government from the labour movement, religious organisations and the intelligentsia. Kaunda was voted out of power and replaced by Frederick Chiluba, who had hitherto been the leader of the trade union movement in Zambia. Following Chiluba's ascendancy to power, media reforms were introduced to stimulate the liberalisation and deregulation of the media industry in line with the Movement for Multiparty Democracy's election manifesto of introducing liberal market reforms in the media industry (Kasoma 1997). However, some observers have noted that this was 'cautious deregulation' as licences were mostly issued to Christian applicants (Banda 2006b). Banda further notes:

> It was this 'Christian determinism' that resulted in a rather skewed distribution of radio broadcasting licences, with the majority given to Christian groupings. The new government of the Movement for Multiparty Democracy (MMD) had replaced the United National Independence Party (UNIP) regime. In embracing a cautious deregulation of the broadcasting market, the MMD wanted to be seen to be reformist, while at the same time remaining firmly in command of broadcasting.

Banda's comments can be supported in view of the fact that the MMD government continued to be not only 'cautious' but also elusive in handling media reforms. For instance, although the MMD government slowly responded to global and regional influence, there was no serious political will after 2002 to implement Acts of

Parliament that were critical pieces of legislation in the deregulation of the media in Zambia. The IBA Act and the ZNBC (Amendment) Act of 2002 are valid examples of this tendency. Similarly, there were no considerable attempts to revise archaic laws that limit the performance of the media as watchdogs against the excesses of governors.

Subsequently to this, Zambia saw the enactment of the 1993 ZNBC Licensing Regulations Act, the 1994 Telecommunications Act and the 1994 Radio Communications Act. These pieces of legislation were all legal instruments designed to liberalise and deregulate the communications sector. However, with the coming of the liberal reforms, a number of radio and television stations emerged to challenge ZNBC's monopoly (Banda 1998: 106).

In 2002, the Independent Broadcasting Authority (IBA) Act had been enacted to provide for independent regulation of the sector. In the same year, the ZNBC Amendment Act had been passed to amend the 1987 ZNBC Act, which vested power in the minister of information and broadcasting to regulate broadcasting in consultation with ZNBC. However, by the end of 2008, Zambia's broadcasting industry, which should have been regulated by an autonomous body since the passing of the IBA Act, continued to be managed, supervised and regulated by the minister of information and broadcasting under the ZNBC Act of 1987.

From 2002 up to the time of concluding this chapter, efforts to have the IBA board established were frustrated by the lack of political will by the MMD government. The names of prospective board members for the IBA had not been submitted to Parliament by the government for ratification. The same applied to the ZNBC, where the old board members appointed by the minister under the 1987 Act continued to operate, effectively defying the provisions of the 2002 ZNBC Amendment Act. This state of affairs had earlier (in 2003) compelled media advocacy groups to sue the government for not appointing members of the IBA and ZNBC boards in accordance with the new laws. Initially the media community won the case, when in December 2004 the Minister of Information and Broadcasting was ordered by the court to send the names to Parliament (Matibini 2006: 139).

However, the government applied for a stay of execution of the judgement and appealed against the ruling in the Supreme Court, which subsequently (in March 2007) overturned the earlier ruling. The Supreme Court observed that, 'the Minister could not be used as a rubber stamp or conveyor belt in the process of appointments of the two boards' (Musenge 2007:1) and declared that the Minister had been within her rights in vetoing some of the recommended names.[2] The media fraternity criticised the decision of the Supreme Court – pointing out that the judges who had sat to review the High Court's decision had trivialised the case by dwelling on the dictionary definition of the word 'recommend' instead of examining broader issues regarding the implications of the Minister's influence on the autonomy of the IBA and ZNBC. When the Supreme Court ruled in its favour, the government became even more reluctant to institute the two boards.

Regarding the print media, Zambia's legal and regulatory frameworks are less strict than those for broadcasting. This, indeed, is the case in many countries the world over (Sawers 2000: 33). In Zambia, the only requirement for publishing a newspaper is to satisfy the provision – under the Printed and Publications Act, Chapter 265 Sec 5 (1) – that requires the publisher to register and deposit a copy of the newspaper with the National Archives. However, there are various laws under the Penal Code (Cap 146) that prohibit the publication of contemptuous, seditious and defamatory material. These clauses have at times been used against media freedom, as in the banning of a *Post* publication in 1996 for alleged defamation of the President.

As in most countries in the region, media freedom is not explicitly guaranteed in the Constitution. Rather, it is implied in Article 20 of the Constitution, which generally describes the freedom of expression of all citizens 'to receive and impart ideas'. Although Zambia's Constitution has been reviewed three times – in 1973 at the introduction of the one-party state, in 1991 at the re-introduction of multi-party politics, and during the 1996 constitutional reforms – no serious attention has been paid to the revision of clauses relating to media freedom. The exception, though, was the 1996 inclusion of a clause that hinders the passing of any law that limits press freedom. Even so, Zambia has more than twenty 'media-unfriendly' laws carrying provisions likely to limit, obstruct or even inhibit the free flow of information and ideas. Among these laws are the State Security Act of 1969, and various clauses on publications, public safety, public order, public health and public morality. Most of these provisions are broad and outdated. The fact that many are vaguely phrased means that they are capable of being used to justify government excesses in dealing with the media (MISA 2007; Banda 2006b: 108).

Impact of technological change on policy and regulatory frameworks

Digitalisation has brought a new dimension to media ecology throughout the world. The impact of computer technology is being felt virtually everywhere, and it can be argued that in the near future nearly all forms of data and information will be produced and stored in interchangeable digital bits. Through the 'information highway', people can have immediate access to all forms of data by using a personal computer (Herman and McChesney 1999: 106). Different media content can now be distributed and shared on a converged communication platform (Steemers 1998). Convergence has brought together media platforms that were once isolated. For instance, content that was conventionally classified as falling under the realm of print media is now also suited to mobile and audio-visual Internet services, while broadcasters are increasingly making data services accessible through the TV set. Therefore, 'content has become *cross-media* or, as generally put, *multimedia*' (Arino & Ahlert 2004: 394–5).

Policy and regulatory frameworks all over the world are under pressure to adopt structures that respond to these changes. Advocates of converged regulation appear to be winning and gaining ground globally. In Africa, South Africa took the lead in 2000 when it established the Independent Communications Authority of South Africa (ICASA), with the mandate of regulating the entire communications industry. Previously, the Independent Broadcasting Authority (IBA) and the South African Telecommunications and Regulatory Authority were responsible for regulating broadcasting and telecommunications respectively (Taylor & Berger 2006).

In Zambia, the pressure on government to enact the 2002 IBA Act was triggered by 'distant influences' (Banda 2006b) that infiltrated the Zambian media environment. Thus the pressure on Zambia's media policy and regulatory frameworks originated both within Zambia and beyond its borders, with South Africa having a critical regional influence. Faced with all these pressures, the government in Zambia yielded and passed the act. (The critical role of Zambian civil activists is described in the section on 'Civil society activism and press freedom' below.)

At the same time, it has to be pointed out that the Zambian IBA Act is a replica of the outdated South Africa IBA Act of 1993. Since its enactment in 2002, there have been suggestions that it be repealed and replaced by an act that considers the converged regulation of all communications sectors (ICT policy: 2005). However, some quarters within the Zambian media fraternity have suggested that the IBA first be implemented, after which the enactment of a converged regulator such as ICASA can be pursued. This argument stems from fears resulting from the suspicion that the government may take advantage of the situation and further delay the liberalisation of the media, especially that of public broadcasting, which has been politically abused by successive governments as a tool to perpetuate their hold on power.

Also, despite the influences from outside the country's borders, Zambia's media policy and regulatory frameworks have not necessarily become replicas of their Western derivatives. Rather, they have taken the form and shape determined by local actors – including politicians and media freedom advocacy groups. More importantly, they have been influenced by the conservative and protectionist attitudes of the ruling elites, who have been wary about the potential ability of new regulatory regimes to undermine the status quo. Besides, it can be argued that the effects of 'distant influences' may at times meet local resistance and may have to be negotiated in line with local conditions relating to socio-economic, cultural and political factors. This indeed has been the case with the political deception surrounding the implementation of the IBA Act and the ZNBC (Amendment) Act of 2002. The same argument can be extended to the Freedom of Information (FOI) Bill, which was thrown out of Parliament in 2002. This was done based on the flimsy reason that it would be inimical to state security given the upswing in global terrorism, which would allegedly be abetted by easy access to sensitive information held in public offices.

The advent of convergence has seen the upswing of a competitive media market in Zambia, especially in the broadcasting sector. The coming of digital satellite broadcast in 1995 opened up cross-border broadcasting in the country. MultiChoice South Africa entered the Zambian airwaves by transmitting analogue and digital satellite pay television for the first time in Zambia. For well-to-do Zambians, this marked a point of departure from permanent exposure to the national broadcaster, ZNBC, whose programming was far inferior to that on the new satellite services – which offered movies, soap operas, live sport, science fiction, comedy and many other types of programmes.

The implication of this challenge was that ZNBC had to re-examine its programming so as to be able to continue attracting the audience, advertisers and programme sponsors on whom it depended for its survival.

This, in effect, forced the national broadcaster to reduce its public-interest programming and to increase its commercial programming. In essence, this was a departure from its obligatory remit as a public broadcaster, which stipulated that it should provide programming of public interest, such as educational, cultural and horizon-widening offerings. The proliferation of community radio and the introduction of new television stations resulted in ZNBC being challenged on all fronts. The American religious network, Trinity Broadcasting, was commissioned in1998, while Muvi TV was launched in 2002. Other stations that have become operational from 2005 include Mobi TV and Copperbelt TV. Subsequently, and as a result of a competitive terrain, ZNBC started in August 2009 to test transmissions in readiness for the launch of a second television channel (TV2) to be dedicated to commercial programming. It is assumed that the original channel (TV1) will eventually be relieved from heavy commercial programming to offer more public interest programmes.

Muvi TV, a free-to-air station, 'claims that it had a viewership in March 2005 of 84 per cent of Lusaka's population, with 54 per cent preferring it to other TV stations' (Banda 2006b: 101). With the entry of new radio and TV channels, and of relatively affordable digital satellite pay TV such as My TV and GTV (defunct at the time of concluding this chapter), the broadcast market opened up to offer the audience a choice of media products that had been non-existent before the liberalisation and deregulation of the media sector.

Community media as alternative media

The liberalisation of the airwaves in the early 1990s owing to international democratic changes propelled the emergence and proliferation of community radio in Zambia. The notion of community radio has played a critical role in promoting an alternative source of information for poor and marginalised communities in far-flung areas of Zambia. Mainstream media have been ineffective in serving such areas.

Community media in Zambia have been used mainly as a vessel for development among poor and marginalised communities, to enable them to access development information (Kasoma 2002). The growth of community media in the country has been remarkable compared to that in other countries in the region, such as Botswana, Angola and Zimbabwe, where the concept is still struggling to take off (Kantumoya 2006). The proliferation of community radio stations in Zambia has been largely supported by international organisations and religious bodies that have established radio stations across the country to serve the Christian faith, especially among Catholics. These religious stations, which were the first form of community radio, now exist alongside stations that are non-religious and are run by indigenous groups within communities.

It should, however, be pointed out that the regulation of community broadcasting has been left to the mercy of the government. For instance, the Ministry of Information and Broadcasting has threatened to revoke the licences of radio stations that are vocal against government or that entertain the opposition. The government generally perceives community radio as a threat that could undermine its popularity within communities. Thus, it closely monitors these stations. If it fails to implement the law in respect of the Independent Broadcasting Authority, the government is likely to continue its unjustified regulation of community radio – just as it persists in influencing the public broadcaster.

International protocols and influence on media policy

Nonetheless, government has been under pressure to implement the IBA Act and to take the FOI Bill back to Parliament for subsequent legislation. Media activists supported by civil society have continued to pressurise the state to implement the IBA Act and also enact the FOI Bill in line with international and regional conventions that support and promote media freedom. During the official opening of Parliament in January 2008, the now late President, Levy Mwanawasa, assured the nation that the FOI Bill would be taken back to Parliament and that the IBA Act would be implemented before the end of 2008 (Phiri & Chanda 2008). However, Mwanawasa died in August of the same year. By the end of 2008, his assurances had not been fulfilled by the new president.

Zambia recognises Article 19 of the United Nations' Declaration on Media Freedom. Furthermore, at the continental level, Zambia is a signatory to the 2002

Banjul African Union (AU) Declaration of Principles on the Freedom of Expression in Africa; and the 2001 Windhoek African Charter on Broadcasting. At the regional level, Zambia has assented to the Protocol on Information of the Southern African Development Community, which is known for its guidelines on the media coverage of elections in the region. The Southern African Broadcasting Association has adopted these guidelines for regional broadcasters to follow in the fair and balanced coverage of all political actors during election time.

At the local level, the Zambian Constitution generally recognises freedom of expression. However, media freedom is not enshrined in the existing (1996) Constitution, even though the media fraternity had submitted proposals for this to happen. Since the establishment in 2007 of the National Constitutional Conference (NCC), mandated to review the Constitution, there have been serious moves by media activists to pressurise and lobby the conference to adopt the proposed submissions to enshrine media freedom in the Constitution.

The NCC was mandated in 2007 to review the existing Constitution by examining all submissions from various stakeholders and interest groups across the nation. Its composition was, however, criticised by the main opposition, and by religious groups and civil society. They boycotted the conference and accused the government of, among other things, deliberately creating an inbuilt membership majority for purposes of influencing decisions through voting within the NCC (Saluseki & Silwamba 2008).

Civil society activism and press freedom

Zambia boasts one of the most robust civil society sectors in the region, one that has played a significant role in championing the democratisation of the media sector. Media freedom organisations such as MISA-Zambia, the Press Association of Zambia, the Zambia Union of Journalists, the Zambia Media Women Association and the Society for Senior Journalists have stood up against repressive media laws and the harassment of media practitioners. They have received support from other civic organisations such as the Oasis forum, a consortium of interest groups consisting of religious organisations, the law fraternity and human rights activists, in pressurising the state to legislate laws that promote media freedom. The enactment of the IBA Act and the ZNBC (Amendment) Act in Parliament can be attributed largely to the work of these organisations (Matibini 2006; Moyo 2006).

By the end of 2008, there were indications that the government was preparing to enact the FOI Act by consulting experts from England on how to manage information and make it available to the public. However, there were also signs that it would make the enactment of the Act conditional upon the statutory regulation of media practice. This was because of concerns raised by Parliament over the media's alleged unethical coverage of the October 2008 presidential elections, in which the former vice-president, Rupiah Banda, emerged as the winner to replace the late Levy Mwanawasa, beating his closest rival, Michael Sata of the Patriotic Front, by a narrow margin.

Another challenge was recorded in 2006, when a motion by the state to increase tax on imported newsprint was introduced in Parliament. The consequence of this proposal would have seen an increase in the price of newspapers at a time when Zambia was preparing to hold joint presidential and parliamentary elections. The timing of the motion was suspect and widely seen as a ploy by the government to deny the masses the information they needed to make informed decisions and choices in this election (ibid).

It was speculated that the move was aimed at neutralising the influence of the vocal, privately owned *The Post* newspaper, which was perceived to be spreading anti-government propaganda. The authorities' fear of *The Post* stems partly from the fact that the paper now commands the largest circulation in the country, and has penetrated far into outlying provinces, directly challenging the state-owned papers such as *The Daily Mail* and *The Times of Zambia*. The media freedom advocacy groups, led by MISA and with support from human rights organisations, successfully lobbied parliamentarians to discontinue the motion, arguing that it would work against the fundamental freedom of all Zambians – and especially of the poor and of marginalised communities – to access information.

In the same election year (2006), media activists rejected the Electoral Commission's regulations on the media coverage of elections. Among other things, the regulations imposed a fine or a jail term for inaccurate reporting, and for expressing opinions about or predicting the outcome of the election (ZEC 2006). Civil society in Zambia continues to play a critical role in shaping media law and policy. Zambia's media advocacy campaign, supported by civil society, is well organised and is recognised in the region (Kantumoya 2006).

Towards a changing media policy and regulatory framework

In analysing media policy in Zambia, this chapter has examined the political economy of Zambia's media landscape. The chapter has described the power relations that exist in the media industry, addressing factors such as state influence and intervention; economic influence, professional journalistic freedom; and the ability of the consumer to access media products. Further, the chapter has noted that the state in Zambia is the dominant actor shaping media policy and regulation. This creates problems particularly in those instances when the state agenda hardly coincides with the public interest.

Media activists and civil society have, however, continued to exert pressure on the state, in attempts to persuade it to formulate media policy and legislation that enhance and sustain media freedom and plurality, and that are also responsive to technological change. This is the type of media policy Zambia needs if it is to respond adequately to the democratic and technological challenges of the new millennium. An ideal policy would boost citizens' access to information and other media products without undue political or economic restraints. Without such changes, the fulfilment of the notion of a public sphere serving the public interest may remain a pipe dream in Zambia for many years to come.

The heightened demand for democratisation in today's societies, coupled with the recent global changes in the communications sector, call for a renewed and committed public-interest approach in the administering of the communications industry. In this way, citizens and consumers will be able to attain their right to access media commodities that are an integral part of their lives. Thus, it is recommended that:

- Policy-makers in Zambia adopt regulatory and policy frameworks that first and foremost conform to the public interest and also consider technological and market changes in the communications industry. Policy-makers and legislators should realise the importance of their functions by formulating media policies and laws that represent the public interest rather than parochial interests. In this way, they stand to benefit even after they have left office.

- The Zambian people should hold the state accountable for any actions that go contrary to its commitments in respect of its resolve to promote freedom of expression, freedom of the media and the free flow of information.

- Civil society should intensify its role of sensitising the masses into recognising their rights regarding the free flow of information, and should hold government responsible for any transgressions.

- Media practitioners should exhibit high standards of professionalism and ethical behaviour, and uphold the media's watchdog role of exposing any excesses on the part of government.

- The SADC should work in unison to check excesses, and to confront states that disregard basic human freedoms such as freedom of information.

- The African Union, through the New Partnership for Africa's Development (NEPAD), should consider broadening the focus areas of the African Peer Review Mechanism (APRM) to include media freedom and performance. Currently, the progress and performance of the four substantive focus areas under the APRM – democracy and political governance; economic governance and management; corporate governance; and socio-economic development – cannot be adequately measured without assessing the functioning of the media, especially the free flow of information.

Conclusion

In spite of the commitments articulated in Zambia's media policy framework, and the new media laws and regulations introduced after the collapse of Kaunda's one party rule, the meaningful democratisation of Zambia's media landscape has continued to be elusive. Notably, the new laws and regulations have been half-heartedly implemented, if at all. This is mostly the result of a lack of political will to implement these policies on the part of the ruling elites who wield power, and has been a common feature among all the succeeding governments since independence in 1964.

There have been only superficial efforts to show that the state is committed to achieving the goals outlined in the policy framework. Broadcasting outreach is yet to penetrate remote rural communities. These remain largely unserved, owing to obsolete or non-existent communication infrastructure, and also their inability to afford radio and television receivers. The case of the print media is even more serious, as the distribution system of newspapers is poor, outdated and unreliable. There is a serious need for the state to address these drawbacks.

References

Ang, I. 1991. *Desperately Seeking the Audience*. London: Routledge.

Arino, M. and C. Ahlert. 2004. Beyond broadcasting: The digital future of public service broadcasting. *Prometheus* 22(4): 394–395.

Banda, F. 1998. Broadcasting in Zambia. In *Up in the Air: The State of Broadcasting in Southern Africa*, ed. A. Opoku-Mensah, 101-118. Harare: Holdings.

——. 2001. *The Media and Political Change in Zambia: A Freedom Forum Report on the Media in Zambia*. Lusaka: Panos.

——. 2006a. Commentary: Negotiating distant influences. *Canadian Journal of Communication* 31: 459–467. http://www.cjc-online.ca/viewarticle (accessed 25 June 2007).

——. 2006b. Zambia. In *Mixed Signals: The State of Broadcasting in Southern Africa*, ed. A. Taylor and G. Berger, 96–113. Lusaka: Panos.

——. 2007. ZNBC: Surviving the competition. *The Post*, 15 August.

Central Statistical Office. Reports for 1994, 1998 and 2006. Lusaka.

Chitala, C. 2009. ICT watchdog coming. *Zambia Daily Mail*, 14 September.

Chitala, N. 2000. GTV subscriber base grows to 4,000. *Zambia Daily Mail*, 7 December.

Collins, R. and C. Murroni. 1996. *New Media, New Policies*. Cambridge: Polity.

Foundation for Democratic Process. 2001. *Report on Zambia's 2001 Tripartite Elections*.

Golding, P. and G. Murdock. 2000. Culture, communications and political economy. In *Mass Media and Society*, ed. J. Curran and M. Gurevitch, 70–91. London: Arnold.

Herman, E. S. and R. W. McChesney. 1999. *The Global Media: The New Missionaries of Corporate Capitalism*. London: Creative Print & Design.

Hoynes, W. 1994. *Public Television*. Boulder, CO: Westview.

Jere, C. 2008. *In Global Information Society Watch. Zambia ICT country report: 202*. Cinnamon, Teal.

Kanyungu, S. 2008. Zesco Fibre Project II to consume $30m. *The Times of Zambia*, 11 April.

Kasoma, F. P. 1997. Communication and press freedom in Zambia. In *Press Freedom and Communication in Africa*, ed. F. Eribo and W. Jong-Ebot, 135–156.Trenton: Africa World.

——. 2002. *Community Radio: Its Management and Organisation in Zambia*. Lusaka: Media Institute of Southern Africa (Zambia).

Kantumoya, L. 2006. The state of broadcasting in Southern Africa: An overview. In *Mixed Signals: The State of Broadcasting in Southern Africa*, ed. A. Taylor and G. Berger, 1–12. Lusaka: Panos.

Levy, D. 2001. *Europe's Digital Revolution: Broadcasting Regulation, the EU and the Nation State*. Suffolk: St Edmundsbury Press.

Macha, H. 2002. *State or Public Service? An Analysis of the Coverage of Political Issues and Debates During the 2001 Election Campaign on Television News in Zambia*. Unpublished MA dissertation, Rhodes University, South Africa.

Mapushi, S. 2007. Supreme Court judgement disappoints media bodies. *The Post*, 16 March.

Matibini, P. 2006. *The Struggle for Media Law Reforms in Zambia*. Lusaka: Media Institute of Southern Africa (Zambia).

McQuail, D. 1994. *Mass Communication Theory*. London: SAGE.

——. 1995. *Media Performance*. London: SAGE.

Media Institute of Southern Africa. 2007. *Southern African Media Directory* 2006/2007. Windhoek: Author.

Moyo, D. 2006. *Broadcasting Policy Reform and Democratisation in Zambia and Zimbabwe: Global Pressures and National Responses*. PhD dissertation, University of Oslo, Norway.

Mukoka, A. 2007. MultiChoice annoys subscribers over coverage of English Premiership. *The Post*, 13 August.

Mulenga, K. 2008. State committed to enacting FOI Act. *Zambia Daily Mail*, 1 April.

Musenge, L. 2007. Minister can veto IBA. *Zambia Daily Mail*, 16 March.

Mushaukwa, L. 2007. Chiluba opts to stand trial in person. *The Post*, 15 August.

Mwale, C. 2008. Bridging the digital divide through ICTs. *Zambia Daily Mail*, 16 January.

Mwanakatwe, J. 1994. *End of Kaunda Era*. Lusaka: Multimedia.

Nyerere, JK. 1979. The process of liberation. In *Politics and the State in the Third World*, ed. H. Goulburne, London: Macmillan.

Peacock, A. 1997. *The Political Economy of Economic Freedom*. Cheltenham: Edward Elgar.

Phiri, B. and M. Chanda. 2008. Zambia is not benefiting from mineral revenue, says Levy. *The Post*, 12 January.

Phiri, B. and D. Powers. 2001. Plurality and power relations in Zambian broadcasting. http://www.wacc.org.uk/wacc/publications/mediadevelopment/archive (accessed 25 June 2007).

Price, E. and G. Verhulst. 1998. *Broadcasting reform in India*. Calcutta: Oxford University Press.

Saluseki, B. and C. Silwamba. 2008. Oasis to petition Parliament over adoption of constitution. *The Post*, 19 July.

Sawers, D. 2000. The future of broadcasting – public service broadcasting: A paradox of our time. *Economic Affairs* 20(4): 33–35.

Siame, S. 2006. *News and advertising content analysis on Zambia National Broadcasting Corporation*. Unpublished.

Sichalwe, N. 2005. Magistrate dismisses Chiluba's objection. *The Post*, 24 August.

Silwamba, C. 2007. Public media shouldn't criticize government. *The Post*, 11 September.

Steemers, J. 1998. *Changing Channels*. Luton: Bookcraft.

Taylor, A. and G. Berger. South Africa. In *Mixed Signals*: *The State of Broadcasting in Southern Africa*, ed. A. Taylor and G. Berger, 65–92. Lusaka: Panos.

The Post. Editorial opinion: Let the MMD government have its constitution, 12 September 2007.

The Post. Editorial opinion: Let's negotiate, compromise, 20 August 2007.

The Times of Zambia. Economic growth to benefit all – Levy, 23 October 2007.

The Times of Zambia. Zambia committed to Freedom of Information Act, 8 April 2008.

Zambia Ministry of Communications and Transport. 2005. *National Information and Communications Policy*. Lusaka.

Zambia Electoral Commission. 2006. *Electoral Regulations*. Lusaka.

Zambia National Broadcasting Corporation Amendment Act, No. 20 of 2002. Lusaka.

Zambia Ministry of Information and Broadcasting Services. 1996. *Information and Media Policy*. Lusaka.

——. 1999. *National Media Policy*. Lusaka.

ZEC *see* Zambia Electoral Commission.

ZMCT *see* Zambia Ministry of Communications and Transport.

ZMIBS *see* Zambia Ministry of Information and Broadcasting Services.

Musical chairs and reluctant liberalisation:

Broadcasting policy reform trends in Zimbabwe and Zambia

9

Dumisani Moyo

This chapter analyses the trajectory of broadcasting policy reform processes in Zambia and Zimbabwe. It looks at the global and regional pressures for reform, and the responses of both state and non-state actors to see how broadcasting reform was negotiated in each of the two countries. The chapter proceeds from the view that the democratisation of broadcasting is essential for citizen participation in the democratic process, particularly in Africa where broadcasting (mainly radio) remains the most widely accessible mass medium. Borrowing from new institutional approaches, I illustrate that contemporary broadcasting policy-making has been heavily influenced by past norms and practices, as well as current ideas, and social, economic, and political developments.

Further, the chapter suggests that despite global and regional pressures, broadcasting policy-making in the two countries continues to be nationally determined, and that despite increased civic activity, the policy-making process continues to be executive-driven. Policy outcomes are analysed and compared in light of principles of democracy and freedom of expression to which both countries have committed themselves though various regional and international charters. I also show that broadcasting reforms in both countries have not contributed much to democratisation as such. In Zambia, the reluctance to liberalise has led to partial reform, while in Zimbabwe the rhetoric of anti-imperialism and anti-globalisation has resulted in a case of playing musical chairs. The study is based on a combination of archival research, secondary literature, document analysis and qualitative interviews.

The background

The wave of democratisation that swept the continent in the 1990s, in what Samuel Huntington (1993) has called democracy's 'third wave', has brought significant changes in the structure and regulation of various social, political and economic sectors. Among these, reforms in the communications sector – notably in broadcasting and telecommunications – have been the most remarkable. The decade of the 1990s saw a radical shift in a number of countries from state monopoly broadcasting and telecommunications systems towards more plural ownership patterns. These changes are linked to similar developments that took place in Western industrialised countries in the 1980s, where technological developments and the desire to strengthen markets led to the rapid liberalisation of both broadcasting and telecommunications (Hesmondhalgh 2002; Humphreys 1996). The broadcasting sectors in Zambia and Zimbabwe are no exception to these changes.[1] This paper analyses broadcasting policy reform processes in the two countries by looking at the global and regional pressures for reform, and the responses of both state and non-state actors in terms of how the reform processes were negotiated in the two countries.

In both Zambia and Zimbabwe, as was the case in many other African countries, the state monopoly broadcasting that had been inherited from the colonial era was justified by the seemingly noble developmental goals of promoting nation-building and forging national identity in the young nations, apart from the tired, old argument about frequency scarcity. A pluralism of media outlets, and criticism and dissent, were all regarded as luxuries that these countries could not afford at that crucial stage. Yet in reality, these institutions were used much less for the goals of nation-building than as propaganda mouthpieces of the ruling elite (Nyamnjoh 2005; Hyden, Leslie & Ogundimu 2002). Through tight content regulation and the direct political appointment of boards running the state broadcasters, African governments of the day ensured that these institutions served their own interests (ibid). As a result, the views of civil society and opposition political parties never saw the light of day.

Broadcasting is of key importance in Africa in the sense that it is the only medium that reaches the widest range of the population with political messages – being perhaps only second to face-to-face political rallies in the run-up to national elections. With the majority of the continent's population living in rural areas, this has meant that newspapers – which require road networks for distribution, some degree of literacy and disposable income to access – and television – which depends on electricity and expensive sets – are not the mass media in the sense that they are in developed countries, as they remain largely urban-centred.

The new media, such as the Internet, and cable and satellite broadcasting, have also remained elitist and confined to the urban areas, not least because of the cost of entry and slow diffusion of these technologies. Radio broadcasting, with its comparatively low cost of receiving transmission and its ability to bridge barriers of literacy, is therefore the only medium that has the potential to create a discursive realm for the majority of Africa's populations. However, broadcasting institutions were hijacked by ruling elites who turned them into what James Curran (2002: 45) has termed 'engines of indoctrination' that, in Habermas's terms, 'draw the eyes and ears of the public under their spell but ... deprive [it of] the opportunity to say something and disagree' (Habermas 1989: 171). Therefore, their potential role of providing a sphere for political debate has never been fully realised (see Ronning 1994).

It is within this broad context that the broadcasting policy reform processes in Zambian and Zimbabwe between 1990 and 2007 are analysed. The study addresses three related questions: first, what were the pressures for broadcasting reform? Second, how did each country respond to these pressures? And third, what explains the different paces in the reform process as well as the policy outcomes in the two countries?

Pressures in favour of reform: Horizontal, vertical and bottom-up

In searching for explanations to the broadcasting policy changes that took place in Southern Africa in recent years, it is important to go beyond what have become shorthand answers that point to neo-liberal hegemony as the only explanatory factor for these changes. Following Levi-Faur and Jordana (2005), this chapter has used diffusion approaches that combine vertical (from global to local), horizontal (country- to-country, or sector-to-sector), and bottom-up (from the domestic to the international) explanations to policy influences and adoption. First, the chapter considers how multilateral organisations such as the World Bank (WB) and the International Monetary Fund (IMF) have imposed the adoption of these policy reforms on developing countries. Second, it looks at how interdependence among countries has led to decisions in one country influencing decisions in another. Third, it looks at how developments in one country have set into motion a wave of imitations or emulations in others, as described in the work of Gilardi (2005) among others. It is not assumed, though, that policy diffusion necessarily leads to policy 'harmonisation' or 'convergence'. As Gilardi himself points out, 'the new "transplants" are being adapted to their new homes and in the process may acquire new meanings and uses' (2005: 8–9).

Based on the above, it is argued that in both countries, a combination of vertical, horizontal, and bottom-up pressures played a significant role in influencing broadcasting policy change in Southern Africa. Direct global pressure to open up markets, notably through the World Bank/IMF-driven Structural Adjustment Programmes, transnational trade regimes such as the World Trade Organisation (WTO) and the General Agreement on Trade in Services (GATS), and also demands for democratisation from both internal and external forces, have been the most salient vertical pressures for broadcasting reform. Western governments seeking expansion of their domestic markets demanded democratisation as a precondition for investment in African markets. Bilateral and multilateral donors echoed these demands, which they tied to the provision of donor support. With the increasing demand for 'good governance' as a condition to giving aid, Western governmental aid donors have pushed the 'free flow of information' and media reform in general high up on the agenda (Hills 2003: 35).

Global pressures have been channelled through regional and local non-governmental organisations (NGOs) and civic organisations, which have received not only funding but also ideas on how to influence governments in developing countries to undertake certain liberal media reforms. Regional organisations such as the Media Institute of Southern Africa, the Southern African Broadcasting Association and Article 19 have provided launch pads for both the global forces and local pro-reform groups advocating broadcasting reform, not only in Zambia and Zimbabwe but also in other Southern African countries. These organisations, with support from Western governments and donor organisations, have mounted campaigns for broadcasting reforms that have focused mainly on four areas: the opening up of broadcasting ownership to allow private broadcasting (both commercial and community); the introduction of independent regulatory authorities; the transformation of state broadcasters into genuine public broadcasters; and the introduction of access to information laws. These issues gained public prominence across the region, leading to varied degrees of success in the four areas.

Apart from these global pressures, the broadcasting reforms that accompanied South Africa's negotiated liberalisation process have served as a watershed in the history of broadcasting reform in Southern Africa. They provided a model for countries in the region to emulate, thereby creating a horizontal force for change. Notably, the reform process in that country was characterised by unprecedented transparency and civic participation (Horwitz 2001a, 2001b). The liberalisation process transformed the South African Broadcasting Corporation (SABC) from a propaganda mouthpiece of the apartheid regime into a public broadcaster that is relatively autonomous from state interference; and established an independent broadcasting authority that in turn licensed several commercial and community broadcasting channels (see Horwitz 2001a, 2001b). While this development is a product of political compromise, where both the outgoing National Party and the incoming African National Congress were keen to have a broadcasting corporation that had been reconstituted as an independent, non-partisan broadcaster before the landmark 1994 democratic elections, this reform process introduced a new culture of accountability in the South African media sector.[2]

Influence also came from experiences in Eastern Europe and Central Europe, where the expansion of broadcasting struck a major blow for democracy in the sense that it forced the state-controlled media to provide at least some of the information that was being made available by external broadcast sources (Horwitz 2001a; Price et al. 2002). In most African countries, radio broadcasts from external channels such as the BBC World Service and the Voice of America, and the expansion of direct broadcast satellite played an important role in forcing open state monopolies over the dissemination of information to citizens.[3] South Africa's satellite broadcaster, MultiChoice, which could initially be accessed in neighbouring countries through a relatively affordable decoder before its signal was encrypted, also sensitised viewers in the region to what a liberalised media environment could bring.

Within the African continent itself, there was growing recognition of the importance of citizen participation as key to national development. The 1990 African Charter for Popular Participation in Development and Transformation, for example, stresses the importance of popular participation in the policy formulation, planning, implementation, monitoring and evaluation of development programmes.[4] Both Zambia and Zimbabwe are signatories to this and to a number of other declarations and protocols on press freedom, including a number that stress the need for broadcasting reform specifically. The 2002 Banjul Declaration of Principles on Freedom of Expression in Africa, for example, implores member states to 'encourage a diverse, independent private broadcasting sector', adding that, 'A state monopoly over broadcasting is not compatible with the right of freedom of expression.' The declaration further encourages 'equitable allocation of frequencies between private broadcasting users, both commercial and community', and advocates independent regulatory bodies responsible for issuing licenses and ensuring adherence to licence conditions.

While these common sources of pressure for broadcasting reform may explain the broader shift from state monopoly broadcasting towards liberalisation, this chapter argues that they do not account for the different ways in which different countries have responded to them, nor do they explain the different policy outcomes in various countries. By comparing the broadcasting reform processes in Zambia and Zimbabwe, the chapter seeks to explain why the two countries have taken different routes towards reforming their broadcasting sectors, and why they have ended up with different policy outcomes. If the two countries experienced similar global and regional pressures to reform their broadcasting sectors, why is it that these pressures yielded more results in Zambia and fewer in Zimbabwe? Why has one country liberalised while the other has not? One of the key arguments of this study is that while both countries experienced a similar set of external pressures towards broadcasting reform, it is the manner in which the local actors interrogated and negotiated these pressures, and the social, political and economic dynamics obtaining in each country, that influenced the pace and course of the reform process, and its outcomes.

While broadcasting reform in both countries is far from a smooth process of liberalisation or deregulation as often assumed, Zambia's 'reluctant liberalisation' has brought about a fairly enabling environment, evidenced by the mushrooming of new radio and television stations since 1993. Here, early media reforms followed closely on the heels of the 1991 political transition. The case of Zimbabwe, however, has been one of playing musical chairs: here the new legislative environment purported in principle to open up the sector, while in practice the regime ensured that it remained closed.

New institutionalism and the policy-making process

This paper proceeds from the view that broadcasting policy-making is a complex process involving multiple actors who are driven by different interests (John 1998; Sabatier 1999). One way of understanding the process, as Peter John suggests, is to specify the interests, resources, interrelationships, constraints and norms of the actors under study (John 1998: 14). Analysing the policy-making process, as John further argues, necessarily involves 'examining the links between decision-makers as they negotiate and seek influence of the governmental system' (1998: 2). Borrowing from political science, this study explores how institutions, networks, socio-economic factors, interests and ideas interact to influence the broadcasting policy reform processes in the two countries. It is argued that these causal factors interact in different ways in each of the two countries to bring about different policy outcomes.

While early policy scholars tended to look at single approaches and how they explain policy change, the tendency in recent years, typified by scholars of 'new institutionalism', has been to focus on the interaction of the various causal factors – or what has been termed the integrative approach (see John 1998; Sabatier 1991, 1999). This is because single approaches fail adequately to explain policy change and variation, and only provide partial accounts of the reform process. The growing understanding is that policy change and variation emerges out of the interaction of processes. As John points out, the interaction between individual choices and institutions, and between ideas and individual interests, can produce rich explanations of policy changes (John 1998: 167).

Reluctant liberalisation: The Zambian route to broadcasting reform

Zambia's political transition in 1991, from a one-party to a multiparty system, gave impetus for reform in various sectors. Prior to the transition, President Kenneth Kaunda's socialist-style United Independence Party (UNIP) had established near-total control of the mass media (Kasoma 1997, 2000a, 2001; Chirwa 1996; Mytton 1983). The successor government, led by former trade unionist Frederick Chiluba, entered on a pro-reform ticket. It made wide-ranging promises to liberalise the economy and guarantee freedoms that had been denied under the previous regime (Ihonvbere 1996; Phiri 1999). However, it is important to mention that the new government inherited a collapsing economy that had been destroyed by decades of state dominance and mismanagement. The monopoly state broadcaster had also been facing collapse, despite attempts in 1987 to make it economically viable through commercialisation through the Zambia National Broadcasting Corporation (ZNBC) Act.

Early Zambian policy reforms

Among the demands from pro-reform groups was the transformation of the Zambia National Broadcasting Corporation (ZNBC) into a true public broadcaster that was representative of diverse interests, not just the ruling party. The raising of the question of political party access to the state broadcasters in the months leading to the historic 1991 elections meant that by the time the new government came into power, broadcasting reform was already high on the national agenda. The promise to liberalise the economy ('with no sacred cows to be spared', as Chiluba declared) created an anticipation that the entire government media empire, including newspapers and broadcasting, was heading for privatisation. Indeed, in 1992 the Zambia Privatisation Agency and the Ministry of Information and Broadcasting went on to commission a private consultancy firm, Coopers and Lybrand, to do a study on the privatisation and commercialisation of government-owned media and printing companies, as well as the restructuring of the Ministry of Information itself (Kasoma 1997: 119–120). However, the privatisation of state media enterprises was not carried out as was expected.

Two main constraining factors can be identified here. One is that the pro-reform information minister, Dipak Patel, did not have the full backing of other ministers, deputies and other politicians for these liberal ideas (Högberg 1993). The other factor is that the government realised that it needed a mouthpiece through which to communicate its programmes to the citizens. Broadcasting in particular was important as an avenue for its self-presentation and representation to the Zambian public. It was therefore classified, along with other industries such as transport and energy, as one of the 'strategic' enterprises that the Chiluba government was not keen to privatise. Eric Silwamba, then deputy minister of information and broadcasting, summed up the government's position regarding the privatisation of broadcasting when he said:

In broadcasting the emphasis should be on *competition, not selling off* completely. *The government ought to have a mouthpiece to explain government policy to the people.* Under the Constitution the public have a right to information and therefore *the government is obliged to provide information.* If all media are privately owned, they are not obliged to propagate government's views. (Cited in Maja-Pearce 1995: 120–121, emphasis added).

These sentiments fitted into the developmental media theories that held sway during those years. However, experience from the Kaunda regime had proved that such good intentions often veiled an underlying interest in control.

The option of privatisation was thus relegated in favour of partial liberalisation as a way of placating media reform advocates as well as international donors.[5] Thus, instead of repealing the ZNBC Act, the government decided to simply amend the act in 1993 to give the ZNBC powers to license other broadcasters, creating an invidious situation where the broadcaster was both player and referee in the same market. The partial opening up of the broadcasting sector in 1993 in principle brought an end to ZNBC monopoly, as it ushered in new players both in radio and television broadcasting. By 2000, nine private radio stations were operational in Zambia, either with full licences or under construction permits (Wales 2000: 98). Most of them, it is important to note, were church-owned and primarily broadcast religious messages.

First to be licensed was Radio Christian Voice, funded by Christian Vision UK. The Roman Catholic Church was licensed to operate four radio stations: Radio Icengelo (in Copperbelt Province), Radio Yatsani (Lusaka), Radio Maria (Eastern Province) and Radio Chikuni (Southern Province). The rise in religious broadcasting followed President Chiluba's speech in 1994, in which he declared Zambia a Christian nation. A crippling license condition for these religious stations, however, was that they could not air political broadcasts (Banda 2003). In 1994 the Information and Broadcasting Minister, Keli Walubita, threatened to close down any Christian radio station that started broadcasting 'political propaganda' (*Zambia Daily Mail*, 6 December 1994).

These early broadcasting reforms were characterised by four main features: partial and reluctant liberalisation, which ensured that the state broadcaster remained the dominant voice despite the 'opening up'; the lack of an independent regulatory authority, which accounted for the partisan and unaccountable licence allocation system; a policy vacuum, which explained the lack of clear goals in the reform process; and the executive-driven nature of the reforms, which ignored the interests of various groups in society.

Zambia's second wave of policy change

The unsatisfactory nature of these early media reforms triggered unprecedented civic activity from the mid-1990s onwards, with various groups challenging the state to institute genuine media reform. Civil society in Zambia had been given a new lease of life following the political opening that came with the 1991 transition. One notable consequence of this was that the late reform process had to a great degree been opened up to non-state actors. A vibrant private press had also emerged in the run-up to the 1991 elections, and became a strong ally of pro-reform groups in Zambia. Undoubtedly, the most visible of them all was *The Post*, which soon became a thorn in the side of the Chiluba Government, exposing corruption and other forms of abuse of power by senior government officials.

What was particularly notable in the broadcasting reform process in Zambia was the way in which civic organisations, together with opposition political parties and the private media, formed a coalition to advocate media reform. Considerable support in terms of finance and ideas came from Western donor organisations involved in 'democratisation' efforts in the region. The coincidence of interests between local actors and these donor organisations attracted the resources necessary to enable the former to advocate media reform effectively.

The most prominent civic actors included media freedom advocacy groups such as the Media Institute of Southern Africa (MISA Zambia, then known as the Zambia Independent Media Association or ZIMA), the Zambian Union of Journalists (ZUJ), the Press Association of Zambia (PAZA), and the Zambia Media Women Association (ZAMWA). With the help of opposition members of Parliament, these organisations initiated a novel process of drafting their own media bills, which were to be tabled in Parliament as private members' bills. These bills included a Broadcasting Bill, an Independent Broadcasting Authority Bill and a Freedom of Information Bill.

Although the private members' bills were thrown out on the strength that the Zambian Constitution required bills with financial implications to be consented to by the President, through the Vice-President or the Minister of Finance, before they could be tabled in Parliament, they acted as a prod to push the government into action (Matibini 2006). In response the government hurriedly prepared its own draft media bills, namely the Zambia National Broadcasting Corporation (ZNBC) (Amendment) Bill, the Freedom of Information (FOI) Bill, and the Independent Broadcasting Authority (IBA) Bill, which were in many ways similar to those of the rejected private members' bills (Lingela 2002: 10; Rønning 2003: 9). Both the ZNBC (Amendment) Bill and the IBA Bill were passed into law in 2002, while the FOI Bill was thrown out.

The IBA Act establishes an Independent Regulatory Authority whose main function is to regulate the broadcasting industry in Zambia.[6] Section 5(2) states that the functions of the authority shall be to, among other things, promote a pluralistic and diverse broadcasting industry; issue licences to broadcasters and broadcasting signal distributors; manage the broadcasting spectrum to ensure the rational and efficient allocation of frequencies; develop local content regulations; oblige broadcasters to develop codes of practice; develop programme standards for the industry; and receive and adjudicate complaints concerning broadcasting services. One of the key merits of the IBA Act is its emphasis on a transparent and fair system of allocating (and even revoking) licences through public hearings.

The ZNBC (Amendment) Act of 2002 provides for the setting up of an autonomous ZNBC Board, and transfers regulatory duties to the IBA. It creates a provision for the ZNBC to collect license fees to finance its operations, and mandates the ZNBC to, among other things: provide varied and balanced programming for all sections of the populations; serve the public interest; contribute to the development of free and informed opinions and, as such, constitute an important element of the democratic process; defend democratic freedoms; broadcast news and current affairs programmes that shall be comprehensive, unbiased and independent, and commentary that shall be clearly distinguished from news; and reflect, as comprehensively as possible, the range of opinions and of political, philosophical, religious, scientific and artistic trends encountered in the country.[7] This is a remarkable improvement over previous legislation, as it sets the basis for reconstituting the ZNBC as a genuine public broadcaster and also provides reasonably sufficient criteria against which to measure the performance of the ZNBC.

While both acts contribute to the loosening up of ownership regulations, they do not sufficiently provide for the autonomy of both the IBA and ZNBC boards, whose members are appointed by the Minister of Information from lists recommended to him by *ad hoc* appointments committees that he would have put in place. Moreover, the excitement about the potential of the two laws to transform the broadcasting industry in the public interest soon turned into frustration, as it became clear that the government was reluctant to implement the new laws, as evidenced by its refusal to take to Parliament for ratification all the recommended names for appointment on the IBA and ZNBC boards. Several media organisations had to take the government to court to demand that the names submitted by the Appointments Committee be taken to Parliament for ratification. By the beginning of 2009, neither law had been implemented. This reluctance on the part of the Zambian government to 'walk the talk' is a clear indication that the reform process was not driven by sincere belief in the need for change, but was rather viewed as a way of placating critics and donors.

Musical chairs? The Zimbabwean route to broadcasting reform

The beginning of the twenty-first century has seen a flurry of activity in terms of media policy reforms in Zimbabwe. Notably, the broadcasting law reforms introduced have in principle brought an end to almost 50 years of legal monopoly broadcasting in Zimbabwe. Yet in practice nothing much has changed, as the new regulations have allowed a *de facto* monopoly to prevail. Instead of democratising the Zimbabwean broadcasting sector, these new laws have further narrowed it by entrenching government dominance and control. The broadcasting reform efforts in Zimbabwe can be put into two distinct phases: the enthusiastic reforming phase; and the authoritarian backlash phase.

The enthusiastic reforming phase

Several dynamics – other than the vertical, horizontal and bottom-up pressures discussed earlier – propelled Zimbabwe towards liberalisation of the broadcasting sector. By the mid 1990s, there were strong indications that the government of Zimbabwe was considering ending the monopoly enjoyed by the state broadcaster, the Zimbabwe Broadcasting Corporation (ZBC), and was opening up the airwaves to competition. Initial indications came from pronouncements by successive information ministers in the 1990s, stressing government commitment to opening up the airwaves – starting with David Karimanzira in 1996. This was followed by more concrete steps. A consultant, Peter Ibbottson, was commissioned to undertake a study and advise the Ministry of Information on how to proceed with the commercialisation of the ZBC ahead of the impending liberalisation. The drawing up of the Draft Communications Bill of 1997 – which aimed to liberalise both the broadcasting and the telecommunications sectors – was another strong signal that at this point the government was committed to reforming the broadcasting sector.

A combination of factors can be attributed to this softening of position. First, the ZBC was going through a phase of heavy financial loss and gross mismanagement.[8] The period 1991–1996 in particular was characterised by general instability at the ZBC, with successive ministers of information hiring and firing new director generals and boards of governors at will. Sometimes the corporation was allowed to drift along without a substantive director general for months. As a Parliamentary Committee report revealed:

> Successive Ministers of Information have contributed immensely towards the instability of the Corporation in that they seem to enjoy intervening directly in the day-to-day running of the organisation when there is no Board of Governors. This leads to untold chaos. (Ad Hoc Committee 1999)

Second, the adoption of the World Bank/IMF-prescribed Economic Structural Adjustment Programme (ESAP) in 1990/91 required reduced government public spending; hence the government was no longer keen to continue providing financial support to the corporation – despite the fact that the government still expected ZBC to continue operating as its official mouthpiece. Such incompatible interests – the desire to commercialise the ZBC on the one hand and a strong penchant for retaining political control of the corporation on the other – contributed to the ambiguity of government policy towards broadcasting in those years. But most importantly, the adoption of these neo-liberal reforms led to a degree of political liberalisation that saw, for example, the suspension of the emergency powers that had been in place since the liberation war era of the 1970s.

Further, there was increased pressure for plural broadcasting from civil society organisations, including the Zimbabwe Union of Journalists, the Federation of African Media Women in Zimbabwe, the Willie Musarurwa Memorial Trust, the Zimbabwe Media Council, the Christian Communicators Association of Zimbabwe, and the national chapter of the Media Institute of Southern Africa, MISA-Zimbabwe.

As was the case in Zambia, the MISA chapter in Zimbabwe was the most prominent of these groups. It was far better organised than the rest, and enjoyed a regional network that allowed it to learn from experiences in other countries. The MISA project dovetailed with the agenda of global forces pushing for the spread of liberal democracy in the region, and hence was able to attract the necessary resources to launch sustained campaigns for broadcasting reform in the various member countries.

These pressures should also be viewed in the context of the winds of political liberalisation and democratisation that swept across the continent in the early 1990s. Internally, there was growing resistance to the one-party state and demand for pluralism from various quarters, including students' unions and the Zimbabwe Congress of Trade Unions.

In Zimbabwe as in many other African countries, the liberalisation of the telecommunications sector provided a test case for advocates of broadcasting reform. In 1998, the successful legal challenge by Strive Masiyiwa's Econet Wireless against state monopoly in the telecommunications sector created a strong precedent for advocates of broadcasting reform. Borrowing a leaf from this experience, they challenged state monopoly in the courts.

Finally, there was also growing anger among ZBC viewers and listeners in response to poor programming. Angry letters to the editor in various newspaper columns, plus the consumer boycott in poorly serviced parts of the country such as Mutare and Beitbridge, are testimony to this (see Moyo 2006).

Partial or pseudo privatisation?

While the Ibbottson Report had recommended the complete privatisation of TV2 and Radio 4 by 1999, the government chose, instead, to lease TV2 to three private broadcasters, namely LDM, the Munhumutapa African Broadcasting Corporation (MABC) and Joy TV (also known as Flame Lily Broadcasting). Leasing was preferred for the obvious reason that it would ensure that the government remained in control of TV2. This strong interventionist streak meant that the drive to introduce private/commercial broadcasting was never synonymous with deregulation – or even liberalisation. The fact that these private broadcasters did not have full licenses and were dependent on the goodwill of the ZBC and those who controlled it was in itself a hindrance to their freedom of operation.

Although no specific rules were laid down regarding what the private stations could or could not broadcast, the contracts were drawn in such a way that these broadcasters had to restrain themselves in order to avoid offending their 'benefactors'. This meant avoiding local news content, as it was likely to be a source of conflict. MABC, which ventured into documentaries and interviews with people believed to hold anti-government sentiments, paid the price for its daring by getting switched off air. Joy TV, on the other hand, survived by avoiding any local news. They even edited out local content from their re-broadcasts of BBC news (see Maqeda 2000).

The arrangement also gave ZBC the unfair advantage of being both player and regulator in the same market. As indicated in the Parliamentary report, ZBC charged unreasonably high prices for renting out airtime to its three tenants, with the result that all three ended up owing the ZBC huge sums of money (Ad Hoc Committee 1999).[9] The licence conditions for the three private broadcasters ensured that government influence extended beyond the confines of the state-owned ZBC. In terms of providing alternative voices in the true sense of the word, this was in many ways a mere palliative, as the coverage of TV2 was limited to within a 70-km radius of the capital, Harare. Besides, the three stations carried mostly entertainment content. ZBC thus retained its monopoly of 'national coverage', which meant that advertisers naturally preferred it to its new competitors.

While it is clear at this point that a reforming spirit had permeated government in the 1990s, it is also evident that there was still a high degree of uncertainty as to what a fully liberalised broadcasting environment would bring. As such, a strong desire to control the sector continued to exist.

The end of legal monopoly broadcasting and the authoritarian backlash

Concluding that the government was not sincere in its promise to liberalise the airwaves, two private companies, the MABC and Capital Radio, separately challenged the ZBC monopoly in the High Court.[10] It was Capital Radio's legal challenge that eventually led to the Supreme Court ruling that did away with ZBC monopoly in September 2000. The government immediately responded by enforcing the Presidential Powers (Temporary Measures) Act, which allows the President to enact emergency laws that are valid for a period of six months. The resultant legislation, the Presidential Powers (Temporary Measures) (Broadcasting) Regulations of 2000, far from feeding into the euphoria that had surrounded the nullification of monopoly broadcasting, further tightened the conditions of entry into the sector. What was apparent, in the manner in which the government responded to the legal vacuum created by the Supreme Court ruling, was that the government was determined to regain lost control of the reform process, and to ensure that whatever changes were made did not prejudice its stay in power. In a way, this control had been temporarily usurped by civil society – as evidenced by the various debates sponsored by MISA and others between 1997 and 2000.

A series of economic and political developments that took place between 1999 and 2000 can be said to have deflected the Zimbabwe government from the road towards liberalisation of the airwaves. They were the accelerated decline of the economy since the crash of the Zimbabwe dollar in 1997, which caused unprecedented restlessness within the body politic; the launch of the *Daily News*, a hard-hitting anti-government newspaper in March 1999; the launch of the Movement for Democratic Change (MDC) – the first serious challenge to the ruling party since independence – in September 1999; the vote against the government-led constitutional referendum in February 2000; the farm occupations that began in earnest in February 2000; and the rise of Jonathan Moyo, a former liberal political scientist, to head the Ministry of Information. Together these led to a radical shift in media policy, resulting in a renewed desire to tighten control not only of broadcasting, but also of the media in general. The Mugabe government viewed the media as key tools not only in projecting its propaganda, but also in the defence of 'national sovereignty' from the sustained barrage of international condemnation. As a prominent official in the Department of Information argued:

> It [the broadcasting spectrum] is finite, therefore it's a national resource, and whoever has access to it must use it in a way that coheres with the national interest. You cannot use a national resource to undermine the nation. But you have an obligation to use the national resource to further the national interest … Whether doing it for the benefit of ZANU PF amounts to pushing the national interest, that's a different matter, but we start from the premise that when the Zimbabwean sovereignty is under assault, then

necessarily it must muster all its resources. (George Charamba, interview by author. Harare, 22 July 2003)

The link between the re-gearing of media policy and land reform in Zimbabwe merits special mention, for the main reason that land reform became the *raison d'état* for most policy shifts during this period. In the discourse of the ZANU PF ideologues, broadcasting reform became interchangeable with land reform, as both were viewed as finite national resources that required a system of allocation inspired by the 'national interest' – however that national interest might be defined.

A siege mentality: Land reform and the re-gearing of media policy

Mounting international pressure and incessant vilification of the Mugabe government in the international media following the adoption of its controversial land reform thus provided sufficient justification for tighter control of the flow of information. As a result, stringent measures were put in place to bar foreign media from covering developments in the country.[11] Internally, the use of broadcasting as a tool for legitimising the land-reform programme became imperative. The ZBC was therefore optimally used to mobilise the masses to rally behind the Third Chimurenga – as the land reform programme came to be known.[12] Then Minister of Information, Jonathan Moyo, summed up the government's approach in these words:

> We believe that information is a strategic issue which is critical in maintaining a country's sovereignty and you cannot claim to be sovereign if you do not own the means of disseminating information … This is why we removed CNN from ZBC when we came in, in the year 2000 and we will never have it again as long as we are still around … We want to use the media to put across our national views and not those of the United States or Britain or the Voice of America. We wish to put across our views as the Voice of Zimbabwe. (*The Herald Online*, 8 April 2004)

The push for regime change in Zimbabwe, coming particularly from the USA and the UK, thus also created strong justification for using the defence of national sovereignty as a reason to continue controlling the media.

New media laws and the restriction of communicative space

The Mugabe government came up with a battery of restrictive media laws that in many ways restrict the communicative space for its citizens, contrary to its claims of having 'liberalised' or 'liberated' the airwaves. The Broadcasting Services Act (BSA) of 2001, for example, purports to open up the broadcasting sector to competition. Its chief architects in the Department of Information touted it as a hybrid of some of the most democratic broadcasting laws in the world (Moyo 2001).[13] Its provisions for the establishment of a broadcasting authority responsible for regulating frequencies and allocating licences to new broadcasters; the setting up of a three-tier broadcasting system comprising public service, community and commercial broadcasting; and its emphasis on the promotion of national culture, national languages, local ownership and local production industry are all remarkable improvements over the previous colonial legislation. However, a closer look at the act reveals that it in many ways impinges on the communicative rights of Zimbabwean citizens.

The BSA contains several clauses that make it difficult for new players to enter the broadcasting market, which to some extent explains why, several years after its introduction, not a single private broadcaster has been licensed. Further, the act places excessive powers in the hands of the Minister of Information and Publicity, who is the ultimate licensing authority. As stated under section 6, 'Subject to this Act, the Minister shall be the licensing authority for the purpose of licensing any person to provide a broadcasting service or operate as a signal carrier in Zimbabwe.' Among many other powers, the Minister determines at his or her discretion who gets a licence; the terms and conditions attached to an issued licence; whether an issued licence should be amended, suspended or cancelled; and when to take over a broadcasting station (Hondora 2002). The Civic Alliance for Social and Economic Progress, for example, argued that the act was 'a recipe for continued state control of radio and television leading to the silencing not liberation and amplifying of the many unheard voices in our society' (*Daily News*, 7 April 2001).

According to the BSA the Minister of Information, in consultation with the President, appoints members of the Broadcasting Authority of Zimbabwe (BAZ). The BAZ is therefore not independent, and the Minister has the discretion to appoint, terminate, or alter the conditions of service of its members. Such boundless powers are open to abuse, as the Minister can deny access to broadcasting to perceived 'enemies of the state'. The strategic relocation of the Department of Information (which replaced the Ministry of Information) to the President's Office is also evident of the importance attached by the government to the flows of information.

The BSA has also been criticised for inhibiting investment in the broadcasting sector by creating unrealistic licensing conditions, particularly for commercial broadcasting.[14] The prohibition of foreign shareholding, the fact that licensees are prohibited from possessing both a broadcasting licence and a signal-carrier licence, and the requirement that all licensees should make available one hour per week to the government, for example, are some of the notable restrictive clauses that are not investment friendly. Section 11 (5) states that 'a licensee shall make one hour cumulatively per week of its broadcasting time available for the purpose of *enabling the government of the day, at its request, to explain its policies* to the nation' (emphasis added). This provision is open to abuse, as the government of the day can choose this time to communicate its propaganda.

Interestingly, criticism of the act has come from both inside and outside the ruling party. The Parliamentary Legal Committee that assessed the Broadcasting Services Bill in 2001 found several of its sections unconstitutional on the grounds of inconsistency with Section 20 of the Constitution, which provides for freedom of expression.[15] In its ruling on Capital Radio's constitutional challenge to a number of the act's sections, the Supreme Court declared as unconstitutional (1) the requirement that a minister of information, who is an interested party, be a licensing authority; and (2) the requirement to have only one national radio and television station in addition to the public broadcaster across the sector (*Weekend Tribune*, 27–28 September 2003).

In his inaugural speech as a new ZANU PF Member of Parliament, former journalist Kindness Paradza called for the revision of the Broadcasting Services Act and the Access to Information and Protection of Privacy Act, arguing that the two media laws were too restrictive and discouraged potential investment in the industry:

> We need to come up with policies that will make it conducive for our people to invest in information communication technology, broadcasting services and the newspaper industry. Special attention should be paid to the BSA and AIPPA to check whether they do not restrict local investment in broadcasting services. A careful perusal and examination of these laws shows there is no other commercial sector in Zimbabwe that is required to adhere to such stringent conditions. (*The Sunday Mail*, 25 April 2004)

His remarks drew fire from the Department of Information, which described him as 'an ignorant novice parliamentarian' (*The Sunday Mail*, 2 May 2004). However, Paradza's sentiments echoed the argument presented by Justice Wilson Sandura in his dissenting judgement to the ruling that Capital Radio had no basis to challenge the prohibition of foreign funding in broadcasting, in which he said that 'permitting foreign investment in private broadcasting would be more likely to create employment for Zimbabweans than a total ban of such investment' (*Weekend Tribune*, 27–28 September 2003).

A significant change that has come with the Broadcasting Services Act is the establishment of the Broadcasting Authority of Zimbabwe (BAZ), whose function, among many others, is 'to receive, evaluate and consider applications for the issue of any broadcasting licence or signal carrier licence for the purpose of advising the Minister on whether or not he should grant the licence' (BSA, Section 3 (2) (c)). As such, the BAZ does not have licensing powers, and simply serves the function of vetting applicants for recommendation to the Minister. What is apparent is that since its establishment in 2000, BAZ has lacked the requisite clarity concerning what its mandate is. Between 2000 and 2007, BAZ has on a number of times called for applications for broadcasting licenses, but nothing has come of it.[16] Delays have been attributed to the technical problems of drawing up the national frequency map, but many people have dismissed them as time-buying tactics to avoid opening up the sector.[17] As MDC Secretary General and parliamentarian, Welshman Ncube, pointed out:

> … the government has only paid lip service to attempts to licence or introduce other players. The effect is that they created a regulatory authority which does nothing other than playing a delaying game so that for all practical purposes the philosophy has been, if we liberalize the airwaves the alternative voices which had been shut out from speaking on ZBC will not be shut out. And this government – make no doubt about it – will not create independent radio and television stations so long as there is political contest in this country. They are so scared of the alternative voice that they are denying the alternative voices access to information through violence and through laws and through the monopoly of the ZBC which is not a legal monopoly but a *de facto* monopoly. Make no mistake, if there is to be an independent radio station, they will make sure that it is controlled by ZANU PF or people who believe in the same ideology as ZANU PF so it will live by the ZBC code. (Welschman Ncube, interview by author. Harare, 23 July 2003)

These words have proved to be prophetic. As at the beginning of 2009, there was still no serious competitor to the ZBC. Since the nullification of monopoly broadcasting by the Supreme Court in 2000, only one broadcaster, apart from the existing state-controlled ZBC, has been licensed. MultiChoice Zimbabwe Ltd, a subsidiary of MultiChoice South Africa, is a satellite subscription broadcaster, and it obtained its license only on condition that it entered a joint venture with the state-owned monopoly signal carrier, Transmedia, and that it carried the ZBC as part of its bouquet. Although it offers news channels such as CNN, Euronews, SABC Africa, Al Jazeera and BBC World, and several entertainment channels, the contribution of MultiChoice to democratisation is limited in the sense that only affluent urbanites can afford the high subscriptions – which are payable in hard currency – and the receiving equipment required.

The ZBC Commercialisation Act, which provides for 'the formation of successor companies to take over the functions, assets, liabilities and staff of ZBC', is perhaps the least discussed of the new media laws in Zimbabwe, not least because of lack of analytical expertise within civic organisations. Yet the act does something that further distances the ZBC from the ideals articulated by civil society, notably that the corporation be transformed into a true public service broadcaster.[18] Thus, instead of articulating ideas of public interest and democratic citizenship, the act provides for the marketisation of a public institution whose mandate should be the provision of quality service to the public.

In this act too, the contradictory interests of commercialisation and state control are apparent: 'In the performance of their functions, the successor companies shall give priority to serving the needs of the State, to the extent that it is compatible with sound business practice to do so' (Section 4 (3)). Two Harare lawyers, Chibwe and Carr (2002) have noted that this provision seeks 'to establish a state broadcaster rather than a 'public broadcaster' in the true sense.' What further makes the position of ZBC ambiguous is the fact that there are no special obligations imposed upon it (such as a public service or public interest mandate) under either the Broadcasting Services Act or any other legislation (ibid).

Broadcasting, national sovereignty and national culture

Claims have been made that Zimbabwe's new media laws are clones of laws from some of the world's established democracies. If they are indeed replicas of some of those finest laws, what then is peculiar about the Zimbabwean clones? Apart from raising questions about democratic citizenship and communicative space, these new laws also raise fundamental questions about the role of the state in communications and cultural policy-making within a global context. In this regard, the Zimbabwean attempt to restore 'communicative sovereignty' – i.e. the state's exercise of authority over flows of information inside its territory – by restricting ownership of broadcasting (and other media) to Zimbabwean citizens and putting in place stringent local content quotas (75%) may not in itself be a bad thing, nor is it something unique to Zimbabwe.

The European Union, for example requires that broadcasters in member countries devote 51% of their airtime to European content as a way of engendering a 'European identity'. France goes even a step further, insisting that terrestrial TV stations carry 60% of European programming, and that this output include at least 40% of French-made material (Levy 2001: 23). The USA and Canada have some of the world's toughest laws concerning the citizenship of media company owners.[19] What is unique and worrisome about the Zimbabwean 'clones' is that the drive to establish 'communicative sovereignty' is coloured by the self-interest of the ruling party, whose desire is to perpetuate its stay in power. The allusions to western imperialism in the ruling party discourse mask an overriding desire to maintain a tight grip on the media.

Thus the discourse of national sovereignty has been used extensively to justify media laws that in many ways restrict rather than open up communicative spaces in Zimbabwe. At the root of the government's motives is the patronising assumption that it knows what is good and what is bad for the citizens of Zimbabwe, who are frequently accused by the government of having short memories of the liberation struggle.

To conclude this section, it is clear that the reform process in Zimbabwe has been driven largely by the executive branch of government, with political imperatives dominating the nature and direction of the reforms. The political and economic developments at the turn of the century have led to an authoritarian backlash, in which the Mugabe regime has been re-gearing old regulatory structures and deploying new ones in order to strengthen its control of broadcasting instead of opening it up to competition.

A comparative perspective

The presentation of the two cases above illustrates that although Zambia and Zimbabwe were exposed to more or less similar global and regional pressures to transform their broadcasting sectors, their responses to these pressures have been remarkably different. Several factors explain the variations in both the policy directions and the policy outcomes in the two countries. The approach taken in explaining these differences draws partly from 'new institutionalism' – which refers to a wide range of studies that have been integrated to provide rich explanations of policy choices and outcomes (John 1998; Peters 1999). Through the lenses of new institutionalism, I argue that internal dynamics have to a great degree determined the course and pace of broadcasting reform in each of the two countries. I also propose that three main factors account for the divergent routes in policy reform and outcomes in Zambia and Zimbabwe: first, the nature of political systems and ruling elites; second, the nature and role of civil society; and third, the historical legacy in broadcasting ownership and control patterns in the two countries.

The nature of political systems and ruling elites

In his comparative analysis of broadcasting reform in Brazil and Argentina, Hernan Galperin (2000) argued that the nature of political institutions in different countries determines the direction, pace and different outcomes of broadcasting policy reform. This argument is confirmed in the current study. How power is distributed among the executive, the legislature and the judiciary has been crucial in determining the pace and character of reforms in Zambia and Zimbabwe. The dominance of the executive branch in policy-making in both countries, which is a direct inheritance from the colonial era, has meant that legislative decisions play a much smaller role and have far less effect than decisions made by the executive. This trend has been strengthened by the syndrome of a dominant ruling party in both countries. In situations where debate on bills is conducted mostly along party lines, the ruling party is able to introduce policies favourable to its interests, with little and/or inconsequential opposition.[20]

It can be argued that the weakening of the ruling MMD party following the 2001 elections in Zambia explains the vibrancy of the debate both inside and outside Parliament, as well as the significantly liberal legislations passed in 2002; while the continued dominance of ZANU PF in the Zimbabwean Parliament could be said to have resulted in stalling and in the subsequent re-gearing process in broadcasting reform in Zimbabwe. ZANU PF's supreme decision-making organs, the Soviet-style Politburo and the Central Committee, are the central policy-making organs, and their decisions are far more effective than those of the legislature.[21] That the Minister of Information during the heady days of broadcasting reform, Jonathan Moyo, was a member of this inner circle in his capacity of Deputy Secretary for Information and Publicity, is suggestive of the executive-driven nature of those reforms.

In both countries, but particularly in Zimbabwe, the tendency to conflate the ruling party and the state has led to a situation where policies are made purportedly in the name of the 'national interest' when in practice they serve primarily the interests of the ruling party. Further, the liberation party syndrome has allowed ZANU PF to define threats to its own political survival as threats to national sovereignty, hence justifying the tightening of control over broadcasting. This is particularly evident in the way broadcasting has been used to provide a liberation narrative that puts ZANU PF at the centre, while marginalising other actors in the process (see, for example, Ranger 2004). The successful maintenance of such a narrative is predicated upon a hegemonic control over the means of communication, notably the broadcasting system. With President Mugabe having unambiguously stood against private broadcasting when he said, back in 1993 that, 'You don't know what propaganda a non-state radio station might broadcast' (Maja-Pearce 1995: 123), it is not surprising that the Presidential Powers (Temporary Measures) Act of 1986 was invoked to halt the liberalisation that would inevitably have followed the Supreme Court ruling that nullified ZBC monopoly in 2000.

Laws should be seen as part of the institutional framework that limits and constrains the choices of actors in the policy-making process. However, in countries where the rule of law is contested, such as Zimbabwe after 2000, institutional frameworks are often violated by an all-powerful executive. Thus, whereas the judiciary had passed judgement in favour of the de-monopolisation of the broadcasting sector, the Executive intervened in the name of safeguarding 'the national interest' and halted the liberalisation process. Similarly, in Zambia, the constitutional provision that all bills with financial implication must first have the assent of the President or his Deputy, led to private members' bills being thrown out of the House. Such provisions ensure that the executive has the final say in determining policy directions. In its 1999 Governance report, the Chiluba government acknowledged this dominance of the Executive and recommended placing further checks on the media in order to strengthen the state. Its report noted that:

> There is no strict separation of powers in Zambia. Each organ has administrative and decisional autonomy. There is a relationship amongst the three organs of the state that cannot be adequately served on the basis of the strict application of the doctrine of the separation of powers. The Executive determines policy, initiates legislation and maintains law and order and enforces and administers the laws enacted by the legislature. The judiciary interprets the laws and administers justice. (NAZ 1999b: 3)

However, it is important to emphasise that Zimbabwe's Presidential Powers (Temporary Measures) Act is a key distinguishing factor between the two countries, in the sense that it empowers the Executive President to intervene whenever he feels that certain policy proposals pose a threat to his own interests. That it has been used on several occasions in the past decade to deal with 'urgent' issues such as telecommunications, land and broadcasting reform indicates that it is a key instrument in ensuring that the executive will always have its way in any policy sector.

The role of the courts in influencing broadcasting reform has been more significant in Zimbabwe than it has been in Zambia. Taking their cue from the telecommunications sector, where a Supreme Court ruling had ended the PTC monopoly in 1995, broadcasting reform advocates sought recourse with the courts, resulting in the nullification of monopoly legislation. Significantly, in both the telecommunications and the broadcasting cases, the Supreme Court argued that monopolies contravened the principle of freedom of expression enshrined in Section 20 of the Zimbabwean Constitution. In Zambia, the courts played a significant role in the initial 'opening up' period, when rulings were passed in favour of opposition parties demanding equal access to the ZNBC in the run-up to the historic 1991 elections.

Another aspect worthy of mention is the sustained attack by the executive, since the beginning of land reform in Zimbabwe, on the judiciary (and particularly its white members), which led to the resignation of the Chief Justice and of two High Court judges in 2001. The white judges were perceived to be protecting white minority interests at the expense of the black majority, and hence were regarded as a stumbling block to land reform. This judicial purge led to the replacement with ruling party loyalists of judges believed to have been impartial (Taylor & Williams 2002). Although the effect of these changes on media reform cannot be easily ascertained, many commentators have interpreted developments such as the closure of the only private daily, *The Daily News*, and of three other publications, as indicative of a heavily manipulated judiciary.

Change of government can bring about significant political change, as new governments always want to distinguish themselves from their predecessors. The fact that Zimbabwe has been under the same government for some three decades, while Zambia has seen some changes in government, partly explains the continuity of state monopoly broadcasting in the former and partial reforms in the latter. Linked to this is the question of the role of individual human agency in the policy process. Traditional institutional approaches have been dismissive of the whole idea that individuals make rational choices that directly influence the policy process, arguing instead that individuals act within the confines and limits of institutions.[22] However, new institutionalism theorists now argue that 'an empirical theory of the policy process that does not centre upon human agency is unlikely to be able to explain much of what transpires' (Sabatier 1999: 215). I would argue, further, that individual human agency cannot be ignored in Africa, where the respect of ruling elites for institutions is often not consistent. Where it suits them, elites may respect institutions and allow them to play the constraining or enabling role that they are meant to play; where it does not, however, they often seek ways of either going around them or changing them completely to attain their preferred ends.

To a great extent, the ruling elite's ideological persuasion or political culture determines the overall media policy and structure. In Zambia, Kaunda's home-grown socialism (humanism) led to a command economy where media ownership and control were centralised in the hands of the government throughout the Second Republic. Similarly, in Zimbabwe, Mugabe's Marxist-Leninist socialism led to a dominant state-led media empire encompassing both print and broadcasting. It must be pointed out that both Mugabe's socialism and Kaunda's humanism were not as clear-cut as is often assumed. Both were a fuzzy mix of socialism and authoritarianism, driven by the two leaders' strong desire to remain in power. The acceptance of market-liberal reform in both countries evidently led to significant changes in their media environments. In Zambia, the embrace of market-liberal reforms by the Chiluba government has made it impossible to stop the tide of demands for media reform, while in Zimbabwe the turn to the IMF/WB-led Structural Adjustment Programme in the early 1990s saw the mushrooming of a multiplicity of publications as well as the opening of debate on broadcasting reform. However, the fact that Mugabe retained his preferred label of a socialist leader despite embracing market-liberal reform explains the cautious and reluctant economic liberalisation that took place in Zimbabwe. As a result, the Mugabe regime has been able to classify broadcasting, along with a few other state enterprises, as strategic and hence not earmarked for privatisation.

The nature of civil society and the degree of citizen participation

It has been argued that active participation and citizenship are mutually reinforcing conditions of a truly democratic society (Barber 1984; Flew 1997). The extent of citizen participation in the policy process can therefore be taken as a measure of the degree of democratisation in a particular country. Further, better policy outcomes are seen as the product of 'a never-ending process of deliberation, decision, and action' (Barber 1984: 151). To be able to participate in the policy process, however, citizens need to 'organise collectively in order to acquire the material and informational resources necessary to effective participation' (Flew 1997: 94). Owing of the practical problem of scale, however, the participation by all citizens of modern societies in the process of deliberation is not possible; thus civil society becomes the crucial site for this organisation and participation.

One of the main distinguishing features of broadcasting reform in Zambia and Zimbabwe is the nature of civil society and the space it has been able to acquire to enable it to contribute to the policy process in each country. Historically, civil society has operated under a more restricted environment in Zimbabwe than it has in Zambia. Notably, the clampdown on trade unions in Southern Rhodesia during the colonial era left a legacy of state intolerance towards civil society that has persisted up to the present day. Jonathan Moyo (1992a, 1992b) and Makumbe (1998) have illustrated how civic and political activity among the black community was criminalised in Southern Rhodesia, to the point where it was driven underground during the colonial era. The coming of independence in 1980 did not bring much reprieve either. As Moyo wrote (1992: 6):

> Instead of rectifying the situation at independence, the ruling ZANU PF party sought to take maximum advantage of an un- and under-developed civil society by claiming that it was the sole legitimate representative of the people. Under the guise of this claim, the party declared itself as the umbrella organisation of all social movements and went about destroying civil society in the name of the revolution. All 'legitimate' organisations were challenged to join the ruling party as a way of proving their revolutionary commitment.

Although not outlawed outright and not as harassed as it had been during the colonial era, civil society was cowed by the co-optation process after independence. Added to that, laws such as the (now 'repealed') Law and Order (Maintenance) Act, the Labour Relations Act, the Private and Voluntary Organisations Act, the University of Zimbabwe Amendment Act, and, more recently, the Public Order and Security Act, not only cripple but also criminalise various forms of civic activity, including the holding of assemblies, meetings or marches without prior police clearance, going on strike, and engaging in acts of civic disobedience.[23] The proposed Non-Governmental Organisations Bill, approved by Parliament in 2004, which seeks to restrict organisations working on governance and human rights issues and to register all NGOs in the country with an NGO Council, should be seen as complementary to existing laws that limit the activities of civic organisations in the country.

In Zambia, on the other hand, colonial authorities allowed trade union activity to develop among Africans, hence creating the basis for the development of a vibrant labour movement that contributed to the demands for majority rule in the 1950s and 1960s. Although civil society was co-opted and suppressed under Kaunda, it remained alive throughout his 27-year rule – albeit in muted form (Nordlund 1996; Ihonvbere 1996). The central role it played in the political transition that brought the MMD to power in 1991 has been well documented (Bratton and Van de Walle 1997; Nordlund 1996; Ihonvbere 1996). The political liberalisation in 1991 gave civil society a new lease of life, as evidenced by the emergence of a large number of NGOs and civic organisations in the 1990s. The governments of both Chiluba and

Mwanawasa regarded NGOs as 'our co-operating partners in development', which meant that, in comparison to the situation in Zimbabwe, there was less tension between the two parties. Further, the development of civil society in Zambia was aided by the rise of an independent press following the political opening discussed earlier.

The MMD government, like its predecessor, had sought to co-opt the Zambia Congress of Trade Unions as a way of eliminating potential opposition. In 1993, it amended the Industrial Relations Act of 1971 to abolish the 'one industry, one union' clause, thereby ending the era of some of the most formidable labour unions in Southern Africa. The effect, not surprisingly, was to weaken the trade union movement in Zambia (Rakner 2003). However, in the final analysis, it is fair to say that civil society in Zambia has operated in a more tolerant environment than has been the case in Zimbabwe. Added to this, the ability of civic organisations to access resources from Western donors – who were keen to see Zambia become the model of democracy for the continent – provides important explanations as to why there was more vibrant civic activity in Zambia in comparison with Zimbabwe.

It should also be pointed out that media reform advocacy groups in Zambia were far better organised and coordinated than was the case in Zimbabwe. The capacity to form a policy advocacy coalition comprising various civic actors enabled Zambian civic organisations to challenge the state as a united front. Important lessons were also learnt during the successful campaign against Chiluba's intention to stand as President for an unconstitutional third term, when churches, prominent NGOs and leading opposition politicians came together and formed the Oasis Forum as a united front capable of resisting Chiluba.[24] In Zimbabwe, on the contrary, several efforts to coordinate activities around broadcasting reform were to a great extent unsuccessful, not least because of mistrust among the civil society organisations involved. Also, whereas the Zambian campaign for broadcasting reform brought in even non-media civil-society organisations such as Women for Change, the Zimbabwean campaign was characterised by atomised media advocacy groups engaged in overlapping but uncoordinated activities. Donors themselves did not push enough, either, for the establishment of coalition networks. Apart from coming late on the scene, both the Civic Forum for Media Reform and the Civic Alliance for Social and Economic Progress failed to unite the different voices advocating media reform in Zimbabwe.

However, it must be pointed out that the failure of Zimbabwean civil society to make significant gains on the issue of broadcasting reform does not mean that civil society in that country is, in general, weak. Nor does it necessarily mean that it is generally poorly organised when compared with the Zambian one. The weaknesses outlined here are in relation to its response to the specific issue of broadcasting policy reform. In other respects and on the whole, Zimbabwean civil society is by far more sophisticated (and perhaps even much stronger) that civil society in

Zambia. What must be stressed is that a dialectical relationship exists between state and civil society, and that a responsive state will enable civil society not only to exist, but also to contribute meaningfully to the policy process. I argue that when the state is not responsive, as is the case in Zimbabwe, even the most organised civil society sector cannot make significant gains. To its credit, however, civil society in Zimbabwe successfully resisted government efforts to introduce a legislated one-party state in the late 1980s and early 1990s. It also successfully campaigned against the government-sponsored draft constitution in the 2000 referendum.[25]

Media–civil society partnerships in the campaign for broadcasting reform in the two countries have also been a key distinguishing feature. The media's contribution to the gradual maturation of civil society cannot be overemphasised. In both Zambia and Zimbabwe, as in many other countries in the region, the rise of civil society coincided with the rise of private media in the 1990s. By performing its watchdog function, the press strengthened public confidence in the understanding that politicians and public officials should not be shielded from criticism and must be accountable to the public for their actions. The exposure by a government newspaper of the 'Willowgate' scandal in 1988 in Zimbabwe, which led to the dismissal of some Cabinet ministers and the suicide of one of them, is a stark example of this new watchdog role of the press in Africa. The relationship between a burgeoning civil society and a nascent but critical independent press was therefore important for the development of both in the 1990s, to the point where, by the end of that decade, civil society had grown into a force to be reckoned with. In both countries, media-reform advocates held several sensitisation workshops with journalists, to equip them with the ideas and vocabulary of media reform. This ensured that broadcasting reform became a key issue on the national agenda.

Historical legacies in ownership patterns and interactions with the present

The process of broadcasting reform in the two countries, as described above, partly confirms the argument that policies are path-dependent, and that the policy choices taken at the formation of an institution will continue to influence future policy decisions. Broadcasting in both countries started as state monopolies during the colonial era, and was structured along the lines of the early BBC prior to the introduction of competition in Britain. Right from the beginning, policy-making in both countries was centralised in the hands of the ruling elite. The coming of independence in 1964 in Zambia, and in 1980 in Zimbabwe, did not bring to an end either state monopoly broadcasting or the executive-driven nature of policy-making: this was because the new governments found both aspects to work in their favour. State monopoly broadcasting was justified as key to nation-building, with the broadcasting institutions expected to play a major role in promoting development, national unity and national identity; while the centralisation of policy-making in the hands of the executive was generally taken for granted and treated as a norm.

In both Zambia and Zimbabwe, the legacy of the ideas and norms of past regimes continues to be strong, constraining and shaping the pace and nature of broadcasting reform in the contemporary era. However, the two countries' responses to the pressures for reform that started in the late 1980s have shown that the peculiar history of each country interacts with new realities in different ways, to bring about different outcomes. The long history of colonial broadcasting in Zimbabwe meant that at independence that country inherited a more established and fairly more stable broadcasting system than that of Zambia. In those long years of colonial rule, broadcasting was consolidated as a propaganda tool in the service of the colonial state. At the same time, liberation movements were forced by prolonged colonialism and a restrictive environment to start their own broadcasts in exile, which meant that they gained experience in the propagandistic and mass mobilising uses of broadcasting prior to coming to power (see Mosia, Riddle & Zaffiro 1994). This experience had a direct bearing on early post-independence broadcasting in Zimbabwe, where former freedom fighters were brought in to occupy senior positions at the ZBC. Independence, therefore, was not accompanied by the significant policy deflection that many people had expected. Instead, it saw the persistence of the old political logic, as the new government retained the anachronistic legislation giving monopoly status to the ZBC. The elite-driven policy-making process was also retained, in contradiction to the values of democracy that the liberation movement claimed to espouse.

Overall, there have been very few changes in Zimbabwean broadcasting policy in 28 years of independence. The most significant change was the one in 1980, when broadcasting was transformed into a medium addressing the entire citizenry of Zimbabwe instead of (mostly) the hegemonic white settler community. The spectre of ruling party use and misuse of the state broadcaster has, however, persisted up to the present day, despite the new legislation that purports to give the ZBC some autonomy.

In Zambia, as we have seen, the UNIP government consolidated state control of broadcasting at independence, and through the nationalisation process, created a vast state-controlled media empire encompassing both print and broadcasting. The results of the 'reluctant liberalisation' of broadcasting under the supposedly pro-reform MMD government have illustrated that to a large extent, the desire to maintain state monopoly broadcasting has remained persistent in Zambia also. The fact that, of all the newly licensed broadcasting stations, none can claim to be 'national' in the sense that ZNBC continues to be, is a strong indicator of the sustained dominance of this logic. Seen in this light, 'national' broadcasting remains the preserve of the state broadcaster. Further, despite the ZNBC (Amendment) Act of 2002, no practical steps have been taken to distance the ZNBC from the government of the day, meaning that it continues to serve as a government mouthpiece.

Conclusion

Both Zambia and Zimbabwe experienced global and regional pressures to transform their broadcasting sectors in the 1990s – as did other countries in the region. These pressures were part of the globalisation of neoliberal economic ideas, the goal of which is to open up hitherto closed markets to competition. Within the communications sector, telecommunications and broadcasting were the sectors most targeted for liberal reform – mainly because of their economic significance. These pressures converged with the demand for democratisation in the region, by both domestic and foreign actors.

This chapter has established that the pressures for broadcasting reform in the two countries have been multifaceted in nature, taking vertical, horizontal and bottom-up forms. It has argued, therefore, that the globalisation of neoliberal policies is not sufficient to explain the broadcasting policy reforms that have taken shape in Zambia and Zimbabwe. Although the two countries experienced more or less similar global pressures for reform, the pace and degree of adoption of these policies has been shaped largely by local political dynamics, and by the 'dialogue' created by the actors involved. A number of factors explain the different local dynamics concerned. These include the nature of political systems and ruling elites; the nature and role of civil society; and the historical legacies in the ownership and control patterns of the broadcasting sectors in the two countries.

References

Ad Hoc Committee *see* Ad Hoc Committee on Zimbabwe Broadcasting Corporation Affairs.

Ad Hoc Committee on Zimbabwe Broadcasting Corporation Affairs. 1999. *Interim Report*. 23 March.

Banda, F. 2003. *Community Radio Broadcasting in Zambia: A Policy Perspective*. Unpublished PhD dissertation, University of South Africa.

Barber, B. 1984. *Strong Democracy: Participatory Politics for a New Age*. California: University of California Press.

Baylies, C. and M. Szeftel. 1992. The fall and rise of multi-party politics in Zambia. *Review of African Political Economy* 54: 75–91.

——. 1999. Democratisation and the 1991 elections in Zambia. In *Voting for Democracy: Watershed Elections in Contemporary Anglophone Africa*, ed. M. Szeftel, R. Southall and J. Daniel, 83–109. Aldershot: Ashgate

Bratton, M. and N. Van de Walle. 1997. *Democratic Experiments in Africa: Regime Transitions in Comparative Perspective*. Cambridge: Cambridge University Press.

Chibwe, L. and B. G. Carr. 2002. *Broadcasting reform in Zimbabwe: An analysis of the ZBC Commercialisation Act*. Harare: MISA-Zimbabwe. Unpublished.

Curran, J. 2002. *Media and Power*. London and New York: Routledge.

Flew, T. 1997. Citizenship, participation and media policy formation. *Javnost* (*The Public*) 4(4): 87–102.

Galperin, H. 2000. Regulatory reform in the broadcasting industries of Brazil and Argentina in the 1990s. *Journal of Communication*, Autumn, 176–191.

Gilardi, F. 2005. The institutional foundations of regulatory capitalism: The diffusion of independent regulatory agencies in Western Europe. *American Academy of Political and Social Science* 598(1): 84–101.

Habermas, J. 1989a. *The Structural Transformation of the Public Sphere*. Cambridge: Polity.

——. 1989b. The public sphere: An encyclopaedia article. In *Critical Theory and Society: A Reader*, ed. S. E. Bronner and D. M. Kellner, 292–312. London and New York: Routledge.

Hesmondhalgh, D. 2002. *The Cultural Industries*. London, Thousand Oaks and New Delhi: Sage Publications.

Heuva, W., K. Tomaselli and R. Teer-Tomaselli. 2004. The political economy of media in Southern Africa, 1990–2001. In *Who Owns the Media? Global Trends and Local Resistances*, ed. P.N. Thomas and Z. Nain, 97–117. London & New York: Zed Books.

Hills, J. 2003. Regulatory models for broadcasting in Africa. In *Broadcasting Policy and Practice in Africa*, ed. T. Kupe, 34–70. Johannesburg: Article 19.

Högberg, P. 1993. Autonomy of the press in Zambia: A study of media control in a newborn democracy. *Minor Field Study* 23. Uppsala: Reprocentralen HSC.

Hondora, T. 2002. *The Broadcasting Services Act: An Analysis*. Harare: MISA-Zimbabwe.

Horwitz, R. B. 2001a. *Communication and Democratic Reform in South Africa*. Cambridge: Cambridge University Press.

——. 2001b. 'Negotiated liberalisation': The politics of communications sector reform in South Africa. In *Media and Globalisation: Why the State Matters*, ed. N. Morris and S. Waisbord, 37–54. Lanham, Boulder, New York and Oxford: Rowan & Littlefield Publishers.

Humphreys, P. J. 1996. *Mass Media and Media Policy in Western Europe*. Manchester and New York: Manchester University Press.

Huntington, S. P. 1993. Democracy's Third Wave. In *The Global Resurgence of Democracy*, ed. L. Diamond and M. F. Plattner, 3–25. Baltimore and London: Johns Hopkins University Press.

Hyden, G. and M. Leslie. 2002. Communications and democratisation in Africa. In *Media and Democracy in Africa*, ed. G. Hyden , M. Leslie and F. F. Ogundimu, 1–27. Uppsala: Nordiska Afrikainstitutet.

Ihonvbere, J. O. 1996. *Economic Crisis, Civil Society and Democratisation: The Case of Zambia*. Trenton and Asmara: Africa World Press.

John, P. 1998. *Analysing Public Policy*. London and New York: Pinter.

Kasoma, F. P. 1994. The legal constraints of liberalising radio broadcasting in Zambia. Paper presented at the Seminar on Liberalising Broadcasting in Zambia, organised by Zambia's Centre for Development Information in collaboration with the Panos Institute, 5–9 December, in London, England. Unpublished.

——. 1995. The role of the independent media in Africa's change to democracy. In *Media, Culture & Society* 17(4): 537–555.

——. 1997. Zambian media and the change to multi-party politics: Lessons for Africa. In *Media, Democratisation and Identity*, ed. R. Zhuwarara, K. Gecau and M. Drag, 116–126. Gweru: Mambo Press.

——. 2000a. Press and Multiparty Politics in Africa. PhD dissertation submitted to the Department of Journalism and Communication, University of Tampere, Finland. Available at http://acta.uta.fi/pdf/951-44-4968-1.pdf (accessed 31 March 2009.

——. 2000b. Choosing a model for the proposed Zambia Independent Broadcasting Authority. In ZIMA report on a one-day Independent Broadcasting Authority (IBA) advocacy coalition building workshop held at the Pamodzi Hotel in Lusaka, 11 April 2000.

——. 2001. *Community Radio: Its Management and Organisation in Zambia*. Ndola: Mission Press.

Keane, J. 1991. *The Media and Democracy*. Cambridge: Polity Press.

Koenen-Grant, J. and H. Garnett. 1996. Improving policy formulation and implementation in Zambia. In *Case Studies: A USAID Implementing Policy Change Project Publication*, April 1996.

Kupe, T. 2003a. Wanted: Media policies for democratising and developing countries in a globalising world. Paper presented at the Journalism Conference, 11–12 September, University of Stellenbosch, South Africa. http://academic.sun.ac.za/journalism/conferencepapers.html (accessed 2 February 2008).

Kupe, T. ed. 2003b. *Broadcasting Policy and Practice in Africa*. Johannesburg: Article 19.

Levi-Faur, D. and J. Jordana. 2005. The global diffusion of regulatory capitalism. *Annals of the American Academy of Political and Social Science* 598(1): 102–124.

Levy, D. A. 2001. *Europe's Digital Revolution: Broadcasting Regulation, the EU and the Nation State*. London and New York: Routledge.

Lingela, B. M. 2002. Advocacy for media law reform: The case of Zambia. Unpublished.

——. 2004. Possible implications for regulating the broadcasting industry in Zambia under the IBA Act No. 27 of 2002 – A practical perspective. Paper presented at the

Independent Broadcasting Regulation's Sensitisation Workshop for Broadcasting stations, 19 March, Ndeke Hotel, Lusaka, Zambia.

Maja-Pearce, A. 1995. Zimbabwe. In *Who Rules the Airwaves? Broadcasting in Africa*, ed. A. Maja-Pearce and R. Carver, 124–126. London: Article 19 and Index on Censorship.

Makumbe, J. M. 1998. Is there a civil society in Africa? *International Affairs* 74(2): 305–317.

Matibini, P. 2006. *The Struggle for Media Law Reforms in Zambia*. Lusaka: Media Institute of Southern Africa.

Maqeda, N. 2000. *Challenges Faced by Private Broadcasters in a Monopolistic or Semi-Deregulated Environment: A Comparative Study of MABC and Joy TV*. Unpublished MA dissertation, University of Zimbabwe.

Mosia, L., C. Riddle and J. Zaffiro. 1994. From revolutionary to regime radio: Three decades of nationalist broadcasting in Southern Africa. *Africa Media Review* 8(1): 1–23.

Moyo, D. 2004. From Rhodesia to Zimbabwe: Change without change? Broadcasting Policy Reform and Political Control. In *Media, Public Discourse and Political Contestation in Zimbabwe*, ed. H. Melber, 12–28. Uppsala: The Nordic Africa Institute.

——. 2006. Broadcasting Policy Reform and Democratisation in Zambia and Zimbabwe, 1990–2005: Global Pressures, National Responses. PhD thesis, University of Oslo, Norway.

——. 1992. Reflections on the idea of civil society in Zimbabwe. Department of Political and Administrative Studies, University of Zimbabwe. Unpublished.

——. 2001. Address to Parliament on the Occasion of Presenting the Broadcasting Services Bill. 3 April.

Mufune, P. 1996. Industrial strike patterns in Zambia. In *Democracy in Zambia: Challenges for the Third Republic*, ed. O. Sichone and B. C. Chikulo, 129–150. Harare: SAPES Books.

National Assembly of Zambia 1999b. 'Governance: National Capacity Building Programme for Good Governance in Zambia' 26th April 1999. Government Printers. Lusaka.

NAZ *see* National Assembly of Zambia.

Nhema, A. G. 2002. *Democracy in Zimbabwe: From Liberation to Liberalisation*. Harare: University of Zimbabwe Publications.

Norlund, P. 1996. *Organising the Political Agora: Domination and Democratisation in Zambia and Zimbabwe*. Uppsala: Uppsala University Press.

Nyamnjoh, F. B. 2005. *Africa's Media: Democracy and the Politics of Belonging*. London and New York: Zed Books; Pretoria: UNISA Press.

Ongeso, R. 2002. *Liberating the Airwaves: The Zimbabwean Experience*. Unpublished MA thesis submitted to the Centre for Mass Communication Research, University of Leicester, United Kingdom.

Peters, G. 1999. *Institutional Theory in Political Science: The 'New Institutionalism'*. London and New York: Continuum.

Price, M. E. and B. Rozumilowicz. 2002. Conclusion. In *Media Reform: Democratising the Media, Democratising the State*, ed. M.E. Price et al., 254–268. London & New York: Routledge.

Price, M. E., B. Rozumilowicz and S. G. Verhulst. eds. 2002. *Media Reform: Democratising the Media, Democratising the State*. London & New York: Routledge.

Rakner, L. 2003. *Political and Economic Liberalisation in Zambia, 1991–2001*. Uppsala: The Nordic Africa Institute.

Ranger, T. O. 2004. Nationalist historiography, patriotic history and the history of the nation: The struggle over the past in Zimbabwe. *Journal of Southern African Studies* 30(2): 215–243.

Rønning, H. 1994. *Media and Democracy: Theories and Principles with Reference to an African Context: Seminar Paper Series No. 8*. Harare: SAPES Books.

——. 2003. *The Media Situation in Zambia, with Special Reference to the Norwegian Support for Zambian Media: Report Prepared for The Royal Norwegian Embassy, Lusaka, November 2002–February 2003*.

Sabatier, P. 1999. The need for better theories. In *Theories of the Policy Process*, ed. P. Sabatier, 3–17. Colorado and Oxford: Westview Press.

Sabatier, P. and H. C. Jenkins-Smith. 1999. The advocacy coalition framework: An assessment. In *Theories of the Policy Process*, ed. P. Sabatier, 117-166. Colorado and Oxford: Westview Press.

Wales, Z. 2000. *Media Ownership Trends in Namibia, Malawi, Tanzania, Zambia and Zimbabwe*. Windhoek: Media Institute of Southern Africa, Regional Secretariat.

Realising or dreaming?

Vision 2016, media reform and democracy in Botswana

10

As key actors in civil society, African mass media possess an as yet mostly unrealised potential to play beneficial nurturing and mediating roles between state and citizenry. Under the right conditions, electronic media and the press can offer useful opportunities for the transmission and analysis of important political information and ideas. Allowed to flourish, media can function as arenas for political education, debate, and awareness-raising, thereby facilitating wider, deeper political participation, and encouraging greater public accountability by ruling elites. With the requisite social and political legitimacy, resources, and professionalism, mass media can even serve as a bridge across election cycles, when political parties are less visible, organised or active. The key word here is 'potential', however.

This chapter critically examines the nature and impact of contemporary mass media regulation in Botswana, in the context of a rapidly changing society. It argues that Botswana's mass media have yet to live up to their potential to act as agents of political socialisation and catalysts for social capital growth, helping to inform, educate, and empower the citizens of a maturing democratic political culture.

As the senior leaders of the ruling Botswana Democratic Party (BDP) look ahead to 2016, the 50-year mark since legal independence, they have laid out highly ambitious information and media-freedom goals in Vision 2016, the country's long-term strategic plan. Yet the challenges associated with moving from words to implementation are daunting, as a younger, better-educated and highly ambitious generation begins to assume leadership roles within the political and economic system. To what extent are Botswana's mass media positioned to act as agents of positive change on the road to 2016 and beyond?

The early years of the twenty-first century witnessed notable growth in the commercial media sector in Botswana, with three new radio, several television, and eight new press options appearing. Media professionalism is gradually showing signs of improvement, following the opening of a new Media Studies Programme at the University of Botswana and an influx of media workers from abroad. Major obstacles remain, including the state control of public service media, small markets and insufficient financial support for independent media. Rural Batswana are not benefiting from media expansion, as virtually all of it is urban-focused. Eleven of thirteen national newspapers are published, and mainly circulate in, Gaborone (Sechele 2006: 6). Beset by widening global and local economic constraints, HIV/AIDS and paternalistic administrative elites, media outlets may aspire to fulfil their role in realising Vision 2016; however this looks to remain more a dream than an achievable project.

Particular emphasis is devoted to describing and analysing the social and political impact of recent media reforms and regulation efforts. The broad outlines of the political economy of Botswana mass media, from the 1990s through 2016, are explored. Aspects of the problem to be identified and critically analysed include:

- key national, regional, and global socio-economic and political trends and processes shaping Botswana's contemporary media structures, functions, and regulation;

- efforts by government to legislate or administratively impose standards and regulations for broadcasting and the press;

- the responses of Batswana journalists and media managers to government attempts at regulation and management;

- trends and prospects for future media–government relations in Botswana; and

- trends and prospects for the mass media and the democratisation of Botswana politics and society.

Theoretical context

One significant barometer of systemic democracy can be the extent of media involvement in civil society relations with state institutions. Civil society groups need freedom of expression and access to information in order to mobilise, organise and act in the political arena. Sustainable democracy requires sustainable political communication networks. Without them, it is not possible to widen and deepen legitimate, representative political institutions and processes (Bennett 1998: 198, 201–202). Lack of access to political knowledge and information hinders participation, especially by those most in need of empowerment: the poor, the unemployed, ethnic and linguistic minorities, isolated rural communities and women.

As engaged members of civil society, mass media organisations can and do play intermediary roles between state and citizenry (Zaffiro 2000). To be sustainable, however, they must be perceived as legitimate, objective, independent and professional – not only by viewers, listeners, and readers, but also by representatives of the state. This process is gradual and not necessarily unidirectional; it requires a stable, supportive political, economic and social environment. The existence of non-state broadcasting and press outlets guarantees nothing, although it serves as an important indicator of potential success. Ultimately, financial and editorial independence may turn out to be more important than ownership or control.

Nyamnjoh (2005) argues that political, cultural, historical and economic realities determine what form and meaning the discussion and articulation of citizenship and rights assume in any given context. The media reflect and also shape African societies. They can only play an effective role if the law and its applications are democratic and when 'they as institutions acquire and live the virtue of tolerance' (p. 17). While most African governments have done little to encourage media freedom, 'the media themselves must share some of the blame. Many journalists and the publications they work for have been so politicised and disrespectful of the need to base reports on facts and the collection of evidence that their role in promoting democratisation has been very limited' (p. 20). Thus, it is important not only to identify and analyse 'government problems with the newly developed fourth power', but also to look for evidence of 'lack of comprehension by journalists and editors' when it comes to defining the role of the media in a democratic society (p. 23).

A good analytical framework focuses on media–government relations, with media understood as a special type of civil society actor. Media systems co-evolve with the rest of the local political, economic and social biota. Policy-makers and media have often interacted as if each group had arrived from its own, very different planet – and indeed this will continue to be the case until the two begin to accept, work with and eventually trust one another. In post-colonial societies, the liberal democratic media culture paradigm is very powerful; it is further magnified and reinforced by foreign media education, training, and socialisation experiences, again almost exclusively centred on Western media values, attitudes and professional ideologies.

Media roles are especially malleable during times of system transition; they must change in tune with transformed political institutions and processes, articulating the reform efforts of civil society (Wiseman 1996: 55; Bratton and Van de Walle 1997: 292–93). Contemporary African mass media aspire to support civil society efforts to widen and deepen democratic institutions and processes. They will play more positive social and political roles as they start to adapt better within dynamic, rapidly changing societies and political cultures. The same holds for political parties and other civil society groups.

Vision 2016: Dreaming of a 'smooth' social and political transformation

Botswana today is navigating a crucial period of system transition. Civil society is much stronger in 2009 than it was a decade ago; the growth and rising aspirations of the mass media dramatically reflect and support this positive trend. The 1990s witnessed steadily improving conditions for the germination of civil society groups. Top officials in the large information-hoarding bureaucracy became less isolated from citizen thinking than they had ever been before; and some even came to accept the idea that government programmes might work better if the public participated in policy formulation. The issue is two-fold: (a) changing the dominant political culture, which does not include a tradition of interest-group politics; and (b) convincing ruling elites that civil society groups represent mass publics, particularly rural citizens who still, by and large, prefer a more decentralised, grassroots, community-based type of politics (Holm & Molutsi 1992: 82–83, 85). These challenges present special opportunities for public service and commercial media to enhance their roles.

The closest thing to an official blueprint for enhanced democratic governance and media reform is the 1997 Presidential Task Group Report, 'Vision 2016'. It says, in part:

'The society of Botswana by the year 2016 will be free and democratic, a society where information on the operations of Government, private sector, and other organisations is freely available to all citizens. There will be a culture of transparency and accountability' (p. 6).

'The Botswana of the future will be a community-oriented democracy, with strong, decentralised institutions' (p. 11).

'The challenge is to ensure the access of all families to information technology, television, audio and print media, and to develop an environment conducive to the free flow of information among all the communities of Botswana' (p. 20).

'There is an urgent need to develop the media, especially radio and television, [to] communicate the Vision to ordinary people, particularly in areas of low literacy levels. Freedom of the press must be guaranteed in law and practice. The media in Botswana must be deregulated in order to encourage citizen involvement. Media development will require a partnership with the private sector. Media freedom does need to be balanced by sound media ethics and [by] a code of conduct that is enforced by the profession itself' (p. 35).

'Botswana must encourage a degree of transparency so that the reasons for decisions and policies are understood by the population. This will require an open acceptance that mistakes and failures are made and an open discussion about how policies and strategies might be improved. At every level there will need to be free and informed political debate that subjects every decision and policy to careful consideration from those with differing views' (p. 57).

These extracts show that the mass media are clearly identified as major players in this long-term reform process. How did this come about? The 1990s swept powerful global, regional and national political and economic trends into Botswana. The birth of democratic governments and free media in the former communist states of Eastern Europe, the coming of majority rule in South Africa and the rising tide of economic and information globalisation all had a significant impact on Botswana's civil society and government. From a national political standpoint, interest in media reforms intensified amid the growing perception of serious, ongoing system legitimacy problems. These were low public awareness about government activities; citizen apathy about politics; low voter registration and turnout; a culture of administrative secrecy; fragmented opposition parties; persistent poverty; unemployment and economic inequality; angry student protests; and increasingly insistent demands for gender rights.

Reforms at the South African Broadcasting Corporation (SABC) after 1994 and the creation of that country's Independent Broadcasting Authority (IBA) in 1995 (Teer-Tomaselli 1998) sharpened arguments that Botswana's government should grant public broadcasting status to Radio Botswana (RB), allow commercial broadcasting, and proceed with long-standing plans to initiate a national television service. Some media changes followed closely on the heels of significant political reforms. Others were stalled. Following unprecedented opposition gains in the 1994 elections, pressure increased on the ruling BDP to undertake measures designed to make political life more participatory. A 1997 referendum lowered the voting age from 21 to 18 and established an Independent Electoral Commission. The Constitution was amended, limiting sitting Presidents to two five-year terms, and an Office of the Ombudsman was created (Zaffiro 2002: B626).

Support for a public, service-oriented, broadcasting parastatal was growing, both inside and outside government, which was being accused of poor public relations. '... even with a powerful tool like Radio Botswana [it] still cannot communicate effectively with the people', said the newspaper *Mmegi* in October 1994 (p. 19). Faced with an increasingly significant opposition electoral challenge, the BDP had to demonstrate its accountability and transparency. Government media managers put effort into responding to complaints, and also into raising credibility and efficiency while moving towards a self-financing operation. Media interests outside government wanted a more decentralised, pluralistic and non-partisan structure of broadcast management and administration.

The absence of clear legal guidelines was stunting and delaying broadcast development. Applications to government for commercial radio and television broadcasting licenses increased sharply in the mid-1990s, spurred on by fears that broadcast deregulation in neighbouring South Africa would choke out commercial opportunities for locally owned stations. A 1996 court challenge by Patrick Gunda, a licence applicant who also happened to be a government lawyer in the Attorney General's Chambers, brought the matter to a head. Gunda challenged the legality of the refusal, by the Office of the President and the Botswana Telecommunications Commission, to grant his Radio GAGA a radio and television licence on the grounds that no such regulatory legislation existed (*Daily News*, 15 August 1996). Early in 1996, the *Midweek Sun* obtained an internal government discussion document which candidly acknowledged that 'RB is perceived as the voice of government because of the predominantly one-sided presentation of views'. It was 'in government's own interest to allow broadcasting a certain measure of professional and managerial autonomy as a way of building credibility for the system' (24 April 1996). Official acceptance, however, would prove difficult.

The road was growing long and twisted. After false starts in 1994 and 1997, the government agreed to defer the introduction of a proposed media law and to consult with local journalists to re-draft acceptable comprehensive media reform and regulatory legislation. Twelve months of dialogue with representatives from the Botswana Journalists' Association (BOJA) and the local chapter of the Media Institute of Southern Africa (MISA-Botswana) produced a compromise bill in May 1998. Both the product and the process were cited as models for other states in the region (Nkhoma 1998: 2). The National Assembly approved a Broadcasting Act, with provisions for the licensing of commercial and community stations, and a National Broadcasting Board (NBB), responsible for considering licensing requests and the allocation of frequency spectrum resources, 'to ensure the widest possible diversity of programming' (MISA 2004: 24–27). Since 1999, the NBB has been managed by the Ministry of Communication, instead of the Office of the President, where it was initially housed.

Acknowledging the limits of the 1998 statute and responding to the pressure to act on the promise of a national television service, government consultants echoed the calls of media organisations for a comprehensive national mass-media policy, pointing specifically to the importance of clearly spelling out the nature and role of public service media. The result was the controversial 2001 Mass Media Communications Bill, which was withdrawn for further study shortly after its stormy reception in the National Assembly. This bill contained no provision for the regulation of, or access to, public service broadcasting. With Botswana still without effective legal instruments guaranteeing editorial independence, many in the public media continue to practise 'defensive journalism' (for example by trying to second-guess the intentions of the government); and avoid investigative reporting in favour of 'safer' forms of writing, such as relaying the content of ministerial speeches (Fombad 2002: 663, 667).

Media responses to government reform efforts

Historically, the Botswana media have been in the forefront of advocacy for system democratisation and media reform, especially since the emergence of a nascent private press in the country (Zaffiro 1988). Yet, as Nyamnjoh asserts, 'most lawmakers see journalists as potential troublemakers who must be policed (2005: 70). Since the days of the Protectorate, officials have been socialised into an inherited government information culture of 'British-inspired libel, sedition, defamation and official secrets acts' which demands that they 'control and contain' rather than share information about the activities, deliberations, and policy decisions of government. This has resulted in extremely limited access to information, particularly by the private press. Among Vision 2016's most cherished recommendations, from the standpoint of mass media, is that it urges the introduction of a Freedom of Information Act to protect the right of citizens to obtain and use information, the holy grail of Fourth Estate reforms.

Since 2004, Botswana's media workers and managers have stepped up their organising and networking efforts. One result is an increasingly well-articulated campaign of self-improvement, accountability, professionalism, ethics and self-regulation. Media groups now repeatedly call upon government to dialogue directly with them over the specific form that official state media policies, laws, and regulations should take. A major concern is the prevention of legislation mandating the licensing and accreditation of media workers by government, as already exists in some neighbouring states, notably Zimbabwe. In 2004 the new Botswana Press Council drew up a Media Code of Ethics 'for the purpose of regulating standards in the print sector' (MISA 2004: 37–40). The code sets out guidelines for fair and accurate reporting by media practitioners, and creates a Complaints and Appeals Committee aimed at 'hearing complaints and concerns raised by members of the public'. The NBB also announced a draft Code of Conduct, 'to guide broadcasters during coverage of the national elections, to ensure free and fair coverage'. In that same year, Batswana editors from print and electronic, public and private media formed the Botswana Editors Forum to 'deal with issues that militate against their work and operational issues such as editorial independence'. Public sentiment, at least among urban readers and audiences, aligns strongly with the media, as at least one recent survey underscores (Nyamnjoh, Forcheh and Maphanyane 2002).

Media organisations and legal experts in Botswana have long argued that, in the absence of adequate legal safeguards to check government media manipulation, and in the context of a heavily executive-centred constitutional system and a political set-up insufficiently competitive to test the country's democratic institutions, the danger is real that the ruling party will use state broadcasting to its own advantage (Sechele 2000). Sections 3 and 12 of the Botswana Constitution provide for freedom of expression, yet partly nullify the enjoyment or protection of that right by specifying a number of limitations on it, all of which have been extensively relied upon by the state to enact legislation and regulations, and to establish practices, that effectively restrict or inhibit freedom of expression. Even more troubling to media organisations and workers is the lack of constitutional protection for media freedom (Balule & Maripe 2000: 2–4).

Colonial-era laws, some drafted by expatriates (Zaffiro 1989), are no way to regulate, let alone build up and encourage, the '21st-Century Fourth Estate' that Vision 2016 talks about. Although they are rarely used, the government has refused to repeal them. Penal Code No. 2 of 1964 encompasses sedition, defamation and contempt, and can be invoked against published and depicted information, and against citizens and non-citizens alike. Section 47 gives the President absolute discretion to prohibit any publication that, in his opinion, is contrary to the public interest. Section 50(1) criminalises sedition, prohibiting publication of anything that

> brings hatred or contempt, or that cites disaffection against the President or the Government of Botswana or against the administration of justice; or raises discontent or disaffection among the inhabitants of Botswana or promotes ill-will and hostility between different classes of the population of Botswana.

Balule and Maripe (2000) have written a 62-page inventory of 'media-unfriendly laws and practices in Botswana'. The Cinematograph Act of 1970 provides for the censorship of films and publications. The Printed Publications Act of 1968 provides for the registration of certain newspapers. Disabling litigation has been utilised against critics in the independent press. *The Examiner*, *Mmegi*, *Botswana Guardian* and *Midweek Sun* have all been subject to large claims for damages (Good 1999: 51–55).

Statutory limitations to constitutionally protected freedom of expression also surface in more recent laws. The apartheid-era inspired National Security Act of 1986 prohibits 'the publication or communication of any information relating to the defence or security of the country' or publication of any classified material without authority. Section 13(2) 'could potentially be used by the Attorney General to compel journalists to disclose confidential sources of information' (MISA 2004: 30–31). Major government power to limit media freedom also emanates from specific official uses and interpretations of such statutes, and by sweeping limitations and the denial of information access as a matter of policy.

Turning up the heat: Government responses to pressures for media reform

Between the 1999 and 2004 elections, it became evident that an irreversible process of media system reform had been unleashed. Government macroeconomic policy successes were beginning to carry potentially unsettling reform implications for the country's as yet electorally undefeated, but increasingly challenged, ruling elites. One way to characterise the changing national mood, especially in urban centres, was as a growing expectation that more media freedom, openness and participatory democracy, long overdue, must come soon; and that the stability and prosperity of the country might be at risk if nothing changed.

At the same time, intensified external pressures to adopt reforms based on Western liberal democratic ideas about media and freedom of information were being aimed at the Government of Botswana. A prime example of the types of 'soft conditionalities' involved was the USA's offer to promote trade with selected African states in exchange for preferential market access for Botswana's textiles. Naturally, the country's embrace of globalisation made its leaders eager to diversify and expand their own export-oriented economy via new trade, manufacturing and investment opportunities. Similar calls for reform reciprocity emanated from the EU, causing Botswana's ruling elites to respond more quickly and positively to 'calls for legal reforms to abolish or modify restrictive media laws, diplomatic signals or disincentives for using extra-legal measures to harass the press, and ending the state monopoly over media enterprises via privatisation and commercialisation exercises' (Ogundimu 2002: 209).

Yet while touting media freedom in Botswana, cabinet ministers and public service elites still adhere tightly to the idea that the government knows best and has the legal right to regulate and police the fourth estate. In 2006, Deputy Permanent Secretary in the Ministry of Communication, Andrew Sesinyi, warned government media that they should exercise 'maximum patriotic solidarity, collective responsibility, and allegiance to country and nation' in their reporting of controversial issues. This followed a story that appeared in *Mmegi*, a private paper, headlined 'Government media instructed on CKGR', in which Sesinyi was quoted as having instructed government media to ensure that any negative reporting on the controversial relocations of the San people from the Central Kalahari Game Reserve be balanced by government statements, and as lashing out at private media for 'rallying behind the enemy'. In August 2007, the *Tswana Times* newspaper accused the Botswana Telecommunications Corporation (BTC) of denying it advertising support as punishment for publishing an unfavourable report about the corporation on 16 March 2007.

There are a few hopeful signs. Minister of Communication, Pelonomi Venson-Moitoi, seems to represent a genuine softening of the position that the media simply have to accept whatever the government decides. She has won praise for her condemnation of the failure by the police to intervene in physical and verbal attacks on journalists. Even more welcome has been her willingness to consult with media organisations on redrafting the 2001 Mass Media Bill. This legislation would grant recognition to the Press Council of Botswana 'as a self-regulating body that will monitor the activities of the press and ensure the maintenance of high professional standards and responsibility for accreditation of journalists, the handling [of] public complaints, and [the] enforcement of a Code of Ethics' (*Mmegi*, 7 May 2007). Increasingly assertive ruling party backbenchers have stepped up calls for the independence of Parliament from presidential and Cabinet control. Indeed, the urban elements of the wider civil society, led by a more assertive, highly educated and independent-minded younger generation of professionals, are standing up to their hard-working but inaccessible and ageing leaders. They, too, now expect that the fine and often-repeated words about media as the fourth estate and the importance of media freedom will come to have real meaning in practice.

The ruling generation, still attuned to paternalistic democracy, is slowly being forced to give way, or fight a holding action. Most ruling elites remain dubious about the media, holding low opinions of its professionalism, ethics and performance. In December 2007, outgoing President Festus Mogae lectured journalists, noting that the profession 'had grown in volume but was still lacking in quality' (Modise 2007). In March 2008, President Ian Khama inherited the responsibility for dealing with (if not exactly managing) this socially volatile, partly reformed media system, probably until the time when the government finally arrives at some final version of Vision 2016. With the rapid approach of the 2009 elections, his government, like those of his predecessors, is determined to identify, propose and manage all the major mass media and information reforms in its own way and based on its own timeline.

Towards a twenty-first century public-service mass media

For media institutions to play significant roles in system democratisation, there is a need, as Fombad (2002: 650) says, to 'widen and deepen [them as] institutions of voice and accountability' for the audiences they serve. Despite a major influx of new digital information technologies into Botswana, a majority of Batswana still depend upon public service broadcasting, especially Radio Botswana (RB) 'as the main and dominant source of news and opinion for the foreseeable future', because they are within reach of a signal and RB is free. Today, about 80 per cent of the population has access to good quality AM and/or FM signals; and plans to improve reception continue (NDP 9 2003: 360).

Since its birth in the 1930s, broadcasting in Botswana has developed based on two imported models: those of the BBC and the South African Broadcasting Corporation (SABC). Anti-communism, colonial paternalism, anti-nationalism and apartheid all subsequently tainted post-independence national media policies, management and content. Foreign models also bequeathed heavy doses of state-centric elitism and a strong preference for using media to disseminate centralised, top-down, one-size-fits-all ideas about development, all of which still echo and endure right down to the present day (Zaffiro 1989, 2001).

Another legacy is the lack of a commonly accepted agreement about what public service media are, or should be: 'fluctuat[ing] between conceptions based upon paternalism, elitism, and consumerism, with the current trend being towards the latter' (Fombad 2002: 656).

Fombad offers six general principles, largely derived from Western legal-constitutional guarantees of freedom of expression, as relevant to public service media: (1) general availability; (2) a concern for promoting national identity and culture; (3) independence from both state and commercial interests; (4) the promotion of impartiality; (5) the provision of a wide range of programmes; and (6) mixed sources of funding, including state and commercial sources. The only legal clue as to what the public service concept may mean in Botswana is found in Section 2 of the Broadcasting Act of 1998, which speaks of 'a public broadcasting service provided by any statutory body which is funded either wholly or partly through state revenue'(Fombad 2002: 656–58, 661).

As Fombad rightly points out, 'the public media cannot operate in a policy-free zone'. Yet they can 'direct state intervention needs to be revised downwards' (ibid: 670). A survey of National Development Plan 8 (1998–2003) reveals a glaring lack of attention to media policy or specific goals and objectives for developing public service broadcasting, community radio, or greater media pluralism (RoB 1997: 441–42). National Development Plan 9 (2004–2009), like all the previous Plans, emphasises technology upgrades, the expansion of facilities and radio and TV coverage (RoB 2003: 361). Yet even in the absence of any articulated public service vision or policy, some of these projects bode well for what may eventually become a more decentralised, public, service-oriented national mass media system.

Efforts at creating a rural news-gathering and reporting infrastructure have finally begun. By the end of the planning period, the Department of Information and Broadcasting will have three regional offices and nine district offices, each equipped with 'fully fledged newsrooms and studios' to 'cater for publications, BOPA (the national press agency) Radio Botswana, and Botswana Television'. Radio and television programme production equipment will be purchased 'to improve local content and to address [the] imbalance in local/regional news coverage' (RoB 2003: 76–77).

Community radio had been very slow to arrive and government had done little to facilitate its development. The Catholic Church in Mahalapye attempted unsuccessfully to establish a community radio station in 1996 (*Mmegi*, 5–11 April 1996). Another unsuccessful community pilot radio project, financed by China, was proposed in 1998, to empower rural area dwellers in the far western Ghanzi District 'to develop their own programs and messages, and to link scattered communities with common goals' (*Daily News*, 18 August 1998). In November 2007, a group of organisers announced plans to apply for a licence for a community radio station to serve the Old Naledi settlement on the outskirts of Gaborone.

Participants at a May 2007 Article 19 Conference on Policy and Regulation for Media Pluralism in Africa decried the tendency of African governments 'to think they are practising diversity just by licensing a couple of private stations to operate alongside state broadcasters' (Naji 2007). In 2007, the NBB issued licences for nation-wide broadcasts to three commercial radio stations, Yarona FM, Gabz FM, and a new entry in the market, Duma FM, raising the total number of stations in the country to five. Yarona and Gabz were the first commercial broadcasters to be given licences in 1998, for broadcasting within a 30 km–40 km radius of Gaborone. One of the requirements for all licensees is that 40 per cent of content be local. The NBB has the authority to issue and revoke licences. In a call for a more level playing field among its direct competitors, the General Manager of Yarona FM called upon the NBB to also license the government-owned, commercial station, Radio Botswana 2 (RB). As of 2009, RB was not yet licensed.[1]

The NBB, the broadcasting regulatory authority, does not yet have legal jurisdiction over BTV, which remains 'technically a division of the Department of Broadcasting Services, with negative implications for editorial independence and control' (MISA 2004: 8). Government remains reluctant to allow deregulation to move beyond this point. This is bad news, in terms of prospects for the democratisation of existing Botswana media, and the opening up of new communicative spaces.

Media globalisation and the political economy of television in Botswana

Rupert Murdoch has probably never worried about the Botswana media market. Yet by the 1990s, the globalisation of electronic communication was accomplishing what apartheid and wealth in diamonds had not been able to achieve. As commercial television and a deregulated SABC in South Africa made unprecedented headway in the Botswana market, government cost-benefit calculations began to shift rapidly in favour of setting up a national service before foreign commercial competition became unbeatable. M-Net, the international pay-TV station, arrived in Botswana's two main cities in 1993 (Collins 1996). In 1996, in a multi-page advertising supplement in *Mmegi*, M-Net proclaimed that 'Digital satellite television comes to Botswana' (29 March 1996), offering more than 24 pay-TV channels beamed to subscribers from the recently launched PAS4 satellite. Two years later the PAS7, offering more channels, was launched by MultiChoice, M-Net's platform provider. In 1998 M-Net, in cooperation with BBC-TV, offered around-the-clock entertainment and news to its Batswana subscribers (Sechele 1998: 414).

The question of national TV was called by the pressures of the market. TV was coming – had come – to urban Botswana, whether or not government agreed to go forward with its own service. National television arrived late – 34 years after national independence – in Botswana, with the launch of BTV in 2000. A key factor in the decision to introduce a government service was the belief that private or joint venture services would not invest in extending coverage to sparsely populated rural areas (*Daily News*, 5 March 1996). At its inception, officials emphasised that BTV would not be a government mouthpiece. However, BTV News and Current Affairs Director, Chris Bishop, resigned in May 2001, stating that 'I can no longer run a TV news service wit the current level of interference. Journalists at BTV have often been harassed by officialdom' (Nyamnjoh 2002: 2).

Currently, 40% of the population has access to Botswana TV via terrestrial transmitter coverage. Existing satellite systems already allow for national coverage of 100%. Ground reception equipment, especially in the most isolated rural areas, is still very scarce. (RoB 2003: 362). In addition, the Educational Broadcasting Division of the Ministry of Education is now providing BTV and radio programming based on the national primary-level curriculum, and other current affairs and 'Educational Forum' offerings aimed at more general audiences (ibid: 285). In 2007, GTV, another pay-per-view service offering twelve channels, joined the urban market. GBC (Gaborone Broadcasting Company) is the other private commercial service.

Building trust by enhancing professionalism

In 2002, MISA-Botswana undertook a national survey on the level and perception of freedom of expression in Botswana. Asked what could be done to enhance media freedom in the country, 71 per cent of respondents selected 'greater professionalism in news gathering and dissemination'. Almost nine in ten agreed that 'to ensure that all information is true before reporting' should be a guiding principle; over 65 per cent of respondents also agreed that 'be impartial in reporting national and international news', 'relentless pursuit of truth at all costs', and 'seek approval of people before quoting or publishing them' should also be guiding principles (Nyamnjoh 2002: 11–13, 15).

The majority of Batswana journalists are secondary-school graduates, young and inexperienced, with no formal media training. The generally low status accorded to media work as a career, the low salaries, and the lack of access to information sources and key decision-makers, are three key problems that must be addressed. The Botswana media have suffered from chronic turnover, insufficient numbers of approved posts, and lack of trained personnel. Experienced people soon leave for better jobs in administration, public relations or international organisations. UNESCO-organised print and radio training courses have been offered; expatriate trainers have been contracted; and record numbers of scholarships for foreign study and training have been approved (Maswabi 1998: 3). But the recipients have continued to flee.

In May 1998, the University of Botswana announced plans to establish a Department of Media Studies, Journalism and Public Relations. Besides offering degree programmes for aspiring journalists, the programme would target people already working in the media, and others in government and private sector posts who dealt with the media (Basimane 1998: 5). The department finally opened in 2002, and its first crop of undergraduates qualified in 2006. At the time of writing, most media workers continue to rely mainly on in-service training (Sechele 2006:15). Nevertheless, these enhanced opportunities for the professional training and development of journalists represent the single most significant measure capable of improving chances for a more credible, responsive, free and society-serving media sector. To the extent that the resources and time necessary to positively affect the careers of practising and aspiring Batswana journalists are provided, the media-based goals contained in Vision 2016 may yet be realised.

Conclusion

The power to police the fourth estate is the power to grant or deny the development of – and access to – 'communicative spaces' for entire communities, especially economically poor and politically marginalised ones. If Vision 2016 is to move from dream to experienced national reality, and especially to a more transparent, decentralised, informed and participatory civic culture for all Batswana, then public service media are simply 'too important, in terms of reach and accessibility for [them] to be controlled by government' (Fombad 2002: 667–68).

In terms of development, the rural and urban poor have no other recourse but the development of public service media policies and resources aimed to serve their interests and needs. These will help to activate their legal political rights and to shape their responsibilities. The continuing monopolisation of public service media by the government, at this delicate stage of democratic consolidation, puts at risk the long-term political, economic and social development of Botswana.

The widening information divide between digital haves and have-nots is also a freedom of expression divide. Access in low-income and rural areas should be increased, by implementing more proactive education policies and creating rural community centres with television and radio. (These media) should not take a back seat to Internet access. Information should be in multiple languages, not just the principal and the official languages, and appropriate to the age and educational level of the audience. It should include programmes with useful local content created by the users themselves (Thapisa 2003).

Public service media (PSM) are vital for Botswana's poor and disenfranchised. Fombad's five 'fundamental principles for a revised, legitimate public service model' (p. 670) provide strong scaffolding upon which to build a system appropriate to Vision 2016. They are:

- Guarantees of freedom from state control, interference or domination.

- Guarantees of pluralism, diversity, fairness and impartiality.

- Clear rules on elections and political broadcasting.

- Clear rules on funding.

- An independent statutory body to control and supervise PSM.

Independence is critical. The new statutory public service media body will have to make a serious effort to recruit people who genuinely reflect Botswana's diverse population and to address a whole range of interests, including rural, urban, educational, linguistic, gender and commercial interests. At the same time, active members of the public service and elected office holders will have to be excluded from the body. Enabling legislation must contain safeguards against domination of the body by pro-government appointees, the dangers of which are currently dramatically clear in the case of Zimbabwe's Mass Media Trust (Zaffiro 2001b: 103). A workable mechanism for public accountability must also be written into the law, perhaps taking the form of regular National Assembly oversight or of external assessments by professional media regulatory organisations. Lacking popular legitimacy and credibility, any public media authority risks the same fate as an unheard, unwatched or unread media outlet: loss of audience, and social and political irrelevance.

With globalisation, Botswana's leaders cannot prevent 'the extension of the public discourse to communicative spaces outside the realm of direct government control' (Ogundimu 2002: 233). The growing availability of decentralised communications carries its own potential risks and benefits for the democratisation of politics and society. Each year more Batswana have access to e-mail, cell phones, the Internet, foreign stations and satellite broadcast outlets. The freedom to access, share, exchange and scrutinise political information instantly is already making the (urban) political arena in Botswana more open, raising the real possibility that 'policing the fourth estate' may simply become irrelevant as people by-pass it altogether for access to political information and freedom of expression. In that sense, key aspects of Vision 2016 are already out of date.

At its best, media can facilitate and connect, empower and clarify, offer a forum for proposals and serve as a reality check for governing elites. There even appears to be a significant relationship between the degree of media freedom and corruption in a society. One recent empirical study concludes that restrictions on press freedom lead to higher levels of corruption; and that political and economic influences on the media are strongly related to corruption (Frelle, Haque & Kneller 2007). To nurture democracy, the media must acquire the capacity to anticipate and analyse not only the actions of politicians but also policies and their wider social implications (Ngugi 1988: 51). To be able to reach that point, media organisations and journalists themselves need empowerment and support, alongside other crucial but underdeveloped civil society groups. Finally, media cannot successfully play this key role without education, training, and experience (Chimutengwende 1988: 29–45). In advocating for a democratic transformation of the broadcasting sector, Batswana media workers have already benefited significantly from effective regional partnerships with advocacy groups such as the Media Institute of Southern Africa and the Southern African Broadcasting Association, groups which they themselves have a major hand in helping to forge, across the SADC region and beyond.

References

Balule, T. and B. Maripe. 2000. *A Quick Guide to Laws and Practices that Inhibit Freedom of Expression in Botswana*. Gaborone: Media Institute of Southern Africa.

Basimane, I. 1998. University plans to introduce media studies. *Daily News*, 15 May.

Bennett, L. 1998. The media and democratic development. In *Communicating Democracy: The Media and Political Transitions*, ed. P. H. O'Neill, 195–208. Boulder: Lynne Reinner Publishers.

Bojosi, O. 1996. The constitutional rights of the mass media in Botswana. In *Botswana's Media and Democracy*, ed. M. Leepile, 53–66. Gaborone: Mmegi Publishing Trust.

Bratton, M and N. van de Walle.1997. *Democratic Experiments in Africa: Regime Transitions in Comparative Perspective*. Cambridge: Cambridge University Press.

Chimutengwende, C. 1988. The role of communication in the development and democratization of African Society. *Africa Media Review* 2(2): 29–45.

Collins, R. 1996. Reforming South African broadcasting. In *South African Media Policy*, ed. P. E. Louw, 79–100. Johannesburg: Anthropos Press.

Fako, T. and F. Nyamnjoh. 2000. Waiting for Botswana television: Benefits and consequences. *Media Development* 48(3): 37–44.

Fombad, C. 2002. The protection of freedom of expression in the public service media in Southern Africa: A Botswana perspective. *Modern Law Review* 65(5): 649–675.

Frelle, S., E. Hanque and R. Kneller. 2007. A contribution to the empirics of press freedom and corruption. *European Journal of Political Economy* 23(4): 838–862.

Good, K. 1999. Enduring elite democracy in Botswana. In *The Resilience of Democracy*, ed. P. Burnell and P. Calvert, 50–66. London: Frank Cass.

Holm, J. and P. Molutsi. 1992. State–society relations in Botswana. In *Governance and Politics in Africa*, ed. G. Hayden and M. Bratton, 75–95. Boulder: Lynne Reinner.

Maswabi, A. 1998. 68 students go for journalism training. *Daily News*, 3 June.

Media Institute of Southern Africa. 2004. *A Comparative Overview of Media Law and Practice in Botswana, Swaziland & Zambia*. Johannesburg: Konrad Adenauer Foundation.

——. 2008. Controversial media practitioners' Bill announced. 7 July. www.allafrica.com (accessed March 2009).

MISA *see* Media Institute of Southern Africa.

Mmegi. Remarks by the Hon. Pelonomi Venson-Moitoi on World Press Freedom Day, 7 May 2007. www.mmegi.org (accessed March 2009).

Modise, O. 2007. Mogae tips journos on good reporting. *Mmegi* 6 December. www.mmegi. org (accessed March 2009).

Ngugi, C. 1995. The mass media and democratisation in Africa. *Media Development* 4: 49–52.

Nyamnjoh, F. 2005. *Africa's Media: Democracy and the Politics of Belonging*. Zed Books: New York.

Nyamnjoh, F., N. Forcheh and M. Maphanye. 2002. *Survey on the Level and Perception of Freedom of Expression in Botswana*. Gaborone: MISA-Botswana.

Ogundimu, F. 2002. Media and democracy in twenty-first century Africa. In *Media and Democracy in Africa*, ed. G.. Hyden, M. Leslie and F. Ogundimu, 207–238.Uppsala: Nordiska Afrikainstitutet.

Republic of Botswana. 1997. *National Development Plan 8 (1997/8-2002/3)*. Gaborone: Ministry of Finance and Development Planning.

——. 2003. *National Development Plan 9 (2003/4-2008/9)*. Gaborone: Ministry of Finance and Development Planning.

RoB *see* Republic of Botswana.

Sechele, S. 1998. The role of the media in the promotion of the quality of life in Botswana. In *Poverty and Plenty: The Botswana Experience*, ed. D. Nteta, 351–59. Gaborone: The Botswana Society.

——. 2000. *Deepening Democracy or Creeping Authoritarian Rule? Media–Government relations in Botswana in Historical Perspective*. MPA thesis, University of Botswana.

——. 2006. *Botswana: AMDI Research Findings and Conclusions*. London: BBC World Services Trust.

Teer-Tomaselli, R. 1998. The public broadcaster and democracy in transformation. *Canadian Journal of Communication* 23: 145–162.

Thapisa, A. 2003. The use of print and electronic media in Botswana. *Journal of Librarianship and Information Science* 35(3): 153–164.

Wiseman, J. 1996. *The New Struggle for Democracy in Africa*. Aldershot: Avebury.

Zaffiro, J. 1988. Regional pressure and erosion of media freedom in an African democracy: The case of Botswana. *Journal of Communication* 38(3): 108–120.

——. 1989. Twin births: African nationalism and government information management in the Bechuanaland Protectorate, 1957–1966. *International Journal of African Historical Studies* 22(1): 51–78.

———. 2000. Broadcasting reform and democratization in Botswana. *Africa Today* 47(1): 86–102.

———. 2001a. *A Political History of Broadcasting in Botswana.* Colorado Springs: International Academic Publishers. First published in 1991 by The Botswana Society, Gaborone.

———. 2001b. Mass media and the democratization of politics and society: Lessons from Zimbabwe, 1990–2000. In *Media, Democracy and Renewal in Southern Africa*, ed. K. Tomaselli and H. Dunn, 99–122.Colorado Springs: International Academic Publishers.

———. 2002. Botswana. In *African Contemporary Record*, vol. 26, 1996–1998, ed. C. Legum, B625–B637. New York: Holmes and Meier.

Global pressures, local disparities:

Deregulation's false promise and Botswana's domestic digital divide

11

Sethunya Tshepho Mosime and Sarah Chiumbu

Botswana has participated in a significant way in the global process, which began in the 1990s, of liberalising the information and communications technology (ICT) sector. In line with neoliberal orthodoxy, the country has done relatively well in putting in place the 'three components to telecommunications reform', namely privatisation, the introduction of competition and the establishment of an independent regulatory authority (Wallsten 2001). The privatisation of the Botswana Telecommunication Corporation (BTC) is, as we write this chapter, at an advanced stage. Competition has been introduced in the ICT sector through means such as value-added mobile and Internet services. Botswana was also one of the first countries in Africa to establish an independent telecommunication regulator – the Botswana Telecommunications Authority (BTA) – in 1996.

In this chapter, we review the country's telecommunications reform in light of the encounter between the global neoliberal agenda and local developments. Liberalisation is not always a success story, especially in developing contexts. In Africa, this is often the result of frail political systems and weak regulatory capacity.[1] While we recognise Botswana's laudable success in some areas, we observe some early indications that the promise of ICTs becoming the new tools for sustainable development and economic growth may be a false promise (Chiumbu 2008: 4).

First, we provide an overview of Botswana's economic and political context. It is within this economic framework that the country's stark contradictions, characterised by 'a domestic information divide'[2] can be understood. Second, we give a brief overview of the rise of the 'information revolution' discourse in the early 1990s and the new global communication policy paradigm that arose out of it. It is within these new communication policy shifts that telecommunications reform in Africa and the southern African region can be understood. Third, we provide a critical assessment of Botswana's telecommunications reforms since the mid-1990s. With the best policy intentions, the Botswana story reveals early signs of what Thandika Mkandawire (2005) has called 'capturing' – a process whereby policies designed to yield growth and benefit whole populations end up benefiting a privileged few. The last section contrasts the rhetoric of universality and the reality of liberalisation. We explore the possibility that Botswana could be experiencing early symptoms of – to use Mkandawire term – a 'crisis of universalism', where global pressure towards neo-liberalism results in the erosion of social benefits at the local level.

Botswana: Political and economic context

Botswana shares borders with Zambia and Zimbabwe in the north-east, Namibia to the north and west, and South Africa in the south and south-east. At Independence in 1966, Botswana was the second-poorest country in the world after Bangladesh. By the mid-1990s, it was the fastest-growing economy in Africa. Botswana was also labelled a shining exemplar of democracy, particularly during the period of unrest in the southern part of the continent when South Africa, Zimbabwe, Namibia, Angola and Mozambique were experiencing massive internal conflicts (Meyer, Nagel & Snyder 1993). From a Gross Domestic Product (GDP) of US$80 million at Independence (Taylor & Mokhawa 2003), consisting mainly of beef exports to Britain and South Africa, Botswana is now ranked as an upper middle-income economy by the World Bank, at a GDP of over US$12,3 billion.[3] During the 1972/73 financial year, Botswana was able to eliminate its dependence on British grants-in-aid (Tsie 1998). The country's success has been attributed to the mineral sector and to good governance through transparent and accountable public institutions, and also to market-friendly regulation (WEF 2007a). Between 1982 and 1991, the economy of the country grew at an average of 10.1 per cent, making Botswana the fastest-growing economy in Africa for the period.

Tsie (1998), among others, attributes the changing fortunes of Botswana's economy and political stability to the state's developmental character, comparing it to the weak and/or patrimonial states found in most parts of Africa. The first crop of political elite – including the first president of the country, Seretse Khama – created a reasonably competent and honest bureaucracy though measures such as removal of the powers of chiefs and traditional leaders in land allocation, mineral rights, development planning and the collection of stray cattle. Yet Tsie also ascribes the effectiveness of that same bureaucracy – in the absence of strong civil society – to traditional and tribal customs that provide a means of mobilising and expressing opposition. Finally, Tsie attributes Botswana's success to a pattern of capitalist accumulation that judiciously combines private capitalism with state intervention (ibid: 1, 2, 14). Wayne Edge also ascribes Botswana's success to its being a developmental state akin to the developmental Asian states of South Korea, Singapore, Taiwan and China (1998: 333, 334).

Botswana has done very well in recent years in Global Competitive Report rankings provided by the World Economic Forum (WEF). The 2008–2009 report shows Botswana as second only to South Africa in sub-Saharan Africa. Botswana is also rated as the country with the lowest rate of corruption in Africa. However, Botswana was found to be problematic as a business destination by the WEF owing to the 'poor work ethic in [the] national labor force', an 'inadequately educated workforce', 'inefficient government bureaucracy' and an 'inadequate supply of infrastructure'. On the 9th pillar of global competitiveness – 'technological readiness' – Botswana ranked a much lower 89th, although this is still relatively high by African standards.[4]

The current global economic crisis has hit Botswana very hard, owing to the economy's over-reliance on diamonds. Before the crisis, diamonds contributed two-thirds of government revenues and this had already made the country's economic success very precarious. The World Bank projects that the plummeting demand for diamonds and other minerals will cause a substantial decline in Botswana's GDP growth for 2008–2011, from the 3.3 per cent attained in 2007/08.[5] Some mines have been closed, with workers laid off as a result. The World Bank also projects substantial fiscal deficits, and predicts that the balance of payments will shrink substantially from the 19 per cent surplus seen in 2007 (ibid).

Attaining economic growth is one challenge, and spreading wealth evenly is another. The economy has been widely criticised for being skewed against the rural poor; against the distribution of cattle, access to land,[6] and income distribution. By the mid-1990s, although Botswana was enjoying good economic growth, it was estimated that around 60 per cent of the rural population and 30 per cent of the urban population could not meet their basic needs.[7] It was the challenge of uneven development that, among other things, led the government to believe that ICT could go some way towards resolving the problem.

Botswana and the domestic information divide

Internet access in Botswana has remained at a low 3 per cent to 4 per cent of the population. A 'community e-readiness assessment' was carried out in 2004, which identified a 'domestic information divide'[8] in Botswana. The assessment, commissioned by the Ministry of Communications, Science and Technology, revealed that Botswana was 'a contrast of extremes'. In that year, the WEF ranked Botswana 55th in the world in terms of overall national connectivity and 28th in terms of overall infrastructure quality, stating that it had a high penetration of fibre connectivity in urban areas.

Although mobile telephony is growing at a tremendous pace in Botswana (as it is in most other African countries), access to personal computers (PCs) and the Internet has grown very slowly. In 2004, the total ownership of PCs in the country's two cities, Gaborone and Francistown, was a mere 8,633 in a combined population of over 300,000. The scenario was even worse in the rest of the country. Five districts with most of the country's population – Kgatleng, North East, North West, Ghanzi and Kgalagadi – had a total of only 1,447 PCs. By 2007, the total number of people in the whole country subscribing to broadband Internet access was only 1,600, or 0.1 per cent of the population (AIUPS 2007). By early 2008, data on the number of websites and Internet hosts in Botswana was still scanty. Only 24 per cent of households had electricity; and most of those were in urban areas.

The situation of unequal access to ICTs is informed by several factors. Firstly, at the international level, ICTs and services are concentrated in the industrialised countries of the North. Developing regions, including Africa, are right at the bottom (Ya'u 2006). Ya'u characterises the digital divide in terms of the dependency of Africa on American and European backbone providers for access to the Internet. He also recognises that, within Africa itself, access to ICTs is uneven; it is available mostly to urban dwellers, with women having less access than men.

The information revolution and local responses

Botswana's telecommunications reforms cannot be understood outside the broader global political economy of communication (Mosco 1996). The Internet was commercialised in 1992 and this led many Western countries to review their communication and information polices (Cogburn 2003; Servaes 2003; Chakravartty & Sarikakis 2006). ICT policies, aimed at responding to the new information age and focusing on infrastructure and technology were put in place, first in the USA and then in Europe. These developments in the West impelled a flurry of national and regional ICT policies in Africa and other parts of the developing world. (Moore 1997; Lovelock 1999; Sum 2003). Multilateral and bilateral donors urged African countries to come up with national ICT policies in line with the prevailing telecommunications developments taking place across the continent (Cogburn 2003; Chiumbu 2008).

As in many other parts of the developing world, there has been pressure on Botswana to become a part of an 'information revolution' and an 'information highway'. This imperative did not brew from within. Telecommunication reforms attempted from the late 1980s were a response to global pressures to secure 'a key position in the emerging global information society', 'become a part of a 'global marketplace', and enjoy 'global connectivity'.[9] We place Botswana's response to global pressures within the country's unique socio-cultural context. Our position is not that Botswana is just an innocent victim of a systematic grand design by the West to mislead and disempower developing countries, in the manner of the world system approach propounded by Immanuel Wallerstein. The chapter locates

Botswana's attempts to become a part of the information highway within the broader global pressure to deregulate. More importantly, it places the country's efforts and challenges within its own, specific local agendas.

Global pressures for telecommunication reforms

Daniel Wanjau Muriu (2002) has described the last decade of the twentieth century as a period that saw the world shift from state-command economies and welfare states to market-driven economies. This is part of a general trend that started in the 1970s in the developed world, where principles of organisation shifted from 'public' to 'private' as public enterprises began to be ideologically associated with wasteful and inefficient bureaucracies (Hall 1997). Thus, the post-World War II view of 'embedded liberalism' founded on Keynesian economic management gave way to the ideology of privatisation (Schiller 1997; Morton 2003). The telecommunication reforms that took place in the West in the 1980s and 1990s can be located in these structural changes. The US and UK governments were prompted to liberalise and privatise their telecommunication sectors in 1984 and 1985 respectively. This trend was followed by nearly all governments in Europe, Asia and North America over the next few years (Schiller 1997).

The telecommunication regulatory reforms in the West gave major impetus to similar reforms in Africa (Hills 1998). In many African countries, the reforms were tied to International Monetary Fund (IMF)-driven economic restructuring that linked loans to progress in reorganising existing ministries of posts, telegraphs and telephones. Many African governments were reluctant to open up the telecommunications sector for fear of losing control of what they saw as a major source of revenue. However, they were pressured to liberalise because the World Bank and the IMF tied telecommunication reforms to aid and loans (Petrazzini 1995; Noam 1999; Wilson 2006, cited in Chiumbu 2008: 87).

The reform agenda was premised on deregulation, liberalisation and privatisation, and ran parallel to ICT policy reforms. The prevailing argument within this framework states that liberalisation of the telecommunication sector is a must if the full benefits of ICTs are to be derived by countries on the continent. Liberalisation has consistently been used as one of the indicators of preparedness for globalisation: countries must develop an edge in the form of a market-friendly policy framework in order to position themselves favourably in an increasingly competitive global environment (WEF 2007a).

Telecommunication reforms: The regional context

The issue of telecommunication reform formally entered the African policy agenda in 1990, when the International Telecommunication Union (ITU) held the first African Telecommunication Development Conference, in Zimbabwe.[10] The meeting created a task force that drafted the 'African Green Paper: Telecommunication Policies for Africa', adopted by African policy-makers in 1996. The main message of this paper, which was inspired by the 1987 European Green Paper, was that African countries should follow the example of what had been done elsewhere and formulate explicit policies that shifted away from government ownership and management of public companies towards the establishment of a policy, legal and regulatory framework for competition. (Chiumbu 2008: 87).

In the Southern African region national telecommunication regulatory regimes were adjusted according to the dictates of market liberalisation through the mediation of the Southern African Development Community (SADC), led by an assertive 'new' South Africa. A neo-liberal agenda of liberalisation and privatisation shaped a range of regional regulatory and policy frameworks for telecommunication development (Barnett 1999: 104–105). In 1998, the African Connection Initiative, an intergovernmental framework agreement for the liberalisation of telecommunications, was signed by African communications ministers. This was followed in the same year by the formation of the Telecommunications Regulators' Association of Southern Africa. These initiatives – supported by the United States Agency for International Development's Regional Telecommunications Restructuring Programme – reflected the need to harmonise telecommunication regulatory frameworks across national markets in order to enhance the attractiveness of the region to international markets (Barnett 1999; Mazango 1999). On the back of broader World Bank/IMF economic reforms and these regional initiatives, countries in Southern Africa opened up their telecommunications and broadcasting sectors, which up till then had been dominated by the State. Although the regional initiatives emphasised the harmonisation of telecommunication policies and the integration of markets, countries nevertheless adopted different models of telecommunication reforms.

Liberalisation of telecommunications in Botswana

Botswana, like other countries in the SADC, embarked on the IMF/World Bank-supported telecommunication reforms in the 1990s, which all followed a model advocated by the World Trade Organisation. Essentially this involved separating telecommunications from postal services and the separation of government regulatory and operator duties (Zibi 1998).

The first wave of liberalisation in Botswana started in 1996, following the adoption of the Telecommunications Policy Framework for Botswana in 1995. Prior to this, the Botswana Telecommunication Corporation (BTC) had been a monopoly in the provision of telecommunications services. Once a Telecommunications Act was in place in 1996, a Botswana Telecommunications Authority (BTA) was established. Between 1999 and 2008, BTA issued over 40 Internet service provider (ISP) and data licenses. It also licensed three public telecommunication operators providing fixed telephone services and cellular service: Orange Botswana, Mascom Wireless and the BTC.

This second wave of liberalisation, announced by government in 2004, was made necessary by convergence – where previously separate media platforms came to overlap as a result of digital technology. UUNET, then a leading ISP in the Southern African region, was one of the bodies that exerted pressure on the government to liberalise; it labelled convergence and liberalisation 'brothers in arms' (UUNET 2005). The argument was that international case studies had shown that for the benefits of convergence to be fully actualised, it was necessary for government to liberalise the industry. This would help cut down costs, improve service efficiency to business and therefore reduce prices for consumers. ISPs in Botswana also successfully lobbied for further liberalisation.

In 2004, the BTA commissioned a team of three consultants – Robert Hall, David Lewin and Claire Milne – to advise it on how to proceed with further liberalisation. Hall and Lewin submitted their final report, entitled 'Recommendations on further liberalisation of the telecommunications industry of Botswana', in 2005. Their proposals were that the national fixed services markets be fully liberalised by September 2005 and the international markets by June 2006, including a lifting of the Voice over Internet Protocol (VoIP) ban. The consultants expected that with value-added services, ISPs would be able to offer more attractive packages to customers. It was argued that there was a huge and growing demand for telecommunication services and products that could not be satisfied by one operator. Competition was expected to encourage service improvement, innovation and efficiency, and also to accelerate the speed of market coverage. Lower prices would be achieved as well as new and better services for consumers, while total industry revenues would go up.

The number one justification for further liberalisation was to end BTC's monopoly in the provision of telecommunications services. In June 2006, the Minister of Communications, Science and Technology, Pelonomi Venson-Moitoi, announced in a policy directive that the government was moving towards a service-neutral licensing Framework on 13 March 2007.[11] On 13 June 2007, BTA awarded mobile phone operators – Mascom Wireless Botswana and Orange Botswana – the service neutral licenses.[12] Before the neutral licensing regime was introduced, BTC was a de facto monopoly as far as the provision of international voice services was concerned. The two operators were now permitted to build their own backbone infrastructure or gateways to carry their traffic instead of being compelled to use the BTC infrastructure. The government also announced that it would lift the restriction on the provision of VoIP for all ISPs. The latter would henceforth be able to provide value-added network service (VANS), including voice service, nationally and internationally. The service had previously been provided only by BTC, Mascom Wireless Botswana and Orange Botswana.

Botswana's national information and communication technology (ICT) policy

In 2007, the government of Botswana launched Maitlamo, Botswana's national policy for ICT in recognition of the role of new technologies in driving social, economic, cultural and political transformation. Like most African ICT policies, Botswana's version stresses poverty reduction and development plans (see Chiumbu 2008). The Long Term Vision for Botswana – Vision 2016 (1997: 5), espouses a vision of Botswana as an educated and informed nation where 'all Batswana will have access to the media through national and local radio, television and newspapers'.

As well as an ICT vision for the country, Botswana's ICT policy includes a number of specific goals. Its two main objectives are to create an enabling environment for the growth of the ICT industry, and to provide universal service and access to suitable technology. The policy also identifies several programmes to accelerate the spread and use of ICTs in the country. These 'fast-track' initiatives are viewed as quickly implementable; and as able to improve both access to and the use of ICTs in the areas of governance, education, health, economic and infrastructural development, security, and legislation and policy. (NICTP 2007: 4, 9–10).

Another aim of Maitlamo is to propel the realisation of universal access set out in the Telecommunications Policy for Botswana adopted in 1995. The policy document states that Universal Service Access (UAS) to telecommunications should be taken to mean access to basic telecommunication services as a citizen's right, comparable with the right to basic education and primary health care (1995: 11). In terms of the policy, the ideal situation would be a telephone in every household that wanted one – at an affordable price. In 2002, the BTA took steps to develop a National Universal Service and Access policy/strategy to ensure that all citizens had access to efficient, effective and affordable telecommunications services. UAS is described in the document as 'a situation where every person has reasonable means of getting access to information and communications, on a non-discriminatory basis, via a public telephone or any other innovative community-based access point' (BTA 2002: 2).

The ITU does not prescribe a fixed definition of UAS. Each country is allowed to establish its own criteria according to its social and economic requirements and conditions (ITU 1998). Generally, though, UAS can be seen as assuming affordable access to basic voice telephony for all people who request it, regardless of their geographic location (ibid). It also usually refers to people being within a reasonable distance of a public telephone or 'payphone', even though the accepted distance is defined differently from country to country. For example, in South Africa – the first country in Africa to come up with a UAS Agency – access is taken to imply a working public telephone within a 30-minute walk of a person's home (Gyamfi 2005: 24).

The 2007 National ICT Policy proposes to improve universal access through the establishment of Community Access Centres (CACs) under the Connecting Communities Programme – which aims to achieve universal access to information and telecommunications. The CACs intend to provide affordable access to computers and the Internet for residents of rural, remote and urban communities – especially those who do not have these facilities in their homes or workplaces. To make universal access more of a realistic and practical goal, policies in most of Africa are designed to provide ICT services on a shared basis, such as at community or village-based level. To this end, many of the African countries have established telecentres and community multi-purpose centres (CMCs). In Botswana, the centres are spreading to every part of the country.

In recognition of the fact that the provision of telecommunications services to rural and remote areas is not commercially viable, the Botswana government announced that a universal service fund (USF) would be established to subsidise services in rural areas (Venson-Moitoi 2007). First proposed by Hall, Lewin and Milne in 2004, the USF was intended to raise income from all operators according to their revenues – resulting in more funds being available for universal access facilities (Hall, Lewin & Milne 2004). According to the 2007 Draft Universal Access and Service Policy for the Communications Sector in Botswana, the targeted services would include fixed and mobile telephony, data services, radio and television broadcasting, postal services, print media and the Internet (BTA 2007). The USF would be managed by the BTA, and one of the provisions of a standard service provider's licence would be to make a contribution to the fund.

The rhetoric and reality of liberalisation

The current global economic climate will no doubt have a negative impact on Maitlamo and Botswana's universal access strategy. However, even outside the current crisis, there were already indications that the fruits of liberalisation and the attempts to universalise the telecommunications sector would not bring the results expected. Proponents of liberalisation argue that deregulation puts an end to high tariffs and helps to provide affordable access to rural and peri-urban areas. Liberalisation and deregulation are also said to bring about competition, thereby enabling network growth and improved services. Although there is no denying that liberalisation and privatisation have to some extent led to improved services in Botswana, the benefits are not clear (Njuguna 2006). In Botswana, the false promise of liberalisation is shown, inter alia, in the intra-country digital divide, the challenges facing universal service/access and the 'capture' of small ISPs by big telecommunications companies.

Further liberalisation: The 'capture' of Internet service providers (ISPs)

Because of the small size of the Botswana market, liberalisation has only served to force small businesses out while increasing market share for the bigger telecommunications companies such as BTC, Orange Botswana and Mascom Wireless. The market dominance of the big groups is more apparent in the Internet service sector. Botsnet, as BTC's subsidiary, enjoys a competitive advantage over other ISPs thanks to the larger bandwidth it was allocated. The Managing Director of Botsnet, speaking at the end of 2007, said that Internet service provision per se was no longer the focus of the company, which was exploring ways to exploit the possibilities ushered in by the service-neutral licenses. (Oteng Mudongo, interview by author. Gaborone, 18 December 2007). Because of its advantaged position, Botsnet has, since its formation in 1999, been at the root of what has been called an 'electronic cold war' between its mother company, BTC, and other ISPs in the country. This situation reached the point where other ISPs formed the Botswana Internet Service Providers' Association (BISPA) in order to press their case against BTC with BTA. BISPA argued that, as a monopoly that was the only gateway for Internet access provision in Botswana, BTC kept prices for its services unreasonably high, forcing many of its competitors to close down. Worse still for the member ISPs, by establishing Botsnet, BTC was doubling as the access provider and an ISP. The concern was that Botsnet was enjoying an unfair advantage, getting better terms and quality of service from BTC than competing ISPs (For-Mukwai 2000).

Within a four-month period from 13 June 2007 (the day on which Mascom Wireless and Orange Botswana were granted the service-neutral licenses) to 12 October 2007, 16 new VANS were licensed by BTA. This was exponential growth, considering that in the previous year (2006), no new ISP had been licensed. Before that, between November 1999 and August 2005, a total of only 18 ISPs had been registered. The year 2008, however, saw a significant decline in the number of new entrants, with only nine new companies being licensed.[13] The initial euphoria regarding further liberalisation faded fast among most local ISPs. According to BISPA, although some ISPs had applied for and obtained the new VANS license, this had not led to growth. The objectives of further liberalisation, increasing competition, reduced prices, increasing local content and improved access for the average person were nowhere near to being met. As far as BISPA saw it, instead of increased competition, further liberalisation had thus far served only to take many small ISPs out of business. William H. Melody (1999) has warned that value-added Internet services do not always guarantee growth – in fact the experience can be quite the opposite in some liberalised markets.

The limited amount of local content available online, according to BISPA, was another major disincentive for people to subscribe to ISPs. Contributing to this dearth of local content was the fact that the multinational corporations such as banks operating in Botswana had not invested very much in providing local content on their websites. Just a quick comparison between the websites of First National Bank Botswana and its counterpart in South Africa showed that South Africans had much more information to access compared to Botswana where the content was limited to the bank's products. Another setback was the increasing costs of Internet. By 2008, Internet costs had also gone up by as much as 100 per cent as a result of increasing landline call costs. ISPs tried to reduce Internet connection fees, but call costs forced people to abandon their Internet subscriptions. Because it was not only very expensive but also offered almost no content about their country, local consumers had very little incentive to connect to the Internet. Call prices had gone up by as much as 100 per cent over a few years. Even when the Internet connection price was reduced by the ISPs, the call costs forced people to abandon their subscriptions. Clearly, if further liberalisation was negatively affecting the small operator in the local telecommunications industry, the situation for the average citizen could only be worse. As far as BISPA was concerned, although the BTA's liberalising strategy looked good on paper, it did not translate into gains for the average person in the street. According to Stuart Brown, an executive member of BISPA, the strategy only benefited the top 5 per cent of the market. (Telephonic interview by author, 18 December 2007).

Challenges of achieving universal access

Liberalisation and deregulation in Botswana have not necessarily resulted in greater efficiencies and lower prices for the country's people. In most cases, the private sector operations have contributed to the widening digital divide between the urban and rural areas. These developments have had implications for universal access and equity. Botswana's experience with deregulation has negatively impacted on universal access service and so far has not benefited its citizens. This is the case in many African countries – while competition has brought better services and improved connectivity in some urban areas, there has also been considerable market consolidation. The shift has been from the previous government monopoly to a private sector monopoly, instead of from a monopoly situation to an open market (Mureithi 2003; Ya'u 2006).

In making recommendations for further liberalisation, consultants Hall, Lewin and Milne took note of the fact that Botswana had an extremely scattered rural population, which made it disproportionately costly to reach the last five or ten per cent of people (Hall, Lewin and Milne, 2004: 68). The report also noted the inadequate and expensive electricity supply, and the growing income inequality in Botswana's society, as the main challenges. It also observed that the infrastructure was generally poor, particularly so in the telecommunications sector. In addition, fixed telephony was very restricted and expensive, directly limiting Internet access. For this reason, the report argued that further liberalisation could mean intensified competition for the more attractive sectors, neglect for the less attractive ones, and a failure to expand unprofitable services where they were needed – especially into rural and low-income households (Hall, Lewin & Milne 2004).

The final consultants' report, submitted by Hall and Lewin, acknowledged that liberalisation might succeed at the expense of efforts to bring affordable, good quality telecommunications to everyone in Bostswana. They suggested that government could raise revenue for universal access through a universal service fund (USF), which would help to subsidise the provision of ICT facilities where these were not commercially viable. The USF would raise income from all operators according to their revenues – which would result in more funds being available for universal access facilities.

The government adopted most of the recommendations of the Hall and Lewin report, including the idea of a USF, as discussed in some detail under the section 'Botswana's national information and communication technology (ICT) policy' above.

Several African countries have set up such a fund as part of their national ICT policy. However, it is becoming evident that the implementation of universal access programmes in much of Africa has failed. In many cases, access does not go beyond introducing connectivity to rural areas. Crucial issues that are often neglected are the costs of new technologies; the availability of relevant content; the skills needed to use the technology; access to reliable and affordable electricity to power the connectivity; and the use of appropriate technology for the connection. This neglect is why telecentres and CMCs have failed in many African countries (Benjamin 2001; Dralega 2008). One of the first steps in the drawing up of Maitlamo was a benchmarking exercise in 2004 to assess the number of people in communities with access to technologies, and how they were using them. It was discovered from the exercise that countries in Southern Africa were doing much worse in terms of ICT use and access than countries in Asia and Europe with comparable domestic incomes, such as Malaysia and Estonia.[15] Several factors are responsible for this, such as the levels of literacy and infrastructural development in Southern African countries. South Africa, the first country on the continent to establish a Universal

Service and Access Agency in 1996, has had only limited success. The agency has been weakly embedded within South Africa's regulatory space, owing to a lack of adequate funding and of operational independence (Gardner 2003).

Universal access strategies: A crisis of universalism in the age of liberalisation

There is ongoing debate about whether universal access to the Internet and other ICTs is a necessity in the developing world. One-time World Bank economist, Charles Kenny, describes the call for universal access to the Internet as 'development's false divide' (Kenny 2003: 77). He argues that, while the push to give Internet access to the world's poorest people is probably premised on noble motivations, this will be too costly and at the same time will achieve little. Because of pervasive poverty in the developing world, the costs cannot be justified in terms of potential revenues. Kenny does not see how sufficient subsidies could be raised to achieve universal access to Internet services. To him, access is more than the physical presence of facilities; and so he sees the lack of requisite skills as blocking the way to countries' ability to achieve adequate access. Also, content that is relevant to the communities concerned would have to be developed, and that would not come cheaply. Although universal service access to other forms of communication may be justified, Kenny does not believe that access to the Internet, in particular, will be of significant benefit to the poor.

However, an important issue to consider is the place of universal service and access strategies in a liberalised economy. Mkandawire has warned of a 'crisis of universalism', because, historically, market liberalisation has proved to be incompatible with social welfare policies such as universal access (2005: 2). In addition, experience with the liberalisation and commercialisation of services has shown that these developments do not automatically guarantee investment in service sectors such as telecommunications (Ya'u 2004). The Draft Universal Access and Service Policy for the communications sector in Botswana is premised on the hope that the new deregulated environment will bring in more players to compete and also to contribute towards the USF. However, as Van Audenhove et al. (1999) warn, the experience in South America was that revenue returns from privatisation or liberalisation are very modest. Fiscal limits or economic incapacity on the part of governments – according to Mkandawire – are partly responsible for the crisis of universalism. Botswana is particularly challenged because of its small and widely distributed population (1.8 million people occupying 582,000 square kilometres). This, according to the draft National ICT Policy, makes it 'disproportionately costly' to reach the neediest, especially to provide telecommunications.[15]

John Browning (1994) goes even further, arguing that in the twenty-first century universal service provision is an idea whose time has passed. Browning warns that unless there is a shift away from universal service, 'it could, in fact, derail the entire information economy'.[16] Universal access, for him, tends to harm rather than enhance access to information and communication. It encourages the telecommunications market to concentrate in fewer and bigger companies while forcing small businesses out. Browning advocates the 'open access' model, whereby small, new competitors get to use the existing telecommunication infrastructure on the same terms as the entrenched monopolies that built it – which effectively debases their monopolistic status. Universal access, on the other hand, tends to reduce choices for consumers and limits opportunities for innovation.

The debate about using the 'open access' model as an enabler of 'universal access' has resurfaced on the international policy agenda as a result of the failure of many universal access strategies. Open access entails allowing a wide variety of physical networks and applications to interact in an open architecture. In other words, anyone can connect to anyone else in a technology-neutral framework that encourages innovative, low-cost delivery to users (InfoDev 2005). In Africa, fibre optic initiatives such as the NEPAD Broadband Project (formerly the East Africa Submarine System (EASSy) cable project),[17] operating on open access principles, should make it affordable to connect thousands of additional users (AITEC 2006).

One failure of universalism in information and communication services arises from the conflation of access to a service and the availability of a service. In the 2006 Budget Speech for Botswana, the Minister of Finance and Development Planning announced that the master plan for the national radio and television transmitter network had been completed; coverage of both electronic media would be improved by installing additional facilities to cover all parts of the country. At the time, 81 per cent of the population had access to good-quality medium-wave transmissions, and about 77 per cent to frequency modulation (FM) radio signals. Television was accessible to about 64 per cent of the population (MFDP 2006:19). Availability of a service *per se*, particularly with reference to information and communication, can simply mean availability of transmission technology, and may not necessarily include access.

Mkandawire argues that in developing countries, universalism is also often compromised by its urban bias. More disturbingly, however, universalism has tended to be derailed by the creation and widening of an economic gap between a privileged few and the marginalised majority. 'What had been touted as policies that would eventually encompass the whole society appeared as exclusive privileges "captured" by a few in privileged sectors bent on blocking the extension of these programmes to other sections of the population' (Mkandawire 2005: 4).

The general shift in developed countries is away from universalist policies towards some kind of diagnostic criteria capable of identifying the beneficiaries of social policies (ibid: 1). In developing countries, poverty remains a serious challenge, necessitating some degree of universalism in selected areas such as health, education, information and communication. The other option – selective targeting – tends to be complex and expensive to manage, prone to information distortion, incentive distortion and corruption, among other problems (ibid: 11–12).

Conclusions

In Botswana, the desire to offset the monopoly of BTC in the provision of telecommunications services motivated the decision to further liberalise the sector in 2006. The result of this has not been encouraging. After obtaining the service and technology-neutral Public Telecommunications Operator (PTO) licence in March 2007, BTC has expanded its dominance into converged fixed, mobile, and broadband services. By the end of 2007, the initial euphoria surrounding further liberalisation was fading among most of the local ISPs. According to BISPA, although some ISPs had applied for and obtained the new VANS license, this had not resulted in their growth.

Mkandawire (2005: 4) has noted that a policy touted to benefit the whole society can be 'captured' by a privileged few. This is exactly what appears to have happened to small ISPs after the second wave of liberalisation in the telecommunications industry in Botswana in 2006. The telecommunications and ICT market continued to be dominated by three big companies – the government-funded BTC, Orange Botswana and Mascom Wireless Botswana.

As Botswana vigorously pursues liberalisation, it has also renewed its intention to achieve universal access service through the recently launched Maitlamo, its draft national information and communications technology policy. Many governments in the developing world, including Botswana, have found the idea of universal service appealing, but their record of providing equal and free access to information and communication for all citizens has not been very good. Although it is still too early to effectively evaluate Maitlamo and also the recently launched universal access strategy, there are already indications that liberalisation is slowing down attempts to provide universal access.

Telecommunications liberalisation and attendant ICT policy reforms promised to spread communication services to a much larger number of people in Africa and to reduce tariffs. Indeed, while liberalisation has led to an increase in teledensity and mobidensity, on the whole the fruits of liberalisation have not been widespread, especially not in peri-urban and rural areas.

To reduce the increasing digital divide between urban and rural areas, many governments in Africa have adopted universal access and service policies that are meant to extend access to telecommunications and ICT services to all their people. However, universal access policies within a deregulated and liberalised environment have led to a situation in which operators ignore the provision of uneconomical services to communities. Although universal service funds have worked well in some African countries such as South Africa and Uganda, they have not met the challenge of providing telephones and ICTs to rural Africa (Padania & Silvani 2005).

Since universal service funds have not yet become a reality in Botswana, it is difficult to estimate the revenue that might be raised through them. However, the only major contributors to the fund are likely to be BTC, Mascom Wireless Botswana and Orange Botswana. The very few local radio and television broadcasters are either government-owned or too small and straitened to make much of a contribution.

Liberalisation means that governments run the risk of diminishing their ability to align their telecommunications policies with national and social policies (Van Audenhove et al. 1999). Thus the national aspirations contained in the government's long-term vision for Botswana – Vision 2016 – may end up being lost to the dictates of the market.

References

Africa Internet Usage and Population Statistics. http://www.Internetworldstats.com/africa. htm#bw (accessed 14 December 2007).

African IT Exhibitions and Conferences. 2006. EASSy cable to be operational in 2008 despite recent setbacks. *Computing Communications*. http://new.aitecafrica.com/node/430#heading30 (accessed 9 January 2007).

AITEC *see* African IT Exhibitions and Conferences.

AIUPS *see* Africa Internet Usage and Population Statistics.

Barnett. C. 1999. Uneven liberalisation in southern Africa: Convergence and democracy in communication policy. *The Public* 6(3): 101–114.

Benjamin, P. 2001. *Telecentre and Universal Capability: A Study of the Telecentre Programme of the Universal Service Agency in South Africa, 1996–2000*. Unpublished PhD thesis, Aalborg University, Denmark.

Bill Gates Foundation. 2006. Permanent Secretary in the Ministry of Labour and Home Affairs, Mothusi Bruce Palai, accepting the Gates Foundation grant to Botswana for expanded global libraries. Initiative increases access to information. http://www.gatesfoundation.org/GlobalDevelopment/GlobalLibraries/Announcements/Announce-061130.htm (accessed 11 December 2007).

——. 2006. Expanded global libraries initiative increases access to information by helping public libraries provide free Internet services and training: Foundation launches $328 million initiative with grants to Botswana, Latvia, and Lithuania. http://www.gatesfoundation.org/global development/global libraries/ Announcements/Announce-061130.htm (accessed 14 December 2007).

Botswana Telecommunications Authority. Annual Report for the Year Ended 31 March 2007. http://www.bta.org.bw/pubs/AnnualReport/2007/BTA%20Annual%20 Report%2007_Pages.pdf (accessed 28 January 2008).

Botswana Tourism Board. 2007. Geographical info. http://www.botswanatourism.co.bw/about/geographical_info.html (accessed 14 December 2007).

Browning, J. 1994. Universal service (An idea whose time is past). *Wired.* http://www.wired.com/wired/archive/2.09/universal.access_pr.html (accessed 21 April 2008).

BTA see Botswana Telecommunications Authority.

Chakravartty, P. and K. Sarikakis. 2005. *Media Policy and Globalisation.* Edinburgh: Edinburgh University Press.

Chiumbu, S. 2008. *Understanding the Role and Influence of External Actors and Ideas in Policy Formulation and Implementation: The African Information Society Initiative.* Oslo: UniPub.

Cogburn, D. 2003. Governing global information and communication policy: Emergent regime formation and the impact on Africa. Telecommunications Policy 27: 135–153.

Dralega, C. 2008. *ICT-Based Development of Marginal Communities: Participatory Approaches to Communication, Empowerment and Engagement in Rural Uganda.* Oslo: UniPub.

Economic Freedom of the World. 2003. Annual Report, Exhibit 2: Summary Economic Freedom Ratings, 2001. http://www.freetheworld.com/2003/1EFW2003ch1.pdf (accessed 28 January 2008).

Edge, W. A. 1998. 'Botswana: A developmental state' in *Botswana: Politics and Society,* ed. W. A. Edge and M. H. Lekorwe. Pretoria: Van Schaik Publishers.

For-Mukwai, G. F. 2000. Botswana ISPs form group, call Telco unfair. Computer World, the voice of IT management. http://www.computerworld.com.au/index.php/id;1733872502;fp;;fpid;;pf;1 (accessed 11 December 2007).

Freedom House. Map of press freedom, Botswana 2006. http://www.freedomhouse.org/template.cfm?page=251&year=2006 (accessed 3 December 2007).

Gardner, S. 2003. *The Effect of Commmercialisation, Privatisation and Liberalisation on Universal Access in South Africa.* Unpublished MA thesis, Rhodes University, Grahamstown, South Africa.

Government of Botswana. 2005. Facts on Botswana. http://www.gov.bw/docs/FACTS_ON%20BOTSWANA_the%20book.pdf (accessed 11 December 2007).

Gyamfi, A. 2005. Closing the digital divide in sub-Saharan Africa: Meeting the challenges of the information age. *Information Development* 21(1): 22–30.

Hall, R., D. Lewin and C. Milne. 2004. Recommendations for further liberalisation of the telecommunications industry of Botswana: e/draft final report – further liberalisation of Botswana telecommunications industry. http://www.bta.org.bw/pubs/final%20report%20%20-%20liberalisation.doc (accessed 3 December 2007).

Hall, R. and D. Lewin. 2005. Recommendations on further liberalisation of the telecommunications industry of Botswana: A final report to the Botswana Telecommunications Authority. http://www.bta.org.bw/pubs/final%20report%20%20-%20liberalisation.doc (accessed 19 February 2008).

Hills, J. 1998. Liberalisation, regulation and development in telecommunications. *International Communication Gazette* 60 (6): 459–476.

InfoDev. 2005. *Open Access Models: Options for Improving Backbone Access in Developing Countries (with a Focus on Sub-Saharan Africa).* An InfoDev Technical Report. http://www.infodev.org/content/highlights/detail/2568.

International Telecommunication Union. 1998. *World Telecommunications Developments Report 1998: Universal Access.* Geneva: ITU.

ITU *see* International Telecommunication Union.

Kenny, C. 2003. Development's false divide. *Foreign Policy* 134: 76–77.

Lovelock, P. 1999. *The Evolution of China's National Information Infrastructure (NII): A policy-making Analysis.* Unpublished PhD thesis, University of Hong Kong.

Mansell, R. 2001. Digital opportunities and the missing link for developing countries. *Oxford Review of Economic Policy* 17(2): 282–295.

Mazango, E. 1998. Telecommunication Sector Reform: Liberalisation and Universal Service Policy in Zimbabwe. MPhil thesis, University of Oslo, Norway.

MCST see Ministry of Communications, Science and Technology.

Melody, W. H. 1999. Telecom reform: progress and prospects. Telecommunications Policy 23(1): 7–34.

Meyer, J. W., J. Nagel, and C. W. Snyder. 1993. The expansion of mass education in Botswana: Local and world society perspectives. *Comparative Education Review* 37(4): 454–475.

Ministry of Communications, Science and Technology. 2003. Connecting Communities. http://www.maitlamo.gov.bw/docs/archives/draft-policies-2003/appx-a-connecting_communities_revised_nov.pdf (accessed 14 February 2008).

——. Benchmarking Report 2004. Executive Draft. http://www.maitlamo.gov.bw/docs/benchmark-report/2.1-icts-in-communities.pdf (accessed 14 December 2007).

——. 2004. Community e-Readiness Assessment. http://www.maitlamo.gov.bw/docs/e-readiness/volume-1/appx-a-community_e-readiness-july_16_ver2_re_5th_aug_04.pdf (accessed 19 February 2008).

——. 2005. Draft National Information and Communications Technology Policy. http://www.maitlamo.gov.bw/docs/draft-policies/ict_policy_draft_jan_2005.pdf (accessed 30 April 2009).

——. 2007. National Information and Communications Technology Policy as approved by the National Assembly. Gaborone: Government Printer.

Ministry of Finance and Development Planning. 2006. Botswana Budget Speech 2006. http://www.botswanaembassy.org/pdf/2006Budgetspeech.pdf (accessed 5 February 2008).

——. 2008. Botswana Budget Speech in Brief. Gaborone: Republic of Botswana.

Ministry of the Office of the President. Relocation of Basarwa. http://www.gov.bw/index. php?option=com_content&task=category&sectionid=10&id=23&Itemid=52 (accessed 12 June 2006).

Ministry of Works, Transport and Communications. 1995. *Telecommunications Policy for Botswana*. http://www.bta.org.bw/pubs/Botswana%20Telecommunications%20 Policy.pdf (accessed 14 February 2008).

Mkandawire, T. 2005. Targeting and universalism in poverty reduction. Social and policy development programme paper no. 23. United Nations Research Institute for Social Development. http://www.unrisd.org/80256B3C005BCCF9/(httpAuxPages)/955FB8A5 94EEA0B0C12570FF00493EAA/$file/mkandatarget.pdf (accessed 9 April 2008).

Mmegi/The Reporter. 2006. Basarwa going back to CKGR. Mmegi Online. http://www. mmegi.bw/2006/December/Thursday14/index.html (accessed 14 February 2008).

Mmegi/The Reporter. 2007. I Promise to Be Myself – Lippe. *Mmegi/The Reporter*. Posted 5 March. http://allafrica.com/stories/200703051534.html (accessed 28 January 2008).

Mogae, F. 2003. Voice of America news conference, 13 November. http://www. botswanaembassy.org/111303_1.html (accessed 11 July 2006).

Moore, N. 1997. Neo-liberal or dirigiste? Policies for an information society. *The Political Quarterly*. Oxford: Blackwell Publishers.

Morton, A. 2003. Social forces in the struggle over hegemony: Neo-Gramscian perspectives in international political economy. *Rethinking Marxism: A Journal of Economics, Culture and Society* 15 (2): 153–179.

Mosco, V. 1996. *The Political Economy of Communication*. London: Sage.

Mureithi, M. 2003. Evolution of telecommunications policy reforms in East Africa: Setting new policy strategies to anchor benefits of policy reforms. *The Southern African Journal of Information and Communication*, 2 (1). http://link.wits.ac.za/journal/ journal3.html (accessed 8 May 2005).

Muriu, D. W. 2002. Paying lip-service to the principles of regulation: A comparative critique of Kenya's telecommunications law. *Journal of African Law,* 46 (1): 14–30.

Njuguna, E. 2006. ICT policy in developing countries: Understanding the bottlenecks. Paper delivered at the Pacific Telecommunication Council Conference, 18 January, in Honolulu, Hawaii, USA. http://www.ptc.org/events/ptc06/program/public/proceedings/ Emmanuel%20Njuguna_paper_w143.pdf (accessed 4 March 2007).

Noam, E. 1999. Introduction. In *Telecommunications in Africa*, ed. E. Noam, 3–12. New York & Oxford: Oxford University Press.

Nulens, G. and L. Van Audenhove. 1999. An information society in Africa? An analysis of the information society policy of the World Bank, ITU and ECA. *International Communication Gazette*, 61(6): 451–471.

Padania, S. and F. Silvani. 2005. Local radio in the information society: Technology, participation and content in Africa. In *Information and Communication Technologies and Large-scale Poverty Reduction: Lessons from Asia, Africa, Latin America and the Caribbean*. London: Panos Institute & Swiss Agency for Development and Cooperation.

Petrazzini, B. 1995. *The Political Economy of Telecommunication Reform in Developing Countries: Privatisation and Liberalisation in Comparative Perspectives*. Westport, Connecticut & London: Praeger Publishers.

Quiggin, J. 2005. *Interpreting Globalization: Neoliberal and Internationalist Views of Changing Patterns of the Global Trade and Financial System*. Overarching Concerns Paper no. 7. United Nations Research Institute for Social Development.

Schiller, D. 1999. *Digital Capitalism: Networking the Global Market System*. Massachusetts: Massachusetts Institute of Technology Press.

Servaes, J. 2003. ed. *The European Information Society: A Reality Check*. Bristol: Intellect.

Sum, N. 2003. Informational capitalism and US economic hegemony: Resistance and adaptations in East Asia. *Critical Asian Studies* 35(3): 375–398.

Survival International. 2008. http://www.survival-international.org/tribes/bushmen/; intercontinentalcry.org/kgeikani-kweni-are-still-not-home; http://www.iwant2gohome. org/ (accessed 14 February 2008).

Taylor, I. and G. Mokwawa. 2003. Not forever: Botswana, conflict diamonds and the Bushmen. *African Affairs* 102: 261–283.

Touré, H. 2007. Competitiveness and information and communication technologies (ICTs) in Africa. http://www.weforum.org/pdf/gcr/africa/1.5.pdf (accessed 5 February 2008).

Transparency International. Corruption Perceptions Index 2005. AFRICA, http://www.transparency.org/news_room/latest_news/press_releases/2005/ cpi_2005_18_10_05 (accessed 11 July 2006).

Tshukudu, P. 2002. Empowering people to cross the digital divide: A gender dimension. Paper presented for the Emang Basadi Association at the World Telecommunication Day, 17 May, in Gaborone, Botswana. http://www.bta.org.bw/news/Empowering%20 people%20to%20Cross%20the%20Digital%20Divide%20-%20A%20gender%20 Dimension.pdf (accessed 10 September 2007).

Tsie, B. 1998. The state and development in Botswana. In *Public Administration and Policy in Botswana*, ed. K. R. Hope and G. Somolekae, 1-20. Lansdowne: Juta Academic.

United Nations Development Programme. 2008. Country fact sheets 2006. Human Development Report 2007/2008. http://hdr.undp.org/hdr2006/statistics/countries/ country_fact_sheets/cty_fs_BWA.html (accessed 10 July 2008).

Universal Service Administrative Company. 2008. http://www.universalservice.org/ default.aspx (accessed 7 February 2008).

UUNET. 2005. Convergence and deregulation – brothers in arms! http://www.uunet. co.zm/_about/news/backbone/backbone.asp?intNewsletterId=74#748 (accessed 7 February 2008).

Van Audenhove, L., J. Burgelman, G. Nulens and B. Cammaerts. 1999. Information society policy in the developing world: A critical assessment. *Third World Quarterly* 20 (2): 399–404.

Venson-Moitoi, P. 2006. Further liberalisation of the telecommunications sector. Press statement by the Minister of Communications, Science and Technology, 21 June. http://www.bta.org.bw/Liberalisation/Press%20Statement%20-%20Liberalisation%203.pdf (accessed 24 April 2008).

———. 2007. Minister of Communications Science and Technology, press statement to Director, Information Services Broadcasting Services, Botswana Press Agency, dated 13 April, 2007. http://www.bta.org.bw/Liberalisation/Press%20Statement%20-%20 Liberalisation%203.pdf (accessed 11 December 2007).

Wallsten, S. 2001. An econometric analysis of telecom competition, privatization, and regulation in Africa and Latin America. *Journal of Industrial Economics* 49(1): 1–19. http://web.ebscohost.com/ehost/pdf?vid=2&hid=12&sid=6b67e9e1-735f-478e-8d9b-690df8593607%40sessionmgr109 (accessed 10 February 2009).

———. 2003. Regulation and Internet use in developing countries. Policy Research Working Paper 2979, The World Bank Development Research Group, March. http://wwwwds.worldbank.org/external/default/WDSContentServer/IW3P/IB/2003/03/29/000094946_03031804031839/Rendered/PDF/multi0page.pdf (accessed 19 February 2008).

WEF see World Economic Forum.

World Audit. Botswana: World Democracy Profile. http://www.worldaudit.org/press.htm (accessed 10 July 2006).

World by Map. Mobile Cellular Telephones of the World. http://world.bymap.org/MobilePhones.html (accessed 24 April 2008).

World Economic Forum. 2007a. The Global Competitiveness Report 2006–2007: Country Highlights. http://www.weforum.org/en/fp/gcr_2006-07_highlights/index.htm (accessed 3 December 2007).

———. 2007b. Africa Competitiveness Report Top Ten. http://www.weforum.org/en/initiatives/gcp/Africa%20Competitiveness%20Report/2007/index.htm (accessed 14 February 2008).

———. 2008. *The Global Competitiveness Report 2007–2008*. http://www.weforum.org/en/initiatives/gcp/Africa%20Competitiveness%20Report/2007/index.htm; http://www.weforum.org/pdf/gcr/africa/botswana.pdf (accessed 14 February 2008).

World Education Forum. Education for All 2000 Assessment: Country Reports, Botswana. http://www.unesco.org/education/wef/countryreports/botswana/rapport_1.html (accessed 10 February 2008).

Ya'u, Y. Z. 2006. Confronting the digital divide: An interrogation of the African initiatives at bridging the gap in Africa and development challenges in the new millennium. (The NEPAD debate.) http://www.codesria.org/Links/conferences/Nepad/yau.pdf (accessed 21 April 2008).

Zibi, G. 1998. The successes and failures of African liberalisation models. Paper delivered at the Sub-regional Workshop on Technological Convergence and Telecommunications, 5–8 May, Johannesburg, South Africa.

Namibia:

The paradox of broadcasting reform in an emerging democracy[1]

12

William Heuva

The Namibian democratic transition has in a sense been quite unique. While it took place within the broader process of globalisation, it was itself a process of decolonisation at the local level. The movements of globalisation and decolonisation signalled the end of an autocratic era and promised political and economic renewal, characterised by democratic reforms. However, these processes were contradictory, and in some respects, radically so.

Having achieved political emancipation in 1990, Namibia set out to reconstruct a new society from the ashes of a destructive apartheid colonial system. The new society and its institutions were to be based on the principles of nation-building and democratisation. These principles would be associated with the ideals of equity, peace, fairness, social justice and access to universal and affordable services – all values that sought to promote and enhance citizenship, public interest and common concerns. Nevertheless, over-emphasis of the project of nation-building tended to undermine the process of democratisation.

Globalisation, on the other hand, tended to promote universal capitalism and uphold market values of consumerism, individualism and private interest, all aspects that tended to pull in an opposite direction to the driving forces of nation-building and democratisation. Capitalist markets, as Okwudiba Nnoli (2000) notes, are individualistic, self-seeking and deal purely with private interests to the detriment of nation-building and the welfare of nations. More importantly, globalisation promotes the commercialisation of public institutions – including broadcasting organisations – with negative effects on public service imperatives. Thus, the commercialisation of public institutions compromises the provision of public services, the reason being that these services become inaccessible because they are unaffordable to marginalised people.

The paradox experienced in Namibian broadcasting reform is rooted in attempts to balance the conflicting objectives posed by the processes of globalisation and decolonisation, and by extension between the imperatives of commercialisation and democratisation. This contradiction beset the Namibian transition process and impacted on the character of communication policies and regulatory practices as the country embarked on the transformation of its broadcasting sector.

This chapter focuses on the political economy of the Namibian communications sector in general and the transformation of the broadcasting sector in particular. The chapter pays attention, inter alia, to the contradictions that emerged in the broadcasting transformation process and highlights the successes and failures experienced.

Colonial broadcasting policy and practice

It is necessary to explain briefly colonial broadcasting policy and practice in order to contextualise the efforts made by the new government to transform the broadcasting system in the post-independence era. The first task of the government was to address colonial media policy. Media protocols are based on the ideologies that underpin the political and socio-economic foundations of societies. Namibian colonial broadcasting policy was constructed on apartheid ideology that was at the core of pre-independence society. Apartheid prescribed the exclusion and marginalisation of the black majority from access to mainstream economic resources and political institutions. As Chris Tapscott (1993: 29) notes, apartheid 'served to reify racial and ethnic divisions throughout society, to the extent that different communities were segregated geographically, economically and socially'. Colonial broadcasting reflected and perpetuated these divisions in Namibian society.[2] Moreover, the broadcasting system served as the apartheid state's hegemonic apparatus promoting the 'colonial discourse', which is defined as 'all the utterances written, spoken and iconographic aimed at affirming the superiority of a dominant group or class over others and justifying such a domination to perpetuate it' (Charles 1995: 135).

The organisational structure and programming of the colonial broadcasting service promoted both the 'crude' and 'reformed' apartheid systems in Namibia. Introduced from the mid-1970s, 'reformed apartheid' attempted to construct a 'neo-colonial' dispensation. It sought to restructure both the 'apartheid superstructure' by repealing petty apartheid laws, and the apartheid economy through the establishment of state-owned enterprises to provide 'basic' services to 'the people'. However, the provision of these services remained skewed, since they continued to be provided on the basis of race, class and ethnicity. It is interesting to note that the provision of the broadcasting services was also based on this division, as is illustrated below.

Not long after the establishment of its broadcasting system in the mid-1930s, South Africa started beaming broadcasting signals to South West Africa.[3] However, it was only in 1956 that the South African Broadcasting Corporation (SABC) established permanent broadcasting facilities in the territory. The initial SABC programmes targeted the white settler communities and the resident South African administrators. A radio service in the vernaculars – 'Radio Bantu' – was introduced in 1969 (De Beer 1975: 33). However, it was only in 1979 that the colonial national broadcaster, the South West Africa Broadcasting Corporation (SWABC) was established (Amupala 1998; Heuva 2000).

Based on the Broadcasting Act (Act 73 of 1976) the SWABC was modelled on the pre-1994 SABC. The latter was an arm of the apartheid state and reflected the National Party's political agenda. The network vigorously promoted apartheid ideology in its programming and editorial practices, even though it was sometimes seen as a 'putative public broadcaster' (Horwitz 2001: 38). The SWABC retained the character of the SABC and thereby remained a mere extension of its mentor (Swapo 1985: 24). Describing the mode of operation of the SWABC, Ellen Dyvi (1993: 65) says that it was:

> … controlled by, and designed to serve, a select few. It largely disenfranchised the majority of Namibians through its programming content which almost solely promoted the attributes of colonialism, suppressed freedom of speech and advocated white, Calvinistic conservatism.

While claiming to be imbued with the Reithian public service ideals of information, education and entertainment, the SWABC – like its mentor, the pre-1994 SABC – discharged these functions in terms of its own parochial ethnic confines. The corporation maintained that it needed to contribute towards the 'spiritual and material welfare of the different communities in the country by utilising its scarce resources to satisfy the communities, each with its own needs and interests' (SWABC 1979: 7). The emphasis on the different communities in broadcasting service provision presumes a 'minoritarian' broadcasting system promoting a 'plurality of diverse publics rather than a single integrated national audience' (Barnett 2001: 47).

Post-independence broadcasting policy initiative

The foregoing description characterises the colonial broadcasting system that the new Namibian government set out to transform and restructure at the dawn of political emancipation. The government did not formulate a broadcasting policy *per se*, but adopted a holistic 'Information Policy' to redress apartheid information policy and practice. Adopted in 1991, the policy provided the theoretical and philosophical foundation of the role and place of the post-independence media systems. However, the formulation of this policy was an elitist process designed overwhelmingly by politicians without public input. It was merely a 'desk study' done by senior officials in the Ministry of Information and Broadcasting (MIB).

Arguably, the urgency to have a policy in place to transform the inherited colonial media institutions did not allow time for consultation with stakeholders (Mathew

Gowaseb, interview by author. Windhoek, 23 July 2002). However, the democratic governance to which the new Namibian government aspired required public participation in decision-making on issues that affected citizens. Since broadcasting was fundamental to a democratic public life, it was essential for citizens to have their say before the policy was finalised. The need for public participation in policy-making was critical to the realisation of democratic communication systems and other societal institutions that would influence citizens' socio-economic and political lives.

Apart from the Information Policy, the government enacted the Namibian Broadcasting Corporation Act (Act 9 of 1991) and the Namibia Communications Commissions Act (Act 4 of 1992) as the basic legal instruments to regulate the inherited broadcasting sector. Moreover, the reform of the entire information and communication sector was constructed on the liberal constitutional provisions adopted at independence. These provisions were derived from the so-called 'constitutional guidelines'[4] proposed by the five Western countries – the USA, the UK, Canada, Germany and France – that negotiated the independence of the territory under United Nations Resolution 435. The guidelines prescribed a liberal political system based on multiparty democracy, adherence to the rule of law, the separation of powers of the legislature, the executive and the judiciary, the adoption of fundamental human rights, the acceptance of a free market economy and the protection of private property (Saunders 2001).

Some of these constitutional provisions have a direct bearing on the media sector and need to be examined briefly. Article 98 of the Constitution provides for a mixed ownership in the economy and by extension, mixed ownership of the media sector. Article 95 obliges the State to provide public services to those who were denied them during the colonial era, and therefore compels the State to expand information and communication infrastructure and services to reach all citizens. More importantly, Article 21 guarantees 'fundamental freedoms', of which sub-article (1)(a) provides for 'freedom of speech and expression, which shall include freedom of the press and other media' (Republic of Namibia 1990: 13). Freedom of the media is a fundamental expectation in a liberal democracy. Media policy is concerned with the freedom of communication – which can be broken down into freedom of expression plus the free flow of, and access to, information. Drawing from the libertarian media perspective, the Information Policy upholds three important journalistic tenets, namely: the right to publish and freely express views and ideas; the right not to disclose sources of information; and the right of access to information (MIB 1991: 8).

In practice, of course, freedom of expression and freedom of the media are not absolute and the Namibian constitution provides parameters to demarcate the space in which these freedoms can be exercised. For instance, sub-article (2) of Article 21 notes that:

The fundamental freedoms referred to in Sub-Article (1) hereof shall be exercised subject to the law of Namibia, in so far as such law imposes reasonable restrictions on the exercise of the rights and freedoms conferred by the said Sub-Article, which are necessary in a democratic society and are required in the interests of the sovereignty and integrity of Namibia, national security, public order, decency or morality, or in relation to contempt of court, defamation or incitement to an offence. (Republic of Namibia 1990: 14)

The parameters prescribe the principle of free but responsible media. The conclusion we can draw is that there is a limit on the freedom to communicate in all democracies, despite the notion that communicating beliefs, ideas and views is central to democracy (Feintuck 1999: 9). Drawing from this constitutional provision, the Information Policy embraced the social responsibility perspective, which obliges the media to act responsibly in executing their duties.

The role of broadcasting in the transition process

The Information Policy urges the media to be the 'catalyst for nation-building and socio-economic development', in addition to performing their traditional role of providing information, education and entertainment. To this end the media have to raise 'people's awareness of, and active interest in the country's development programmes and projects' (MIB 1991: 4, 5). The role of the media in the development of the country has been a critical priority of the new government, to the extent that it enjoys a prominent place in its macro-economic policies. For instance, the government's Transitional National Development Plan (1991–1994) calls for the establishment of a 'vigorous mass media system' (NPC 1993: 227). Articulating the role of the media in the development of the country, the government argues, among other things, that:

Namibia has adopted a democratic political system. In order for this young democracy to flourish, the Namibian electorate must be adequately informed to be able to make sound judgments. The development of a flourishing mass communication system is crucial in facilitating the implementation of educational and economic development programmes. The mass media must be deployed to combat illiteracy and to create the necessary social and psychological pre-conditions for fundamental change. Information must illuminate the path for development (ibid: 227)

The government considered the media as crucial to nation-building because the media have the responsibility of 'holding together the social system and thereby nurture the young democratic State and its institutions' (ibid: 75). Broadcasting, more particularly, had to 'instil in the people a sense of belonging and loyalty to a single motherland; unite them and foster in them patriotic sentiments around which their productive energies can be galvanised for socio-economic and political development' (MIB 1991: 5). The government emphasised that 'unless the population as a whole shares a common field of reference in terms of news and information gathered and circulated, there cannot be meaningful sharing of ideas and national ideals' (ibid: 4). The idea behind these arguments was to counter divisions among the citizens created by apartheid ideology. Moreover, the contentions were based on the notion that the media constituted the cultural arm of the nation-building effort, and provided focus on the political and cultural integration of a nation by acting as sources of common meanings, agendas and imagery (Chadha & Kavoori 2000: 425).

Creating unity among the citizenry was another objective the media had to facilitate. To counteract the ethnic, tribal and racial divisions perpetuated by the racist apartheid ideology, the media – and more particularly the national broadcaster – had to foster new values and norms to unify the divided people. This would provide them with hope for the future and a common destiny as a free and united people. In addition, the media had to contribute to the process of democratisation. The media are arguably vital for the functioning of democracy, since they provide the crucial channels that enable citizens to participate in the political and economic decision-making processes (Hamelink 1999). It is important to have well-informed citizens, to nurture a democratic culture in a young nation.

These additional roles of nation-building, development, unity and democratisation are based on the development communication paradigm, which draws on the structural–functionalist modernisation perspective (Melkote & Steeves 2001: 72–102). This paradigm, promoted by Western 'development experts', considers the media to be indispensable tools in the process of development and nation-building. Developing countries emerging from autocratic rule and under-development have tended to organise and operate their media systems within the broader context provided by this communication model (Eko 2000). Namibia was no exception. However, the political elite's uncritical acceptance of the paradigm, together with its desire to achieve political hegemony, brought forth fierce opposition from civil society. Despite the politicians insisting on developmental journalism, critical and independent media practitioners and media houses – many schooled in the liberal media tradition – have defended the role of the media as watchdogs over the state and its organs. Thus, critical media reports directed at government policies, programmes and projects on nation-building and development have been rejected by the political elite as being contradictory to the national interest. This challenge is captured lucidly by Robert Martin (1998: 69), when he argues that 'critical reporting about the activities of the government and party leaders is not considered as part of the development journalism; rather, to engage in such reporting is viewed as opposition to development.'

Apart from setting out the role and functions of the media in 'new' Namibia, the Information Policy makes provision for fundamental human rights and freedoms, although somewhat half-heartedly. In the next section we will examine the provisions of the 'right to know', the free-flow of information and the expansion of media infrastructure, and also the principles of media diversity, pluralism and empowerment.

The right to know

The Information Policy makes provision for the principle of access to information, or of citizens' right to know, although it lacks clear strategies for the implementation of this basic human right. The policy does not propose the translation of this objective into concrete reality. As a result, no legal instruments have been introduced to enforce this goal – despite acknowledgement by the government in its White Paper on Sectoral Development Programmes that without guaranteed access to the sources of information, media freedom will remain 'a privilege enjoyed by a few' (NPC 1993: 75).

In mature democracies, the right to know is underpinned by 'freedom of information' legislation, which compels public and private institutions to provide information to citizens on request. In the absence of such legislation, governments disseminate information they deem to be in the national interest, even if it is not necessarily what the citizens want. Jan van Cuilenburg and Paul Slaa (1993: 151) call this information provision a 'top-down information flow'. Describing this practice in sub-Saharan Africa, Paul Ansah (1992: 56, cited in Morrison and Love 1996: 66) notes that:

> Communication patterns … tend to be top-down, unidirectional, paternalistic and manipulative rather than being participatory, dialogical, horizontal and providing awareness of genuine feedback and interaction. The existing situation has been described as one in which 'the few talk to the many about the needs and problems of the many from the standpoint of the few'.

The top-down information provision can best be interpreted as a mobilisation exercise by governments to oblige citizens to support their (government's) policies and programmes – which translates into the propaganda function of governments. In the Namibian context the mobilisation function is illustrated lucidly in the Information Policy. There the government admits that the state-owned media have a 'distinct function to prepare, package and deliver the government's nation-building messages to the public and to mobilise the people for active participation in the country's development tasks' (MIB 1991a: 11). The emphasis in this statement is placed on the preparation and packaging of government information before it is delivered to the public. This implies that information is tailored in such a way as to ensure a positive reading – or what Stuart Hall calls a 'preferred reading' – from the citizens (Hall 1980).

The free flow of information

Linked to the notion of the right to know is the principle of 'free flow of information'. Both these discourses are based on the strong link connecting communication to democracy (O'Neil 1998:1). Namibia's Information Policy prescribes the free flow of information to facilitate the dissemination of information within society in order to nurture democracy. Under apartheid, information was both controlled and restricted by the state. This was done by applying a battery of legal instruments that inhibited freedom of expression and the free flow of information. Severe restrictions were imposed directly on the gathering, production and dissemination of information (Louw 1993), and indirectly through self-censorship on the part of the media organisations (Oosthuizen 1989: 45). The Namibian government sought to redress this restrictive media environment, but fell short of realising the objectives of the right to know and the free flow of information.

Firstly, it failed to speedily repeal or amend certain apartheid laws and to enact new legislation that would enhance the above-mentioned ideals.

Secondly, the government attempted to enact restrictive laws reminiscent of those in the apartheid era. For instance, the Protection of Information Act (Act 84 of 1982) –Section 4 of which prohibits public servants from disclosing government related information – has remained on the statute books. Section 4 seeks to safeguard national security by protecting state secrets. While the government amended some of the provisions of the Criminal Procedure Act (Act 51 of 1977) through the Criminal Procedure Amendment Act (Act 24 of 2003), it did not amend Section 205 that gives power to judges and magistrates to compel any person (including journalists) to reveal the sources of their information at the request of a public prosecutor. Media rights organisations and practitioners are of the opinion that this legal provision may undermine the journalistic practice of maintaining the confidentiality of sources (Kandjii 2004).

In 1996 and 1997 Namibian lawmakers attempted to curb media freedom and freedom of expression by proposing the inclusion of restrictive provisions in the draft Powers, Privileges and Immunities Bill. These provisions not only sought to compel citizens, including journalists, to reveal the sources of their information to parliamentary standing committees, but also wanted to prohibit journalists from interviewing parliamentarians on matters that still needed to be tabled in Parliament. However, strong opposition from civil society forced the lawmakers to abandon these proposed amendments.

Pluralism, diversity and empowerment

Namibia's Information Policy provides for the liberalisation of the broadcasting sector, and thereby for the creation of a plurality of broadcasting outlets. However, it fails to make provision for the support and encouragement of a diverse media environment. For instance, it does not seek to empower citizens in terms of the ownership, production, consumption or dissemination of communication media. Despite the rhetoric of 'empowerment' in the broader economic sector, the government has done very little to realise this objective in the media sector.

While the government has been reluctant to assist communities in the establishment of their own local media outlets, it has – at least at policy level – committed itself to setting up the Universal Service Fund to help expand telecommunication facilities and services across the country. However, the same government has not yet considered the establishment of a similar fund for the broadcast and print media to promote diversity in this sector. Nevertheless, a few community-based media have emerged – set up by the communities themselves with financial and technical support from donor organisations.

The lack of media diversity, as Andrew Calabrese (2004: 7) notes, tends to undermine the breadth, depth and quality of public knowledge and this is true of the Namibian situation. Thus, the failure by the Namibian government to promote media diversity has negated the development of vibrant and diverse voices that could have contributed to the nurturing of the young democracy.

Expansion of infrastructure

The expansion of information and communication infrastructure has been another priority of the Information Policy. Here, the policy draws from Article 95 of the Constitution, which requires the State to provide public services and utilities, including broadcasting infrastructure and services, to all its citizens. The expansion of this infrastructure became an integral part of the democratisation process. The government believed that only when the majority of the people had access to infrastructure and services could they participate fully in the activities of their society (NPC 1993: 74).

In order to achieve this objective, the government proceeded to narrow the communication gap between urban and rural dwellers. This would have the effect of integrating the rural communities into the mainstream economy through the information and communication sector. With this in mind, the government, through its agencies and assistance from international donors, had been allocating resources to acquire the necessary communication technologies. However, as noted above, the provision of additional communication infrastructure and services did not seek to promote diversity, but only the expansion of the government's top-down information strategy.

Liberalisation of the broadcasting sector

Namibia introduced competition in its broadcasting sector by opening it to private and community operators in 1992. The introduction of competition was informed by the neo-liberal policy of liberalisation adopted by the State in 1990. Drawing from Article 98 of the Constitution, which guarantees a mixed form of economic ownership, the Information Policy extended the mixed ownership rationale to the broadcasting sector. This led to the emergence of private-commercial and non-profit community-based broadcasting operators (see Table 12.1). This policy reform was remarkable, since the provision of broadcasting services was confined to the SWABC during the colonial era, while private broadcasting (both commercial and community) was prohibited prior to independence.

The emergent mixed broadcasting system comprises the dominant national/public broadcasting system – exemplified by the NBC – and the relatively small (in terms of penetration in society), privately-owned system, comprising the commercial and community broadcasting sub-systems. The dominant public system is directly regulated by the State through the Namibian Broadcasting Corporations Act (Act 9 of 1991), while the Namibia Communications Commission (NCC) regulates the privately-owned sub-system through the provisions of the Namibian Communications Commission Act of 1992. The public system is partially tailored along the lines of Robert McChesney's (1997: 66) public service broadcasting model, which is said to be accountable, non-profit, non-commercial and independent from the state and from business. However, Namibia's dominant public service broadcasting model has not been independent from either.

'Managed liberalisation'

While the broadcasting sector is liberalised and thus open to competition, it has not been entirely thrown open – some restrictions are still imposed on foreign ownership, which is limited to minority shareholding. In terms of this 'managed' or 'controlled' liberalisation, broadcasting licences are issued only to Namibians or to a 'company of which at least 51 per cent of the shareholding is beneficially owned by Namibian citizens, and which is not controlled directly or indirectly by persons who are not Namibian citizens' (Republic of Namibia 1992: 10). This strategy can be understood in terms of Linda Weiss's (1999) notion of 'managed openness', which is aimed at controlling the impact of globalisation at the local level.

Despite this limitation on foreign ownership – coupled with a relatively small advertising contribution – Namibia has managed to attract a handful of foreign investors to its broadcasting market, mainly from South Africa. South African broadcasters, apart from being inspired by historical and cultural links, have also benefited by extending their reach to the Namibian business market, which is dominated by South African retail companies. The lack of local content requirements

Table 12.1: Post-independence broadcasting market structure

Station	Type/ Orientation	Ownership	Language
NBC Radio Service	Non-profit/ public/ national	State/ public	English, Afrikaans, German, Otjiherero, Oshiwambo, Lozi, Gciruku, Setswana, Damara/ Nama, !AH Radio (San dialects)
Radio 99	Commercial	Private	English
Radio Wave	Commercial	Private	English
Radio Kudu	Commercial	Private	Afrikaans
Radio Energy	Commercial	Private	English/ Oshiwambo
Radio Omulunga	Commercial	Private	Oshiwambo
Radio Ecclesia	Non-profit/ religious	Private (Catholic Church)	English
UNAM Campus Radio	Non-profit/ students' radio	Private (University of Namibia)	English
Channel Seven	Non-profit/ religious	Private (Media for Christ)	Afrikaans/ English
Katutura Community Radio (KCR)	Non-profit/ community	Private	English
Ohangwena Community Radio	Non-profit/ community	State/ public (regional government)	English/ Oshiwambo
Erongo Community Radio	Non-profit/ community	Private	English
Cosmos	Commercial	Private	English/ Afrikaans
Trinity Broadcasting Radio	Non-profit/ religious	Private	English/ Afrikaans
Windhoek-Paris FM	Commercial	Public/ private	English/ French
NBC Television Service	Non-profit/ public/ national	State/ public	English
MultiChoice Namibia	Commercial	Private	English/ Afrikaans
DEStv [5]	Commercial	Private	English
One Africa TV	Commercial	Private	English
GTV	Commercial	Private	English
Reho-TV	Community	Private	Afrikaans

Source: Namibia Communications Commission

in Namibia has allowed programmes produced for the South African audience to be re-broadcast to additional customers. Thus, economies of scale are achieved through the re-use of the same programme material to a new and expanded audience at no extra production cost (Van Loon 1996).

Commercialisation in the broadcasting sector

The government policy of liberalisation has ushered the broadcasting sector into the mainstream economy by introducing competition into the sector. While competition resulted in a plurality of voices and thus more choices for the consumer, it inadvertently depressed the revenue stream of the national broadcaster. The change from monopoly to a competitive market meant that the limited advertising revenue had to be shared among the operators. Faced with budgetary cuts from the State and the mismanagement of resources, including finances at the company level, the NBC was forced to commercialise its operations in order to fund its public service mandate.

In fact, the government has persistently encouraged the corporation to increase its revenue generating activities, such as licence fee collection and advertising income, in order to ease the latter's burden on the Treasury. Faced with an urgent need to reduce the 'social deficits' created by apartheid, together with demands by donors to reduce State funding on social services, the government had to continually decrease its subsidy to the corporation during the transition process. Public service broadcasting in general was threatened by neo-liberal orthodoxy, which advocated a lean and mean government in terms of providing basic services to the citizens (McChesney & Schiller 2003: 5).

Aida Opoku-Mensah (1998: 5) aptly describes the dilemma of national service broadcasters in sub-Saharan Africa and other developing countries in the era of globalisation by arguing that: 'having theoretically relinquished direct control of the formerly state-run broadcasters, governments are cutting their subsidies to these corporations and forcing them to survive in increasingly crowded commercial marketplaces'.

This is the broader context in which the NBC had to contribute to nation-building, socio-economic development, unity and democratisation. At the same time it had to perform its traditional role of informing, educating and entertaining the public. In order to fulfil this mandate, the corporation had to cut costs. A number of strategies were adopted to achieve this, among them the streamlining of the corporation's operations; the downsizing of the staff complement; the outsourcing of non-core functions; and the divesture of assets and properties. The NBC restructured itself several times and adopted business plans to transform itself into a commercially viable institution with a public service mandate. However, it was not successful in all these measures. A number of reasons can be advanced for this failure, but suffice it to say that political control, inadequate public funding and the mismanagement of resources continued to thwart its process of transformation.

Regulating the broadcasting sector

Regulation is understood as comprising the rules, procedures and institutional mechanisms for negotiating power relations between the media, the political sphere, the market-place and the public (Hamelink 1999: 13). After having formulated a fairly liberal Information Policy to steer the transformation of its information and communication sector, the government proceeded to restructure the inherited broadcasting system by establishing a new regulatory framework. It dismantled the state monopoly over the broadcasting sector, but transferred state control from the apartheid regime to the post-independence government. In 1992 the government established a new agency, the Namibia Communications Commission,[6] to regulate the sector. Established under Section 2 of the Namibia Communications Commission Act (Act 4 of 1992), as amended, the Commission is tasked with the responsibility of licensing private broadcasters and regulating their activities. The 1992 Act replaced legal instruments such as the Broadcasting Act (Act 73 of 1976), the Radio Act (Act 2 of 1952), and the Post Office Act (Act 44 of 1958) and a host of media and security legislation that were used to regulate the sector during the colonial era (see Hachten & Giffard 1984; Herbstein 1985; Stuart 1990).

Despite the rhetoric of an 'independent' regulator, the Commission has not been independent or autonomous. Rather, it is positioned to serve as an appendage of the government. The Commissioners are appointed by a government minister in terms of Section 3 of the 1992 Act, and they account directly to the government instead of to the public whose interests they are supposed to serve. Secondly, the Secretariat of the Commission consists of a Directorate in the MIB. The broadcasting sector needs regulatory bodies that are independent of the state and business, but still accessible to all stakeholders with interests in the sector. 'Independence', as William Melody (1997: 19) argues, does not necessarily mean independence from state policy. Instead, it implies the freedom to make one's own decisions within the broader policy framework set by the state, but without interference from it or from other stakeholders. The state must lay the ground rules in terms of policy and permit the regulator to operate within these rules without interference. In fact the state, in consultation with the broadcasting industry and the public, is responsible for overall policy formulation, while regulatory bodies are tasked with the design and practical implementation of regulations. Thus, for regulatory bodies to perform their function effectively and without undue influence or bias, they have to operate independently and autonomously from the state and the industry. Independence and autonomy allow regulators to avoid being 'captured' by government or the industry. Arguments on the role of the state could be further grounded in theory, as these were part of a larger global debate on 'rolling back the state'.

The above-mentioned shortcomings in the regulatory regime are not unique to Namibia. I would argue that these challenges are common throughout the world, wherever attempts are made to establish independent regulatory authorities. Describing the shortcomings of African regulators in particular, Ernst Wilson III and Kelvin Wong (2003: 166) note that:

> Most African countries had virtually no experience with effective independent regulatory agencies. Instead, all regulation was done by in-house ministry officials. Most lacked adequate training and money. They frequently lacked the autonomy necessary for effective enforcement that facilitates privatisation and competition. Thus, while many African countries established formal regulatory agents for the ICT sectors, in most cases the Regulators were understaffed and lacked the expertise necessary to run effective regulatory agencies.

Thus, like other developing countries, Namibia has as yet to establish an effective regulator that can design and implement competitive rules relevant to a dynamic information and communications sector in a rapidly changing political and economic environment. Apart from the question of independence and autonomy, an effective and credible regulator must have its own sound financial basis, skilled and professional staff and the necessary tools to monitor compliance. Namibia's regulator does not meet these requirements. It does not have its own source of income for conducting operations, but is provided with a budget from the State Treasury. This is allocated through the MIB, while income from licence fees is paid back to the State. Most tellingly, the Commission is dogged by inadequate staffing and a lack of expertise to meet the demands and challenges of the ever-changing information and communication sector.

It is also expected that a regulator should be legitimate. Legitimacy is established through transparency and accountability. Transparency means that the regulatory process and decisions taken by the regulator are open to public scrutiny. The public is, therefore, allowed insight into regulatory decisions, while the regulator facilitates public consultation and challenge. Accountability means that the regulator is answerable to the citizens and their political representatives in Parliament for its decisions and rulings. The Namibia regulatory process fails this test. Its decisions are not subjected to public input and scrutiny. It does not hold public hearings on licensing, despite the fact that it gazettes pending licences in the *Government Gazette* for public attention. The commission is accountable only to Cabinet through the minister and not to the public with regard to its decisions. This situation indicates that the regulator operates entirely at the pleasure of the government and has no independent voice.

Some of Namibia's neighbours – notably Botswana, South Africa and Zambia – have already appointed 'independent' regulatory bodies, mainly through a fairly transparent process of public nominations. The regulatory bodies of these countries, and more particularly the Independent Communications Authority of South Africa (ICASA), have adopted fairly democratic procedures whereby the public is consulted through various methods. Open hearings are conducted and the public, including stakeholders and civil society organisations, is afforded opportunities to comment on the draft regulations through oral and written submissions. Thus, the public interest is taken fully into account in these regulatory procedures.

Challenge to the regulator's independence

The independence and autonomy of the Namibian Regulator has been a contested issue between the State and other stakeholders in the broadcasting sector. Civil society organisations, among them the Namibian Chapter of the Media Institute for Southern Africa (MISA), have called for the independence of the Regulator. MISA-Namibia frequently criticises government's control of the commission and has been calling for the appointment of an independent regulator as well as independent directors for the national broadcaster. This can be facilitated through a transparent and participatory process in terms of the provisions of the Windhoek Declaration and of the SADC Protocol on Culture, Information and Sport – instruments that the Namibian government has embraced.

The demand for an independent regulator stems partly from the perception that states have concurrent interests in the broadcasting sector as owners, producers and consumers of communications, and cannot therefore be independent arbiters or regulators (Schiller 1969/1992, cited in Mosco 1996: 92). In situations where states assume such conflicting responsibilities in terms of broadcasting, they cannot be expected to mediate effectively and fairly between the opposing interests and demands of the various stakeholders in the sector.

In spite of calls by stakeholders to have an independent regulator in place, the government does not seem ready to heed this call. Addressing a workshop on the Information and Communications Bill that was drafted to replace the Namibian Communications Commission Act, a former minister of information and broadcasting made the government's position very clear with regard to the establishment of an independent regulator. He argued, among other things, that:

> One of the major expectations among stakeholders is to see an independent and fully autonomous regulator in place soon after the Bill becomes an Act. On this point, I have to disappoint you. In view of the numerous fraudulent activities that have been uncovered at State-Owned Enterprises lately, the Ministry of Information and Broadcasting, as line ministry dealing with the regulator, does not see its way open

to immediately surrender its oversight role over the regulator that will be created as a State-Owned Enterprise (Mbumba 2003: 3).

Interestingly, the Information and Communications Bill initially proposed the retention of the regulator by the Minister, although the latter will now select the commissioners from 'a list of suitable candidates' prepared by a selection panel. Ironically, the same minister will appoint the panel, the majority of whose members will be civil servants. This clearly indicates that the government is not prepared to allow the establishment of independent regulatory bodies, despite the fact that it has ratified a number of international instruments that provide for such bodies in the broadcasting sector. Nevertheless, civil society organisations continue to challenge the government on this omission.

The State's direct regulation of the national broadcaster

Despite some profound reforms undertaken in the broadcasting sector, the government has not abandoned state control over the national broadcaster (NBC). The NBC is regulated by the Namibian Broadcasting Corporation Act (Act 9 of 1991) and not by the Namibian Communications Commission Act of 1992. Section 29 of the latter Act makes this clear:

> This Act shall not apply to the Namibian Broadcasting Corporation established by Section 2 of the Namibian Broadcasting Corporation Act, 1991 (Act 9 of 1991), or in respect of the broadcasting activities carried on by that Corporation (Republic of Namibia 1992: 19).

Although Namibia sought to establish a new national broadcaster different from the old, colonial one, the government did not do away with the fundamental provisions of the legislation on which the colonial broadcaster's policy had been based. As a matter of fact, it retained most – if not all – of these provisions. Even the Administrator General's Broadcasting Act Amendment Proclamation (AG 16 of 1979) to the South African Broadcasting Act of 1976 did not change the fundamental political control provided in the earlier Act. The amendments proposed by the Administrator General (AG) were at best cosmetic, and contained terms such as 'Administrator General' instead of 'Minister' and 'South West Africa' instead of 'South Africa'. Thus, the Broadcasting Act of 1976 remained the basic legal instrument on which the SWABC was regulated, and continued to be the foundation on which the Namibian Broadcasting Act of 1991 was crafted, despite the considerable fanfare about a 'new Act'. The pattern of control inherited from the colonial Act was transferred *in toto* to the 'new Act'.

To understand the similarities between the two pieces of legislation, we have to examine the control structures of both the SWABC and the NBC. The SWABC operated under political control exercised by the AG, who was appointed by the South African government to implement an internal political settlement in Namibia. He assumed what was called 'allocative power' with regard to the Corporation, while the operational power was dispensed by the directors he appointed and who reported directly to him. With the establishment of the Transitional Government of National Unity (TGNU) in June 1985 following the implementation of the 'internal political settlement', the power to allocate resources and duties was symbolically transferred to the TGNU. During the brief life of the transitional government, the Minister of National Education assumed responsibility for the Corporation. In this arrangement, the SWABC accounted to and reported directly to the Minister, who in turn reported to Cabinet and the National Assembly of the TGNU. Following the implementation of the United Nations Peace Plan (Resolution 435), which led to the internationally supervised elections in the territory on 1 April 1989, the TGNU was dissolved and the AG resumed direct control of the Corporation.

After ascending the ladder of power in 1990 the new government retained these patterns of control. In terms of the Namibian Broadcasting Act of 1991, the Minister of Information and Broadcasting appoints the directors who are accountable to him/her for the management of the NBC. Apart from appointing the directors, the Minister has the power to approve major decisions of the Corporation ranging from financial matters to programme content. The Minister has to approve any co-operation between the Corporation and other operators. For instance, the NBC needs written permission from the Minister in order to be able to enter into agreements with other broadcasters when it wants to co-broadcast, or to supply or receive, information, news or programmes. Loans, investments and any other financial transactions also have to be approved by the Minister (Republic of Namibia 1991: 24, 25). While some of these obligations are of an administrative nature, they have nevertheless had serious implications for the independence of the Corporation. The Namibian Broadcasting Act therefore does not allow for autonomy of the NBC, nor does it provide checks and balances to prevent political control of the Corporation.

The regulation of private broadcasters

While directly controlling the national broadcaster, the government has had an arm's length relationship with private broadcasters. As indicated above, private broadcasters have been regulated in terms of the provision of the Namibian Communications Commission Act of 1992. Nevertheless, the Minister of Information and Broadcasting formulates regulations for private broadcasters based on the recommendations of the Commission, in terms of Paragraph 27 of the Act. The first set of such regulations was promulgated in the *Government Gazette* of 25 February 1994. In addition to these ministerial regulations, various provisions of the Namibian Communications Commission Act set out a number of duties and responsibilities to be observed by private broadcasters.

Some of these regulations deal with general administrative matters relating to application procedures and licence requirements, including licence conditions and fees. Others pertain to the performance of private licence holders. They set down rules and responsibilities in terms of professional standards, advertising, political reporting and the promotion of national identities. Like broadcasters elsewhere, Namibian private stations are required to observe professional standards of factual, accurate and impartial reporting. 'Counter-version' facilities must be provided to people and institutions affected by false or unfair reporting. The principle of 'counter versions' is based on the 1949 Fairness Doctrine of the Federal Communications Commission in the USA, which required that free airtime be allocated by broadcasting corporations to individuals and groups negatively affected by their broadcasts (a requirement unfortunately suspended in America in 1987) (Harvey 1998: 542).

The 1992 Act also seeks to regulate broadcasting content. Content regulations define 'limitations imposed on what cannot and must be broadcast' (Feintuck 1999: 51). This has been a thorny issue in broadcasting regulation. It relates to the question of media 'externalities'. Like other media, broadcasting markets are said to have externalities (both positive and negative) that refer to 'those costs paid by society and not by the seller or buyer' (McChesney 2003: 131). Because they use public resources (airwaves), broadcasters have to be held accountable to the citizens, who are the ultimate owners of these resources. For instance, Namibian private broadcasters are obliged to limit their advertisements to 20 per cent of their total daily broadcasting time. They are also prohibited from carrying advertisements for alcoholic beverages and tobacco products in programmes aimed at audiences younger than 18 years. They are further held accountable to the Commission in terms of the content and scheduling of their sponsored programmes.

Interestingly too, private broadcasters are prohibited from carrying advertisements 'intended for or related to party political purposes' or from broadcasting 'any programme which has as its predominant tenor, the advancement of the interests of any political party', except during election times (Republic of Namibia 1992: 13). During elections, private broadcasters are required to follow certain guidelines. For example, they are allowed to grant airtime to all political parties, but only during the six weeks before polling day. If they choose to cover a presidential election, they have to allocate equal time to all the candidates. In local, regional and parliamentary elections, they have to allocate 40 per cent of the 'political airtime' equally to all participating parties. The remaining 60 per cent must be divided among contesting parties in accordance with the number of votes received in the previous election (Republic of Namibia 1994: 3). It is interesting to note that while the government prescribes the coverage of political reporting by private broadcasters, it does not do so for the national broadcaster. The NBC is allowed to draw up its own election guidelines in consultation with political parties.

An important dimension of the Namibian regulatory regime was its intention to ensure that private broadcasters provide a high percentage of public service programming at the expense of commercial content. However, this principle has not been successfully implemented since the liberalisation of the sector in 1992. In fact, the commodifying of the broadcast space in the age of globalisation has seen a marked shift from public service ethos to a commercially motivated outlook. The need to compel private broadcasters to air public service-oriented programmes has been an attempt to balance the public and commercial interests in the sector. The Namibian regulatory regime has sought to achieve this objective by, for instance, compelling private broadcasters to observe the socio-cultural norms and values of the nation. Paragraph 18 of the Namibian Communications Commission Act obliges them to:

(a)   encourage the development of Namibian expression by providing a wide range of programming that reflects Namibian attitudes, opinions, ideas, values and artistic creativity by displaying Namibian talent in entertainment programming insofar as it is practicable to do so and with due regard to the nature of the service pertaining to the licence holder;

(b)   serve the needs and interests and reflect the circumstances and aspirations of Namibian men, women and children in a multicultural society;

(c)   make maximum use of Namibian creativity and other resources in the creation and presentation of programming, unless the nature of the service provided renders that use impracticable or the resources and expertise are not available in Namibia;

(d)   contribute through programming to shared national consciousness and identity, but with the due regard to the nature of the service pertaining to the licence holder;

(e)   provide programming that caters for culture, arts, sports and education, but with due regard to the nature of the service pertaining to the licence holder (Republic of Namibia 1992: 12–13).

In spite of the fact that Namibia adopted what can be seen as a progressive regulatory approach, the Commission has yet to enforce provisions of this regulatory mechanism. As indicated earlier, the Commission is dysfunctional. It suffers from a shortage of resources including funds, personnel and equipment, all of which impinge on its ability to enforce and monitor compliance with the regulations. Moreover, the conditions attached to these responsibilities are self-defeating. As can be seen above, the government has made adherence to the obligations conditional on the type of service provided, as well as on the availability of resources and expertise. These 'opt-out clauses' have proved to be the regulatory regime's Achilles heel because they allow broadcasters to abuse them. This oversight, together with the lack of domestic (local) content requirements, has allowed broadcasters to transmit foreign programme material with insufficient consideration for the production and screening of programmes with domestic content. It is instructive to note that owing to the absence of local content requirements, the first two television stations to be established after the liberalisation of the sector – Desert Entertainment Television and One Africa Television – during their formative stages opted to trade shares in their companies plus advertising revenue for television programme material from foreign television channels.

Conclusion

This chapter has highlighted the successes and shortcomings of Namibian broadcasting-sector reform in the post-independence era. The government has largely succeeded in ending the State monopoly by liberalising the broadcasting sector and thereby opening it up to more players. It effectively scrapped some of the restrictive legislation that inhibited the realisation of a democratic media environment in the pre-independence era. However, liberalising the sector brought it into the sphere of the economy, where operators have to compete for audiences and advertising revenue. The government's failure to fund the national broadcaster adequately – owing to its neo-liberal policies of reduced funding for social services – has inhibited the successful transformation of the NBC.

The government has also adopted a fairly liberal Information Policy to steer the transformation of its broadcasting sector during the transitional period. However, as I have indicated, the formulation of this policy was not informed by public debate. As a result, the government failed to democratise the broadcast policy-making process – which partly inhibited the emergence of a democratic communication system in the post-independence era. Moreover, the Information Policy lacked implementation strategies. Thus, while important tenets related to media rights and freedoms are recognised in the country, no concrete mechanisms are provided to implement them. The Information Policy is outdated and does not meet the standards set in the SADC Protocol on Culture, Communication and Sport; or in the SADC Protocol on ICT; or in the African Commission's Declaration of Principles on Free Expression in Africa, to mention but three examples.

It is worth noting that while the government dismantled state monopoly in the broadcasting sector, it retained state control over the national broadcaster by adopting a regulatory mechanism similar to that used by the colonial administration. Therefore, despite the 'rearrangement' of the broadcasting sector, the policy legacy of the old broadcasting dispensation has remained strong. This has restricted the transformation of the former state broadcaster into a truly public service broadcaster.

In addition, the new regulator, the Namibian Communications Commission, is not an independent body, but remains a government agency.

Perhaps the most contentious aspect of the Namibian broadcasting sector reform process relates to the need to balance the conflicting demands of the 'national interest' and the 'public interest'. It has been demonstrated in this chapter that the broadcasting sector has to perform developmental roles in addition to its traditional responsibilities. It is expected of the sector to do more than just inform, educate and entertain citizens. It has to propagate the government's policies and programmes of national development, national identity, unity and the democratisation of the new society. The dissemination of these imperatives has been a very sensitive issue for government and any challenge to it has been viewed as a threat to the 'national interest'. The promotion and protection of the 'national interest' has led to direct and indirect political interference in the operations of the national broadcaster. This has not only undermined its transformation into a credible public broadcaster, but has also impacted negatively on the broader democratisation process of society.

In post-colonial Namibia, the ideals of democratic and independent regulatory mechanisms in the broadcasting sector have not been realised. Since the country generally moved away from the autocratic apartheid regime of the pre-1990 era, many of the problems relating to the transformation of the broadcasting system can be associated with the challenges of the democratisation of society and its institutions. In this context the public service broadcasting system still remains an ideal and is not a working reality. In the main, this is the result of State control over the Regulator and the national broadcaster. The liberalisation of the broadcasting sector in the post-independence era led to the emergence of private, commercial and community broadcasters that offered opportunities for promoting diverse views and broader public debate. Nevertheless, political control continues to undermine the ideal of a fully democratic public broadcasting service.

References

Amupala, J. 1988. Development of broadcasting in Namibia. Unpublished paper presented at the Namibian Press Centenary Conference, 12–13 October, in Windhoek, Namibia.

Barnett, C. 2001. Media, scale and democratisation. In *Media, Democracy and Renewal in Southern Africa*, ed. G. Tomaselli and H. Dunn, 14–53. Colorado Springs: International Academic Publishers.

Calabrese, A. 2004. Towards a political economy of culture. In *Towards a Political Economy of Culture: Capitalism and Communication in the Twenty-First Century*, ed. A. Calabrese and C. Sparks. Lanham, Maryland: Rowman & Littlefield Publishers.

Chadha, K. and A. Kavoori. 2000. Media imperialism revisited: Some findings from the Asian case. *Media, Culture and Society* 22 (4): 412–432. London: Sage.

Charles, A. 1995. Colonial discourse since Christopher Columbus. *Journal of Black Studies* 26(2), 135–152.

De Beer, S. 1975. Die werksaamhede van die SAUK in Suidwes Afrika. *SWA Jaarboek*. SWA Administrasie.

Dyvi, E. B. 1993. *Radio and National Identity in Namibia: A Study of the Namibian Broadcasting Corporation*. Unpublished dissertation for the degree of Cand. Polit., University of Oslo, Norway.

Eko, L. 2000. Public broadcasting in a changing political and regulatory environment: the case of Africa. *Ecquid Novi* 21(1): 82–97.

Feintuck, M. 1999. *Media Regulation, Public Interest and the Law*. Edinburgh: Edinburgh University Press.

Hachten, W.A. and C.A. Giffard. 1984. *Total onslaught: The South African Press Under Attack*. Johannesburg: Macmillan.

Hall, S. 1980. Encoding and decoding. In *Culture, Communication and Language*, ed. S. Hall, D. Hobson, A. Lowe and P. Willis, 18–27. London: Hutchison University Press.

Hamata, M. 2001. Defence media restrictions 'not new'. *The Namibian*, 28 September 2001.

Hamelink, C. J. 1999. *Preserving Media Independence: Regulatory Frameworks*. Paris: Unesco.

Harvey, S. 1998. Doing it my way – broadcasting regulation in capitalist cultures: The case of 'fairness' and 'impartiality''. *Media, Culture and Society* 20(4): 538–547.

Herbstein, D. 1985. Namibia: How South Africa controls the news'. *Censorship* 4: 24–29.

Heuva, W. E. 2000. *A Decade of Broadcasting in Independent Namibia*. Basler Afrika Bibliographien Working Paper No. 6. Switzerland: Basler Afrika Bibliographien.

Horwitz, R. B. 2001. *Communication and Democratic Reform in South Africa*. Cambridge: Cambridge University Press.

Kandjii, K. 2004. Namibia. In *Undue Restriction: Laws Impacting on Media Freedom in the SADC*, ed. R. Louw, 53–63. Windhoek: Media Institute of Southern Africa.

Louw, R. 1993. 'Foreword'. In Louw, P.E. (ed.). *South African Media Policy: Debates of the 1990s*. Bellville: Anthropos.

Mampone, L. 2005. The SABC – 70 years of broadcasting. *City Press*, 4 December 2005.

Mbumba, N. 2003. A statement by Honourable Nangolo Mbumba, Minister of Information and Broadcasting, at the final workshop on the draft Communications Bill for the Republic of Namibia. Nampower Convention Centre, Windhoek, 24 July.

McChesney, R. W. 1997b. *Corporate media and the threat to democracy*. Open Media Pamphlet Series. Cresskil (New Jersey): Hampton Press, Inc.

McChesney, R. W. and D. Schiller. 2003. *The political economy of international communications: Foundations for the emerging global debate about media ownership and regulation*. Technology, Business and Society Programme, Paper 11, October. United Nations Research Institute for Social Development.

Melkote, S. R. and H. L. Steeves, L. 2001. *Communication for Development in the Third World: Theory and Practice for Empowerment*, 2nd ed. New Delhi: Sage Publications India.

Melody W. H. 1997. *Telecom Reform: Principles, Policies and Regulatory Practices*. Den Private Ingeniorfond: Technical University of Denmark.

MIB *see* Ministry of Information and Broadcasting.

Ministry of Information and Broadcasting. 1991. *Namibia's Information Policy*. Windhoek: John Meinert Printing.

Morrison, A. and A. Love. 1996. A discourse of disillusionment: Letters to the Editor in two Zimbabwean magazines, 10 years after Independence. *Discourse and Society* 7(1): 39–75.

Mosco, V. 1996. *The Political Economy of Communication: Rethinking and Renewal*. London: Sage Publications.

National Planning Commission. 1993. *Transitional Development Plan: 1991–1992 to 1993–1994*. Windhoek: John Meinert Printing.

Nnoli, O. 2000. Globalisation and democracy in Africa. In *Globalisation and the Post-Colonial African State*, ed. D. W. Nabudere. Harare: AAPS Books.

NPC *see* National Planning Commission.

O'Neil, P. H. ed. 1998. *Communicating Democracy: The Media and Political Transitions*. London: Lynne Rienner Publishers.

Oosthuizen, L. M. 1989. *Media Policy and Ethics*. Cape Town: Juta & Co.

Opoku-Mensah, A. 1998. Broadcasting in Southern Africa: An overview. In *Up in the Air? The State of Broadcasting in Southern Africa*, ed. A. Opoku-Mensah, 18–27. Lusaka: Panos Southern Africa.

Republic of Namibia. 1990. *Constitution of the Republic of Namibia*. Windhoek: John Meinert Printing.

——. 1991. Namibian Broadcasting Act. *Government Gazette* No. 223, Windhoek, 19 June.

——. 1992. Namibian Communications Commission Act. *Government Gazette* No. 384, Windhoek, 3 April.

——. 1994. Regulations under the Namibian Communications Commission Act. *Government Gazette* No. 802, Windhoek, 25 February.

——. 2002. Defence Act. *Government Gazette* No. 2749, Windhoek, 7 June.

——. 2003. Criminal Procedure Amendment Act. *Government Gazette* No. 3123, Windhoek, 30 December.

Republic of South Africa. 1976. Broadcasting Act. *Government Gazette* No. 5138, Cape Town, 26 May.

Saunders, C. 2001. From apartheid to democracy in Namibia and South Africa: Some comparisons. In *Transition in Southern Africa: Comparative Aspects. Discussion Paper No. 10.* Uppsala: Nordic Africa Institute.

Schiller, H. I. 1969/1992 (2nd updated ed.). *Mass Communication and American Empire.* Boston: Beacon Press.

South West Africa Administration. 1979. Broadcasting Amendment Act (AG 16 of 1979). *Extraordinary Official Gazette* No. 3942, Windhoek, 27 April 1979.

South West Africa Broadcasting Corporation. 1979. *Annual Report, 1978-1979.*

South West Africa People's Organisation. 1985. Mass media in occupied Namibia. *Swapo Information Bulletin,* June. Luanda: Department of Information and Publicity.

Stuart, K.W. 1990. *The Newspaperman's Guide to the Law.* Durban: Butterworths.

Tapscott, C. 1993. National reconciliation, social equity and class formation in independent Namibia. *Journal of Southern African* 19(1), March.

Van Cuilenburg, J. and P. Slaa. 1993. From media policy towards a national communication policy: Broadening the scope. *European Journal of Communication* 8(2): 150–158.

Van Loon, A. 1996. Global trends – global solutions? In *Media Ownership and Control in the Age of Convergence,* ed. V. MacLeod, 27–33. London: International Institute of Communications.

Weiss, L. 1999. Managed openness: Beyond neoliberal globalisation. *New Left Review* 238, Nov./Dec.

Wilson III, E. J. and K.Wong. 2003. African information revolution: A balance sheet. *Telecommunications Policy* 27(1–2): 155–177.

Swaziland struggles for media freedom

13

Richard Rooney

Swaziland's media policy is closely connected to the general polity in the kingdom. Swaziland is not a democracy and is ruled by sub-Saharan Africa's last absolute monarch, King Mswati III. Freedom of expression is limited in the kingdom and human rights are constantly under attack. The kingdom had been under a state of emergency since 1973, when a royal proclamation suspended the then existing Constitution.

Following international pressure, a new Constitution, which allowed freedom of speech and freedom of association, came into effect in 2006. The same international pressure that resulted in the new Constitution encouraged a raft of draft government bills to democratise the media in Swaziland. These bills, introduced in 2007, have yet to be finalised or enacted.

On the face of it, these changes are encouraging. A non-democratic kingdom appears to be undergoing radical change with the purpose of creating an open society with freedom of expression and media operation. However, what we actually have is a situation of change but no change. Swaziland has a dual legal system – the official modern system and the traditional cultural system. The first of these is the modern law that is enshrined in the Constitution. It allows individuals and the media the 'right of freedom of expression and opinion' (Section 24). Then there is Swazi law and custom, presided over by 'traditionalists', which places the monarch at the top of a legal system that is administered through chiefs and other advisors appointed by the monarch. The role of the traditionalists as advisers to the king is enshrined in the Constitution (Section 231).

In the present situation, the traditionalists appear to have the upper hand. Freedom of expression is still restricted, most of the media houses in Swaziland remain under State control, and the changes that are enshrined in the Constitution have not been forthcoming in practice (Rooney 2007).

This chapter looks at what has been happening to media policy in Swaziland since the Constitution was signed in 2006. It begins with a brief introduction to Swaziland as a country and the media landscape within it. A critical discussion of the specifics of the Constitution in the area of freedom of expression follows. This includes an overview of the operations of the media since the Constitution came into force, and highlights the continued restrictions they face. It then discusses the draft bills, detailing their contents and discussing the likelihood of their implementation. It concludes by arguing that the bills, in keeping with the constitution that spawned them, are unlikely to themselves lead to a democratisation of media in Swaziland.

An important part of the debate in Swaziland at present surrounds the subject of public service broadcasting. Broadcasting in Swaziland is mostly state controlled, but there have been some initiatives – supported by civil society – to shift towards a public service paradigm. Although the state claims to welcome such a move, the evidence on the ground is that the undemocratic ruling elite has no intention of making change a reality. Citizens in Swaziland have played an important role in the broadcasting debate, despite the fact that they are marginalised in the decision-making process. The problems this raises form the final substantive part of this chapter.

Country background

Swaziland is among the smallest countries on the African continent and is landlocked between South Africa and Mozambique. It has a population estimated at fewer than a million, and is a middle to low income country, ranking 137 out of 177 on the UNDP Human Development Index. The economy has been hard hit by the HIV/AIDS pandemic and also by droughts that have caused severe food shortages, with about 60 per cent of the population relying on donated food aid (Rooney 2007).

The population is ethnically homogeneous, with approximately 97 per cent of the people being Swazi. Most of this population is rural – only 23 per cent of people live in urban or suburban areas (Rooney 2007).

Swaziland has one of the highest income inequalities among middle to low income countries – with a Gini coefficient of 0.61.[1] Corruption is a major problem and members of parliament engage in fraud and graft (Ndlovu 2006). The king and members of his set spend lavishly (in 2005, King Mswati purchased two $500 000 Maybach limousines and a fleet of 10 BMW cars for his wives) while presiding over a population of which about 70 per cent live on an income of less than $1 per day.

A private consultant estimated that the government loses 40 million emalangeni (about $6.5 million) per month to corrupt practices (Freedom House 2006). An anti-corruption unit was established in 1998 but has failed to produce a single indictment. In 2005, Transparency International (TI) assessed Swaziland for the first time; it ranked 103rd out of 159 countries surveyed in TI's corruption perceptions index (ibid).

The media landscape

Most of Swaziland's news media are state controlled and the rest have been subjugated to the needs of the monarchy. There are two principal groups in the newspaper sector, both of which have dominated for the past 35 years. The first is the Loffler family, based in Namibia; it owns African Echo, the holding company of the *Times of Swaziland* (published on weekdays*)*, *Swazi News* (published on Saturday) and the *Times Sunday*. These newspapers – the first of which, the *Times*, was established in 1897 – are the only major news sources in the kingdom that are free of government control (Rooney 2007; SADC 2004: 45–47).

The second major player is the corporation, Tibiyo Taka Ngwane, which is controlled by the Swazi royal family and owns the Observer Media Group, publisher of the *Swazi Observer* and its companion, the *Weekend Observer*.

One independent monthly comment magazine, *Nation*, manages to continue publishing despite government opposition and a small circulation. A free government-produced newssheet, *Swaziland Today*, has very little credibility.

There are two free-to-air television stations in Swaziland – Swazi TV and Channel Swazi (Channel S). Swazi TV is the state broadcaster and dominates the airwaves. Two Acts of Parliament have resulted in a monopoly by state-owned radio and television. Broadcast licensing is the prerogative of Swaziland Posts and Telecommunications, which has the sole authority to issue licenses (Maziya 2003: 91).

Swazi TV has one channel with multiple national repeaters. The government allowed Channel Swazi, a pro-establishment medium, to begin operating domestically in 2001 (SADC 2004: 45–47).

The king supported Channel S to show that his regime was democratic and respected human rights. However, the station's offices were raided by police after it screened a report deemed too critical of the king. Any hint of independence at Channel S was immediately reined in by the authorities (Reporters Sans Frontières 2003).

There are two radio broadcasters in Swaziland: the Swaziland Broadcasting and Information Services (SBIS) and Voice of the Church, a private Christian radio station that is a local franchise of TransWorld Radio. Voice of the Church is the only privately owned radio station in Swaziland. The SBIS is a state-run national radio service with one siSwati-language channel, one English-language channel, and one information services channel.

Access to international news

The ordinary person in Swaziland has next to no access to news and information from outside the kingdom. No news organisation in Swaziland employs foreign correspondents.

The state-controlled television and radio stations do not air reports prepared by overseas news agencies in their news bulletins. The only foreign news broadcast is 'Headlines', read live by newsreaders. The main source of outside news is the USA-based CNN, which Swazi TV carries during the early morning, but even this window on the world was reduced in 2007 when Swazi TV launched its own home-based breakfast show.

SBIS radio broadcasts about three hours' worth of material per day from the BBC World Service and the Voice of America.

Radio and television broadcasts from neighbouring South Africa seep over the border and are available in some parts of Swaziland, but the mountainous terrain in the kingdom makes it impossible for most people to receive adequate signals.

For the wealthy viewer, the South Africa-based satellite broadcaster, MultiChoice, operates in Swaziland, providing subscribers with access to television services including CNN, BBC World, Al Jazeera and Sky News.

Swazi newspapers tend to carry a full page of foreign news each day, supplied by international news agencies. Foreign sport, especially European football, dominates the sports pages. The entertainment pages are full of material about Hollywood celebrities and products, even though most of them are unknown in Swaziland (Rooney 2007). There is no cinema in the kingdom, and many of the movies and TV shows featured in the entertainment pages do not air in Swaziland – not even on satellite TV.

Newspapers and magazines from Johannesburg, South Africa, are available without restriction in urban centres in Swaziland. The availability of these publications is largely unproblematic because they do not report or comment on events inside Swaziland. However, in 2007, there was a call to ban *Drum* magazine after it published a critical article on the extravagances of King Mswati's birthday party (Ndlangamandla 2007).

The Internet has very limited use in Swaziland. Electricity does not reach much of the kingdom and people are too poor to afford computers. It is estimated that in 2007 only 41 000 people (3.7 per cent of the population) used the Internet (Internet World Stats).

The existing legal framework

It is estimated that there are more than 30 pieces of legislation in Swaziland that could be regarded as restrictive to media freedom. According to Vukani Maziya, these restrictive laws have resulted in a lack of growth in the media industry, harassment and intimidation, strained relationships and mistrust between government and the media, weakened media organisations and lack of professionalism (Maziya 2003: 86–88).

The principal statutes that impact on media freedom in Swaziland include the Proscribed Publications Act of 1968; the Obscene Publications Act of 1927; the Books and Newspaper Act of 1963; The Official Secrets Act of 1968; The Cinematograph

Act of 1920; The Sedition and Subversive Activities Act of 1938; and the Swaziland Television Act of 1983. These Acts of Parliament impose restrictions that can be detailed as follows:

- The Proscribed Publications Act allows the state to ban certain publications and to require that they may only be imported and possessed under licence. The act applies to newspapers, books, periodicals, pamphlets, posters and other printed matter. Section 3 empowers the Minister for Public Service and Information to ban publications 'if the publication is prejudicial or potentially prejudicial to the interests of defence, public safety, public order, public morality or public health'.

- The Obscene Publications Act restrains and prohibits the dissemination of indecent and obscene publications. The Act explicitly applies to the print media. There is currently no restriction on obscene material transmitted over the Internet as this medium was not within the ambit of the legislation when it was drafted. The Obscene Publications Act makes it an offence to import into Swaziland, manufacture, produce, sell, distribute, possess or deal in indecent and obscene objects or publications. The Act does not define what it means by the terms 'indecent' or 'obscene'.

- The Books and Newspapers Act licenses newspapers. It defines a newspaper as 'any printed matter containing news, or intelligence, or reports of occurrences of interest to the public or any section thereof, or any views, comments or observations thereon printed for sale or distribution and published periodically'. Section 4 prohibits anyone from printing or publishing a newspaper in Swaziland unless the editor of the newspaper is resident within Swaziland and holds a registration certificate issued by the Registrar of Books and Newspapers. Where a newspaper has more than one editor, the chief editor has to be resident in Swaziland. The effect of this is that newspapers have to be locally controlled and registered in order to be distributed in Swaziland.

- The primary purpose of the Official Secrets Act is to protect official secrets from disclosure. The Act is of general application and does not specifically apply to the media.

- The primary purpose of the Cinematograph Act is to control the making and public dissemination of films, as well as of pictures and posters relating to the films. It is prohibited for anyone to make a film showing African gatherings or African life without the prior permission of the Minister for Public Service and Information. The Act further prohibits the production of films depicting certain Swazi cultural celebrations – namely Incwala Day, the King's Birthday, the Umhlanga (Reed Dance) and the Somhlolo (Independence Day) – without the Minister's written consent. The Minister has unlimited discretion to grant or refuse consent and to declare any picture objectionable if he believes that scenes depict any of the following: ridicule or contempt for any member of the King's naval, military or air forces; scenes tending to 'disparage public characters'; scenes calculated to 'affect the religious convictions or feelings of any section of the public'; 'suggestive' scenes of executions and murders; and 'other revolting scenes' of immorality or indecency.

- The primary purpose of the Sedition and Subversive Activities Act is to provide for the suppression and punishment of criticism of the king and the government of Swaziland. Section 4 makes it an offence for any person to do anything, or even to attempt to do anything, with seditious intent. It is also an offence to conspire with anyone who wants to do anything with seditious intent. This includes the utterance of seditious words as well as the printing and dissemination of seditious publications. The importation of seditious publications is also an offence, except when the importer had no reason to believe that the publication was seditious.

Section 3(1) defines a 'seditious intention' as an intention to bring the king into hatred or contempt, or to excite disaffection against the king, his heirs, his successors and the government of Swaziland; cause inhabitants of Swaziland to 'procure the alteration, otherwise than by lawful means, of any matter in Swaziland as by law established'; bring the justice administration system into hatred, contempt or disaffection; promote 'feelings of discontent amongst the citizens and inhabitants of Swaziland; or promote ill-will and hostility between different classes of the population of Swaziland'.

- The Swaziland Television Authority Act established the Swaziland Television Authority (STA), which is empowered, among other things, to establish and operate television broadcasting stations in Swaziland and also to issue and withdraw licences. The effect of this is that the STA wears two caps – it acts both as the regulator for the television broadcasting industry and as the public broadcaster under the guise of the Swaziland Television Broadcasting Corporation (STBC).

  The STA Board of Control monitors programming content to ensure that it complies with 'acceptable moral standards'. Section 9 empowers the Minister to appoint all the members of the Board of Control.

  In fiscal matters, the STA is directly accountable to the Minister rather than to Parliament. The Swaziland Television Authority Act also requires the STA to report annually to the Minister on the performance of its functions during the past year and on its intended future operations. The Minister, rather than the STA, has the final say over the granting of television broadcasting licences. Section 17 states that the STA may grant licences subject to the approval of the Minister.

The licensing of radio broadcasting is regulated by the Swaziland Radio Regulations of 1992, which modified the Posts and Telecommunications Corporation Act of 1983. Effectively, it is the Minister of Natural Resources and Telecommunications who holds the regulatory powers and the authority to issue licences. Under Section 12 of the regulations, both the licensing authority and the Minister (effectively the same person) may at any time revoke or suspend a broadcasting licence if the licensee fails to comply with any of the provisions of the act or the regulations, or with any condition of the licence; or where it appears that such revocation or suspension is expedient in the public interest. There is no right of appeal against decisions.

Experiences under existing legislation and regulations

In both the state and the private sectors, the government has generally kept a tight reign on media in recent years. A Commonwealth election monitoring team criticised Swaziland's lack of press freedom and expressed disappointment at government-owned Radio Swaziland's reporting on the 2003 elections. The monitors commented that restricted campaign coverage reduced voters' knowledge of the candidates and harmed their ability to hold the candidates accountable (Campaign to Protect Journalists 2003).

In April 2003, the newly appointed Information Minister, Abednego Ntshangase, announced a censorship policy for state media, saying that 'the national television and radio stations are not going to cover anything that has a negative bearing on government'. Ntshangase mentioned specifically that State broadcasters would not be allowed to cover the controversy surrounding the government's plans to purchase a luxury jet for King Mswati (International Press Institute 2003).

The ban on negative content was directed toward the SBIS – which operates the only news-carrying radio channels in the country – along with Swazi TV (Campaign to Protect Journalists 2003).

In May 2006, Mswati III banned newspapers from writing about his wives without his permission – even while they were covering official events – after the *Times Sunday* interviewed one of his wives (with her consent) while she was sick in hospital. This was the second time in 12 months that the king had attempted to gag journalists from reporting on royalty. In 2005, he ordered the media to stop writing about his lavish spending after they published the fact that he had purchased luxurious vehicles to the value of $500 000 for his 13 wives (Ndlovu 2006).

The media, especially at organisational level, seem to accept that government is a stakeholder on national issues; and that in spite of weaknesses apparent on both sides, coexistence and mutual co-operation are possible (Campaign to Protect Journalists 2003).

Under Swazi law and custom, there are issues related to King Mswati III that cannot be reported on. These issues include his wealth, his health and matters relating to what goes on at traditional ceremonies that he might attend (MISA 2007b: 31). Maziya (2003: 95) reports that much of the interplay between media ethics and Swazi law and custom has been linked to reports about the royal family.

The new Constitution of Swaziland

Swaziland finds itself in a confusing situation in terms of its new Constitution. The Constitution became effective in 2006, but the ruling elite has largely ignored its provisions. This means, for example, that although the Constitution allows for freedom of assembly, political parties remain banned.

Section 24 of the Constitution, dealing with Protection of Freedom of Expression, states that '… a person has a right of freedom of expression and opinion; a person shall not, except with the free consent of that person, be hindered in the enjoyment of the freedom of expression, which includes the freedom of the press and other media, that is to say,

• Freedom to hold opinions without interference.

• Freedom to receive ideas and information without interference.

• Freedom to communicate ideas and information without interference (whether the communication be to the public generally or to any person or class of persons); and

• Freedom of interference with the correspondence of that person.'

Although the Constitution appears to state the position clearly on freedom of expression, the media still struggles to exercise these rights. In March 2007 the Times of Swaziland group of newspapers was forced into publishing an abject apology to King Mswati after the *Times Sunday* ran a news commentary sourced from the international news agency, Afrol News, in which the following appeared:

> Swaziland is increasingly paralysed by poor governance, corruption and the private spending of authoritarian King Mswati III and his large royal family. The growing social crisis in the country and the lessening interest of donors to support King Mswati's regime has also created escalating needs for social services beyond the scale of national budgets.

Such open criticism of the king is not allowed in Swaziland (not even in so-called independent newspapers like the *Times Sunday*). The publisher was summoned to the royal palace and told that unless he published an unreserved apology his newspaper group would be closed down. The apology was forthcoming (MISA 2007b: 10–11).

In October 2006, Parliament ordered the *Times of Swaziland* to apologise for the opinion expressed in the newspaper that a select committee investigating the operations of the Swaziland Broadcasting and Information Service operated as a 'kangaroo court'. The newspaper declined to apologise, citing its right to freedom of expression under the Constitution (MISA 2007a: 73).

In June 2007, the Minister for Health and Social Welfare, Njabulo Mabuza, banned health workers from talking to the media in response to a number of stories highlighting the impact of a critical drug shortage (MISA 2007b: 37). Workers were forbidden to have any type of communication on the subject, including interviews and casual or 'indiscreet' conversations, whether at clubs, hotels, bars or private parties. Journalists were also barred from Mbabane Government Hospital, the country's key medical facility.

There may be some hope for the media's right to freedom. In October 2007, a Swazi House of Assembly select committee was set up to investigate the editor of the *Times Sunday* for contempt of Parliament, following a comment article he wrote in his newspaper criticising the Speaker of the House of Assembly.

The select committee cleared the editor of contempt charges, citing his rights under the Constitution. However, this victory was far from total as the select committee went on to recommend that all journalists who report on Parliament should be accredited (presumably, as this was not made clear in the report, by Parliament itself). The committee criticised journalists for being ignorant of parliamentary procedures and journalistic ethics, and suggested that workshops be held to sensitise them to the issues. The committee also called for the reintroduction of a defunct Media Council Bill, which among other things would require journalists to be qualified and registered with some central body (House of Assembly 2007).

Emerging legal framework

In 2006 the Information and Media Policy was adopted, after ten years in the making. This policy provides a framework for the development of an information and media sector. To support this initiative, the Ministry of Public Service and Information engaged Commonwealth consultants to review and update restrictive media laws in consultation with stakeholders (MISA 2007a: 68).

The move to create new policy also followed international trends. Since the end of the Cold War, there have been advances in the causes of liberalisation, deregulation and promoting greater respect for human rights, including freedom of expression (Kantumoya 2006: 5). According to Kantumoya, Southern Africa has not experienced the impact uniformly, 'but it is evident that global trends are influencing its laws, policies and regulatory and institutional frameworks in a fundamental way' (Ibid).

In Swaziland, as a result of consultants' work, a number of draft bills were published in 2007. These include the Freedom of Information and Protection of Privacy Bill, the Swaziland Media Commission Bill, the Books and Newspapers (Amendment) Bill, the Swaziland Public Broadcasting Corporation Bill and the

Swaziland Broadcasting Bill. The Freedom of Information and Protection of Privacy Bill is explicit in its objective to:

> Encourage a culture of openness, transparency and accountability in public bodies by providing for access to information held by these bodies in order to enable every citizen to fully exercise and protect their constitutional right of freedom of expression.

If such a bill were brought into law and actually acted upon, it would completely change the presently oppressive Swazi society.

Along the same vein, the Swaziland Media Commission Bill intends to 'Establish a Media Commission for the purpose of promoting and preserving the freedom of the press in Swaziland; and promote, supervise and maintain responsible standards of journalism.'

The Books and Newspapers (Amendment) Bill would replace the Books and Newspapers Act of 1923; the Swaziland Public Broadcasting Corporation Bill would establish the Swaziland Public Broadcasting Corporation; and the Swaziland Broadcasting Bill would oversee television and sound programme services, and provide for the content and scheduling of programmes and advertising.

State versus public service broadcasting

On the face of it the draft bills are an attempt to open up the restricted society that is Swaziland. The introduction of public service broadcasting is another area of possible advancement towards a more open media environment.

At present, the Swaziland Broadcasting and Information Services controls broadcasting in the country. SBIS is a government department under the Ministry of Public Service and Information. A legal notice of 1991 gives the department responsibility for radio and television broadcasting services; newspapers, magazines and other printed publications; government information services; and the accreditation of foreign news reporters and correspondents operating in Swaziland.

The 'mission' of SBIS is to be 'responsible for disseminating news and information aimed at educating, informing and entertaining the Swazi nation effectively and impartially for the purposes of development and social welfare through radio broadcasts and publications' (GKS undated).

This 'mission' is supported by a 'vision' that 'by the year 2000 the SBIS shall be a fully fledged Public Service Broadcaster, a vehicle for providing comprehensive information for development and social welfare to all sectors of the Swazi society'. Despite this vision and a clear date for its implementation (2000), SBIS has made no progress towards implementing a public service broadcasting model in Swaziland. Its lack of commitment can be seen in the fact that it has not even bothered to revise the target date of 2000, even though at the time of writing the deadline had been exceeded by several years.

The reality is that the overall role of the SBIS is to 'assist the Government of Swaziland', and since Swaziland is not a democracy, there is no impetus from ruling elites to change the status quo. Put simply: the ruling elite will get no benefit from a change to public service broadcasting and since the ruling elite's authority is not under threat, there is no need to change.

Despite the bleakness of prospects for change, the Swaziland Chapter of the media advocacy group, the Media Institute of Southern Africa (MISA), has been campaigning for public service broadcasting in the kingdom. It sponsored a workshop on broadcasting transformation in 2007.

Public service broadcasting (PSB) provides access to a wide range of information and ideas, and can serve as an instrument of popular empowerment through its programming. The main problem faced by MISA and other reform advocates is that this empowerment goes against the grain in Swaziland, which is not a democracy. The country's broadcasters serve the interests of its ruling elite and not those of the people. And because broadcasting is state-controlled, no criticism of the status quo is allowed on the airwaves. Any censure of the ruling class is seen as 'un-Swazi'. The Prime Minister is editor-in-chief of the radio station, SBIS, and can decide what goes on the air and what does not.

PSB cannot exist in a state-controlled environment. This is because, in order to work, it has to keep a distance from vested interests. Radio and television stations need to be left alone to make their own decisions regarding their business and the content of their channels. If State money is to be used to finance any public service broadcasting, there needs to be a clear understanding (preferably set down in law) that the contribution does not confer a right on the State to interfere in the affairs of broadcasting stations.

Recently, the present Ministry of Information and Public Service publicly embraced PSB as the way forward for Swaziland. At MISA's 2007 workshop, Martin Dlamini, the Director of Information and Media Development, supported the concept of PSB, describing it as 'a public policy instrument that gives concrete expression to the fundamental right to freedom of expression'. Yet these are empty words. In reality, despite a new Constitution coming into force in 2006, Swaziland is a closed society. There is limited freedom of association, freedom of expression and freedom of action. Cultural norms restrict what people can say and how they behave. Cultural elites can decide what is permissible or what is 'un-Swazi' and therefore not permissible. Journalists speak of the considerable restraints they work under – for example, they are regularly followed by the police (MISA 2007b: 6–7). PSB is incompatible with all these restrictions because it is a medium that allows access to all, caters for minority tastes and views (and more importantly, opinions) and encourages questioning and democracy.

The role of civil society in advocating media policy reform

Civil society generally has been marginalised in Swaziland and the media sector is no exception. The manner in which the Swazi Constitution was written and approved testifies to this.

Pressure had been building for several years to modernise the political system and particularly to draft a constitution containing a bill of rights. This pressure was mostly from an international community that had witnessed the successful transformation of Swaziland's neighbour, South Africa, from an apartheid state to a fully-fledged democracy.

To facilitate the writing of a constitution, King Mswati in 1996 appointed a 30-member Constitutional Review Commission (CRC) to examine the constitutional system, determine citizens' wishes regarding a future form of government and make recommendations on a new constitution. This process took five years (International Bar Association 2003: 3–5).

The CRC's terms of reference initially provided that it would draft a new constitution, but these terms were subsequently amended to the drafting of a report, which was completed in August 2001. The terms of reference of the Commission did not expressly allow for group submissions, and they were apparently not entertained. NGOs *per se* were therefore effectively prevented from commenting, depriving the CRC of much valuable input.

The extent to which individual Swazis were consulted has also been questioned. The CRC did not keep records of the submissions it received and media coverage of this aspect was apparently banned. The International Bar Association (IBA) reports that there is no formal record of how Swazi citizens presented their views and of what they said to the CRC. Records of the proceedings were not made available to any person other than members of the committee, the Attorney General, experts assisting the committee and members of the secretariat. Members of the Swaziland judiciary were not consulted either.

Furthermore, information was elicited in a highly charged atmosphere. Individuals were reportedly asked – in the presence of chiefs – whether they wanted to retain the king or whether they preferred political parties to govern the country. The IBA reported that the process led to the conclusion – not surprisingly – that the present system of government must continue. The ban on political parties, it was said, should be maintained, the executive powers of the king retained and the position of traditional advisers to the king strengthened. It was also apparently desired that Swazi customs and traditions should have supremacy over any contrary international human rights obligations.

The lack of any meaningful consultation on the drafting of the Constitution has had a demoralising effect on civil society in Swaziland. In fact, there is suspicion that consultations are meaningless, especially since the views of 'traditionalists' will prevail in any debate between traditionalists and modernisers.

An example of this occurred in March 2007, when a stakeholders' workshop on the various draft media and access to information bills discussed previously in this chapter was held with a consultant from the Commonwealth Secretariat who had been responsible for writing the bills. The unpublished minutes of the three-day workshop offer some revealing insights (Anon. 2007). The meeting was so poorly attended that the few present considered abandoning it altogether. There was particular concern at the absence of 'traditionalists'. Attendees decided to continue on the grounds that they were there anyway. The consultant then expressed disappointment that stakeholders had not forwarded submissions and feedback on the bills as had been requested. This underlined the general lack of commitment by stakeholders to the consultation process.

Conclusion

There will need to be changes in Swazi society before there can be real changes in media policy, and the most obvious change needed is the advent of democracy. People who cannot understand the principles of democratic life cannot fully appreciate how a free media model differs from a state-controlled one.

The king and the elite that supports him are entrenched in power and there are no obvious signs that this will change. Opposition within the kingdom is marginalised and political parties are banned (the Constitution allows this). The international community largely ignores Swaziland because it has no geopolitical significance in international affairs. Unlike its neighbour, South Africa, Swaziland has no strategically important seaports and no mineral wealth worth mentioning.

This should not stop media freedom advocates in the international community from exerting pressure on the kingdom. They should continue to ask for proper editorial freedom for the media, and for legislation that protects and promotes the public interest. The public interest should extend beyond the interest of powerful groups to include the poor, powerless and voiceless.

It might be that in a kingdom such as Swaziland, the best vehicle to achieve this is radio. The reach of radio should be extended by dismantling the state controlled SBIS and encouraging the creation of small community-run stations that are better able to cater for the expression of a range of opinions of public concern. Commercial media, supported by advertising, would have a limited impact in Swaziland since the majority of people are too poor to be viable prospects for advertisers.

It is difficult to be optimistic about change in Swaziland. It took ten years for the Constitution to be written and enacted and also ten years for the kingdom's Information and Media Policy to be published, so not much movement on the new draft bills published in 2007 can be expected in the foreseeable future.

References

Anon. 2007. Unpublished minutes of the workshop to review the draft media and access to information bills for the Kingdom of Swaziland, held in Mbabane 26–28 March. Workshop organised by the Media Institute of Southern Africa.

Campaign to Protect Journalists. 2003. Attacks on the press. http://www.cpj.org/attacks03/africa03/swazi.html (accessed 30 October 2007).

Freedom House. 2006. Freedom in the world – Swaziland. http://www.freedomhouse.org/template.cfm?page=22&year=2006&country=7065 (accessed 30 October 2007).

GKS *see* Government of the Kingdom of Swaziland.

Government of the Kingdom of Swaziland. About the Swaziland broadcasting and information services. http://www.gov.sz/home.asp?pid=2568 (accessed 30 October 2007).

Government of the Kingdom of Swaziland. 2005. *The Constitution of the Kingdom of Swaziland Act*. Mbabane: Government Printer.

House of Assembly. 2007. *Report of the House of Assembly Select Committee Investigating Contempt Charges Against the* Times Sunday *Editor*. Mbabane: Government of the Kingdom of Swaziland.

IMF *see* International Monetary Fund.

International Bar Association. 2003. *Striving for Democratic Governance: An Analysis of the Swaziland Constitution*. London: International Bar Association.

International Monetary Fund. 2007. IMF Country Report No. 07/132. http://www.imf.org/external/pubs/cat/longres.cfm?sk=20616.0 (accessed 30 October 2007).

International Press Institute. 2003. World Press Freedom Review. http://www.freemedia.at/cms/ipi/freedom_detail.html?country=/KW0001/KW0006/KW0178/&year=2003 (accessed 30 October 2007).

Internet World Stats. Internet usage statistics for Africa. http://www.internetworldstats.com/stats1.htm (accessed 14 February 2008).

Kantumoya, L. 2006. Broadcasting in Southern Africa: An overview. In *Mixed Signals: The State of Broadcasting in Southern Africa*, 1–12. Lusaka: Panos Southern Africa.

Maziya, V. 2003. Swazi media: A bridge over troubled waters: Journalistic views on restrictive media laws. In *Restrictive Media Laws in Swaziland*, ed. T. Khumal. Mbabane: Media Institute of Southern Africa.

Media Institute of Southern Africa. 2007a. *So This Is Democracy? State of Media Freedom in Southern Africa 2006*. Windhoek: Author.

Media Institute of Southern Africa. 2007b. *African Media Barometer: Swaziland 2007*. Windhoek: Author.

MISA *see* Media Institute of Southern Africa.

Ndlangamandla, M. 2007. Drum littered with fools. *Swazi Observer*, 4 May 2007.

Ndlovu, N. 2006. Swaziland: King Mswati III gags the media. *African News Dimension*, 9 May. http://www.andnetwork.com/index;jsessionid=51423FC9FB14EAECAE5B9A4 9863101DF?service=direct/1/StoryList/item.viewStory&sp=l33938 (accessed 31 May 2006).

Reporters Sans Frontières. 2003. Swaziland – 2003 Annual Report. http://www.rsf.org/ article.php3?id_article=6453 (accessed 30 October 2007).

Rooney, R. 2007. The Swazi press and its contribution to good governance. *Global Media Journal – African Edition* 1. http://academic.sun.ac.za/gmja/Aca4.htm (accessed 29 October 2007).

SADC *see* Southern African Development Community.

Southern African Development Community. 2004. *Media Law: A Comparative Overview of Media Laws and Practice in Botswana, Swaziland and Zambia*. Johannesburg: Konrad Adenauer Foundation.

Epilogue:

Media reforms in Africa – A theoretical commentary

14

Fackson Banda

If 'theory' is a systematic articulation of our epistemological and ontological assumptions about the African media condition (see Du Plooy 2001; McQuail 1987), then we must conclude that it is not often easy to present media-policy reform debates in Africa in terms of neat theoretical scaffolding. Much literature on the subject is often a mishmash of different theoretical trajectories. A sizable proportion of academic work on the subject tends to espouse a critical political–economic tradition (see Tomaselli & Dunn 2001; Lesame 2005). Other works, though not focused specifically on Africa, assume a more liberal–pluralist, 'public interest' theoretical interjection (cf. Buckley, Duer, Mendel & Siochru 2008). Within the critical political economy can be discerned more localised or indigenised strands that seek to domesticate the Western theoretical propositions of mostly liberal democracy in a way that allows for Afrocentric agency (cf. Nyamnjoh 2005; Banda 2008).

The reasons for such a mishmash of theorising African media-reform debates are several. Firstly, Africa, with or without the Maghreb region, is so chequered a continent that its media policy reform experiences cannot so easily be theoretically accounted for. Secondly, the historical route that general media development has followed in Africa is so scarred by different legacies of colonialism – British, French and Portuguese – that it is impossible to theoretically present Africa as a homogenous whole. Thirdly, debates about African media are but an extension of Western debates about media in general. This is a function not only of the European colonisation of Africa but also of the ongoing global imbalance in knowledge production and distribution. Africa's media scholarly work is underpinned by Western epistemic and ontological assumptions; hence many books on African media policy and reform processes mirror Euro-American analytic categories (Banda 2008a).

As a consequence, this present book is an assemblage of essays whose theoretical assumptions are indicative of the multi-theorising that must necessarily arise from the multi-faceted African media condition.

A common thread running through such multi-theorising, however, is that of *critical* reflection, from different vantage points, of the ways in which media policies and other media reform processes in Africa have been, and continue to be, crafted and executed. But we must underscore the fact that the idea of *critique* underpinning all the essays attests to the fact that this book goes beyond the boundaries of what is referred to as *critical theory*. In other words, if being *critical* means 'including variant readings and scholarly emendations' (Merriam-Webster Online Dictionary 2009), then the generic act of *criticising* is not the preserve of *critical* theory. By implication, other theoretical traditions, such as the positivistic notion of liberal pluralism that seems to underpin some of the essays here, can mount a critique of their own. Such an elastic perspective of theorising allows for a reflexivity of the mostly Euro-American theoretical pastiche that characterises many African scholars' analytical work.

It would appear, then, that a multi-theoretical perspective of African media policy-reform debates allows for an onto-epistemic sophistication that eschews the singularism or binarism often evident in Western theorising. For instance, we cannot reduce the chequered, often problematic, experiences of African media to either a *positivistic* liberal pluralism or a *critical* political economy. In fact, even in Western philosophy, the softening of the Marxist doctrines of economism and historicism and the tempering of the excessive celebration of liberal pluralism have given rise to a kind of liminal critical pluralism (Branston & Stafford 2003: 117–133), indicating the continuing epistemological tension between the two 'meta-narratives' of society (cf. Fourie 2007: 146). In his essay in this book, Wallace Chuma seems to embrace elements of critical pluralism when he calls for a 'regulated pluralism' in media policy reforms in Zimbabwe.

In fact, as a result of the inadequacy of Western theorising to account comprehensively and definitively for the diversity of African media cultures, Fourie (2007: 174–177) is compelled to introduce into his study of Africa's mass communication such elements of critical theory as post-colonialism, Afrocentricism and *ubuntu* (cf. Banda 2008a).

The critical theoretical tradition espouses a specific form of critique, often associated with Marxism and forms of neo-Marxism. This branch of critical theory has a variety of leaves, such as critical political economy, cultural and feminist cultural studies, queer theory, etc. A Western philosophical anti-thesis of positivism, critical theory would look at the processes of formulation, implementation and evaluation of African media policies in terms of their interconnection with Africa's entrenched political and economic interests (cf. Fourie 2007). Such a form of critique, manifest in critical political economy, is evident in several of the essays assembled here.

For example, Duncan and Glenn, in their chapter on *Turning points in South African television policy and practice since 1990*, appropriate Pierre Bourdieu's concept of symbolic capital to demonstrate how power habituated in the various societal fields of politics, economics, religion, journalism, etc. imposes structural limitations on the workings of the media (cf. Bourdieu 1998). It is important to note that the generality of the authors' analytic thrust is political–economic in that it characterises the totality of South African television experience in terms of the interface between commerce, state and television.

Nevertheless, by invoking Bourdieu, the authors go beyond classical Marxist economic determinism in the *first instance*. They recognise how power to define media policy reforms is located in the interface between different social formations or fields – broadcasting, business, etc. Such formations, especially when they become overly commercialised and politicised, can accumulate symbolic power in such a way that they dispossess the public of its legitimate claim to a representative and democratic public sphere. An important point here is the two authors' recognition of how these different fields articulate in the enunciation of media policy reforms in South Africa.

There are other articles that have a more descriptive political economic strand. They include Caeser Jere's essay, *Towards a changing media policy and regulatory framework in Zambia*, and William Heuva's article, *Namibia: The paradox of broadcasting reform in an emerging democracy*. These two, and also Isaac Phiri's *Zambia: Policies of a media-phobic state*, are indicative of a political economic strand that emphasises the murky politics of the African state. Not so much a capitalist state (and sometimes tending towards a developmental state, as in the case of South Africa), the African state is a smorgasbord of interlocking political interests, often manifesting itself through the centralisation of power in the ruling elite. As such, the African state's influence on media policy processes, for example, is much greater than that of private media corporations in Africa. Africa, perhaps with the exception of South Africa, Egypt and Nigeria, does not have the kind of complex media corporations that the industrialised world boasts of.

More often, in fact, the few privately owned large media corporations in Africa almost always collide with the State. As Horwitz and Currie's essay on *Politics, privatisation and perversity in South Africa's telecommunications reform programme* demonstrates, the influence of the state's doctrine of *managed liberalisation* on telecommunications policy in South Africa would appear to be indicative of the ANC government's distrust of 'independent institutions supporting constitutional democracy', including the Independent Communications Authority of South Africa (ICASA). The overriding state influence over ICASA does not augur well for most media corporations.

Such a statist emphasis can be contrasted with Noam Chomsky's and Edward Herman's radical strand of political economy – posited in the revised propaganda model (Herman 1999) – which would seem to stress state–media *collusion*, and not collision.

This point of experiential differentiation between the American and African brands of political economy is important to highlight because, as Shakuntala Rao (2000: 98), citing Edward Said's essay, 'Traveling theory reconsidered', puts it:

> 'To pull a theory from one sphere or region to another' must be done with care and not with a sense of borrowing or adapting. One must fully understand the political and cultural affiliations of the theory from whence it originated, and the conditions of its creation and writing, before one can make it travel. To prevent a theory from becoming a relatively tame academic substitute for the real thing and to avoid such domestication, one must see the profound potential of theory to 'move beyond its confinement, to emigrate'.

Statist control – in what might emerge as an Afro–statist strand in the political economy tradition – emerges as a common theme throughout this book. A more historical-descriptive elaboration of this strand is evident in Elaine Windrich's article on *Broadcasting in Zimbabwe: An historical perspective*. Phiri's essay, in particular, demonstrates this tendency in the context of Zambia. By highlighting what he sees as a 'media-phobic state', Phiri gets to the core of what moves the African state to play an over-determining role in Africa's media reform processes. In other words, theorising African media and policy reforms must reckon with the frequent political insecurities of the African state. This problem is highlighted by almost all the other papers in this book.

Also discernible in this ensemble of work is the cultural studies tradition, itself a spin-off of critical theory but less concerned with the singularity of economic determinism. Last Moyo's essay, *The dearth of public debate: Policy, polarities and positional reporting in Zimbabwe's news media*, exemplifies this theoretical tendency. Taking us away from the economic determinism of classical Marxist political economy, Moyo attempts to open up questions about ideology and/or hegemony and how human institutions, including the media, serve as its mediators. The spotlight is shone, not on the economic determinants of the media as such, but on which messages are socially constructed in the process of mediation, and how. This focus on the hegemonic enables us to comprehend the multiplicity of human players who influence the structures and processes of mass communication in Zimbabwe.

By eschewing the oppositional media representations of nationalism and imperialism on the one hand and of human rights on the other, Moyo invites us to consider the complexity that is the Zimbabwean Question, and how it is (re) presented in the form of totalising or grand narratives that leave no room for the historical and social complexity of the Zimbabwean media condition. In other words, Africa cannot be reduced to the kind of binary oppositions that oversimplify what is an otherwise complex situation. This, in itself, is an acknowledgement of the need to deploy a multi-theoretical perspective on the African media situation, recognising both the structure and agency of mediation.

An important point to note, however, is that even Moyo seems to succumb to the rather political–economic proposal for a media policy intervention that addresses the 'structural and institutional problems that characterise Zimbabwe's polarised media landscape'. This would appear to be an attempt at constraining the journalistic agency that he sees as 'now part of the crisis'.

James Zaffiro embraces a 'civil society' theory of African media reforms, locating his analysis in the 'extent of media involvement in civil society relations with state institutions.' Although this is not exactly a liberal–pluralistic theoretical trajectory, it is underpinned by many of the assumptions of liberal pluralism in which various interest groups exert checks and balances on each other, creating, in Zaffiro's words, a 'systemic democracy'. But in arguing for such a civil-societal approach to the media reform agenda, Zaffiro recognises the influence of the political–commercial complex over the media policy reform process – evidence that even here political–economic assumptions are at play.

The next theoretical trend, not so explicitly stated in many of the essays but worthy of mention, is that of development journalism. Clearly, not much optimistic work has been carried out in this tradition. There are a few exceptions, however (cf. Banda 2007). But given the emergence of the developmental state in South Africa, coupled with the pressing developmental challenges faced by many countries on the continent, it seems reasonable to resuscitate scholarly work on the reconceptualisation of development journalism, viewed as an emancipatory form of journalism that transcends the institutional strictures of both commerce and state power. Most Western treatises on development journalism have tended to emphasise aspects of state control, de-emphasising some of the participatory tendencies of subsequent conceptual formulations of development journalism (Banda 2007).

Finally, the analyses presented here can be seen as signalling the interconnection between the global and the local – a process that Roland Robertson (1995) would rather refer to as 'glocalisation'. Although many scholars of African media policy reform tend to refer to this as globalisation, to an extent suggesting that something is being done to Africa, there is a need for a more nuanced analysis that allows for the kind of policy hybridity or melange that is likely to emerge when the global (more accurately the Euro-American) collides with the local African media context. For example, the very idea of South Africa embracing a policy of *managed* liberalisation in telecommunications implies a rejection of the non-statist values of Euro-American neo-liberalism.

Indeed, when Chuma calls for a *regulated* pluralism in Zimbabwe, he recognises the need for public-media policy interventions that can tame the run-away processes of deregulation, liberalisation, privatisation, commercialisation and internationalisation that come in the wake of the 'globalising' of African societies. In other words, the African State *is* a player despite the claim that globalisation results in the receding of the state. It is important, then, to recognise that the policy effects on African media landscapes of what we call globalisation are not uniform or even (Banda 2006). The process of globalisation tends to be so murky and unpredictable that its outcomes are equally murky and unpredictable. Elsewhere, I have argued that 'glocalisation can be seen as the unpredictability of globalisation' (Banda 2008b: 132).

Whenever we examine those media policies adopted on the basis of the promise of globalisation, we witness this unpredictability. In the 1990s, it was fashionable to say that liberalising the media industry would result in quality media products. While we have seen a quantitative increase in media outlets across Africa, we yet have to see a great deal of *qualitative* improvements in the content churned out by most media outlets.

We can argue that this view of globalisation as glocalisation is a repudiation of the suggestion by some radical political economists that globalisation results in media and/or cultural imperialism. As such, it leans more towards the notion of cultural studies. In addition, as I demonstrate in my works on the subject, the view powerfully invokes the postcolonial theoretical idea about a conscious rejection of imperial discourses of African media cultures (cf. Banda 2008a; 2008b). In the end, it reinforces my point about the need for multi-theorising Africa.

It is clear, then, that most treatises on media reforms in Africa reflect a decidedly political–economic perspective. There are, however, variations in emphasis, with most reflections demonstrating that the African state is a key determinant of most of the media reform agenda. To varying degrees, the economic in political economy features in treatises on media reforms, especially in such middle-income countries as South Africa. There is also evidence of a cultural studies tradition that attempts to go beyond economic determinism and raise questions of human agency. Such a theoretical tendency gets caught up in a range of perspectives, including those that look at the place of local African culture in media reform (cf. Nyamnjoh 2005; Banda 2008a, 2008b). What this means is that theorising media reform in Africa is a complex affair, inviting a multi-theoretical approach.

References

Banda, F. 2006. Negotiating distant influences – globalization and broadcasting policy reforms in Zambia and South Africa. *Canadian Journal of Communication* 31 (2): 459–467.

——. 2007. An appraisal of the applicability of development journalism in the context of public service broadcasting (PSB). *Communicatio* 33(2): 154–171.

——. 2008a. African political thought as an epistemic framework for understanding African media. *Ecquid Novi: African Journalism Studies* 29(1): 79–99.

——. 2008b. Negotiating journalism ethics in Zambia: Towards a 'glocal' ethics. In *Media Ethics Beyond Borders: A Gglobal Perspective*, ed. S. J. A. Ward and H. Wasserman, 124–141. Johannesburg: Heinemann.

Bourdieu, P. 1998. *On Television*. Trans. P. Ferguson. New York: New Press.

Branston, G. and R. Stafford. 2003. *The Media Student's Book*. 3rd ed. London: Routledge.

Buckley, S., K. Duer, T. Mendel and S. O. Siochru. 2008. *Broadcasting, Voice, and Accountability: A Public Interest Approach to Policy, Law, and Regulation*. Washington, DC: The World Bank Group.

Du Plooy, G. M. 2001. *Communication Research: Techniques, Methods and Applications*. Lansdowne: Juta.

Fourie, P. J. 2008. Approaches to the study of mass communication. In *Media Studies: Media History, Media and Society*, ed. P. J. Fourie. 2nd ed., 90–183. Lansdowne: Juta.

Herman, E. 1999. *The Myth of the Liberal Media*. New York: Peter Lang Publishing.

Lesame, N. C. ed. 2005. *New media: Technology and Policy in Developing Countries*. Pretoria: Van Schaik.

McQuail, D. 1987. *Mass Communication Theory: An Introduction*. 2nd ed. London: Sage.

Merriam–Webster Online Dictionary. 2009. *Critical*. [0]. http://www.merriam-webster. com/dictionary/critical (accessed 27 January 2009).

Nyamnjoh, F. B. 2005. *Africa's Media: Democracy and the Politics of Belonging*. London & New York: Zed Books.

Rao, S. 2008. Postcolonial theory and global media ethics: A theoretical intervention. In *Media Ethics Beyond Borders: A Global Perspective*, ed. S. J. A. Ward and H. Wasserman, 90–104. Johannesburg: Heinemann.

Robertson, R. 1995. Glocalization: time-space and homogeneity–heterogeneity. In *Global Modernities*, ed. M. Featherstone, S. Lash and R. Robertson, 25–44. London, Thousand Oaks and New Delhi: Sage.

Tomaselli, K. and H. Dunn, eds. 2001. *Media, Democracy and Renewal in Southern Africa*. Colorado Springs: International Academic Publishers.

NOTES

Chapter 2

1 The authors wish to acknowledge that portions of this chapter appeared previously in *Telecommunications Policy*, vol. 31, issue 8/9 (September/October 2007): 445–462.

2 This overview is necessarily compressed and thus imprecise. In fact, the process of institutional reform in South Africa had begun well before the 1994 election, rooted in the actions and politics of the internal democratic civil-society and organised-labour structures that had carried on the anti-apartheid struggle during the 1980s while the ANC was in exile. The communications sector was an early focus of institutional reform. Deliberations over the status of broadcasting, initiated by media-sector civil society groups, were taken directly into the national constitutional political negotiations known as the Convention for a Democratic South Africa (CODESA) in the 1990-1994 transition period, largely because the South African Broadcasting Corporation (SABC), the putative public broadcaster, had served for decades as a National Party-aligned apartheid bulwark, and its transformation was deemed mandatory in the lead-up to the election period to come. See Horwitz (2001).

3 Telkom engaged in a post-paid billing system and did not understand how to demand payment from customers who did not have a mailing address. Requiring rural customers to pay their bills at the nearest post office meant the extra expense of a taxi ride to a location that may have been rather far away. Billing practices were one reason for the huge customer churn and eventual disconnection in the rural areas (Nkenke Kekana, former chair for the ANC of the Parliamentary Portfolio Committee on Communications, interview by author. Johannesburg, 8 September 2006).

4 In fact the number of main (fixed) lines to subscribers is lower even than reported, because Telkom's figures include several hundred thousand integrated services digital network (ISDN) channels. Note that Telkom itself has a 50 per cent position in Vodacom, the leading mobile operator.

5 President Thabo Mbeki (2005) himself commented critically on high telecommunication costs on a number of occasions, most prominently in his 'State of the Nation' address to Parliament in 2005.

6 See the fine work on these matters by Alison Gillwald and other members of the Link Centre at the University of the Witwatersrand, especially the sector performance reviews (Gillwald & Kane 2003; Gillwald & Esselaar 2004). A good compilation of reports and relevant news articles can be found at the website, hellkom.co.za. Telkom tried to shut down this critical, sarcastic website on grounds of intellectual property infringement, but was not successful.

7 In economics, rent-seeking is the process by which an individual, organisation or firm seeks to gain through manipulation of the economic environment, rather than through trade and the production of added wealth. Rent-seeking behaviour can be connected

with, but should be understood as distinct from, corruption. BEE in South Africa should be seen as rent-seeking within a particular political context of redirecting wealth and opportunities toward the previously disadvantaged black population through state contracts and tenders, etc., although it is increasingly being seen as corruption *per se* (Institute for Justice and Reconciliation 2006). Indeed, widespread criticism of BEE as enabling only the emergence of a very small, very wealthy black elite prompted the passage of the Broad-based Black Economic Empowerment Act (Republic of South Africa 2004).

8 Although the White Paper, like the Telecommunications Act, gave Telkom a five-year period of exclusivity to fulfil a universal service mandate (the Act offered an optional sixth year), two elements of the White Paper would likely have opened the sector relatively quickly, without damaging Telkom. The resale of communications services by other private entities was to be permitted after three years, and the self-provision of links to the backbone network was always to be permitted if and when Telkom could not accommodate the request with reasonable quality in reasonable time.

9 This is in some respects an arbitrary list, as many other telling episodes mark the failure of policy and regulation in the sector. For example, the third mobile telephone licence episode (too long and complicated to recount here) involved serious allegations of improper ministerial intervention in a regulatory matter (Nape Maepa, former chair of SATRA, interview by author. Johannesburg, 4 September 2006). The character and timing of the Minister's intervention into the licensing process, to wit, her insistence that a licence award be made by a particular date, and that the award went to the Saudi backed Cell-C consortium, led many observers to speculate about a possible quid pro quo link between the Minister's intervention and the contemporaneous effort by the South African Government to sell arms to Saudi Arabia. Accounts of the various incidents of regulatory and policy breakdown can be found in, among others, Cohen (2003), Gillwald (2003), and Makhaya and Roberts (2003). Press accounts are chronicled on hellcom.co.za.

10 Certain incidents are revealing in this regard. Minister Naidoo asked Koos Klok, a knowledgeable old-hand from the old Department of Posts and Telecommunications, then advising the Minister on the translation of the White Paper into draft legislation, whether the Minister would have more or less power under the White Paper policy. When Klok answered 'Less,' Minister Naidoo responded: 'This is unacceptable.' (Koos Klok, interview by author. Johannesburg, 27 October 1997). In the final stages of the writing of the draft legislation, Andile Ngcaba, then the Postmaster General, said that he would never allow the Regulator to have power (Koos Klok, interview by author. Pretoria, 15 September 2006).

11 Myers contends that the South African Government at that time was inexperienced at drafting legislation of this type and relied on the expert advice SBC was only too happy to provide. Indeed, the lack of experience of the new Department of Communications (reorganised and renamed from the old Department of Posts and Telecommunications in the wake of the passage of the Telecommunications Act) was so great that SBC and Telkom lawyers and advisers – pointedly *not* Government officials – wrote Telkom's 25-year Public Switched Telephone Service (PSTS)

licence, modelling it after the licence that the British government had signed with BT (Gabriele Celli, Telkom executive of regulatory and public policy, interview by author. Johannesburg, 16 September 2006).

12 SBC's share of the US$1.2 billion bid for 30 per cent of Telkom came to $770 million. During the third quarter of 1998 SBC sold its interest in MTN to the remaining shareholders for $337 million, realising a pre-tax gain of $250 million (US Securities and Exchange Commission 2000). Looked at in terms of SBC's South Africa overall investment profile, after clearing $250 million profit from the sale of its stake in MTN, SBC won effective control of Telkom for a mere $470 million. Also worth noting is the fact that, of the $1.2 billion Thintana paid for its 30 per cent stake, $1 billion stayed in the sector to be used for the network roll-out.

13 To get a sense of Thintana's profits, consider an admittedly rough calculation for a sample year: 2001. Assuming that Thintana took 30 per cent of Telkom's R1.641 billion net profits in 2001 (as corrected in Telkom 2003), this would have amounted to R452.3 million. Add the 'management fee' of R260 million and the 'strategic services personnel fee' at a conservative estimate of US$50 million (the annual average 2001 exchange rate was 8.29 rand to the US dollar, thus the figure is in the region of R414.5 million). Thintana's profit in 2001 was of the order of R1.127 billion.

14 Nape Maepa, the first Chairman of SATRA, was advised by staff at the US Federal Communications Commission to watch out for SBC, on the grounds that SATRA should expect much litigation from Telkom because of its SBC partner (Nape Maepa, interview by author. Johannesburg, 4 September 2006).

15 Lewis (2005: 14) cites ISPA's allegation that Telkom pricing levels were up to 40 per cent lower than the rates charged by existing ISPs. Suspicions were that Telkom could not in fact account for its rates for SAIX or Intekom, very much in keeping with the international experience regarding incumbent network operators whose services are bundled within their vertically integrated networks. One way to cope with this problem is to require such operators to create separate subsidiaries for their services that encounter competition. This practice was not employed in South Africa. Makhaya and Roberts (2003: 54) argue correctly that the lack of costing information in general makes it impossible for the Regulator to judge whether Telkom's pricing decisions are in fact part of the elimination of cross-subsidies (as the company claims) or are its response to existing and prospective competition.

16 Looking at the situation in a report commissioned by the Department of Communications in late 2003, the Yankee Group noted that the ITU had placed South Africa seventy-eighth on its Digital Access Index, below peer countries such as Poland, Hungary, the Czech Republic, Brazil, Mexico, Chile and Malaysia. The ITU noted that South Africa had fallen more than any other country but one among the 40 countries that it had previously surveyed in 1998 (Finnie et al 2003: 2).

17 A VPN is a private communications network often used within a company, or by several companies or organisations, to communicate confidentially over a publicly accessible network and to which access is controlled by firewalls and secure tunnels

to enable private and secure use by authorised users. The growth profile of VPNs is very strong internationally and in South Africa (Ibid: 44–45).

18 The question of access to the backbone network got embroiled in the process of amending the Telecommunications Act in 2001, as well. A curious moment transpired when the Minister of Communications, Ivy Matsepe-Casaburri, announced that two new fixed network operators would be licensed and broadband providers would be liberalised – essentially replicating the DTI's wish list. Soon thereafter this direction was reversed and it was stated that only a second network operator would be licensed – one of several reversals the media dubbed 'Ivy's "flip-flops"'. The Minister's first announcement was seen as having contributed to the significant reduction of the share value of Telkom when the Government was getting ready for its IPO. Protecting the share value was not unrelated to the power of Thintana. The Shareholders' Agreement reportedly gave Thintana the right to sell one share for every share Government would take to market. Thus, in order for the IPO to be financially viable, Thintana needed to be appeased so that it would not exercise its rights (Minister of Communications 2001; Republic of South Africa 2001; *Business Day* 2001).

19 Hirsch, however, makes no mention of the notorious 1999 arms deal, which cost the country R30 billion (US$4.8 billion) for what most considered a non-existent military threat, even as government enforced tight-fisted fiscal rectitude everywhere else. See the documents collected at The Arms Deal Virtual Press Office (www.armsdeal-vpo. co.za).

20 One caveat has to be addressed here. Government's suspicion of the independence of the Regulator and desire to maintain control over it may have been born in part from its experience of the IBA's credit card scandal of 1995. The perception was created that it had been the IBA's independence that had abetted corruption and that such independence therefore needed to be trimmed. Even if credence is accorded to this argument, the Government's action of casting aspersions on the regulatory agencies as organisational entities, instead of criticising and punishing corrupt individuals, served only to weaken the organisations and the institution of independent regulation.

21 Suzanne Vos, a member of the Parliamentary Portfolio Committee on Communications for the Inkatha Freedom Party, said that some ICASA councillors were so beholden to their ministerial sponsors that they supported the Ministry's bid to limit their own independence and power in the ICASA Amendment Bill hearings (Suzanne Vos, interview by author. Cape Town, September 12, 2006).

22 In this regard, the original SATRA council may have suffered from the fact that its chair had less political capital than its Department-aligned councillors.

23 Sometimes the political pressure brought to bear on people and institutions was not subtle at all. Those – even solid ANC members in regulatory or oversight positions – who asked tough but appropriate questions were attacked as troublemakers, or derided as Democratic Alliance supporters in an effort to bully them into silence (Yasmin Carrim, former ICASA councillor and now a member of the Competition Tribunal, interview by author. Pretoria, September 15, 2006). The Director General of the DoC, Andile Ngcaba, would occasionally impugn the commitment and even

patriotism of his opponents in affairs of policy. In the 2000 interconnection fracas between SATRA and the Ministry discussed previously, Ngcaba responded to SATRA's 'defiance' as 'the last kick of a dying horse', adding that 'We don't have time for individuals who don't have the interest of the industry and government at heart' (*Business Day* 2000). Earlier examples of this political dynamic include the parliamentary debates around the Telecommunications Act of 1996. Minister Jay Naidoo was not averse to deploying anti-apartheid struggle rhetoric to cast aspersions on those who defended the independence of the Regulator (Republic of South Africa 1996f). And when Koos Klok helped the Telecommunications Forum express dissatisfaction with the changes to the White Paper in 1996, Ngcaba, at that point the Postmaster General, wrote Klok a letter advising him that he could be charged with sedition and that his position in the department was being reconsidered (Koos Klok, interview. Pretoria, 14 September 2006). The point is that ANC political culture has not adapted fully to liberal democratic politics. In a fusion of morality and politics, the ANC leadership often demonises opponents both internal and external to the party as foes to be destroyed rather than challengers to be confronted, engaged, and perhaps bested. For a theory-based perspective on the general phenomenon of what she calls antagonistic versus agonistic politics, see Mouffe (2000).

24 Productivity factors typically range between 5 per cent and 10 per cent at this stage in a telecommunications reform process, according to long-time comparative telecoms scholar William H. Melody (2002). For purposes of comparison with South Africa's 1.5 per cent figure, the productivity factor was set at 7.5 per cent for British Telecom during the 1990s; 6.5 per cent in the USA; 7.5 per cent in Australia; and 3.0 per cent in Mexico (cited in Gillwald & Esselaar 2004: 23).

25 The former chair of ICASA's council, Mandla Langa conceded that ICASA's decision to withdraw from litigation on the rate regime had been a big mistake (Mandla Langa, interview. Johannesburg, 5 September 2006).

26 In a devastating critique of Telkom's tariffs, veteran industry scholar William H. Melody (2002) argued that the 1.5 per cent productivity factor was remarkably low by comparative standards and was clearly belied by the productivity gains Telkom itself trumpeted in its annual report of 2002 (11 per cent for its fixed line network and 29 per cent for its mobile investment in Vodacom). Evaluating Telkom's proposed price increases to come into effect in 2003, Melody criticised the company's use of inflation data as well. Although the 12.5 per cent figure Telkom used to justify its tariff increase did reflect a momentary rise in the customer price index (CPI), the effect of inflation on its costs was immaterial – indeed, the company was experiencing declining costs in its major purchases of the latest technology equipment in international markets. Very high tariffs (and profits) were not the province of just Telkom. Interconnection fees paid by Telkom to the mobile operators, though according to regulations cost-based, in fact were – and continue to be – priced well above costs, resulting in high fixed-line to mobile call charges and an entry barrier for would-be entrants into the mobile and fixed-line markets (Hodge 2005b: 13–19).

27 Government raised R4.3 billion from the 2003 listing (*Business Day* 2004). Under the Khulisa scheme, historically disadvantaged individuals were offered a discount of 20

per cent on the IPO share-offering price. Khulisa share-buyers who held onto their shares for two years were to qualify for a loyalty bonus of one extra share for every five shares they owned. All other South African citizens were allowed to buy shares at a discount of 5 per cent on the offering price (Gush & Ginsberg 2003).

28 Calculating the consequences of Telkom's dominance and high telecommunications costs on the South African economy in any definitive way is problematic, but most economists argue that the negative effects have been significant. One report by telecommunications consultant Paul Cole, commissioned by the Universal Service and Access Agency of South Africa, calculated that in sample year 2002 consumers were forced to pay US$ 586 million more than they would have paid in a competitive market. The estimate of a "lost" US$ 2.23 billion to the South African economy was caused by lost foreign investments and extra expenditures on telecoms by consumers (Regulateonline.org 2006). Another recent estimate, by Efficient Research chief economist Dawie Roodt, indicated that the lack of competition and Telkom's monopolistic behaviour in the telecommunications arena between 2001 and 2006 had cost the economy at least R50 billion in lost growth (MyADSL 2006). Telkom itself, continuing to build telephone lines to reach the poor at great expense even when it was apparent that they were disconnecting and buying mobile phones, wasted about R17 billion (Hodge 2005b: 3).

29 See, for example, Mokaba (1997) and the much more measured and subtle ANC (1996). President Mbeki himself believed that a black capitalist class was one of the pillars of democracy in South Africa. He stated to a group of business leaders in 1999, 'As part of our continuing struggle to wipe out the legacy of racism, we must work to ensure that there emerges a black bourgeoisie, whose presence within our economy and society will be part of the process of the deracialisation of the economy and the society' (cited in Gumede 2005: 224).

30 In fact, Jordan himself ascribed his sacking to political differences with Mandela over the appropriate form of discussion and decision-making process that should prevail in the ANC's National Executive Committee and in Cabinet. Jordan wanted more openness; Mandela adhered to the caucus-based democratic centralist model (*Mandela: The Authorised Portrait* 2006: 296–297).

31 ANC Treasurer-General Mendi Msimang wrote a letter to Thintana, assuring the company that the Government endorsed the Elephant Consortium bid (Piliso 2006b).

32 Suzanne Vos, Member of Parliament for the Inkatha Freedom Party, interview. Cape Town, 12 September 2006; Dene Smuts, Member of Parliament for the Democratic Alliance, interview. Cape Town, 12 September 2006. Vos asserted that political negotiations around CODESA and the first couple of years after the election had been tough, but cooperative and productive. The previous few years, she said, had been different, all about ANC control and major business deals among ANC comrades. Not mincing her words, Vos described the political system of the moment as a 'thugocracy'. Smuts, whom everyone acknowledges as having a keen understanding of the communications sector, was less pejorative but no less critical. 'In the first five years, this was a powerful Parliament,' she stated. She then went on to say that 'ANC

MPs have lost their courage since 1999; this is now the second or third tier of ANC talent in Parliament.' Yet even in the better years, Smuts asserted, Parliament had been subservient to Government, with Ngcaba essentially giving instructions to the ANC caucus in the Parliamentary Portfolio Committee.

33 The newly passed Electronic Communications Act (ECA) addresses some of the problems presented in this article, but it will very likely take a long time to fix them (Republic of South Africa 2005). As prominent telecommunications lawyer Lisa Thornton declared, given the economic stakes and the propensity of the players – especially Telkom – to go to the courts, it will probably take ten years of litigation to resolve some of the most basic provisions of the ECA (Lisa Thornton, interview by author. Johannesburg, 6 September 2006).

34 In 2006 Parliament appointed an ad hoc committee, under the chairmanship of the respected Kader Asmal, to review Chapter 9 and associated institutions. Underscoring the widespread assessment of the concentration of political power in the post-apartheid period, the committee supported the independence of Chapter 9 institutions. It took special note of the perception that ICASA lacks independence, and declared both the perception and the realities behind it undesirable. The committee recommended the appointment of ICASA councillors by the President instead of the Minister, and also a revision of ICASA's funding model in order to support its independence (Republic of South Africa 2007: 194, 202).

Chapter 3

1 Marketisation could be defined as the use of market-based solutions for political, social or economic problems. The hostile view of 'marketisation' or 'libertarian' views has been expressed in South Africa by P. Eric Louw and others. See, for example, Louw (1993: 101): 'The claim that a libertarian ("free enterprise") media guarantees a "free market place of ideas" is not borne out by the facts.'

2 This backlash is evident in part in the policy pronouncements of the ruling ANC. See, for instance, the ANC's discussion document for its 2002 National Conference, which stated that the reliance of many media on advertising 'places direct limitations on the ability of media to expand and reach the majority of South Africans. Commercial considerations are at the apex of consideration of what market to target and what content to deal with and what perspectives reflected [sic]'… [Patronage] by the advertisers skews the media landscape and consequently distorts the democratic process and debate.' (African National Congress 2002: 4–5). In an attempt to address this problem, the ANC resolved that a publicly funded model for the SABC should be established by 2012, and that public funds should be set aside for regional television. In its 2007 conference, the ANC lamented the lack of progress in this regard (ANC 2007: 1).

3 By 1990, advertising accounted for 68.3 per cent of its total income, with the licence fee accounting for 28.8 per cent. This situation was virtually unprecedented, matched only by Television New Zealand, which derived 76 per cent of its income from advertising (McKinsey 1993: 6).

4 This development coincided with the apartheid government's review of its economic policy, given its realisation that its 'Keynesianism for whites only' economic system was not sustainable, and that the economy had to become export-orientated along neo-liberal lines. To this end, it developed its Normative Economic Model (NEM), an array of policies designed to restructure the economy along neo-liberal lines (Marais 1998: 85).

5 For a history of COM and the CIB, see Tusi Fokane's chapter in *The Broadcasting Independence Handbook* (FXI 2008).

6 The problem with an advertiser-driven funding model is that it skews SABC services towards servicing audiences that advertisers consider to be attractive financially, and also forces SABC services to chase audience ratings, at the expense of genres that may be crucial to the public mandate, but may not deliver large economically well-off audiences (such as religious programmes focusing on minority denominations or children's programmes).

7 The Applied Broadcasting Centre, the Community Television Consortium, the Film and Television Federation, the King Luthuli Transfomation Centre, Lawyers for Human Rights, the National Arts Coalition, the National Community Radio Forum, the Personal Managers Association, the South African Council of Churches, the South African Communications and Development Institute, the SACHED Trust, the South African Students' Press Union and the Universal Brotherhood Consortium (MBC 1994: 1).

8 In making these arguments, the group of 13 organisations considered global trends impacting on broadcasting policy, including technological advances coupled with globalisation, fuelling counter-veiling tendencies towards regionalisation and localisation. According to the organisations, 'the restructuring of public broadcasting services must be done in a way that gives attention to all three levels of change that are occurring in the late twentieth century – the global, the national and the local. Neither [sic] of these levels can be ignored in the restructuring process. They have to be simultaneously addressed [sic] and dealt with dynamically and not defensively.' (MBC 1994: 44)

9 This funding was for the cost of provincial split time on radio stations, the cost of increasing African languages and local content, and the cost of funding the Education Ministry/SABC Task Team recommendations on educational broadcasting (Portfolio Committee on Communications 1996: 3).

10 For more information on the impact of GEAR on broadcasting, see Duncan (2002 & 2006).

11 These reasons were as follows:

- a loss in advertising revenue after the re-launch of its channels;

- growing competition from M-Net for ad spend and audiences;

- the implementation of the decision by the IBA for the SABC to spin off its signal distribution arm, Sentech, into a separate company, resulting in the loss of this revenue stream;

- the loss of advertising revenue from the privatisation of its six radio stations, which led to the government claiming the proceeds from the sales; and

- the government's reneging on a commitment by the Independent Electoral Commission to pay the SABC R30 million for the coverage of the 1994 elections (Duncan 2002: 126).

12 A broadcaster with in-house production capacity, which produces and broadcasts programmes.

13 A broadcaster that outsources all its programme production, and merely operates a channel for content that has been developed by independent production companies.

14 This review involved the prime-time prioritising of news and drama, and also family entertainment programmes such as soaps, sitcoms and game shows, primarily in English (SABC strategy team 1997).

15 Even at the time when the Broadcasting Act was passed, there were indications that the SABC was simply unable to afford self-sufficiency. In the 1999/2000 financial year, the Corporation posted a deficit of R28 million, compared with the surplus of R120 million for the previous year. In addition, of the 19 divisions, only seven were shown to be profitable at an operational level. In a report commissioned by the SABC in May 2000, Gemini Consulting estimated that the Corporation would run up losses of between R200 million and R300 million per annum until 2006, unless significant government funding or debt financing were made available. The public broadcasting division would be unprofitable, with losses escalating to R441 million per annum by 2004. The public commercial division, which is meant to cross-subsidise the public services, would only be profitable in 2002, when it would make negligible profits. So at that stage it was clear that the public commercial services were simply unable to cross-subsidise the public services (Gemini Consulting 2000).

16 By 2002, with respect to television, 44 per cent of the population attracted 60 per cent of ad spend; with respect to radio 34 per cent of the population attracted 59 per cent of ad spend; and with respect to newspapers, 60.9 per cent of the population attracted 68 per cent of ad spend (Wortley and Bolton 2002).

17 '[I know] that amongst many middle class people and would-be middle class people, there is a snobbish attitude which says that it is enough if our languages are used in families and communities, in churches and in prayer. We don't need to bother about having our languages developed to the extent where, for example, that English or to a lesser extent perhaps, Afrikaans, are already developed. I know that. But I want to warn, I want to say that if we are going to continue on that road, I want to repeat what I always say when I address this question, we are condemning ourselves to perpetual mediocrity.

The reason I say that is if we want a sub-stratum of people, of masses of people who are creative, spontaneous, self-confident, then the languages of the people have got to be seen as languages of power, languages of empowerment, they've got to be seen to be languages that are subtle, sophisticated, languages that open the world to us. And unless we use the SABC and other media to do this, we condemn ourselves to perpetual mediocrity. There is no nation in the world that has thrived on the basis of a foreign language, on the basis of a third language or even a second language. There is no nation in the world that has thrived. And we've got to take this lesson to heart. The SABC must take this lesson to heart.'

18 According to ICASA, '[Broadcasting] South African content is not regarded as a burden. Indeed, broadcasters see South African content as an opportunity to meet changing audience needs and to grow the South African industry, while contributing to the emerging democratic culture of the country' (ICASA 2002: 27).

19 ICASA also introduced a weighting system for neglected genres such as drama, through which broadcasters are required to meet a drama score. The score is calculated using a format factor. For instance, four (the highest factor) is awarded for one-off dramas, three for a series produced at a rate of one hour or less per week, and two for a series produced at the rate of more than one hour per week (ICASA 2002). Extra points are awarded to dramas in African languages, although dubbing is not incentivised.

20 Rene Smith has argued that while the series was 'a highly textured narrative that is open to multiple interpretations', its representation of young women and gender-based violence 'perpetuate the dominant patriarchal ideology, thereby obliterating the series' counter-hegemonic potential' (Smith 2002: 261).

21 According to the SABC's editorial policies, the SABC has a constitutional duty to treat all languages equitably, and with equal respect. However, the broadcaster also needs to address the marginalisation of indigenous languages and sign language, in recognition of the impact of the previous systemic marginalisation of these languages. The policies identify XiTsonga, Tshivenda, Siswati and SiNdebele as languages that are more marginalised than larger languages such as SeSotho and IsiZulu (SABC 2004: 26–34).

22 By July 2007, *Generations* stood at 4 654 700 in viewer ratings, followed by *Muvhango* at 2 248 200 (Ngudle 2007).

23 According to *Muvhango*'s producer, Duma Ndlovu (Ngudle 2007), 'I must admit *Muvhango* was perceived to be a rural soapie but the concept was the conflicting interests of affluent, culturally bound people living in the 21st century. In order to appeal to a younger market, we had to adopt the glossy culture, but we still don't want to lose our cultural footprint.'

24 Paterson argued that the United States (US) influenced South Africa's broadcasting transition, by encouraging liberalisation rather than a public-service-orientated system. He stated that the success of the US in selling liberalisation '[opens] the door to US and European media conglomerates that have been falling over themselves to flood South Africa with their productions' (Paterson 1994: 22).

25 The process of commercialisation is described in detail in Tleane and Duncan (2003).

26 This term is contested. In its narrower sense, it involves mobilising journalism to bolster national development efforts. It is thus a form of journalism that can easily be captured by national governments, since journalism is required to serve patriotic

objectives. A broader reading of development journalism would locate it in the tradition of emancipatory journalism, where journalists critically examine the aims of national development. For a thorough analysis of the competing definitions of development journalism, see Banda 2006.

27 In 2006, allegations surfaced in the media that the Managing Director of News and Current Affairs, Snuki Zikalala, had blacklisted certain political commentators who were critical of the government. The SABC appointed a commission of enquiry to investigate the matter, which found that Zikalala had excluded certain commentators on grounds that were not objectively defensible. The commission also found that the extent of delegation of editorial control was not clear, leading to a situation where Zikalala intervened in the day-to-day business of editorial decision making in a seemingly ad-hoc and inconsistent manner, whereas his role was primarily a management one (Commission of Enquiry 2006). These incidents pointed to the ongoing problem of the lines between editorial and management functions being blurred, leading to confusion and demoralisation in the newsroom.

28 Possibly the most significant study in this regard was undertaken by Media Tenor, which involved a five-year content review of SABC television news from 2002 to 2006. It found that reporting on the President had been balanced, and that while the ANC received significantly more coverage than other parties, this coverage was not necessarily positive (Media Tenor 2006). A more recent Media Monitoring Project (MMP) report stated that over 96 per cent of all news items monitored over a two-month period (August–September 2006) had been fairly reported. The MMP research project monitored news for credible and well-sourced reporting, ethical coverage, adequate coverage of events, and quality of information; and monitored e.tv, Lesedi, Metro, Motsweding, SABC 3, SAfm, Thobela, Ukhozi and Umhlobo Wenene (Skinner 2007: 97–148). These findings are borne out by the statistics of the Broadcasting Complaints Commission of South Africa's (BCCSA) concerning complaints against the SABC, which stated that in 2005/6, the SABC enjoyed a 95 per cent success rate (SABC 2006: 27–28). The greatest proportion of complaints was lodged against SABC 3, followed by SABC Television News, 5FM, SABC 2 and SABC 1. Most complaints involved allegations of indecency. After these came complaints against biased information, offensive language, and invasions of privacy and dignity.

29 In August 2005, a freelance cameraman working for the SABC failed to record the booing of the Deputy President, Phumzile Mlambo-Ngcuka, by Jacob Zuma supporters. An enquiry conducted into the incident found that the cameraman did witness the incident, but considered it to be 'irrelevant' and therefore did not film it. The enquiry's findings also questioned the SABC's editorial integrity, quoting Acting Head of Television News, Amrit Manga, as stating that the cameraman may not have sent the footage because he did not want to upset his bosses, whom he assumed would hold pro-Mbeki sympathies (*Sunday Independent* 2005).

In December 2005, the SABC cancelled a planned interview with Jacob Zuma on the eve of his rape trial. The SABC's stated reasons were contradictory. It maintained that his response to a request to participate had come too late: an argument Zuma's aide, Ranjeni Munusamy, contested. The SABC cites as a second reason that it had received legal advice not to flight the programme, as the interview had the potential of violating the sub-judice rule (*Sunday Independent* 2005): a reason that would not have been relevant had the first reason been true. Then in February 2006, Ukhozi FM withdrew a pro-Zuma song from its play list, on the basis that it asserted Zuma's innocence on charges of rape and corruption (*News24* 2006). In May 2006, the SABC decided not to show a documentary on Mbeki, citing editorial changes that had not been made by the producers, and possibly defamatory content. Another documentary in the same *Unauthorised* series, on Irvin Khoza, was apparently also altered (*Mail&Guardian* 2006).

30 In his book *The Structural Transformation of the Public Sphere – An Enquiry into a Category of Bourgeois Society*, Jurgen Habermas described the emergence of a new civic society in the eighteenth century, based on rational-critical debate and discussion. This civic society constituted a social arena where 'the public' was constituted, and where matters of common concern could be debated. Habermas argued that such a public sphere must be reconstituted in order to keep a check on political and economic power (Habermas 1989).

31 The first, dubbed the 'Northern service', would cover North West province, as well as Limpopo, Gauteng and the Free State, and would broadcast programmes in Setswana, Sesotho, Sepedi, Xitsonga and Tshivenda. The second service, dubbed the 'Southern service' would cover Northern Cape, Western Cape, Eastern Cape, Mpumalanga and KwaZulu-Natal. These services were to be established as separate corporate entities, with the state as sole shareholder. In time, the government would decide whether to invite public or private equity.

32 For the purposes of marketers, South African audiences are defined according to a market segmentation tool called the Living Standards Measure (LSM). This segments the South African market according to people's living standards, using criteria such as salary levels, degrees of urbanisation, and ownership of cars and major appliances. Marketers use it to target particular markets according to their LSM profile, with LSM 10 being the highest, and LSM 1 the lowest. The higher the LSM, the more attractive the audience is to advertisers (Tleane and Duncan 2003: 14). South African audiences are skewed towards the lower LSMs.

33 What is noteworthy is the fact that the number of people located in LSM 5 and below is decreasing over time. In 2004, 63.6 per cent of the population fell into LSM 5 and below, in 2005, 61.2 per cent, and in 2006, 59.3 per cent. LSM 1 has experienced the biggest drop (from 9.1 per cent in 2004, to 6.1 per cent in 2006, and 2 and 3 have also declined, but less dramatically. LSM 4 and above have all increased. This suggests that poverty is declining. The crucial policy question, though, is the significance of this decline.

34 The trend towards increasing state control is not dealt with in depth in this chapter. For an analysis of the erosion of the independence of the IBA, ICASA and the SABC since 1997, see Duncan (2008).

35 Local content was meant to account for 10 per cent of broadcast time in January 1999, escalating to 30 per cent of broadcast time by 2000 and 45 per cent in its third broadcast year.

36 Currently, 60 per cent of the channel is owned by Naspers, and 40 per cent by Avusa (previously Johnnic Communications).

37 This will be a period when both analogue and digital signals will be available.

38 According to the African Charter on Broadcasting, 'The legal framework for broadcasting should include a clear statement of the principles underpinning broadcast regulation, including promoting respect for freedom of expression, diversity, and the free flow of information and ideas, as well as a three-tier system for broadcasting: public service, commercial and community.'

39 Bourdieu's notion of 'symbolic capital' relates to the symbolic power that people enjoy by virtue of their social position, which is generally reproduced through education that transfers specific beliefs and behaviours. Using symbolic power against another implies symbolic violence, and may take such forms as judging and dismissing the person as inferior. This power may be dispensed without words, using physical symbols and behaviours (such as 'looking down one's nose'). Symbolic capital engenders a sense of duty and inferiority in others, who look up to those who have that power. Bourdieu developed this concept in an attempt to explain how power is reproduced in institutions (see Bourdieu 1984).

40 Harvey's concept of 'accumulation by dispossession' describes a process of accumulating wealth by robbing people of their rights. This form of accumulation differs from accumulation through production, where wealth is created through productive activity. Such accumulation may take place by dispossessing people of property, or invading countries to capture key resources, but it may also take less dramatic forms. These include privatisation, where public goods are handed to the private sector, financialisation (which redistributes money upward) and state redistribution through instruments such as regressive taxation (Harvey 2003).

41 According to Langa Zita (2000), the realities of globalisation have 'significantly proscribed prospects of progressive manoeuvrability. ... Contrary to the implied thesis that we give up the progressive project, the ANC government has grasped the essential nettle of the moment, to fight to open the market internationally as a necessary condition for advancing transformation domestically. Consistent with this perspective the ANC, both as movement and as government, has sought to mobilise global forces, organisations and institutions to achieve a people-centred global economic order.'

42 Some statistics are available on the extent of social instability in the country, in the form of statistics on the number of protests. In response to a Parliamentary question put by Member of Parliament for the Independent Democrats, Patricia De Lille, on 9 November 2007, the Minister of Safety and Security released figures on the number of protests for 2005/2006 and 2006/2007. These statistics point to a sharp increase in protest action since the release of the 2004/2005 figure of 5,800 protests: in 2005/2006, an estimated 10,763 recorded protests took place, and in 2006/2007, an estimated 9,446 protests. The largest number of protests took place in KwaZulu-

Natal, with the province accounting for about one fifth of the recorded protests for 2005/6 (National Assembly 2007).

Chapter 4

1 The newspaper chain was purchased from the Argus Press using a US$2 million Nigerian contribution.

2 See the *The Standard* column, 'Standard Plus', for criticism of 'The Dead BC'.

3 See Geoffrey Nyarota, *Against the Grain,* for the best account of the press in Zimbabwe.

Chapter 5

1 This is the acronym for the Zimbabwe African National Union Patriotic Front, Zimbabwe's ruling party since independence in 1980.

2 The Catholic Church-owned *Moto* magazine was banned by the Rhodesian state for its anti-colonial editorial line and for its support of the liberation struggle.

3 In 1991 Zimbabwe implemented the Economic Structural Adjustment Programme (ESAP) at the behest of the International Monetary Fund (IMF) and the World Bank (WB), as a way of revitalising an economy that was experiencing stagnation, rising unemployment, a shortage of foreign currency and a ballooning budget deficit.

4 See Zimbabwe Human Rights NGO Forum (1999).

5 Sithole was given an administrative post within Zimpapers that had nothing to do with editorial functions at *The Herald.* He was replaced by former Director of Information, Bornwell Chakaodza.

6 For a comprehensive discussion of the debate about the war, see Horace Campbell's *Reclaiming Zimbabwe* (2003).

7 This is the acronym for the Patriotic Front Zimbabwe African People's Union. PF Zapu was the largest opposition party in Zimbabwe until its merger with Zanu PF in 1987.

8 Republic of Zimbabwe. 2002. Zimbabwe Parliamentary Debates 28(46), 29 January. Harare: Government Printer.

9 William Chikoto, interview by author. Harare, April 2004.

10 Innocent Chofamba Sithole, interview with author. Harare, April 2004.

11 This discussion of the South African policy process is not meant to be extensive, but is instead intended to highlight its key aspects for comparative purposes. It is important to mention that there is ongoing debate about whether the practice of South African media reflects the intentions of policy, especially in the wake of increasing commercial pressures on both the print and the broadcast media. Also debated is the relationship between the state and the public broadcaster, amid allegations of

undue ANC influence on the functions of the SABC (for further discussion on this, see Duncan and Glenn in this volume). Academics and civil society alike have been actively engaged in this debate, including Prof. Guy Berger (Rhodes University), Prof. Tawana Kupe (University of the Witwatersrand [Wits]), and Prof. Anton Harber (Wits); Joe Thloloe, the Chairman of the South African National Editors' Forum; and Jane Duncan of the Freedom of Expression Institute.

12 Chapter 20 (1) of the Constitution of Zimbabwe only makes reference to 'freedom to hold opinions and to receive and impart ideas and information without interference, and freedom from interference with [the citizen's] correspondence'.

13 The Independent Communications Authority of South Africa (ICASA), the statutory regulator, is accountable to Parliament and in principle operates autonomously, free from undue political and commercial influence. There is, however, much debate around the independence of ICASA as well as the effectiveness of the three-tier system in South Africa. In this volume, for example, Duncan and Glenn argue that South African broadcasting policy has produced a television system characterised by uneven development, where the commercial model dominates both public-service and community media. This is a valid argument, but applies mostly to television. Community and public-service radio in South Africa are the most pervasive media, and act as key institutions of the public sphere.

14 In 2005 ZUJ, IJAZ and the Media Institute of Southern Africa (MISA) produced a blueprint Code of Conduct as part of their negotiations with the government aimed at creating a voluntary regulatory body for journalists. At the time of writing, however, the Code remains non-binding on media organisations.

15 For a discussion of the shortcomings of the ZIMCO training programme, see Nyahunzvi, T. (1996).

Chapter 6

1 Newsnet is the subsidiary of the national public broadcaster, Zimbabwe Broadcasting Holdings (ZBH). Its major task is to provide news and current affairs programming to ZBH radio, TV and online services.

Chapter 7

1 Kasoma passed away in 2003. He received a posthumous presidential award in 2007 for his contribution to media scholarship.

Chapter 8

1 Sinha in Price and Verhulst (1998) points out that the Indian government had, by virtue of its dominance of the country's political economy, been the biggest threat to public-service broadcasting for forty-five years.

2 The then Minister of Information and Broadcasting, Mutale Nalumango, was uncomfortable with a number of recommended names, especially those of civil society members perceived to be anti-government.

Chapter 9

1 Zimbabwe and Zambia provide interesting cases for comparison in the sense that apart from being neighbouring countries, both are former British colonies, and both were part of the short-lived Central African Federation. Thus their broadcasting industries share a common cradle.

2 Although the autonomy of the SABC and the independent regulator (the Independent Communications Authority of South Africa – ICASA) has been questioned in recent years, it is notable that the founding principles underpinning these institutions have provided space for citizens to keep demanding that their autonomy be restored.

3 By 2002, direct to home satellite TV had reached some 41 countries on the continent (Kupe 2003b: 2).

4 See http://www.chr.up.ac.za/hr_docs/african/docs/other/other3.doc (accessed 25 May 2008).

5 Donors everywhere consider press freedom to be one of the indicators of democracy, and often make the establishment of press freedom a condition for support.

6 Section 4 of the Independent Broadcasting Authority Act of 2002.

7 See Section 7 of the Zambia National Broadcasting Corporation (Amendment) Act of 2002.

8 According to a Parliamentary committee report, the corporation had been posting financial losses since Independence, save for 1994 and 1995, when it realised a profit of Z$1 million and Z$10 million respectively (Ad Hoc Committee 1999: 12–13).

9 LDM was first to withdraw, citing financial constraints; MABC was switched off air, allegedly for failing to pay its bills to the ZBC, although it is argued that it had ruffled some feathers in government through some of its 'political broadcasts' (see Maqeda 2000); and Joy TV was briefly switched off for similar (financial) reasons but was brought back on air. As Maqeda argues, Joy TV enjoyed favourable treatment because people who were closely connected to power owned it – including James Makamba and the President's nephew, Leo Mugabe.

10 It is also important to note that the process of broadcasting-policy reform closely followed developments in the telecommunications sector, where the legal battle by a private entrepreneur (Strive Masiyiwa) to get an operating license became a test case for aspiring private broadcasters in the country.

11 Both the BBC and CNN, for example, have been barred from reporting from Zimbabwe.

12 The First Chimurenga refers to the first resistance to colonial occupation in 1896–97, while the Second Chimurenga refers to the armed resistance to colonialism in the 1960s and 1970s.

13 On presenting the Broadcasting Services Bill to Parliament on 3 April 2001, the Minister of Information, Jonathan Moyo, argued that the principles contained in the Bill resembled those of the broadcasting regimes of most democracies, notably the United States of America, Canada and Australia (Moyo 2001). In other, separate remarks, the Act that resulted from the Bill has been compared to media laws in Sweden and Britain.

14 The original act stipulated that a commercial broadcasting licence was valid for only two years, while a community broadcasting licence would be valid for only one year. This has since been amended to give commercial broadcasters a ten-year, renewable, license.

15 Section 20 (1) of the Constitution states: 'Except with his own consent or by way of parental discipline, no person shall be hindered in the enjoyment of his freedom of expression, that is to say, freedom to hold opinions and to receive and impart ideas and information without interference, and freedom from interference with his correspondence.'

16 See, for example, *The Herald*, 10 July 2001: 'BAZ flooded with applications for licenses'; *The Herald*, 4 August 2001: 'Broadcasting authority calls for submissions'; and *The Herald*, 10 December 2001: 'BAZ invites applications for licences'.

17 See, for example, *The Zimbabwe Independent*, 5–11 June 2001: 'State dallies on opening of airwaves'.

18 The African Charter on Broadcasting, drawn up by the Media Institute of Southern Africa, provides that 'all state and government controlled broadcasters should be transformed into public service broadcasters, that are accountable to all strata of the people as represented by an independent board, and that serve the overall public interest, avoiding one-sided reporting and programming in regard to religion, political belief, culture, race and gender' (see http://www.article19.org/docimages/1019.htm). However, the Charter is not binding on African governments.

19 Rupert Murdoch had to take American citizenship in order to expand his media empire into the lucrative American market.

20 An exception is Zambia after the 2001 elections, when the ruling party won with a narrow margin. In Zimbabwe, the opposition almost took half the parliamentary seats in 2000, but owing to a constitutional provision that allows the President to nominate an extra 30 non-constituency MPs (10 chiefs elected by their peers, 8 governors and 12 non-constituency MPs), ZANU PF retained the majority necessary to push through whatever laws it wanted.

21 The Central Committee is the party's policy-making organ in the interims between the National People's Congresses, while the Politburo, which is appointed by the Presidium, is a standing committee of the Central Committee as well as the organ for implementing party policy. See http://www.zanupfpub.co.zw/ (accessed 3 June 2005).

22 Peters cites James March and Johan P. Olsen (1984, 1989, 1994, 1996) as the leading scholars promoting the removal of human decision-making from the policy process. They argued that rational choice analysis made individuals too autonomous; and that in fact individuals are constrained by institutions (Peters 1999).

23 Although in principle the Law and Order (Maintenance) Act has been repealed, its spirit and intent have been reincarnated in the new law that replaced it – the Public Order and Security Act.

24 The Oasis Forum continued to exist after the third-term debate, as a pressure group advocating constitutional reform.

25 However, the defeat of the government's draft constitution has been interpreted by some as a pyrrhic victory for both civil society and the political opposition, in the sense that the draft constitution was in many ways a great improvement on the current Lancaster House Constitution, and offered opportunities for political change. See, for example, Moyo, J. 2005. The third way: Zimbabwe's last Chimurenga. http://www.newzimbabwe.com/pages/thirdforce7.12895.html (accessed 27 July 2005).

Chapter 10

1 In June 2008 Minister Venson-Moitoi introduced a Media Practitioners' Bill aimed primarily at government regulation of workers in the print media (Media Institute of Southern Africa 2008).

Chapter 11

1 Haggarty, L., Shirley, M. M. and Wallsten S. 2002. Telecommunication reform in Ghana. Policy Research Working Paper 2983. http://www.worldbank.org/external/default/WDSContentServer/IW3P/IB/2003/03/29/000094946_03031804031943/Rendered/PDF/multi0page.pdf (accessed 10 February 2009).

2 *Maitlamo*, Botswana's National ICT Policy National E-Readiness Assessment, June 2004. Volume 1 – E-Readiness Report, Executive Draft. http://www.maitlamo.gov.bw/docs/e-readiness/volume-1/intro-july_22rev_1-3_rel_05_aug_04.pdf (accessed10 February 2009).

3 The World Bank. http://web.worldbank.org/WBSITE/EXTERNAL/COUNTRIES/AFRICAEXT/BOTSWANAEXTN/0,menuPK:322821~pagePK:141132~piPK:141107~theSitePK:322804,00.html (accessed 30 April 2009).

4 World Economic Forum. 2009. Global Competitive Report 2008–09. http://www.weforum.org/pdf/GCR08/GCR08.pdf (accessed 10 February 2009).

5 The World Bank http://web.worldbank.org/WBSITE/EXTERNAL/COUNTRIES/AFRICAEXT/BOTSWANAEXTN/0,,menuPK:322821~pagePK:141132~piPK:141107~theSitePK:322804,00.html (accessed 30 April 2009).

6 Peters, P. E. 1992. Manoeuvres and debates in the interpretation of land rights in Botswana. *Africa* 62(3): 413–434.

7 Arntzen, J. 1995. Economic instruments for sustainable resource management: The case of Botswana's water Resources. *Ambio* 24(6): 335–342

8 Botswana Communities e-Readiness Report. http://www.maitlamo.gov.bw/docs/e-readiness/volume-1/appx-a-community_e-readiness-july_16_ver2_re_5th_aug_04.pdf (accessed 13 December 2007).

9 Draft National Information and Communications Technology Policy, January 2005, p. 6. http://www.maitlamo.gov.bw/docs/draft-policies/ict_policy_draft_jan_2005.pdf (accessed 10 February 2009).

10 Africa Telecom 90, jointly organised by the ITU and the Posts and Telecommunications Corporation of Zimbabwe, held at the Harare International Conference Centre and the Sheraton Hotel, 3–9 December, in Harare, Zimbabwe. http://www.itu.int/AFRICA2001/press/presskit/backgrounders/event90.html

11 Botswana Telecommunication Authority. http://www.bta.org.bw/licensing/Licensing%20Framework%20Public%20doc.pdf (accessed 30 April 2009).

12 Botswana Telecommunication Authority. http://www.bta.org.bw/pubs/newsletter/October_BTA_News.pdf (accessed 30 April 2009).

13 Botswana Telecommunications Authority. http://www.bta.org.bw/licensed.html (accessed 30 April 2009).

14 Commissioned by the Ministry of Communications, Science and Technology, 2004.

15 Draft Botswana National ICT Policy, 2004. http://www.maitlamo.gov.bw/docs/draft-policies/appx-a-connecting_communities_final_jan_7.pdf (accessed 30 April 2009).

16 Retrieved at http://www.wired.com/wired/archive/2.09/universal.access_pr.html (accessed 10 February 2009).

17 The NEPAD Broadband Project is an undersea fibre optic cable network that will link East Africa with the rest of the world. With the existence of the SAT-3/West African Submarine Cable/SAFE, it will provide the last link to a high-capacity fibre optic telecommunications network that will completely encircle Africa. It will also support broadband Internet connection and significantly cut telecommunications costs within Africa.

Chapter 12

1 This chapter is based on a PhD thesis undertaken in the Department of Culture, Communication and Media Studies, University of KwaZulu-Natal, Durban, South Africa, under the supervision of Professor Ruth Teer-Tomaselli. The financial contribution of the National Research Foundation is acknowledged.

2 For the reader who is not familiar with the country, Namibia is a vast southern African country of 825 418 square kilometres with a population of about two million people. It was a German colony from 1884 until the end of the First World War, when it was handed over to the guardianship of South Africa as a mandated territory of the League of Nations, and its successor the United Nations, to be prepared for independence. However, the South African government delayed the granting of independence, contrary to the wishes of the majority of the Namibian people and the international community. Desirous of incorporating Namibia as part of the Republic of South Africa, the government imposed its administration on the territory, treating it virtually as one of its provinces. It also extended its legislation, including media policies and regulations, to Namibia. Owing to opposition to its administration by the Namibian people, the South African government had to exercise its rule using a combination of 'coercion and consent' measures. This was characterised, on the one hand, by the use of 'state apparatuses' such as the law and the occupying army to

suppress opposition; on the other hand, a subtle form of domination was exercised through various methods – including the state media – to achieve hegemony and thereby win the hearts and minds of the Namibian people.

Namibia depicted features of a 'settler oligarchy' in which the colonist community practised what they imagined was democracy, but which excluded the majority of the indigenous people. The white minority governed the territory until 1977 when the South African regime co-opted many of the black traditional and political leaders in a form of neo-colonial administration that encompassed some forms of power sharing. By the middle of the 1980s, the South African government had established an 'internal settlement' that excluded the progressive organisations – among which was the then-exiled national liberation movement – the South West Africa People's Organisation (Swapo). On 17 June 1985 a 'transitional government of national unity' (TGNU), consisting of internal political parties, was inaugurated. The TGNU exercised legislative and executive powers subject to the whims of the colonial government, but did not have jurisdiction over security matters, defence or foreign affairs. The TGNU was, by and large, unacceptable to both the majority of the Namibian people and the international community, despite attempts by the South African government to sell it to the interested parties. It remained an 'interim government' until 'genuine' independence was achieved in 1990 through United Nations Security Council Resolution 435.

3 South Africa first introduced a radio service, named 'JB Calling', on 1 July 1924, broadcasting to Johannesburg and its environs. Similar local radio stations were established in Cape Town and Durban during the same year. In 1927 these three stations combined to form the African Broadcasting Corporation. In 1936 the latter was transformed into the South African Broadcasting Corporation, which was established by an Act of Parliament (Mampone 2005).

4 These guidelines were adopted in 1982 by the five countries and laid down the principles according to which the future constitution of the country should be crafted. Generally, they have been referred as the '1982 constitutional principles'.

5 Desert Entertainment Television (DEStv) was established in 2001 by NamCapital, a fully Namibian-owned black empowerment company. However, it ceased broadcasting in 2004 when the company went into a joint venture with One Africa Television.

6 Unless otherwise stated, I have used the 'NCC', the 'Commission' or the 'Regulator' to refer to the Namibia Communications Commission in this chapter.

Chapter 13

1 The Gini coefficient uses a measurement between 0 and 1 to determine income distribution – the closer to 1, the more unequal a society; the closer to 0, the more equal a society (IMF 2007).

CONTRIBUTORS

Prof. Fackson Banda is SAB LTD–UNESCO Chair of Media and Democracy at Rhodes University, South Africa.

Dr Sarah Chiumbu is Lecturer in the Department of Media Studies at the University of the Witwatersrand, Johannesburg, South Africa.

Dr Wallace Chuma is Senior Lecturer in the Centre for Film and Media Studies at the University of Cape Town, South Africa.

Willie Currie is Communications and Information Policy Programme Manager at the Association for Progressive Communications.

Prof. Jane Duncan is Highway Africa Chair of Media and Information Society, School of Journalism and Media Studies, Rhodes University, Grahamstown, South Africa.

Prof. Ian Glenn is Director of the Centre for Film and Media Studies at the University of Cape Town, South Africa.

Dr William Heuva is Lecturer in the Department of Media Studies at the University of Botswana.

Prof. Robert Horwitz is Professor in the Department of Communication at the University of California, San Diego, USA.

Ceaser Jere is Media Advisor for Panos Southern Africa. He also lectures part-time in communication studies at the Cavendish University in Lusaka, Zambia.

Dr Sethunya T Mosime is Lecturer in the Department of Sociology at the University of Botswana.

Dr Dumisani Moyo is Senior Lecturer and Head of Department of Media Studies at the University of the Witwatersrand, Johannesburg, South Africa.

Dr Last Moyo is Senior Lecturer in the Department of Media Studies at the University of the Witwatersrand, Johannesburg, South Africa.

Dr Isaac Phiri is Lecturer and Coordinator of Graduate Studies in the Department of Mass Communication at the University of Zambia.

Prof. Richard Rooney teaches Journalism and Broadcasting at the Girne American University, Turkish Republic of North Cyprus.

Elaine Windrich is Research Scholar in the African Studies Centre at Stanford University, USA.

Dr James J. Zaffiro is Professor of Political Science at Central College, Pella, Iowa, USA.

INDEX